The Psychology Major

Training and Employment Strategies

The Psychology Major

Training and Employment Strategies

Edited by

Paul J. Woods

Hollins College

 American Psychological Association
Washington, D.C.

Library of Congress Cataloging in Publication Data

Main entry under title:
The psychology major: Training and employment strategies.

  Includes bibliographies.
  1. Psychology—Study and teaching. 2. Psychology—Vocational guidance.
I. Woods, Paul J., 1930– [DNLM: 1. Psychology—Education.
2. Employment. BF77 P9744]
BF77.P76   150'.23   79-19256

ISBN 0-912704-09-8

Published by the American Psychological Association, Inc.
1200 Seventeenth Street, N.W., Washington, D.C. 20036
Copyright © 1979 by the American Psychological Association.

Printed in the United States of America.

Contents —————————————

Part III Training for Careers in Community Service, Mental Health, and Public Affairs

1

Paul J. Woods

Introduction and Overview

Introduction

This book is intended to be a companion to *Career Opportunities for Psychologists: Expanding and Emerging Areas*, which was published by the American Psychological Association in 1976. That book was the result of our concern with the increasing numbers of people going into graduate study in psychology at a time when traditional areas of employment, such as academia, would no longer be able to absorb those coming out of graduate programs. The situation then was, and now is, rather alarming: Namely, the number of people in graduate study in psychology is equal to the entire membership of the American Psychological Association. This means that in about five years or so the number of psychologists in the United States will double! One can be astonished by such a prospect and, if one is entering the job market, frightened. My experience in editing the 1976 book, *Career Opportunities*, however, has led me to be enthusiastic about the future of psychology. It is my considered opinion that in most aspects of the human endeavor on this planet, a person trained in behavioral methodologies and subject matter can make a worthwhile and professionally satisfying contribution. That doesn't mean that the jobs actually exist now (although many innovative careers are being pursued); for the most part, we are still talking about *potential* employment. Various educational institutions, individuals, and committees are working essentially in promotional ways to make such potential careers into realities. Anyone wishing to get a glimpse of the future or to broaden his or her outlook regarding what psychologists can do is urged to examine the book *Career Opportunities for Psychologists*.

Most of the readers of the present book are, for the time being at least, primarily concerned with employment prospects at the baccalaureate level. Those graduating from college with majors in psychology are similar to and different from all other college graduates. They are just as well-qualified and should be as competitive and successful in the general job market as any other liberal arts graduates. But those aspects of their training that deal with the subject matter and methodology of psychology (including experimental methodology and statistics and an appreciation of the relatively unique ways psychologists view human behavior) give them a distinct advantage over other graduates in a variety of job situations. At this level of education we cannot talk about jobs for psychologists; those graduates looking for a job should not expect to find "psychology major" listed in the qualifications or job description. A student graduating as a psychology major cannot expect to be employed as a psychologist any more than a student graduating from a prelaw program, say, can expect to be employed as a lawyer. Yet the psychology major is generally prepared for a wide variety of roles and is specifically prepared to fill many of them better and more competently than people who have majored in other fields.

This book was prepared with two audiences in mind: students and faculty. If students read this book early enough in their college careers—years before they are in the job market—they might improve their qualifications and chances of success by planning their programs differently. Programs can be improved by a judicious selection of electives both within and outside of the field of psychology and by arranging for work and field experience. Several contributors to this book stress the importance of experience from the employer's point of view. Students also might appreciate, before it is too late, the relevance and marketability of some of their courses (e.g., "Why do I have to study statistics and experimental design when I want to work with disturbed children?"). Many courses have the goal not of teaching specific job skills but of making the student more "psychologically minded." And in many jobs this frame of reference will put psychology majors a step ahead in competency and satisfaction. When the time for job hunting does arrive, students will find herein much advice of direct value. Some very helpful chapters on techniques and strategies are summarized more fully below.

Those faculty members who are struggling with students on such issues as required core courses might find this book a helpful ally. They also might find it a source of stimulation for program modifications or additions. It is my impression that with only a little effort and without disturbing the integrity of a basic psychology program, variations can be introduced to improve students' qualifications and competitiveness in the job market. Faculty will also be pleased, I predict, with the help offered by those chapters dealing with techniques and strategies for obtaining employment.

In the process of editing this book, I have had extensive correspondence with a number of people; some of them, while not contributing chapters, made points and reported recollections that deserve mention. A professor at a major university wrote:

I would like to add that our suggestion that students take first courses in accounting, business law, and business management has been widely accepted among our undergraduates, even among those who hope to go to graduate school.

Paul J. Woods is a professor of psychology at Hollins College.

The director of a neuropsychology laboratory at a university medical center reported the following personal experience:

I have no manuscript describing employment of persons with a bachelor's degree (major in psychology), but I have for many years employed people at this level if they could demonstrate exceptional adaptability, flexibility, and multifaceted abilities to cope pleasantly with the complexities of dealing with the public and with patients and patients' relatives in a service delivery, teaching, and research system. Such persons are given on-the-job training to administer an extensive battery of tests according to standard instructions; to conduct structured information interviews; to answer telephone inquiries professionally, sympathetically, and effectively; to search records; to tabulate data accurately; to pursue library searches; and to perform numerous receptionist and clerical duties.

Personal characteristics of cooperation, flexibility, reliability, concern for patients' and relatives' comfort, prudent judgment, and ability to carry through on many needed tasks without constant supervision are, in my view, even more important than the specific formal coursework completed by a candidate for positions such as "psychological technician" or "psychological assistant," because on-the-job training must be given and would usually be quite specific to the operations and needs of the particular employment setting.

Then from a university professor, I received a general recollection:

We have taken a look at what our graduates are doing (not a very systematic look, I am afraid, and our conclusions may be highly biased by the fact that we only know about the activities of those students we could find and who responded to the probings of the Alumni Office—the source of our data). In general, of our locatable and responsive graduates who did not go on to graduate school, slightly more than half are in "people-related jobs"—but people related is pretty loosely defined. Some of them, however, seem to be in jobs that relate fairly closely to undergraduate training in psychology (working in an institution for the mentally deficient, for the Big Brother organization, in a drug crisis center, etc.), but more of the jobs seem to be more peripherally related to psychological training (airline stewardess, salesperson, receptionist, etc.).

And, finally, a college professor wrote:

I will be happy to share with you my own informal survey on where our graduates go. . . . For those who do not go on to graduate school, several have entered the following jobs: biofeedback technician; paramedic; women's health-related occupations, such as contraceptive counseling or family planning counseling; psychiatric aides or counselors at state mental hospitals; group home counselors; geriatric counselors; youth center directors or counselors; transcendental meditation teachers; industry training and apprentice programs; child care workers; various state jobs, either in psychology-related areas like employment counseling or in non-psychology-related areas such as surveying; and finally the ACTION programs.

Overview

Keeping in mind the two major audiences and the various purposes of this book, I have organized the contributions into four sections. Different sections will, it is hoped, suit the needs of particular persons at different times and can be read independently of other sections, although it is recommended that students familiarize themselves with all of the contributions. Students should find within these pages information and suggestions that will have a major impact on their undergraduate programs and career plans.

Preparation and Strategies for Employment

The first section consists basically of "how-to-do-it" chapters. While written especially for the psychology major, it contains valuable guidance and advice for almost everyone at the undergraduate level. The first two chapters should be reviewed and their suggestions considered early in the undergraduate career. One can obtain a broad liberal arts education and still include courses and experiences that will greatly enhance one's employment potential. Chapter 2 brings together some specific suggestions relating to academic preparation, to the building of skills, especially through direct involvement with professors and others outside of the usual course work, and, finally, to the development of a "professional network." A professional network is a collection of persons working in the field that a student gets to know personally and who get to know that student. They can be of great value to one's education and subsequent employment. One strategy for building a professional network while at the same time gaining the valuable *experience* so many employers desire is through volunteering, which is discussed in Chapter 3. Cheap labor for an organization and easy credit for the student are *not* what volunteering is about. Jeanne Foley discusses the value of volunteering in terms of its relevance to the student's goals and calls it "altruism with a plus." Volunteering is one way to determine if one really likes and is suited for a particular line of work before making too much of an investment and too strong a commitment. This chapter should convince everyone of the many benefits connected with volunteering.

The remaining chapters in this first section are more relevant to the task of job seeking, but they have some relevance to career *planning* and, hence, should also be read at an early stage in the undergraduate career. Bruce Fretz's chapter on "Where to Look for Positions" involves a description of career options that may very well broaden the psychology major's usual view that the mental hospital is the only place to obtain work related to psychology. In Chapter 5 the same author offers models for résumés and cover letters and, perhaps even more important, some very specific suggestions on how to conduct oneself in an interview.

This section closes with a chapter on an alternative to the "traditional" résumé. Long before they actually begin to enter the job market, students should read this chapter by Vicki M. Wilson on the qualifications brief. A qualifications brief is far more comprehensive than a résumé and should be developed *during* a student's educational experience rather than merely summarizing it at the end. The extra effort involved in developing a qualifications brief may pay off in important ways. Not only will it help applicants "sell" themselves, it will also help them clarify their real objectives. This excellent chapter should be of value to all undergraduates whether or not they are psychology majors.

Job Prospects: Potential and Real

Some large-scale surveys have attempted to determine where former students have found employment. An ambitious survey conducted by the

American Psychological Association (Cates, 1973) received replies in 1969–1970 from 4,320 baccalaureates. Specific jobs were not cited in the published account of this survey, although they were reported as being extremely diverse. The most numerous jobs cited were teachers (21%) and mental health or welfare workers (18%). In all, 27% of the respondents reported that their work was directly related to their training in psychology, and another 48% stated that it was somewhat related. These percentages are remarkably close to those from a much smaller survey reported by Lunneborg (1974), which covered 312 former psychology majors from a single university. Of those employed, 25% had jobs directly related to psychology, and overall, 53% reported that they were "in psychology" even though their job titles might not reflect it.

The second section of this book contains information from several categories of employers and from former undergraduates who are now employed.

Chapter 7 thoroughly covers job possibilities with the federal government. The author, John Tiedemann, is a psychologist employed by the U.S. Postal Service, and he discusses the federal job situation in specific detail. Opportunities for social science majors in general are quite varied, and Tiedemann points out that applicants may fail to recognize interesting jobs because the titles of advertised positions do not always clearly identify the kind of work performed. Tiedemann has tried to provide a better understanding of the federal job market and has grouped those positions for which persons with psychology backgrounds may qualify into four categories: clinical psychology or social service, research, personnel work, and general management. He then covers how to apply for federal jobs and which agencies hire psychology majors and provides an outlook on the chances of getting a government job.

Chapter 8 reports some encouraging findings from a survey of community agencies. Jerry L. Fryrear contacted over 300 agencies in four southern cities to inquire about openings for baccalaureate psychology majors and about the skills and experience required for these openings. About one third of the agencies contacted were mental health agencies; the other two thirds dealt with a wide range of services. Fryrear reports that 55% of the agencies sampled either have hired or would hire baccalaureates and that each agency averages 5.9 openings with average starting salaries of $7900. The most frequently mentioned skill requirements were interviewing ability, crisis intervention techniques, behavior modification skills, and knowledge of child development. The most frequently mentioned experience requirements were work with the culturally disadvantaged and work with the emotionally disturbed.

In recent years mental health workers below the professional (graduate-degree) level have been increasingly employed in a variety of human service settings. Persons in these roles are most often called paraprofessionals, psychology technicians, or mental health technicians. In Chapter 9 Carol J. Erdwins and Mark B. Mendelsohn report a survey of employment opportunities for such paraprofessionals in a metropolitan area (northern Virginia). They found a total of 322 paraprofessional positions in various human service agencies. The positions required these persons to perform many of the same activities as the mental health professional, although with more supervision; over 95% of the respondents engaged in some kind of therapeutic intervention and liaison work with the client's family. Interestingly, very few positions required the administration of psychological tests. A wide range of salaries was found, with public agencies generally offering higher starting wages. Opportunities for promotion, however, were very limited. Comparable numbers of similar openings can be expected in other metropolitan areas around the country. These authors close with some suggestions to academic departments planning to develop paraprofessional programs.

Edward J. Jordan, Jr., describes the types of jobs in the hospitals and clinics of the Veterans Administration that can be filled by people with a bachelor's degree in psychology. He reports a survey of a sample of VA facilities in which he found that 56% of those facilities employed bachelor's-level psychology technicians. The activities performed by such persons could be classified as psychodiagnostic testing (the most common response), neuropsychological testing, vocational rehabilitation, and research. Jordan points out some negative features of psychology technician positions but concludes that a gradual expansion of these types of positions can be expected in the future.

In Chapter 11 Patricia W. Lunneborg describes a challenge for the enterprising, well-prepared, and dedicated student. For one who has patience and persistence and is willing to start on a volunteer basis, a career in research is possible. Lunneborg describes the cold realities involved in obtaining such work but emphasizes the satisfactions.

The next four chapters involve surveys of students. These are modest in scope compared to the survey of more than 4,000 baccalaureates by Cates (1973), and they deal only with the graduates of particular programs. But they do contain interesting findings, and the reader may "relate" to them at a personal level.

Robert Titley conducted a longitudinal survey of psychology majors one, five, and ten years after graduation. The career patterns he uncovered led to the encouraging conclusion in Chapter 12 that baccalaureates in psychology have fared better in the job market than many have believed and than other surveys have indicated. His findings demonstrate that the career development process continues to operate beyond college. Indeed, given time, work experience, and, in many cases, additional education and training, there is evidence of *upward mobility* among psychology majors in a wide variety of human service and other occupations.

Graduates from the University of New Hampshire over a five-year period were surveyed by James Davis, whose findings are reported in Chapter 13. Davis found that most jobs obtained by bachelor's-level psychology graduates were in business. About one third obtained jobs in areas in which psychology appeared to be *directly* relevant, but over half of the graduates said they would major in psychology again if they had it to do over. Of particular interest to faculty is a discussion in this chapter of curriculum changes that did not require any major revision in the under-graduate program but that resulted in a program significantly more useful in terms of career preparation.

Related to these surveys is another one conducted by James Walsh at the University of Montana. Walsh concludes in Chapter 14 that under-graduate training in psychology constitutes not just a sound educational program but also a good way to get a job after graduation. Work *directly* in the field of psychology is not available for all, but, nonetheless, half of those at the University of Montana desiring such work (which was, however, a relatively small number of persons) did find it within six months of graduation. Furthermore, Walsh reports that students hired as behavior technicians in 1974 were earning over $15,000 several years later.

Finally, a survey I conducted which is reported in Chapter 15 might prove instructive to current students in that it contains "hindsight" reac-tions to undergraduate courses. The respondents (all of whom were women) rated courses as "directly relevant and/or useful" in jobs they had held since graduation. Basic courses such as learning, statistics, and experimental psychology appeared on the list. The jobs respondents initially obtained or advanced to without any graduate training were impressively (and encouragingly) diverse: air traffic control specialist, pro-bation officer, research assistant, adminstrative assistant, caseworker, news audience research administrator, emergency outreach counselor, claims processor, and, even, head bartender.

Training for Careers in Community Service, Mental Health, and Public Affairs

Material in this section should be of interest to both faculty and students; some of these programs and their components could serve as models and sources of stimulation to both audiences.

Sally Fullerton's extremely thorough chapter deals with the prepara-tion of bachelor's-level persons for careers in community service. She describes the generalist professional model that has been developed and evaluated over the past 10 years at the Lila Acheson Wallace School of Community Service and Public Affairs at the University of Oregon. Persons interested in community service work would do well to study this chapter carefully even if they are not planning to enter a formal program of the sort Fullerton describes. She deals extensively with the components of and issues related to the generalist model: (a) generalists versus spe-cialists issue, (b) professional roles and settings, (c) competencies needed, (d) student selection, (e) instructional program, (f) theory–practice integration, and (g) professional identification. She concludes her dis-cussion of the evaluation of the program by citing evidence that students are generally satisfied with their training, that many find jobs directly related to their career interests, that they have sufficient knowledge and skills to perform well in these professional roles, and that the agencies that hire them are pleased with their performance. Chapter 17, by Mary Harvey and Bryan T. Downes, is an extension of Chapter 16 in that it deals with new thrusts in the same Community Service and Public Affairs program at the University of Oregon. These chapters together thoroughly cover training and career issues in this area.

James P. McGee and Benjamin Pope in Chapter 18 (which originally appeared in *Professional Psychology*) trace the development of the use of paraprofessionals in the mental health field. This historical account is an appropriate introduction to other chapters in this section. McGee and Pope are concerned with the more academically oriented mental health worker programs at both the Associate of Arts and Bachelor of Arts levels. They summarize innovative principles that have been incorporated into various undergraduate training programs, describe their own program, and conclude that no technical obstacle exists to the integration of mental health programs with psychology programs.

The variety of community agencies that have developed and expanded since the late 1950s has resulted in an increased need for personnel. Citing other analyses of personnel supply and demand, Raymond P. Lorion notes in Chapter 19 that such services cannot be delivered if professionals are the sole treatment agents. New roles, such as mental health workers, mental health technicians, community aides, and community counselors, have evolved in the human service system. Lorion describes undergraduate training in the human services field and interesting practicum settings. Students reading this chapter should note the benefits stated by one individual who worked in a practicum setting:

The work really increased my interest in mental health. Most of all, it has shown me my strong points, weak points, and even some areas where I know almost nothing. Some of what was in the books makes sense now; some of it seems too distant to be useful. I've learned some important things about what I can do and how I feel about working with people who are very different and more in need of help than anyone I have ever known.

Kenneth M. Shemberg and Stuart M. Keeley in Chapter 20 describe another model for the training of subprofessional mental health workers. Their program is divided into three major phases. Phase 1 is a 10-week introductory course in clinical psychology which serves as a basic background and as a screening program to select the small number of students who will be allowed to continue. Phase 2, also of 10 weeks' duration, is the basis of the training program. The academic component of this phase has goals ranging from mastering the basic principles of operant conditioning and social learning, to acquiring interview and observational skills, to becoming sensitive to ethical problems, to writing reports. Another component of this phase consists of one-day-a-week placement on a clinical team consisting of two PhD clinical psychologists and from four to six graduate students. Finally, Phase 3, the real-world experience, is a 20-week placement in a mental health setting. Experience with their students leads Shemberg and Keeley to believe that this program offers meaningful personal, educational, and intellectual growth.

After experimenting with a five-year double baccalaureate degree program, the Psychology Department at the University of North Carolina at Greensboro developed a program incorporating a supervised practicum resulting in the traditional degree in four years plus a certificate in behavioral technology. This program, described by Robert G. Eason in Chapter 21, was designed to provide the necessary knowledge and skills for individuals to function effectively as behavioral technicians (under appropriate supervision) in service-oriented institutions and settings. This program interferes neither with the traditional requirements for the psychology major nor with the liberal arts program of the university. So far, only a few individuals have completed the program, but feedback from their employing agencies has been "very positive."

Issues such as public housing, highway construction, senior citizen programs, community mental health programs, transportation, rehabilitation, unemployment, pollution control, or preservation all have psychological dimensions that would benefit from the conceptual and analytical approach of psychology. Dean John E. Kerrigan, who is not a psychologist himself, recognizes this fact and is keenly interested in the preparation of undergraduates for careers in the public sector. In Chapter 22 he describes the educational processes of a program for undergraduates in public affairs psychology. It can serve as a model for any department wishing to move in this direction or as an eye-opener for students who are considering career alternatives.

In the final chapter in this section, Thomas J. Kramer and James H. Korn distinguish between their career-oriented program and vocational programs that prepare students for a specific job. Their intention is "to help students develop career-planning and decision-making strategies as skills that will be useful to them later in life whatever their vocation." Their program is related to the needs of their community, and their graduates are uniquely prepared for human service careers in education, government, mental health, and business. This chapter, like others in this book, can serve as a comparison model and source of stimulation for other departments as well as a means of broadening the perspective of the undergraduate.

The Undergraduate Major: Surveys, Models, and Problems

Faculty members are the primary audience for this section, although it also contains material that should interest students. Chapter 24 reports results of a survey of psychology departments by Harry J. Parker and John J. Hedl, Jr. Their survey, which covered institutions in the southwest United States, may have nationwide implications and can serve as a model for persons in other regions. In the survey, department chairpersons were asked to indicate (a) the purposes of the psychology major at their school, (b) the curriculum emphases within the major, (c) the nature of required practica and fieldwork experiences, and (d) the degree of emphasis attached to each of the curricular purposes. Departments that listed "employment of graduates in psychologically oriented occupations" as one of the purposes of the psychology major also listed three specific occupations their graduates had entered.

In Chapter 25 Walter Mink reports on a questionnaire survey designed to tap current practices and expectations of liberal arts college departments and university graduate departments. Faculty sensitive to the need to assess their own programs will find useful information here. (Two thirds of the liberal arts colleges surveyed reported major curriculum revisions since 1972. Almost half of the departments reported an attempt to prepare students for careers at the bachelor's level, and two thirds believe it is appropriate to do so.) Students with either career or graduate study goals should note that in this survey, graduate departments reported that they view research experience as more important than internships and teaching experience when selecting students. The author also cites a related study that reported the value of research and measurement, interpersonal, and communication skills.

Chapter 26, by Thomas J. Kramer and Ellen Harshman, describes a framework for sound internship supervision, which is based on a handbook prepared by Kramer to assist his fellow faculty members at Saint Louis University in supervising undergraduate internships. This chapter is included as a model for faculty consideration and for students at other institutions.

In Chapter 27 Barbara F. Nodine describes a small, college interdisciplinary program that integrates a major in psychology with training in special education. With the bachelor's degree in psychology, students receive state certification to teach mentally and/or physically handicapped children and youth. Job placements of their graduates indicate the program has succeeded in its mission of training generalists in special education.

Relatively small departments can arrive at a consensus to move in a given direction regarding program innovation and can sustain interest and support among the faculty for a reasonable period. Larger, more heterogeneous departments, however, are more likely to be subject to conflicts of interest and competition pressures from incompatible program directions. Departments considering innovative programs would do well to assess their situation in light of the case study discussed by Rosa Lynn Pinkus in Chapter 28. She describes the rise and reasons for demise of a program at a major university that was designed to prepare college graduates for careers in psychology or psychology-related professions. If programs at other universities are likely to succumb to the same forces, one wonders if the exercise is worth the effort.

In Chapter 29 Patricia Keith-Spiegel and David L. Cole spell out some of the areas of resistance to changing the undergraduate training model. Ignoring these problems will not make them go away, and these authors are to be commended for not shying away from controversy.

The final chapter in this section reports on the results of a survey of over 200 undergraduate psychology majors from three different types of institutions: a large state university, a relatively small state college, and a small private liberal arts college. This work was contributed by Lisa Gray-Shellberg, Patricia Keith-Spiegel and Hana Kornwasser. One of their findings truly justifies the need for the current book: Only a relatively small percentage of the students surveyed could be said to have "constructive and useful ideas" relating to how to go about looking for a job in their area of interest in psychology. Other findings in this chapter deserve careful attention: Three out of every four students plan to pursue graduate study in psychology; many students seem to be unaware of the contemporary training and job market issues, overestimating their chances of being professional psychologists; new psychologically related vocations should be created and career programs should be instituted at the baccalaureate level.

Appendixes

The book closes with some information-packed appendixes. The first, by Teresa McDevitt and Douglas Bloomquist, is an annotated bibliography on curriculum and careers in psychology and is a resource for those wishing to go beyond the coverage of this book. In the next appendix, the Qualifications Standards for psychology jobs in the federal government are reprinted for easy access. Following this is a comprehensive listing of Federal Job Information Centers and State Personnel Offices compiled by Bruce Fretz and John Tiedemann. The final appendix is for those who are considering or planning to go to graduate school. The competition is keen, and Vicki M. Wilson and Patricia W. Lunneborg spell out excellent strategies for admission. No one interested in graduate work should fail to study this chapter carefully, and it is hoped that faculty will bring it to the attention of their students already planning on graduate work.

REFERENCES

Cates, J. Baccalaureates in psychology: 1969 and 1970. *American Psychologist*, 1973, *28*, 262–264.
Lunneborg, P. W. Can college graduates in psychology find employment in their field? *Vocational Guidance Quarterly*, 1974, *23*, 159–166.
Woods, P. J. (Ed.). *Career opportunities for psychologists: Expanding and emerging areas.* Washington, D.C.: American Psychological Association, 1976.

Part I

Preparation and Strategies for Employment

2

Steve Saxon, Bruce R. Fretz,
and John G. Tiedemann

Increasing One's Chances of Future Employment While Still in College

This chapter presents some basic preparatory steps that students can take, while still in college, to improve the likelihood of being employed upon graduation. These steps include academic preparation, skills acquisition, and the development of a professional network. Also suggested are courses that improve potential employability, procedures for acquiring skills, and techniques for the building of a professional network.

Academic Preparation

A 1975 survey of faculty and personnel who work in career advisement and placement suggests that psychology students increasingly need to combine psychology with other courses if their education is to lead more directly to employment at the bachelor's-degree level. Those surveyed recommended that students interested in maximizing their employment opportunities need to take two or more courses in at least one of the following areas: economics, business administration, personnel administration, marketing, consumer education, journalism, speech, communications, English composition (for editing, technical writing), biological and ecological sciences, math/statistics, computer science, sociology, and social work. Survey respondents also noted that music, art, and recreation courses pertaining to the therapeutic use of these disciplines are also very valuable.

Courses that don't carry much weight with prospective employers without accompanying skills include history and systems of psychology, theories of management, individual theories of personality, and generalized survey courses.

Advanced courses usually carry more weight than introductory courses, and, although an applicant's proficiency in a certain area is measured by the total number of credit hours he or she has amassed in that area, the courses must show an accumulation of progressively more advanced skills. For example, one applicant for a research psychologist position requiring considerable skills in research design and statistics was disappointed to find that his twelve credits in statistics were evaluated at little more than three credits, because the courses were Introductory Statistics in Psychology, Introductory Statistics in Business, Introductory Statistics in Economics, and Introductory Statistics in the Biological Sciences—all essentially equivalent courses. Students planning their college curriculum with an eye to future employment would do well to move quickly into the advanced courses and to avoid as much as possible courses that offer overlapping material or skills already attained in other courses.

Students should also look at some of the findings in Chapter 15 of this book, entitled "Employment Following Two Different Undergraduate Programs in Psychology." This chapter describes a survey in which former students were asked which courses were directly relevant and/or useful to them in jobs they had held since graduation. The survey also asked which courses students had *not* taken that they subsequently wished they *had*.

Skills Building

Although "think tanks" do exist around the country, most industries, businesses, and government agencies are involved in applying already-established procedures toward solving existing problems. Therefore, especially at the entry level, it is what the applicant can *do* that the prospective employer will buy. Skills are more important than philosophies. Prospective applicants should emphasize their technical, rather than theoretical, knowledge on application forms and in any interviews unless an interviewer specifically leads the interview into a theoretical discussion.

The following are some skills prospective employers are looking for: statistics or mathematics, testing skills (construction, validation, administration, and interpretation), interviewing skills, research design, physiology and biochemistry, survey techniques, data collection procedures, questionnaire design, teaching or training skills, communication skills (both written and oral), briefing techniques, foreign language skills, courses in political or social science, courses in government or business administration (including budget, finance, and law), and automatic data-processing skills.

Students can begin to develop such skills through their coursework, but many of these skills can also be acquired or developed further through direct involvement in such areas as research, consulting, and service delivery. These sorts of experiences can be gained through field placements made with the help of faculty and by contacts developed entirely on the student's own initiative. Such a strategy is discussed in detail in the next chapter.

Steve Saxon is with the Training, Consultation, and Education Division of the Alcoholism, Drug Abuse, and Mental Health Services of the Orange County, California, Human Services Agency; Bruce R. Fretz is a professor of psychology at the University of Maryland; and John G. Tiedemann is in private practice in Washington, D.C.

Another commonly overlooked resource for skills development beyond that gained in formal course work is professors. Most professors have professional involvements outside their academic teaching that are of interest and value to students. They frequently do clinical work, research, program planning, writing, and all sorts of consultation and are often quite willing to involve students in this work. But the student must usually take the initiative in cultivating this resource. Because of their teaching, committee obligations, and professional work, professors often *seem* unreachable, but the student should not assume that they are. And if a first attempt at contact turns up a professor who is reluctant to have an "apprentice," the student should not give up! There are other faculty more approachable and even eager to have students working with them.

Developing a Professional Network

A professional network is a collection of persons working in the field whom the student knows and who know the student. It is a pipeline to jobs, a source of recommendations, a means of expanding the student's professional awareness, and an important means of staying abreast of the field. The sooner the student begins building a network, the better; students should not wait until they are actually looking for jobs.

One of the most underutilized approaches to acquiring experience and making contacts is that of using one's status as a student. (The term *student* is here used in its most generic sense.) The approach is fairly simple: It entails finding someone who is doing something one likes or finds interesting, calling or visiting that person, and stating that one is a student interested in what the person is doing and in working with him or her. First, this approach is flattering and constitutes a compliment to the person one has chosen. Second, as a student one is generally seen as moldable and hence capable of becoming a protegé, something nearly every professional would like to have. Third, a learning environment is created which allows one to ask questions and be ignorant with little likelihood of negative repercussions, since students are supposed to ask questions. Fourth, people will take time with students that they generally won't take with another professional. And fifth, such an approach is helpful in building a professional network and can often lead to some kind of "assistantship."

People are often reluctant to approach well-known professionals. This seems to be especially true for students. "They're too busy," "They don't know me," and "They wouldn't want to bother" are common fantasies that accompany the idea of meeting well-known professionals. This simply may not be true. The "well-knowns" are as approachable as anyone else, often more so. Each year there are visiting professors at universities all over the country whose time and talents go underutilized. Finding them and talking with them will not only expand the student's professional network but will demonstrate the student's initiative and interest as well.

One fact is as true in network building as in skills building: Professors are an overlooked and underutilized resource. As stated earlier, professors often seem unreachable; generally this is untrue. A professor can become a friend or a mentor, in either case a valuable addition to the student's professional network. Professors, of course, have their own professional networks and, when appropriate, can make personal contacts potentially of great value to their students.

Part of building a professional network is knowing other people and what they are doing. One of the best and simplest ways of accomplishing this is to join various professional organizations. The most relevant organizations for psychologists are the American Psychological Association and the state psychological associations. Information on student membership in the American Psychological Association can be obtained by writing to its main office at 1200 17th Street, N.W., Washington, D.C. 20036. From that office can also be obtained the addresses of the membership chairpersons of the state psychological associations. The state psychological associations usually have annual meetings that provide great opportunities to meet professional psychologists from throughout the student's state. The newsletters and journals that these organizations publish are also good sources for identifying people, places, and issues. Most of these organizations have student membership categories, they want student involvement, and the cost is usually minimal. Joining one is a good way to meet people and discover job opportunities while demonstrating one's excitement with the field and expanding one's professional network.

3

Jeanne M. Foley

Gaining Experience by Volunteering: Altruism With a Plus

This chapter, which should be read early in a student's undergraduate career, discusses volunteering and similar activities that provide firsthand experience in psychology. Such experience can be of great value in investigating careers, in obtaining a job after graduation, and for personal development. A final section provides suggestions on how to find and evaluate volunteer placements as well as a discussion of the volunteer's responsibility.

Until recently, volunteers have been regarded as those who donate time and energy to help a group that can not afford to pay staff; altruism has traditionally been the volunteer's primary motivation. Aside from wanting the experience to be worthwhile and reasonably interesting, most student volunteers have given little thought to using such activity to enhance their job opportunities or help them toward careers.

Today, however, although student volunteers still want to help others and to feel useful, there is an added incentive for volunteering. Besides the altruistic aspects, students are discovering a distinctly practical aspect to volunteering that is directly relevant to their personal, academic, and career goals. That is, the motivation for volunteering has changed toward what I like to call "altruism with a plus," a plus that can mean a variety of benefits for the psychology student.

Faculty are beginning to realize that volunteering can represent a valuable learning experience worthy of encouragement and even academic credit. And some psychologists have seriously begun to consider the benefits of volunteering and to develop it from a mere opportunity for cheap course credit to a respectable part of the psychology curriculum.

Benefits of Volunteering

In this presentation of the benefits that can accrue to the student volunteer, I emphasize the advantages of volunteering for deciding upon a career and getting a job. Other practical benefits, such as admission to a graduate program, as well as purely personal benefits, are also described.

And in a final section I provide general comments about volunteering and some ideas on finding and evaluating volunteer jobs.

Before describing some of the benefits, it may be well to note that a number of options fall under the general rubric of volunteer work. Courses may be offered that focus on volunteer activity but that may also include some supervision, class meetings, or assignments; titles of such courses often include the terms *internship*, *field study*, *fieldwork*, or *practicum*. Sometimes students may fulfill more limited requirements for a course through volunteering or may have the option of volunteering instead of doing some other assignment such as writing a paper. Although, by defini-tion, volunteering is something one does without pay, if one is very fortunate it is sometimes possible to be paid for work that others do on a volunteer basis. For example, at the child-care facility at the Loyola University of Chicago, approximately 40 students have volunteered to work with the children for 5 hours each week. However, several students who have already demonstrated their competence and who qualify for the work-study program have been invited to be paid teacher aides. This is cer-tainly volunteering with a plus!

Choosing a Career

Perhaps the most important benefit volunteering offers initially is in help-ing to answer the question, "Would I really like to have a job doing this type of work?" It is one thing to read about schizophrenics, disturbed children, or the aged and to think the subject very interesting; it is another thing to work with these groups on a year-to-year basis. Some students, for example, may like children but may not enjoy working with severely disturbed children for extended periods. Others may discover that they become too emotionally involved. Progress with disturbed children is often excruciatingly slow and, Skinner notwithstanding, behavior modifi-cation does not "work" as fast as students may have been led to believe in class. Or perhaps a volunteer may be repelled by older children who are not toilet trained. As the director of one child-care facility said, "If you feel obliged to wash your tennis shoes after only one has been peed on, you're being too fussy." Finding that one is not suited for work with a particular group is not a reason to feel disheartened—one should simply regard the venture as a learning experience and try a different group. On the other hand, one may discover a real talent for working with a particular group.

It is important to recognize that a job as a volunteer will not be the same as that of a full-time, paid employee, but participation in a particular setting can provide a good opportunity to observe what various members of a staff with different types of training are doing. Whose job is desirable and what training would be needed to obtain a similar position?

Jeanne Foley is a professor of psychology at Loyola University of Chicago and the administrator of its Child Development Center.

As a psychology major the student might look especially closely at the roles of psychologists in this setting—are there jobs for those with bachelor's degrees or does it seem essential to have a master's degree or a doctorate? In some cases graduate school should be the next step for the volunteer.

What other types of professionals are working in this setting? One may have a chance to see what social workers, psychiatrists, physical therapists, occupational therapists, teachers of special education, and others are doing. Their work may suggest approaches through fields other than psychology. As a volunteer the student should be able to talk with these professionals about their satisfactions, dissatisfactions, training, and pay. A polite way to inquire about pay is to ask what a beginner in the field might expect to make and what the upper salary limits are.

Getting a Job

Even though it sometimes seems that school will continue forever, graduation does occur and students must face the problem of getting jobs. Obviously, majoring in psychology is popular, and many other students with similar academic backgrounds will be looking for jobs. Prospective employer's are not overly impressed merely by a background of interesting psychology courses and will want to know what else an applicant has to offer. This is where volunteer experience can really be useful. First, the volunteer has been in a real-life work situation. If applying for a job in an area related to the volunteer experience, the applicant should be able to talk knowledgeably about the work and why he or she wants the job and thinks he or she can handle it well. Even if the volunteer activity is not especially relevant to the desired job, volunteering seems to impress employers. For example, a student who had had a variety of volunteer activities and was about to graduate could scarcely contain his excitement when he got a job as a teacher. As he described it, "I told them about all the volunteering I had done and they were so pleased they didn't even want to see my transcript. And you know how hard it is to get a teaching job!"

As the employer warms to the idea of hiring an applicant, references may be necessary. In this area too the volunteer has an advantage. Although most students will want to ask their teachers for recommendations, it is often especially beneficial to have a letter from the person who supervised their volunteer activities. Needless to say, the person who is asked to write such a letter should have been impressed by the volunteer's qualities of diligence, reliability, pleasantness, and independence. Presumably, this is the type of person an employer would like to hire, and one's chances for employment will be increased.

A few words about recommendations from teachers may be in order at this point. These can be useful for students who have demonstrated laudable qualities and high achievement in class. However, unless a student has managed to have considerable interaction with faculty members outside of class, faculty are largely able to report only on academic achievement, with statements such as "John was an excellent student in my class and received an A. He was highly motivated and was pleasant." This sort of recommendation conveys little that might not be gathered from a transcript. In contrast, a person who has known the applicant in a work situation is likely to have comments about performance that are more pertinent to the concerns of an employer.

It is often possible, of course, to get to know teachers outside of class and to remedy the situation described above. Even if faculty members have large classes and appear to have little time for talking with students individually, it is possible to volunteer to help them with research or other work. An offer like this is sufficiently unusual to create an impression and, after a few moments of incredulity, a teacher may often work something out with the student. Provided the student follows through in a satisfactory manner, such an arrangement can produce excellent material for a letter. And if volunteering is not an option, doing independent study with a faculty member is another good way to become known.

A couple of success stories may help to illustrate the benefit of volunteer work in getting a job. One student in a class on aging volunteered to escort a group of senior citizens from a nearby housing project to a restaurant for dinner and entertainment. The student was responsible for taking the group in a bus and joining them for dinner. Rather to his surprise, he had a great time. He followed up with participation in other activities and attended a monthly intergenerational discussion group involving senior citizens and college students. Although he had previously thought mainly about working with children, he decided he would rather work with the aged. With little difficulty he obtained a job as a counselor for elderly clients at a community mental health center, largely (according to him) because he was the only applicant who had actually had experience working with senior adults. After working there for two years he decided that he needed more education, and he is now completing his master's in social work with a specialization in gerontology.

A second example, although it does not involve a career in psychology, also illustrates the value of volunteer work. A student who had worked with the local alderwoman as part of a fieldwork program in college was hired as her full-time assistant upon graduating. This job paid well and fit with the student's interest in politics.

Of course, not everyone who volunteers is so fortunate, but those who volunteer definitely seem to improve their chances for employment in the areas that interest them. The director of a day shool for severely disturbed children reported that notices are often posted on the bulletin board announcing the availability of paid positions in similar facilities for volunteers when they graduate. The director also noted that volunteers who have demonstrated excellence in working with disturbed children seem more likely to get into graduate programs in psychology than those who have not done such work.

Getting Into Graduate School

This brings us to a related topic—the importance of volunteering in gain-ing admission to graduate programs. The type of credentials needed for admission to graduate school are likely to be different from those needed for employment; those who screen applicants for graduate work are generally more concerned about academic achievement and Graduate Record Examination scores than about volunteer experience. Recom-mendations from teachers who can attest to the student's superior qualities are likely to take precedence over letters from work supervisors. Nevertheless, a school will find it reassuring to know that an applicant for a doctoral program in clinical psychology, for example, is not only intelligent but has good interpersonal skills and shows ability for working with patients, children, or adolescents. A student who was an excellent research assistant on a volunteer basis might also be more likely to obtain as a graduate student an assistantship that provides a stipend and tuition benefits.

Personal Benefits

A good volunteer experience can make coursework more relevant or mean-ingful. Seeing something firsthand makes it seem more real than reading about it in a textbook or hearing about it in a lecture. For example, two teachers of developmental psychology at Loyola University started a day-care center for normal children. One of the motivations for starting the center was to have a facility in which students could observe children. Volunteers worked at the center each week and found that language development, cognitive development, play behavior, and the like all took on new meaning. The students not only enjoyed themselves but learned a number of skills relevant to adult–child interactions and discipline that were both good preparation for parenting. In fact, a study on students' responses to a questionnaire about handling various problems with children indicated volunteers scored higher in terms of presenting accepta-ble child-rearing approaches than those who only attended class. Although those who volunteered may have been more gifted in working with children from the start, a pretest given prior to the volunteer work did not suggest that they had superior knowledge.

One never knows where information gained in volunteering will be helpful. Parenting is an obvious application, but volunteering can also be helpful in graduate studies. One graduate student I knew had considerable volunteer experience in a state mental hospital. While others were trying to memorize the behaviors and symptoms that are diagnostic criteria for Wilson's disease or Parkinson's disease, she thought to herself, "No problem. I just think of Mr. Smith. He had all the symptoms." Whatever diagnostic group the students had to know about, she had seen a typical case.

Volunteers working with adult mental patients and disturbed children have sparked research on the effects that this experience may have on the volunteers themselves and their adjustment. Although volunteers may be different from nonvolunteers, some findings suggest that volunteers develop more positive attitudes about themselves and score better on various personality measures after their volunteer experience.

The considerable emphasis I have placed on the benefits of volunteering for the volunteer should not be read as approval of a "What's in it for me?" attitude. Needless to say, the personal benefits noted above are far less likely to occur if one volunteers simply to get points with supervisors or teachers. The volunteer who is valued and makes a positive impression is the one who is highly motivated, who is really interested in the job, and who is willing to work extra in a crunch. The student who merely "puts in time" or who stands about chatting and drinking coffee might as well stay home.

Hints for Volunteers

Some volunteer jobs are better than others, and it is important to find the right spot. Advice on locating such an opening is not easy to give because possibilities vary a good deal with the size and type of community in which one lives. In a city like Chicago the possibilities are myriad, and it may be quite easy to find work to suit one's interests near home or school. In a small community options are more limited, and the potential volunteer may need to be more resourceful in locating a suitable activity or more flexible in adapting to what is available. Most large, nonprofit institutions, such as hospitals, have active volunteer programs and often have a director of volunteers who is available to discuss opportunities. Clinics, mental health centers, recreational programs, churches and synagogues, and schools (especially for small children or people who are disturbed, retarded, or handicapped) often need volunteers. The area of aging is popular, and work with senior adults in nursing homes, drop-in centers, or recreational programs is likely to yield job opportunities after graduation. Thinking about the age and type of person one would like to work with is a good first step in deciding where to work, but it is important to keep an open mind. Volunteering is a way to *discover* interests and, like the student who rode the bus with the senior citizens, one might just find the focus for a career.

It is quite possible to go knocking on doors and locate volunteer opportunities without assistance; however, as a first step, it is helpful to check with one's university department, especially if it gives credit for field study or volunteering. Such departmental programs usually have a list of approved facilities, and the director may be willing to share sources even with a student not signing up for credit.

Loyola University of Chicago has a Volunteer Action Program that is operated by students. The students locate groups who want volunteers, determine whether the group provides valuable volunteer experience, and then recommend the group to potential volunteers. Each semester the program publishes a list of approved agencies and a description of the type of work available.

For the student trying independently to find placement, checking the phone book, visiting likely facilities, and asking friends or teachers can be helpful. Many faculty members have some type of community involvement or work with groups that would appreciate volunteers.

If none of these suggestions yields volunteer work, the student must then be especially resourceful. The local hospital (or other organization) may not have a volunteer program, but it might like one. Even if a community already has adequate opportunities for volunteers, developing a new volunteer program can have great advantages.[1] There are also many projects of less scope that might be developed to meet a specific need. Children are an appealing group, and numerous programs already exist for them. However, the needs of older persons have received little attention in the past, and many volunteer services could be helpful to them. Elderly persons who live alone in the community might enjoy visitors or a daily phone call to see that they are all right. Many senior citizens can handle independent living quite well but need an occasional helpful hand (or strong arm) for carrying groceries, trips downtown, household repairs, or a trip to the doctor.

As a final consideration, it is important to locate an organization that knows how to work with volunteers so that both it and the volunteer benefit. Some groups regard volunteers as cheap help and take advantage of them by loading them with work without providing adequate training or supervision. The opportunity to learn is minimal in such a setting. A responsible organization recognizes that the job should be a learning experience for volunteers even though this takes staff time. Those responsible for volunteers should recognize their level of training and competence and should not place them in situations that are too demanding; however, neither should all of the menial and dull jobs be assigned to volunteers. A balance of challenging and less stimulating work should be the aim.

At the other extreme are organizations in which the staff seems reluctant to let the volunteer do more than stand around and watch the professionals. Observing a good model is certainly a useful training procedure, but the volunteer also needs activity. If an organization does not have jobs that can be handled by college students, it should not enlist such volunteers.

Fortunately, many organizations are sensitive to these issues and treat their volunteers well—although they may need to be reminded that some supervision or instruction would be welcome. The volunteer should

---

1. The Volunteer Action Program at Loyola University was started by an undergraduate in cooperation with one of her psychology professors. After its first year of operation, they both received an award from the state of Illinois for developing the program. The student, who has since received her PhD, has become an expert on volunteers. She gained experience and made money to help finance her graduate education by planning and supervising the training of volunteers and by doing the research evaluation for a federally funded project involving student volunteers working with disadvantaged children. Her successor in the Volunteer Action Program was hired immediately after graduation by the state to work with their volunteer programs.

be aware of these potential problems, however, particularly if placement is sought without a list of recommended facilities checked by a department or school.

As a final word—volunteering is a two-way street, and volunteers also need to recognize their responsibilities. Anyone inspired to rush out and sign up for volunteer work should think about time and commitments. If there is any single thing that distresses organizations about volunteers, it is their lack of reliability and punctuality. A volunteer who is needed and valued is expected to be dependable. Students should not skip their volunteer work whenever there is a test, a quiz, or a paper due or because it seems like a good morning to sleep late. Emergencies do arise, but one prone to emergencies should not volunteer.

Volunteering has many advantages for the student and potential job seeker. Even if it does not produce any career magic, the satisfaction of altruism is itself a reward.

4

Bruce R. Fretz

Where to Look for Positions

There are many employment opportunities for psychology majors besides the ones in mental hospitals and related institutions and agencies to which students often feel restricted. This chapter should broaden the student's perspective on this question and could profitably be followed by a reading of Chapters 12 through 15, which deal with surveys of graduates and report a wide variety of jobs that actually were obtained by people at the bachelor's-degree level.

Students often think of mental hospitals as the only places for employment for those interested in work related to psychology. Listed below are positions to be found in many other types of agencies and settings. In various sections of the country, persons with bachelor's degrees have found interesting and challenging positions like these that utilize their knowledge of psychology.

1. Community Relations Officer: works either for business or government in promoting good relations with the local community.

2. Affirmative Action Officer: works for recruitment and equal opportunities for minorities; employed by business, industries, schools, and government.

3. Recreation Worker: plans and supervises community recreation facilities. (Increasing number of opportunities available for therapeutic recreation workers, often requiring coursework in therapeutic recreation.)

4. Urban Planning Officer: deals with city planning and renewal.

5. Personnel Administrator: works with employee relations, selection, promotions, etc.

6. Advertising Copywriter: researches audience and media, writes text of advertisements.

7. Media Buyer: researches product and audiences to select most effective media for advertising.

8. Health Educator: gives public information about health and disease.

9. Vocational Rehabilitation: counsels persons with handicaps and illnesses in preparation for new vocations. (Some states require a master's degree for this position.)

10. Psychiatric Assistant: administers routine tests, helps with patients under supervision of psychiatrist.

11. Director of Volunteer Service: responsible for volunteers—recruits, supervises, trains, and evaluates volunteers.

12. Public Statistician: collects and interprets data on health and disease and community relations.

13. Customs Inspector: serves at international borders and airports in investigations and inquiries.

14. Probation and Parole Officer: persons with psychology backgrounds are often preferred for such positions, especially with adolescent parolees.

15. Newspaper Reporter: social science, psychological interest areas.

16. Technical Writer: researches and writes material dealing with social science and psychological knowledge for magazines, newspapers, and journals.

17. Sales Representative: major publishers of psychological books often seek out undergraduates with psychology majors for these positions on college campuses.

18. Opinion Survey Researcher: does opinion polls and interprets results.

19. Daycare Center Supervisor: supervises and coordinates activities of preschool children with working parents.

20. Research Assistant: assists in the collection and analysis of data for major investigations. Positions usually available only in large hospitals, businesses, and government.

21. Laboratory Assistant: psychology background preferred for students working with animal behavior research, especially primate laboratories.

22. Scientific Instrument Salesperson: opportunities in sales and development for companies specializing in psychology apparatus.

I have *not* listed the numerous kinds of "counselor" roles that are available to many students with a bachelor's degree in a variety of social work service and mental agencies. Opportunities of this type are most abundant in the inner city and rural areas. Usually the student can find out about such opportunities through contacting local community service agencies (e.g., half-way programs for alcoholic or drug addicts, former prisoners, former mental hospital inmates, and former institutionalized retardates). Many of these programs provide interesting live-in possibilities with adequate pay; while they often do not offer much of a future as a career, for a beginning postbachelor's-degree position they can be quite challenging.

Once a general idea of which kinds of positions might be possible has been obtained, the student can begin to identify potential employers. The placement or career library on campus probably contains descriptive

---

Bruce R. Fretz is a professor of psychology at the University of Maryland.

employment brochures, manuals, and pamphlets for many companies and government agencies. These materials often provide information about the location of positions, wage scales throughout the country, and companies' histories, outlooks, and needs. Local chambers of commerce and state employment agencies are also significant sources of information for the student's local area. A worthwhile project for any Psi Chi chapter or psychology club wishing to develop better knowledge of local employment resources for its members would be a survey of all the agencies in its area that employ people in any of the occupations noted above. Much useful information might be gained by a series of telephone calls and/or letters to the personnel departments of area businesses, hospitals, research institutes, newspapers, advertising agencies, market research departments, professional and technical journals, public relations firms, test development corporations, military bases, departments of correction, adoption and child care centers, mental health agencies, and all service agencies listed in the brochures of the United Fund or other local charity groups.

State Government. State government employment opportunities will vary from state to state, although merit or civil service systems are established in all of the states. Addresses of State Personnel Offices appear in Appendix C. Students should write or call the appropriate agency or office in their state for information. State job qualifications are similar to those adopted for federal positions. Thus, education, experience, and examination performance will determine merit rating for state jobs.

Federal Government. There are extensive opportunities at the federal-government level as well. Full coverage of this area can be found in Chapter 7 in the next section.

5

Bruce R. Fretz

Presenting Yourself

This chapter provides specific suggestions on crucial components of the job-seeking process: the résumé and its cover letter, the interview, and the follow-up. Included are samples of a cover letter and two résumés, a list of interviewing behaviors and characteristics that often lead to an applicant's rejection, and a list of questions frequently asked during employment interviews. All those entering the job market should study this chapter carefully and then review the section on the interview when they have one scheduled. Actual role playing of interviews with friends is suggested.

In seeking a job, three presentations must be made: (a) the résumé (vita), (b) the cover letter, and (c) the personal interview. The quality of these presentations, especially when positions are limited, is critical. A few helpful hints follow.

The Résumé

A résumé is a brief sketch aimed at enlisting an employer's interest in a potential employee. The résumé should include the candidate's name, address, and telephone number; education and employment record; references (including both faculty and employers); and career objectives. Pertinent extracurricular activities and interests might also be included. The résumé should be kept to one page unless an applicant has an unusual amount of past employment experience. It should be neat and well typed. Candidates applying for several very different kinds of positions may want to prepare a different résumé for each type of position, since one of the useful pieces of information on the résumé is the career objective, which may differ according to setting. Sample résumés are provided at the end of this chapter. Applicants may also wish to consider the more demanding but potentially more valuable alternative to the traditional résumé, the qualifications brief, which is presented in the next chapter.

A cover letter should be specific and concise. Since a résumé will be included with it, it should not repeat information on the résumé. The letter should begin with a reference to the specific position for which the candidate is applying and should briefly state how the position fits the candidate's career objective. A mailing address and phone number should definitely be included in this letter. (See the example at the end of this chapter.)

The Interview

The employment interview may be one of the most important events in the job seeker's experience, for the obvious reason that the 20 or 30 minutes spent with the interviewer may greatly alter the entire future course of his or her life. Yet interviewers are continually amazed at the number of applicants who drift into job interviews without any apparent preparation and only the vaguest idea of what they are going to say. Their manner says, "Well, here I am," and that is often the end of it in more ways than one.

Others, although they undoubtedly do not intend to do so, create an impression of indifference by acting too casually. With the tight labor market existing at this time, job candidates bear the responsibility of projecting themselves in an enthusiastic, positive manner in order to appear competitive.

Still other applicants work themselves into a state of mind in which they feel as if they are being marched into a medieval inquisition chamber. When they arrive for the interview they are in the last stages of nervous fright and are unable to do much more than gulp and answer in monosyllables. It is important for this type of applicant to realize that the recruiter is also a human being and in most cases a very pleasant one.

Prior to the interview, students should research the organization to which they have applied. The types of positions and programs the organization has to offer should be matched against the applicant's interests. Information about the organization's size, locations, services, and products will give candidates something besides themselves to talk about during the interview and can provide material to form pertinent questions. Information about major companies and employers may be found in references such as *Standard and Poor's Register* (1978), *Moody's Industrial Manual* (1978), and other technical and professional journals or in materials available in college libraries and career-center or placement-office libraries.

It is difficult to actually rehearse for an upcoming interview because it is impossible to know what cues will be given. Relying on native courtesy and good sense is the best strategy, although practice in interviewing with friends may increase an applicant's confidence. However, there are some basic rules and situations common to many interviews that may be of help to the applicant who knows about them ahead of time.

1. It is essential to be on time.
2. Correct pronunciation of the interviewer's name should be determined in advance.

Bruce R. Fretz is a professor of psychology at the University of Maryland.

3. Cues should be taken from the interviewer at the start. If the recruiter moves to shake hands, the applicant should do so—but not unless the recruiter makes the first gesture. Applicants should normally wait until offered a chair before sitting down.

4. Chewing gum or smoking should be avoided unless an invitation to do so is extended.

5. At least one surprise question right at the start of the interview should be expected. A few interviewers favor such openers as "What can I do for you?" "Tell me about yourself," or "Why are you interested in this organization?" These are not easy questions to answer without some previous thought, and preparation for them will pay off.

In answer to the first question, the candidate should respond by stating that he or she would like to apply for a job in a certain operation of the organization and would like to progress into a more advanced phase. Interest in progress with the organization should be expressed as specifically as possible. If the recruiter asks the candidate to talk about himself or herself, the candidate should mention personal characteristics that relate to the particular job. Candidates must learn to articulate personal strengths and assets and to be informative without boasting or telling their troubles. If asked why they are interested in the organization, candidates who have studied the organization's literature will not be at a loss for words.

6. Applicants should look the interviewer directly in the eye and continue to do so from time to time during the conversation. This is important, as nearly every interviewer is conscious of such eye contact. Applicants should also remember to smile frequently, at appropriate occasions.

7. A few interviewers like to do most of the talking and to judge applicants by their reactions—that is, by the interest, comprehension, and intelligence demonstrated. Other interviewers hardly speak at all, and for an amateur interviewee these are the hardest to deal with. Applicants who get the impression that an interview is not going well and that they have already been rejected, should not let their discouragement show. There is nothing to lose and maybe much to gain by continuing the appearance of confidence. The last few minutes often change things. Sometimes an interviewer who is genuinely interested in a candidate's possibilities may seem to discourage the candidate in order to test his or her reaction. By remaining confident and determined, the candidate will probably make a good impression.

8. Applicants should convey their good points to the interviewer. Such traits won't become apparent unless the applicant brings them into the discussion, but this should be done in a factual and sincere manner. These qualities are highlighted best if they can be related to a concrete example. For example, saying "I paid for 75% of my college expenses through part-time employment" is better than saying "I am a hard worker and want to get ahead." The first statement establishes the point more convincingly than the second.

9. Most interviews follow a rather simple question-and-answer format. If such is the case, the ability to answer quickly and intelligently is of great importance. Confused and contradictory answers insure failure. The greatest preventive measure for contradictory answers is the plain, umembroidered truth. A frank answer, even if it seems somewhat unfavorable to the applicant, is better than an exaggeration.

10. Applicants should conduct themselves as if determined to get the job being discussed. The recruiter is aware that candidates usually have other irons in the fire, of course, but the recruiter should be convinced that the applicant wants a position with that organization.

11. Applicants should avoid giving the impression of having come in to look over the possibilities without yet being sure of what they want. Statements such as "I'll do anything if I'm given the chance to learn" or "I don't know what I want to do—I hope that you can suggest something" should also be avoided. Whenever possible, candidates should apply for a specific job or field of work. Even if no opening exists in that area, the candidates presentation may lead the interviewer to suggest another job or department, perhaps even better than the one sought. For this reason it is not advisable to go too far out on a limb by considering only one certain job.

12. If the interviewer does not indicate when an applicant will be notified, the applicant should ask if he or she may call in a week or two.

13. All interviewers should be thanked for their time.

14. If no definite offer is made or no specific salary is discussed, an applicant should not be discouraged. The recruiter will probably wish to communicate with the office first or interview more applicants before making any offers.

15. If a first interview is unsuccessful, the applicant should remember that interviewers, companies, and jobs differ greatly. Much can be learned from the first interview, and succeeding ones will almost certainly be better. The important thing is for the applicant to keep trying.

Poor Interviewing Behaviors

Following are a number of negative factors evaluated during the employment interview that frequently lead to an applicant's rejection.

1. Poor personal appearance.
2. Overbearing, overaggressive, conceited, superiority complex, know-it-all.
3. Inability to express self clearly—poor voice, diction, grammar.
4. Lack of planning for career—no purpose and goals.
5. Lack of interest and enthusiasm—passive, indifferent.
6. Lack of confidence and poise, nervousness, ill-at-ease.
7. Overemphasis on money—interest only in best dollar offer.
8. Unwilling to start at the bottom—expects too much too soon.
9. Makes excuses, evasiveness, hedges on unfavorable factors in record.

10. Lack of tact.
11. Lack of maturity.
12. Lack of courtesy—ill mannered.
13. Condemnation of past employers.
14. Lack of social understanding.
15. Indecision.
16. Merely shopping around.
17. Little sense of humor.
18. Lack of knowledge of field of specialization.
19. No interest in company or in industry.
20. Emphasis on whom one knows.
21. Cynical.
22. Inability to take criticism.
23. Lack of appreciation of the value of experience.
24. High-pressure type.
25. Asks no questions about the job.
26. Indefinite response to questions.

Frequently Asked Interview Questions

Applicants who think about answers to the following questions *before* the interview can greatly enhance their chances for future employment.

1. What are your future vocational plans?
2. In what school activities have you participated? Why? Which did you enjoy the most?
3. How do you spend your spare time? What are your hobbies?
4. In what type of position are you most interested?
5. Why do you think you might like to work for our company?
6. What jobs have you held? How were they obtained and why did you leave?
7. What courses did you like the best? Least? Why?
8. Why did you choose your particular field of work?
9. What percentage of your college expenses did you earn? How?
10. How did you spend your vacations while in school?
11. Do you feel that you have received a good general training?
12. What qualifications do you have that make you feel that you will be successful in your field?
13. What extracurricular offices have you held?
14. What are your ideas on salary?
15. Do you prefer any specific geographic location? Why?
16. What do you think determines an employee's progress in a good company?
17. What personal characteristics are necessary for success in your chosen field?
18. What have you learned from some of the jobs you have held?
19. Can you get recommendations from previous employers?

20. What was your record in military service?

21. How long do you expect to work?

22. Have you had any serious illness or injury?

23. Are you willing to go where the company sends you?

24. Is it an effort for you to be tolerant to persons with a background and interests different from your own?

25. What types of books have you read?

26. Have you plans for graduate work?

27. What jobs have you enjoyed the most? The least? Why?

28. What are your own special abilities?

29. What is your idea of how industry operates today?

30. What are the disadvantages of your chosen field?

31. What have you done that shows initiative and willingness to work?

32. What specifically have you done while in college that has enhanced your leadership qualities?

33. Are you having other interviews?

The Follow-Up

Follow-up is essential. Any verbal arrangements made (in person or by phone) with an employer before, during, or after the interview should be backed up with confirming correspondence. Following the interview, applicants may wish to write a brief note to the interviewer, expressing thanks for the interviewer's consideration and a continued interest in the organization. If no word is received on the status of an application within the amount of time specified in the interview, the applicant should call or write the interviewer and ask if a decision has been made. Such a letter might include a sentence or two to review the applicant's abilities in relation to the employer's needs and to express continued interest in the position.

When an offer of a position is received, applicants should acknowledge the offer, express appreciation for it, and provide a date by which they will advise the organization of their decision. In declining an offer, applicants should be brief and polite no matter what their view of the offer. Some day they may want to be considered again by that employer.

REFERENCES

Moody's Industrial Manual. New York: Moody's Investors' Service, 1978.
Standard and Poor's Register of Corporations, Directors, and Executives. New York: Standard and Poor's Corporation, 1978.

SAMPLE COVER LETTER

March 10, 1979

Mr. Olson James
304 Huey Street
Beltsville, Maryland 20705

Dear Mr. James:

I am interested in applying for the health statistician position advertised in the March 4 issue of the Baltimore *Sun*.

As indicated on my résumé, I will receive a BA degree in psychology in May 1979. I believe that my background and experience in statistics and social science qualify me for this challenging type of work.

I would be most happy to meet with you at your convenience to further describe my qualifications for and interest in the position. Letters of recommendation are available from the references listed in my résumé.

Please contact me at:

John Doe
721 Main Street
College Park, Maryland 20742
301-937-4189

Thank you for your attention.

Sincerely,
John Doe

SAMPLE RÉSUMÉ A

Name	William Ingloff	*Social Security No.*	097-30-9004
Address	408 Haberside Drive	*Date of Birth*	June 16, 1957
	Largo, Florida 33540	*Place of Birth*	Manhattan, Kansas
Phone	813-365-7843		

CAREER OBJECTIVE
Advertising copywriter, researcher

EDUCATION
1975:   Graduated from Manhattan-East High School, Manhattan, Kansas
1979:   University of Missouri, Columbia, Missouri
        Degree: Bachelor of Arts
        Major: Psychology
        Minors: Journalism, Advertising

EMPLOYMENT HISTORY
Research: Summer 1978, Co-investigator with Professor James Marks on critical color variables in males' clothing preferences
Teaching: September 1977–June 1978, Review Assistant for introductory psychology course, University of Missouri, Department of Psychology
Part-time: June 1976–May 1977, Bank Teller, Columbia Federal Savings & Loan, Columbia, Missouri 65201

EXTRACURRICULAR ACTIVITIES
September 1978–Present: Volunteer tutor at emotionally disturbed children's home
September 1976–Present: Advertising editor, campus newspaper

HONORS AND AWARDS
Phi Kappa Phi (Senior Honor Society), 1979
Psi Chi (Psychology Honor Society), 1978

REFERENCES
Professor Martha Locke, Department of Psychology, University of Missouri, Columbia, Missouri 65201
Professor James Marks, Department of Psychology, University of Missouri, Columbia, Missouri 65201
Mr. William Inge, Vice President, Columbia Federal Savings & Loan, Columbia, Missouri 65201

SAMPLE RÉSUMÉ B

Name	Jacqueline S. Connors	*Social Security No.*	079-03-4090
Address	37 Brookside Drive	*Date of Birth*	May 15, 1957
	Northampton,	*Place of Birth*	Bethesda, Maryland
	Massachusetts 01060		
Phone	413-257-8195		

CAREER OBJECTIVE
Child care specialist

EDUCATION
1975:   Graduated from Walt Whitman High School, Bethesda, Maryland
1979   Smith College, Northampton, Massachusetts
     Degree: Bachelor of Arts
     Major: Psychology
     Minors: Human development, music
     Fluent in conversational Spanish.
     Focus of program was on developmental psychology, supplemented by
     courses in family relations, early childhood education, and art for children.

EXPERIENCE
Summer intern (1978) at Schenectady Family Services Program. Served as assistant to coordinator for summer educational and recreational services for underpriviledged children.

Served as camp counselor at Camp Adirondack for handicapped children, summer 1977.

Served as educational skills tutor for four children, aged 8–10, during academic year 1976–1977.

Served as review assistant for introductory child psychology course, 1978–1979, Smith College.

EXTRACURRICULAR ACTIVITIES
Smith College Choir, September 1976–December, 1978.
Field hockey team, fall 1976 and fall 1977.
Psi Chi (Honor Society in Psychology) vice president, 1977–1978.

HONORS AND AWARDS
Psi Chi (Psychology Honor Society), 1976.

SPECIAL SKILLS
Certified American National Red Cross Life Saving and Water Safety instructor.

REFERENCES
Will be furnished upon request.

6

Vicki M. Wilson

The Qualifications Brief: An Alternative Résumé

This chapter describes an alternative to the traditional résumé for psychology majors. The qualifications brief stresses individual strengths and is valuable for new graduates without extensive work histories. First, advice and resources are provided to help students decide upon and write a career objective. Questions are then used to elicit abilities, qualifications, accomplishments, experience, and education, all of which can be developed to support this objective. Finally, a step-by-step explanation of the format of a functional qualifications brief is included, as are effective writing tips, a sample qualifications brief, and an annotated bibliography on résumé writing.

A written description of a job applicant has two primary purposes: to ensure that the employer knows the applicant's identity, goals, and abilities and to encourage the employer to interview the applicant. This is where the traditional résumé often fails because it is an extensive, neatly margined *list* of experiences and education with no elaboration of the applicant's qualifications and abilities. Thus, a highly qualified but newly graduated psychology major can send out hundreds of résumés with no results. A potentially more successful presentation is the *qualifications brief*, which stresses qualities, accomplishments, and abilities backed up, but not overshadowed, by experience and education.

Writing an effective qualifications brief requires a good deal of time and energy; but such initiative is essential in the psychology job market today. Consider the following facts:

1. Only about one out of five jobs is actually publicized through private or public employment agencies (Lathrop, 1977), and for psychology's many social service positions this proportion is even smaller. In most college placement bureaus the primary recruiters are business, education, and engineering organizations; very few, if any, social service recruiters are to be found.

2. Of those surveyed in a January 1973 U.S. Manpower Administration study (Rosenfeld, 1975), 63% obtained their current jobs either by directly applying to an employer without referral or by asking friends and relatives for tips.

3. Of the estimated 75,000 psychology graduates in 1976, only from one-fourth to one-third continued for advanced study (American Psychological Association, 1976; Kulick, 1973); most of the others were in competition for *available* jobs.

4. Most employers are not trained in hiring techniques; their expertise usually lies in fields other than employment. Thus they are not necessarily skilled in drawing out an applicant's qualifications.

All of this means that job applicants must take the initiative and be able to express exactly what they want to do, where they want to do it, and why they are the best persons to do it. Time and energy devoted to preparing a qualifications brief will bring career goals into perspective (at least for the immediate future) and result in a concise, concrete analysis of abilities, qualifications, education, and experience to support those goals. The truly successful job hunter knows what he or she wants and goes after it, and writing a qualifications brief is a good first step.

Three decisions face the psychology graduate writing a first qualifications brief: (a) What is the career objective? (b) What qualifications support that objective? and (c) What is the most effective way to organize this information?

The Objective

The objective is a concise statement of a job applicant's career goals, the applicant's qualifications, and how these qualifications were acquired. Not all authorities on résumé writing agree on the style of the objective or even on the need for one. However, I believe the objective is a necessity for psychology majors with liberal arts backgrounds. Psychology graduates can be qualified for any number of entry-level positions depending on their interests, the type of psychology courses they took, and any supplementary courses that may qualify them for other areas (e.g., art for art therapy, business for organization management, speech and communications for public relations, or social work for counseling). Simply stating that one has a psychology degree provides little information to potential employers. It is up to applicants to state parsimoniously what they want to do, where they want to do it, and why they are qualified to do it—all in one sentence!

Before writing the objective, job seekers should first decide exactly what they want to do and where they want to do it. Until these questions can be answered concretely, it will be impossible to go any further. A typical statement among psychology graduates is "I want to work with people." Does this mean personal, vocational, academic, rehabilitative, or parole/probation counseling? Will the counseling be with normal, mentally retarded, emotionally immature, or physically disabled people, and will

Vicki M. Wilson is currently academic counselor at the Department of Psychology, University of Washington.

they be children, adolescents, or adults? Is the desired location a community mental health center, hospital, group home, or school? Is the goal to negotiate, instruct, supervise, persuade, or serve? Is one more interested in data (information, knowledge, concepts) or things (inanimate objects, substances, or materials) than in people? All of these questions must be answered before starting to write the objective.

Many resources and techniques can help in finding the answers. For those completely in the dark, *What Color Is Your Parachute?* (Bolles, 1977), *The Quick Job-Hunting Map* (Bolles, 1975), *Where Do I Go From Here With My Life?* (Crystal & Bolles, 1974), and *Who's Hiring Who* (Lathrop, 1977) will help in gaining a sense of self and of place in the world of work. More specific job information, including titles and work requisites, can be found in the *Dictionary of Occupational Titles* (U.S. Department of Labor, 1977), the Bible of vocational counseling. Browsing through federal, state, and local job specifications and the Yellow Pages can also be of help. These resources are not the gospel on what can and cannot be done by psychology graduates, however. Lunneborg, for example, in a later chapter of this book indicates that the unlikely area of psychological research is open to those with bachelor's degrees. Other traditionally "closed" areas may actually be available to the persistent job seeker.

Many psychology graduates find employment in, the following worker trait groups (as characterized by the *Dictionary of Occupational Titles*): administration, child and adult care, education (particularly special education and instructional support services), guidance and counseling, interviewing, information giving, and social-science, psychological, and related research (Lunneborg, Note 1). Keeping these areas in mind, job seekers can consult college career planning and placement centers, psychology departments, booklets printed by United Way that describe social service agencies, and articles in the *American Psychologist* and *Vocational Guidance Quarterly* for information on the types of agencies most relevant for psychology graduates.

After deciding general career goals, the job seeker can acquire more specific data on a number of occupational areas by informational interviewing and volunteering. Lathrop (1977) refers to informational interviewing as CORE (career opportunities research). This activity consists simply of talking with people who have jobs one might be interested in to find out what those jobs are really like. Receptionists can help locate the right persons in agencies to talk to. After obtaining a name, call the person directly, explain that one is researching occupations, and try to arrange a 20-minute appointment to ask questions about his or her job. Emphasize that employment is *not* being sought. Questions should be considered ahead of time and typed before the interview. Good questions include the following: What are your typical day and week like? What type of background is necessary for your position? What is your background, that is, education and experience? What do you like most and least about what you do? What rewards (personal, social, material) come with your position? Where do you see this position leading in your career?

Volunteer work is another good method for getting an accurate picture of a particular job. For a full coverage of the strategy of volunteering see the earlier chapter by Jeanne M. Foley.

The exercises suggested by Bolles (1975, 1977), Crystal and Bolles (1974), and Lathrop (1977), supplemented by informational interviewing and volunteering, can provide general ideas for the career objective. But in focusing on a specific objective, it is better to think in terms of immediate rather than long-term goals and to keep things tailored to short-range plans. The finalized statement should be a concise, one-sentence description of an immediate, short-range objective. It should be stated in terms of an applicant's highest abilities and accomplishments as proven by education and experience to date. Since its purpose is to convince an employer of the applicant's suitability, it should be written in line with the employer's goals and should stress what the applicant has to offer, not what the applicant wants. No job titles should be mentioned; doing so would only limit the job possibilities.

Following are some examples of objectives:

1.   Public relations work in hospital setting where knowledge of hospital procedures and problems, oral and written expertise, and interest in and ability to deal with the public can be used.

2.   Recreational therapy with physically handicapped persons of all ages where background in recreational program development, ability to understand special problems of the handicapped, and broad sports and crafts skills will be of value to insure program growth and maximum client participation.

3.   Research position in social service agency needing highly motivated, persevering, conscientious, objective, detail-loving individual with strong theoretical and practical background in statistics, research design, and program evaluation.

Any one of these objectives could be that of a new psychology graduate looking for a first formal job. Each objective is based on personal experience and interests, courses used to supplement the psychology degree, and related volunteer work. For example, the first writer started work during high school as a candy striper at the local hospital and later became a volunteer assistant to one of the hospital administrators. In college this person excelled in writing and worked on the college newspaper. Finally, during the senior year the student volunteered several hours a week with a local consumer protection office.

To summarize, an effective objective should (a) be a concise, parsimonious statement of the desired career and location, (b) include the applicant's abilities and accomplishments as proven by experience and/or education, (c) avoid specific job titles, and (d) stress what the applicant can offer the employer, not what the employer can give the applicant.

Support of the Objective

Once the objective has been written, rewritten, and finalized, a clear picture of one's abilities, qualifications, accomplishments, experience, and education is needed to back it up. The most relevant of these should be carefully selected for inclusion in the qualifications brief. The following exercises may be helpful in choosing the best qualifications to support the objective.

Job Experience

Each paid and volunteer job held since high school should be listed on a separate sheet of paper. The ten questions below can be used as guides in writing everything that can be remembered about each position. It is important to be specific and yet not omit anything of possible relevance to the current career goal. Answers to these questions should definitely be written rather than merely thought about. In this way, when the time comes to rewrite the qualifications brief (and it will), all the information can easily be reviewed and that relevant to the new objective selected. No employer will ever see this information, but it can be continually added to in moving from job to job on the way to an ultimate career goal. The following questions should be answered for each job held:

1. What specific *activities* made up a typical day?
2. What specific *activities* made up a typical week?
3. What *activities* were involved in any specific assignments or projects delegated or asked for?
4. What *skills* and *abilities* were used in these daily, weekly, and special activities? What determined selection for special projects?
5. What were one's *accomplishments* in this job? What changes were made as a result of one's work? Are they still in effect? What did they mean (in as quantifiable terms as possible) to the agency?
6. What new *skills* and *abilities* were gained as a result of this job?
7. What part of the job was most enjoyable? What activities were being performed and what skills were being used?
8. What were the personal, social, and material (salary, benefits, etc.) rewards of this position?
9. What was the job title, and what were the dates of employment?
10. What was the reason for leaving?

Some of these questions can be answered fairly straightforwardly; others will require some hard thinking and going beyond the surface. For example, was selection for special assignments due to one's availability or to a special talent for dealing personally with frustrated, angry people? Was the job left because school was starting or would one have left soon anyway? Why?

Among the most difficult for most people are answers that describe major accomplishments and changes made as a result of their work. An appropriate type of change to mention is illustrated in the following example of a receptionist in a day-treatment facility. Since the receptionist spent much time near the client waiting room, she noticed that the clients spent many hours in useless activity. As a result of her observations, a new program was implemented for those waiting to be seen that enhanced the agency's therapeutic goals.

Education

A second writing session should be devoted to education, with the focus on college and any supplementary work such as workshops. The following questions should be answered:

1. What formal degrees were earned, and in what area(s) (e.g., Bachelor of Arts in Psychology and Communications, Bachelor of Science in Psychology, Bachelor of Science in Psychology and Biology)?

2. What was the general theme of the psychology courses selected (e.g., ethological, developmental, social, experimental, organizational)?

3. What coursework was taken to supplement the psychology degree (e.g., art, social work, business, wildlife sciences, education, communications, mathematics)?

4. What relevance does this additional background work have for a career objective?

5. What special honors were awarded (e.g., Phi Beta Kappa, cum laude, an academic scholarship, graduation with honors)? If a local scholarship was received, a *brief* description of it should be written since not everyone may be familiar with its title.

6. What types of courses were most enjoyed and why?

7. What school-related extracurricular activities were participated in (e.g., debate club, school newspaper, organization of student protests)? What special skills were developed as a result of these activities?

8. To what professional associations did one belong? What work was published and what presentations were made?

Personal Experience

The final area that can be used to support the career objective is personal experience. What situations or skills unconnected with employment or academic training are relevant?

Organization of Information

There is no one *best* principle for organizing all of this information; individuals should use whatever approach emphasizes their high points and minimizes their low ones. However, the three most common approaches are (a) the conventional or chronological, (b) the problem-solution-result, and (c) the functional. The conventional, probably the most familiar approach, consists primarily of a chronological listing of past positions. This style is most appropriate for someone with extensive experience in a series of well-defined jobs, not generally the case for newly graduated psychology majors. Likewise, the second option is primarily for those with an extensive work background who are able to focus on three or four major problems faced in previous jobs, how they resolved the problems, and what the results meant to the company in quantitative terms (i.e., time saved, money saved, efficiency improve). This type of approach is used primarily in business as opposed to social service.

The functional qualifications brief is generally thought to be the most appropriate for those without long, consistent job histories, for those who have tendencies to change jobs frequently, and for those newly graduated. It is suited to such individuals because of its stress on strengths, abilities, and accomplishments rather than job history.

Writing the Functional Qualifications Brief

To help new graduates without extensive work histories, the rest of this chapter is devoted to writing functional qualifications briefs.[1] After the objective has been written and ideas for its support gathered, the following format should guide the remainder of the functional qualifications brief:

Vital Statistics

The applicant's name, address, and phone number and the date are essential. Surprisingly, some people spend hours polishing the language in their qualifications briefs and then forget to include their names. Since an employer may want to contact a job applicant immediately, the applicant who cannot be reached directly by phone should include a number for messages.

Strengths

What is one's strongest skill, ability, accomplishment, or experience and how does it support the objective? What is the second strongest? The third strongest? After considering these questions, the applicant should select up to four strengths relevant to the career objective as headings for the qualifications brief. The work, education, and personal-experience histories written for a previous exercise can be drawn upon for this purpose, and those strengths that best prove an ability to perform for a specified employer can be located. The goal is to create an image of the person best qualified to meet the employer's needs. Applicants might start with the most qualifying *experience* (not necessarily the most recent) that supports

---

1. If another organizing format will better show one's qualifications, it should be used. The annotated bibliography at the end of this chapter lists some of the better reference books on résumés. Most of the guides on the market address themselves primarily to aspiring business executives, and it may take a little imagination for psychology graduates to make the examples relevant to their own job searches. However, the suggestions on style, organization, and what to include are applicable to any person looking for employment. The two most helpful books listed are those by Bostwick (1976) and Lathrop (1977).

their objective, then continue with the next best, and so on. Or an applicant might decide that *skill* headings (e.g., ability to deal with different clients, writing proficiency, public-speaking expertise) may better reflect his or her qualifications. Or perhaps a combination of experiences and qualifying abilities should comprise the strength headings. Whatever form these headings take—experiences, abilities, skills, accomplishments, problems-solutions-results—the success of the qualifications brief will depend on their relevance to the career objective and how closely the objective matches a prospective employer's needs.

A paragraph following each strength heading should describe what form that strength has taken and how it is relevant to the employer's needs. Too many qualifications briefs start off on the right track only to get lost in a jumble of rambling, irrelevant tales. The key to a concise, effective qualifications brief is a careful review of the previously prepared histories and, with the career objective in mind, a selection of the three or four *most* qualifying strengths and the data to support them.

Simple, direct language should be used so the facts can speak for themselves. Although there should be no large, unaccounted-for periods of time in education or experience, dates should be de-emphasized; the quality of what an applicant has done is far more important than when it was done. Further, the qualifications brief should reflect successes, not failures. Whenever possible examples of success and even praise by supervisors should be cited. Applicants should attempt to portray the scope and effect of their work, their accomplishments, the abilities they have gained and used, and the results they have produced.

Education

For some people, educational background may be the most qualifying experience. If so, it should be listed first to catch the reader's attention. Is one's psychology background directly related to the objective? How? Is supplementary work directly related, and if so, how does it support one as the best person for the job?

Professional information such as membership in organizations and lists of publications or presentations may also be included here if it is relevant to the objective. But if such items are a *major* contribution to the qualifications for the position being sought, they may deserve a separate heading altogether. To merit this importance, however, they must be outstanding strengths of utmost import to the position sought.

Personal Information

Most personal information (birth date, marital status, health, sex) has little to do with the qualifications for a particular job, but it often involves small details with big implications. Personal information should be included when it will enhance the applicant's prospects for obtaining a position; otherwise it should be left out. For example, for a public-relations position that requires much traveling applicants might simply state that they would enjoy a position in which travel is an integral part and that they have few personal obligations to interfere with travel time. But in most cases, the only essential personal information is name, address, and phone number.

References

Experts agree that letters of reference should not be included with the qualifications brief. Authorities are about equally divided, however, on whether to actually list references or to state that they will be furnished on request. But since the goal is to convince the employer of one's suitability for the job, it is logical to make it easy for the employer to gather additional information by including the names, addresses, and phone numbers of references so they can be contacted directly and immediately.

Style of the Qualifications Brief

Several points of style should be kept in mind regardless of the format chosen by the applicant. First, the qualifications brief should be no longer than two pages, preferably one. No matter how extensive an applicant's background, if the crucial information can't be summarized in two pages, most employers won't be interested. They simply have neither the time nor the energy to sift through superfluous information to get at the facts.

Second, one's work, education and personal-experience histories must be kept up-to-date. Qualifications briefs need revising as job prospects change; the order or even the type of functional headings may need to be altered. Also, as the career objective changes, so should the emphasis of the qualifications brief. If these histories are up-to-date, it will be a simple task to review and select the most relevant data to support the new objective. In addition, if the qualifications brief and histories are kept current, they can be tremendous confidence builders in dealing with present as well as prospective employers. One will always be ready with a persuasive self-presentation and thus avoid having to develop a qualifications brief on short notice when one is least likely to do a good job.

Third, no matter how proficient one's writing ability, a friend, counselor, or relative should edit the finished product. This person should look for any misspelled words, grammatical errors, or unclear meanings. Someone unfamiliar with the finished product will often find problems the writer might miss.

As a last guide, I have included a sample qualifications brief for a newly graduated psychology major with no formal, paid experience but with excellent qualifications to back up her objective. The following points should be kept in mind when reading through it:

1. The brief should reflect the applicant's character and personality. One should never adapt someone else's qualifications brief to fit one's own experiences nor have anyone else, particularly a professional resume-writing business, prepare it. An ability to "sell" oneself is essential, and to do so in person one must first be able to get the facts down on paper.

2.   The writer should make the final decision on which style emphasizes his or her strong points.

3.   The objective should be stated in terms of the strongest abilities, experiences, and qualifications.

4.   The information in the brief must support the objective.

5.   The most qualifying experience, ability, or accomplishment should be described first, followed by the next most qualifying, and so on.

6.   Abilities and accomplishments should be emphasized more than duties and responsibilities.

7.   Specific examples of successes and accomplishments should be given.

8.   The focus should be on the employer's needs, not the applicant's.

9.   The brief should consist of short words, sentences, and paragraphs. The addition of irrelevant padding will not fool anyone.

10.   Dates should be de-emphasized.

11.   The brief should create an image of a self-starter with ideas, a person who gets things done.

12.   The active voice should be used wherever possible.

13.   The word *etc.* should never be used.

14.   The final product should be neatly typed, correctly spelled, and carefully edited, with wide margins and bold headings for emphasizing strong points.

15.   The qualifications brief is not the place for modesty; its aim is to "sell" the writer's qualifications.

A functional qualifications brief is not easy to write. It would be much less difficult to simply list a string of dates and duties. Writing an effective qualifications brief means taking time to research the market carefully, evaluate one's assets realistically, and target specific individual goals. Someone who just wants a job should not bother with a qualifications brief. But if a career that uses one's abilities and experience and leaves room for potential growth is desired, the time and effort involved will be well worth the result.

Annotated Bibliography on Résumé Writing

Angel, J. L. *Why and how to prepare an effective job résumé.* New York: World Trade Academy Press, 1972.

Provides structured formats but gives examples of résumés for a variety of people, including social scientists, teachers, counselors, business administrative personnel, persons over 50, and recent college graduates. Contains three sections: (a) merchandising one's skills, (b) writing résumés according to occupational classification, and (c) writing résumés for specialized groups.

Bostwick, B. E. *Résumé writing: A comprehensive how-to-do-it guide.* New York: Wiley, 1976.

New, up-to-date guide on résumé writing intended for all job seekers. Provides examples of at least 10 different résumé styles including the basic, chronological, chronological with summary page, functional, Harvard, functional-by-company (institution), creative, narrative, professional, and accomplishment. Summarizes what a résumé is, who uses résumés, and why one should write a résumé. Gives good examples. Excellent reference.

Irish, R. K. *Go hire yourself an employer*. Garden City, N.Y.: Anchor Books, Anchor Press/Doubleday, 1973.

Contains a good chapter for job seekers on first "getting it together" and then writing an effective résumé.

Irish, R. K. *If things don't improve soon I may ask you to fire me*. Garden City, N.Y.: Anchor Books, Anchor Press/Doubleday, 1976.

Chapter 5 on résumés and the résuméd is written from a manager's/employer's point of view; discusses what employers look for in a résumé. Easy reading with good examples; gives a view of job seeking from the other side.

Lathrop, R. *Who's hiring who*. Berkeley, Calif.: Ten Speed Press, 1977.

Offers a unique approach to the writing of résumés or, as the author refers to them, qualifications briefs. Very good approach to new ways of catching the employer's eye. Traces the steps of preparing the brief. Excellent, easy-to-read book.

New York State Employment Service. *Guide to preparing a résumé*. New York: Department of Labor, 1976.

Handy guide designed to help evaluate one's "selling points" and present them in an organized manner.

Payne, R. A. *How to get a better job quicker*. New York: New American Library, 1975.

Referenced in *A Guide to Career Alternatives for Academics*. Provides solid, practical advice on interviewing and résumé writing.

Zambrano, A. L., & Entine, A. D. *A guide to career alternatives for academics*. New Rochelle, N.Y.: Change Magazine Press, 1976.

Chapter 3 on the résumé provides a concise approach to the dos and don'ts of résumé writing for academics seeking academic appointments or wishing to enter the business world. Contrasts two styles, the academic and the business oriented.

REFERENCE NOTE

1. Lunneborg, P. W. *What can you do with a degree in psychology?* (Tech. Rep. 77-1). Seattle: Department of Psychology, University of Washington, March 1977.

REFERENCES

American Psychological Association. *Graduate study in psychology for 1977–1978*. Washington, D.C.: Author, 1976.

Bolles, R. N. *The quick job-hunting map*. Berkeley, Calif.: Ten Speed Press, 1975.

Bolles, R. N. *What color is your parachute?* Berekely, Calif.: Ten Speed Press, 1977.

Bostwick, B. E. *Résumé writing: A comprehensive how-to-do-it guide*. New York: Wiley, 1976.

Crystal, J. C., & Bolles, R. N. *What do I go from here with my life?* New York: Seabury Press, 1974.

Kulick, J. A. *Undergraduate education in psychology*. Washington, D.C.: American Psychological Association, 1973.

Lathrop, R. *Who's hiring who*. Berkeley, Calif.: Ten Speed Press, 1977.

Rosenfeld, C. Jobseeking methods used by American workers. *Monthly Labor Review*, 1975, *98*(8), 39–42.

U.S. Department of Labor. *Dictionary of occupational titles* (4th ed.). Washington, D.C.: U.S. Government Printing Office, 1977.

SAMPLE QUALIFICATIONS BRIEF

Sandra F. Johnson

October 15, 1977
4200 East Elroy
Seattle, Washington 98167
(206) 982-0417

OBJECTIVE

RECREATIONAL THERAPY with physically handicapped persons of all ages where background in recreational program development, ability to understand special problems of the handicapped, and broad sports and crafts skills will be of value to insure program growth and maximum client participation.

STRENGTHS

Program evaluation and development. Of primary interest are evaluating, developing, and implementing recreational programs to meet leisure and therapy needs of handicapped people. Work with the Seattle Park Department evaluating basketball and track programs for the physically disabled highlights these interests. Concern was with lack of program participation. As a result of my evaluation of times offered, skills taught, values and behavior rewarded, and from results of a personally developed survey (80% response rate by center's clientele), new basketball and track programs were started. Under my guidelines, the new programs emphasize skills to increase coordination, encourage self-sufficient behavior, and stress enjoyment and development of caring, interpersonal relations skills. Each team now has a waiting list. Numerous letters were received from players, parents, and counselors congratulating and confirming our success. August 1976–August 1977.

Understanding the handicapped. From work in a center for physically disabled adults I gained an understanding of their problems. Even though I initiated daily group activities to maintain muscle tone, coordination, and interest in day-to-day living, my major accomplishment was a daily ball game and literary discussion with one older woman. Initial conversations with her lead to comments like "Don't waste your time." As a result of our interaction, however, she is now the most active of the center's members and is currently lining up its first competitive wheelchair volleyball team. September 1975–June 1976.

Sports and crafts skills. Active participation in numerous individual and team sports, e.g., volleyball, basketball, swimming, baseball, soccer, and track has led to coaching and a concern with methods of teaching sports skills. My latest coaching effort is the Eastside Bullets, a wheelchair basketball team in its third season. Most rewarding here is not the team's winning record but the waiting list of interested persons (a second team is now being organized).

When not playing or coaching, I spend my time in crafts, including knot-tying, painting, pottery, drawing, and glass cutting. These activities were shared with members in the center for handicapped adults. Center supervisors expressed appreciation for this added dimension to their program.

Sandra F. Johnson
Page Two

EDUCATION

Bachelor of Arts, Psychology, University of Washington—August 1977. Emphasis on personality and developmental; special attention to deviant and abnormal development. Extensive supplemental work in special education, recreation, and counseling. Awarded scholarship in senior year by Seattle Handicapped Citizens Center for interest in and work with disabled persons.

PERSONAL

Highly paid summer construction work enabled me to quickly earn yearly college expenses and thus devote major energy toward the two years of volunteer experience previously described. This work, along with having a physically disabled sister, has shown me that carefully planned sports and crafts skills programs can go a long way toward enhancing interpersonal skills and developing self-confidence for physically handicapped persons.

REFERENCES

John H. Greene
Seattle Park Department
2301 1st Avenue N.E.
Seattle, Washington 98671
(202) 889-8345

Felix Alwith, PhD
Department of Psychology
University of Washington
Seattle, Washington 98195
(206) 567-7890

Elena Jones
Seattle Handicapped Citizens Center
5607 N.E. 82nd
Seattle, Washington 98706
(206) 671-5678

Job Prospects: Potential and Real

7

John G. Tiedemann

Federal Government Jobs for Social Science Majors

The federal government offers individuals with training in the social sciences generally, and in psychology in particular, a broad spectrum of employment opportunities. The purpose of this chapter is to assist the social science major in exploring opportunities in the federal service and, perhaps, to give college psychology departments a little more insight into what the job seeker with a social science background will need to be able to compete effectively for a federal job. The chapter discusses the categories of jobs open to social science majors, how to apply for federal jobs, which federal agencies hire psychologists and social science majors, and the chances of getting a government job.

Federal Jobs Open to Social Science Majors

Because the opportunities for social science majors in the federal sector are so varied, beginning job seekers may fail to recognize interesting jobs available to them. Such job seekers must learn to identify the kind of work performed from the title of the position being advertised. In order to give the reader a better understanding of the federal job market, positions for which applicants with psychology backgrounds may qualify are grouped into four categories.

Clinical Psychology or Social Service

Most positions in the category of clinical psychology or social service require a degree in psychology or at least 24 credit hours in the social sciences. They usually involve direct patient–professional interaction in areas such as testing, individual counseling, therapy, family counseling, or remedial training. Other positions involve the administration of federal grants to government and nongovernment organizations doing clinical work or clinical research. Persons interested in this type of work should look for such position titles as psychologist (including such subspecialty descriptors as clinical, counseling, developmental, personality, social, experimental and physiological, and personnel measurement and evaluation), social scientist, social science administrator, social science analyst, grants management specialist, public health adviser, head start program specialist, education specialist, social worker (candidates must have a master's degree), and correctional treatment specialist.

Research

The research category includes both basic and applied research that may be performed in a clinical, social, cultural, military, or organizational-industrial setting. Most of these positions emphasize systems or operations analysis, human factors in human–machine systems, research design, data collection, statistical analysis, and report writing. Position openings may be in the continental United States or in other countries. Interested persons should look for such job titles as psychologist (with a subspecialty descriptor such as engineering, general, or experimental), operations research analyst, systems research analyst, technical information specialist (biological or social sciences), industrial engineering technician, and human factors specialist.

Personnel Work

Positions in personnel work involve the application of psychological tools and principles in an organizational or industrial setting. Incumbents work in areas such as personnel testing, selection, classification, training and development, employee motivation and morale, and counseling. Some personnel-type positions may involve research, but most do not. When required, such research is usually in the form of cost-versus-benefits analyses, effectiveness studies, equal employment opportunity (EEO) impact studies, comparisons of personnel selection procedures (i.e., written tests vs. work history), or statistical tabulation.

Applicants with degrees in personnel, public, business, or commercial administration have slightly better chances for employment in this area, but applicants with a degree in psychology or the social sciences would qualify academically for these positions at the entry level. Interested persons should look for such position titles as personnel staffing specialist, personnel management specialist, position classification specialist, industrial relations specialist, education and/or training specialist, employee development specialist, civil rights counselor, equal rights counselor, test development specialist, position review specialist, management analyst, and recreation specialist.

General Management

The general management category includes all positions for which a bachelor's degree in any area of study is sufficient academic qualification. Most of these positions are nonprofessional in the sense that they do not

---

John G. Tiedemann has worked in government service for over 25 years and is in private practice in Washington, D.C.

require a specialized academic degree, licensing, or certification. Most federal employees in the positions in this category are hired at the entry level (Grades 5, 7, or 9) and are trained either on the job or through special training programs conducted by the hiring agency. Interested persons should investigate such positions as management analyst, program analyst, program manager, industrial hygienist, statistician or statistical assistant, administrative officer or assistant, budget officer, contract representative, customs inspector, writer or editor, tax technician, or law enforcement officer.

The positions listed under each of the four categories above do not exhaust the total number of position titles that could be listed, and, of course, as in any arbitrary categorization, some positions could fit equally well into two or more categories, depending on which duties the incumbent performs most frequently. Position titles alone do not describe the duties to be performed. If the job seeker is in any doubt about the type of duties performed in a particular position, he or she should request a position description from the federal agency advertising the job. This description will help the job seeker determine if the position really involves the type of day-to-day work he or she wants to do.

Positions with the same title but from different agencies may or may not involve the same duties, depending on the mission and function of the agency. Even when the position descriptions of two different agencies list essentially the same duties, one agency may emphasize the research nature of the work, and the other agency may emphasize the counseling aspects.

A word of caution is in order: Federal agencies with well-established programs are notorious for not updating position descriptions as the duties of a position evolve. The job seeker should check on the accuracy of the description with a knowledgeable personnel specialist from the agency advertising the position or with someone who works in the office to which the vacant position is assigned. This precaution will give the candidate a distinct advantage on his or her application or in the interview for the position.

How to Apply for a Position

Although the majority of positions of interest to psychologists are in the executive branch of government, both the legislative and judicial branches hire individuals with psychology or social science backgrounds. Positions in the legislative and judicial branches involve personnel, general administrative, or investigative, rather than research or clinical, duties. Courts also may hire individuals with psychology backgrounds to be probation officers, social workers, child development specialists, family counselors, domestic relations specialists, and psychologists specializing in criminal rehabilitation. Both the legislative and judicial branches have hiring procedures that are not governed by the Office of Personnel Management (formerly the Civil Service Commission).[1]

Positions in the executive branch are either in the competitive service or the excepted service. Positions in the competitive service, regardless of the agency in which they are located, come under the civil service merit system administered by the Office of Personnel Management. Excepted service jobs are located in agencies having their own merit systems such as the Foreign Service of the Department of State, the Department of Medicine and Surgery of the Veterans Administration, the Postal Service, or the Tennessee Valley Authority. The excepted service also includes some specific occupations such as chaplin, lawyer, or administrative law judge. Individuals interested in an excepted service job should not apply to the Office of Personnel Management or one of its Federal Job Information Centers but should contact the particular agency directly. Federal Job Information Centers maintain a complete list of establishments in the excepted service.[2]

Appointments to jobs that come under the civil service merit system are made on the basis of ability to do the work as demonstrated in competition with other applicants—hence the name competitive service. Since most of the positions of interest to psychologists are in the competitive service, the serious job seeker should understand the civil service examining system. The examining system functions through area offices of the Office of Personnel Management called Federal Job Information Centers. These are located in centers of federal population throughout the country. These centers announce and conduct examinations, evaluate an applicant's work experience, training, and aptitude, and then place the names of applicants who meet prescribed qualifications on a list, or register, of qualified applicants. If an applicant is applying for a position at Grade 8 or below, the Federal Job Information Center receiving the application will evaluate the application. These applicants are notified of the status of their applications by the office to which they applied. The notice usually includes the applicant's rating score (with 100 being the highest obtainable score without the addition of veterans' preference bonus points), what grade or grades the applicant is qualified for, and how long the applicant's name will remain on the register (usually 12 months). When the Federal Job Information Center provides the hiring agency with a list of the top candidates on the register from which the agency is to choose the best qualified, the "Rule of Three" applies. The rule of three means that the hiring official of the agency with the vacancy, by law, does not have to

---

1. Persons interested in working within the judicial branch should contact their nearest federal court or should write to Director, Administrative Office of the United States Courts, United States Supreme Court Building, 1 First Street, N.E., Washington, D.C. 20544. Persons interested in working for the legislative branch should contact their representative in the House or their senator or should write to Select Committee on Government Operation, Office of Placement and Management, Washington, D.C. 20515.

2. Appendix C contains a list of federal job information centers.

choose the top person, but has a choice of any of the top three candidates. This explains why a person whose name is at the top of the register some-times doesn't get a job when people lower on the list may.

Registers or lists exist for each occupational specialty; for example, psychologists are qualified under the 180 series, personnel officers under the 201 series, and statisticians under the 1530 series. Federal agencies hire from different registers depending on what skills they require. Appli-cants may be listed on more than one register; for example, a job seeker with a major in psychology and a strong minor in statistics may apply for both the psychologist and the statistician registers. However, applicants must submit a separate application for each register on which they are seeking placement. Registers may be open or closed. Registers are open when agencies have indicated to the Office of Personnel Management that they have openings for individuals with certain qualifications and when the current register does not have sufficient names to provide a competi-tive basis for selection. Registers are closed when no agencies are indicat-ing an interest in hiring individuals with that occupational specialty, or when the register has an adequate number of names on it from which a good selection can be made.

The Office of Personnel Management, through its Federal Job Information Centers, issues announcements that tell what registers are open, what jobs are available, what experience and education are necessary for an application to be accepted, whether a written test is required, where the jobs are located, what the pay is, etc. Psychologist positions and other positions requiring a college degree usually do not require a written examination but do require a list of courses taken and grades obtained in order to evaluate an applicant's training. Applications generally will be accepted from students who expect to complete within nine months courses or degrees that would permit them to meet the quali-fication requirements of the occupational specialty for which they are applying. Applicants should read these announcements carefully and should not apply if they do not meet all of the qualification requirements, or if they do not want to work where the jobs are located.[3]

Applicants for most scientific positions and most jobs at Grade 9 and above do not receive a rating at the time the application is processed; it is sent to a Federal Job Information Center. They do receive a letter acknowledging the receipt of their application and their names are placed on a list along with others who have applied for similar work. Applicants

---

3. Persons interested in a civil service job are strongly urged to contact their nearest Federal Job Information Center and ask for such pamphlets as *Working for the USA* (BRE-37), *Directory of Federal Personnel Offices, Veterans Readjustment Appointments, The Employment Picture for College Graduates,* any announcements (open or closed) for which social science majors may qualify, an *Application for Federal Employment* (Standard Form 171), *Professional and Administrative Career Examination* (PACE), and any other literature available that may help them apply for a federal position. If a Federal Job Information Center is not listed in the telephone book under United States Government, one can dial (800) 555-1212 for the toll-free number of the nearest center.

have no numerical standing on these lists. When a specific vacancy occurs, the applications of persons on the occupational specialty list will be sent to the hiring agency for evaluation and ranking by the hiring agency. Applications that are submitted to Federal Job Information Centers will be distributed to any agency requesting a list of qualified applicants if the application appears to meet the requirements submitted by the hiring agency. An applicant may also apply directly to any agency that has, or may have, vacancies for which the applicant feels qualified. The typical system used by most agencies for ranking applications is discussed in a later section.

Persons who have majored in the social sciences but who are not necessarily restricting themselves to a career in one of the social science specialties may want to consider the Professional and Administrative Career Examination (PACE). For those with a college degree or equivalent experience, this examination offers the opportunity to compete for a wide variety of jobs in federal agencies across the country. About 85% of these positions are filled outside of the Washington, D.C., area.[4]

The PACE program is directed toward individuals having, or soon to have, a bachelor of arts or higher degree. Another program, the Junior Federal Assistant (JFA) examination, is directed toward the junior-college graduate or four-year college undergraduate and is used to fill technical and administrative support positions located throughout the Washington, D.C., metropolitan area. These positions are generally involved in the administration of programs in such areas as science, education, urban development, defense, social sciences, law enforcement, and environmental protection. All applicants interested in positions covered by JFA must pass a written test with a score of 70 and have a minimum of two years of college or two years of progressively responsible experience, or a combination of both that totals two years.[5]

Individuals interested in working for the federal government in a particular location or for a particular agency should check with the specific agencies in which they are interested. An agency's personnel office can advise the job seeker of current vacancies open to the aspirant and how many openings are likely to occur in various job categories during the upcoming 6–12 months. If the agency has position openings of interest to the job seeker, or is likely to in the immediate future, interested persons can submit an Application for Federal Employment, or Standard Form (SF) 171, directly to the agency. (SF 171's can be obtained from the particular agency.) The application can be for a specific vacancy listed by the agency in an announcement, or it can be a general application for consideration for several types of jobs. Whether the agency receives an SF 171 directly from the applicant or from a Federal Job Information Center in response to a request for a register listing, the agency will evaluate each

---

4. Interested persons should check with their nearest Federal Job Information Center for test dates and application information.

5. Information and assistance can be obtained from a Federal Job Information Center.

application according to the specific requirements listed in the vacancy announcement and return the application if the applicant does not meet the qualifications or is not selected for the job. If an application is submitted to the agency for *any job for which qualified*, the agency usually holds the application on file for 6–12 months and evaluates it whenever a vacancy occurs for which the applicant appears to be qualified. After 12 months, the application usually is sent back to the applicant for updating. Whether it is sent back or not, interested persons should keep their applications current, that is, less than one year old.

An applicant may indicate on an application for a specific vacancy that he or she wishes to be considered for that vacancy and, if not selected, for certain other optional positions and, if not selected for one of these, that the application be kept on file for future consideration. Such a request produces the maximum mileage out of one application; however, an application written for one type of job may not emphasize the skills the applicant has that are more germane to another type of job. Usually, the most successful application is the one tailored to a specific job. Filling out the SF 171 *carefully* is probably the most important single thing the federal job seeker can do to assure his or her fullest consideration. When one looks at the government's selection process, one truly realizes the importance of the application form, so perhaps a description of that process is in order.

Selection Process

Each vacant position is identified by a position description (often called a PD) that describes (a) the title, grade, salary, and location of the position; (b) the duties, responsibilities, and reporting relationships of the incumbent; and (c) the training, experience, and skills or aptitudes required to perform the duties. Using the position description as a guide, the personnel office develops a vacancy announcement, that (a) describes the job and the duties involved (though usually not in as much detail as the position description), (b) lists the training, skills, and experience requirements to meet the minimum qualifications for the job, and (c) specifies where and when to apply. The announcement may also indicate how much weight is given to each requirement during the evaluation process. Prospective applicants would do well to obtain a copy of the announcement and the position description, if possible, before attempting to fill out the application. These two documents can serve as guides to the qualities that must be specifically covered in the application.[6]

---

6. Appendix B describes the qualification standards for positions in the psychology series as published by the U.S. Office of Personnel Management in its *Qualifications Standards Handbook* (X-118). Titles included are clinical psychologist, counseling psychologist, personnel psychologist, engineering psychologist, psychologist, psychology aid, and psychology technician. Most agency position descriptions and vacancy announcements for psychologists incorporate these qualification standards, plus any necessary additional qualifications.

Once the agency has received applications, either from the Federal Job Information Center in response to a request for a register list, or directly from interested applicants, the selection process begins. Five hurdles face each applicant:

1. *Application acceptance.* When the agency's personnel office receives an application, a clerk compares each application to a checklist made up from the position description and the vacancy announcement and categorizes the applications either as those that meet minimum requirements for the job or those that fail to meet minimum requirements for the job. In the latter case, the clerk sends a form letter to the applicant that indicates which deficiency disqualified the applicant. The clerk reviewing the application may not be the most careful or perceptive reviewer nor have a very extensive understanding of that occupational specialty. He or she may be inundated with applications to be processed in a short time or may just be having a bad day; therefore, the application must show clearly that all prerequisites and the essential qualifications for the job are met. If the clerk has difficulty finding the information that supports fulfillment of the requirements, he or she may reject the application prematurely, and consideration of that applicant for the job stops right there.

2. *Highly qualified rating.* Applications that meet the minimum requirements are sent to a review panel or selection committee of from three to five evaluators who read and then rate each application as highly qualified, qualified, or marginally qualified. (Not all agencies use the marginally qualified rating.) The primary source of information for this evaluation is the SF 171, supplemented with references and a supervisor's evaluation of the applicant's current performance, if the applicant is employed. The SF 171 is more important than the references or supervisor's evaluation to achieve a high rating. Laudatory references and outstanding performance evaluations help, but they do not overcome deficiencies in training or experience. Mediocre or nondescript references and fair performance evaluations may harm the applicant more than outstanding references and evaluations may help. Rating panels tend to look as much for shortcomings that would indicate weak capability as they do for indicators of strong capability. From a pile that may include 100 or more basically qualified applicants, the panel must identify from 5 to 10 as the best qualified. The panel members eliminate the less qualified applicants on the basis of (a) weaknesses and deficiencies in training and experience that they detect on the SF 171 and (b) mediocre or poor references or performance evaluations. The selecting or hiring official then decides if the rating panel or the hiring official will interview the best qualified applicants.

3. *Placement on candidate list.* When the rating panel has completed its evaluations of all applicants, it sends to the selecting official a list of from 5 to 10 candidates that it believes are the best qualified. This list may contain all of the candidates who were rated "highly qualified" or just the 5 or 10 who were ranked highest. If no applicant was evaluated as

"highly qualified," or if very few were, the list may also include the best candidates from the "qualified" group. The list seldom includes marginally qualified applicants unless the agency is desperate to fill the position.

4. *Successful interview.* The selecting or hiring official (a) reviews the SF 171, references, performance evaluations, and the rating panel's comments about each candidate on the list submitted by the rating panel, and (b) decides who to interview. So far, each applicant has been considered only on the information supplied on the SF 171, on references, or on supervisor's evaluations. Applicants who get as far as the personal interview will have a chance to clarify or expound their qualifications for the job. Because only a few applicants have this opportunity, the information on the SF 171 and its clarity and appropriateness are very important. Most interviews last from 15 to 45 minutes. In this time the interviewer describes what the job will require of the selected candidate and expounds on any details that were not fully covered in the vacancy announcement. The applicant describes his or her work interests, training, experience, and skills acquired since submitting the application. Most interviews also include a short question-and-answer session to see how the applicant handles interpersonal relationships.

5. *Final selection.* When all applicants have been interviewed, the selecting official chooses the successful candidate and notifies the personnel office. Before notifying the selected candidate, the personnel office must verify the information submitted by the applicant on the SF 171 and on any other documents submitted. If all information is correct as stated, the selected candidate is notified by the personnel office and a reporting date is agreed upon. All other candidates are notified of their nonselection via a form letter. The new appointee must now serve a probationary period of from 6 to 12 months, depending on the job and the agency. During the probationary period the appointee can be terminated for any reason the agency feels justifiable, and the appointee has no appeal rights. Appointees who successfully complete the probationary period acquire "career conditional" status. When they have completed three years of satisfactory government service, they acquire "career status."[7]

Federal Agencies Hiring
Psychologists and Social Science Majors

The executive branch hires most of the applicants who seek positions that require or accept psychology or social science backgrounds. Some agencies employ few, while others, such as the Veterans Administration, the Department of Health, Education, and Welfare, the Department of Defense, and the Office of Personnel Management, employ several

---

7. Information reg'rding probationary periods and career–conditional and career status can be obtained from the U.S. Office of Personnel Management, a Federal Job Information Center, or the personnel office of any federal agency.

hundred. The following list, while not intended to include every agency hiring psychologists or individuals with psychology backgrounds, covers the major departments and agencies.

Department of Agriculture
14th Street and Independence Avenue, S.W.
Washington, D.C. 20250

Through 4-H Clubs and community education programs, the Department of Agriculture's Extension Service helps the public learn about and apply to everyday activities the latest technology in home economics, nutrition, youth development, child development, home management, family relations, and agricultural and animal husbandry.

Department of Commerce
14th Street between Constitution Avenue and E Street, N.W.
Washington, D.C. 20230

National Bureau of Standards (NBS). Although the NBS is primarily concerned with physical measurement systems and the establishment of physical standards, its overall goal is to strengthen and advance the nation's science and technology and to facilitate their effective application for public benefit. The bureau uses psychologists in programs involving testing and measurement in the behavioral sciences and the application of such tests and measurements for public benefit. (Contact the Personnel Office, NBS Headquarters, Washington, D.C. 20234.)

Bureau of the Census. The bureau is a general-purpose, statistical agency that collects, tabulates, and publishes a variety of statistical data about the people and the economy of the United States. It employs social psychologists and social science majors to develop and conduct its decennial and special surveys. (Contact the Personnel Office, Bureau of the Census, Department of Commerce, Washington, D.C. 20233.)

Department of Health, Education, and Welfare (DHEW)
300 Independence Avenue, S.W.
Washington, D.C. 20201.

The DHEW is composed of five major elements, each of which has numerous offices, bureaus, institutes, or centers. The department is one of the largest federal employers of psychologists and social science majors. Positions include those in social, psychological, and mental health research; testing; therapy; training and education; and grants administration. The various offices and bureaus cannot be described here in detail, but the titles listed below will give some insight into each unit's special interest. (For further information on the particular functions and opportunities in each element of the department, contact the Personnel Office, DHEW, 330 Independence Avenue, S.W., Washington, D.C. 20201.)

Office of Human Development
    Administration on Aging
    Office of Child Development
    Office of Youth Development
    Office for Handicapped Individuals
    President's Committee on Mental Retardation
    Office of Native American Programs
    Rehabilitation Services Administration
    Office of Manpower
    Office of Volunteer Development

Education Division: Office of Education
    Bureau of School Systems
    Bureau of Occupational and Adult Education
    Bureau of Education for the Handicapped
    Bureau of Postsecondary Education
    Office of Indian Education
    National Institute of Education

Public Health Service
    Alcohol, Drug Abuse and Mental Health Administration
      National Institute on Alcohol Abuse and Alcoholism
      National Institute on Drug Abuse
      National Institute of Mental Health
    Center for Disease Control
    Food and Drug Administration
    Health Resources Administration
      Bureau of Health Manpower
      Bureau of Health Planning and Resources Development
      National Center for Health Services Research
      National Center for Health Statistics
    Health Services Administration
      Bureau of Community Health Services
      Bureau of Quality Assurance
      Indian Health Service
      Bureau of Medical Services
    National Institutes of Health
      National Institute of Child Health and Human Development
      National Institute of Environmental Health Sciences
      National Institute of General Medical Sciences
      National Institute of Allergy and Infectious Diseases
      National Institute of Neurological and Communicative
        Disorders and Stroke
      National Institute on Aging
      Clinical Center
      Fogarty International Center
      Division of Research Resources
      Division of Research Grants

Social and Rehabilitation Service
    Office of Child Support Enforcement
    Community Services Administration
Social Security Administration

Department of the Interior
C Street between 18th and 19th Streets, N.W.
Washington, D.C. 20240

Bureau of Indian Affairs. The principal objectives of the bureau includes training and encouraging Indian and Alaska native people in the full development of their human resource potentials through education and social and community development programs. (Contact the Personnel Office, Bureau of Indian Affairs, Department of the Interior, 1951 Constitution Avenue, N.W., Washington, D.C. 20245.)

Department of Justice
Constitution Avenue and 10th Street, N.W.
Washington, D.C. 20530

Bureau of Prisons. The bureau is responsible for the care and custody of persons convicted of federal crimes. It operates a nationwide system of security prisons, halfway houses called community treatment centers, and community program offices. Psychologists assist in the rehabilitation process. (Contact the Personnel Office, Bureau of Prisons, 320 First Street, N.W., Washington, D.C. 20534.)

Immigration and Naturalization Service. The service provides education and social assistance to aliens seeking naturalization and to those legally residing in the United States. (Contact the Personnel Office, Immigration and Naturalization Service, Department of Justice, 425 I Street, N.W., Washington, D.C. 20536.)

Drug Enforcement Administration (DEA). The DEA conducts domestic and international investigations of major drug traffickers. (Contact the Personnel Office, DEA, Department of Justice, 1405 I Street, N.W., Washington, D.C. 20537.)

Law Enforcement Assistance Administration (LEAA). This branch assists state and local governments in strengthening and improving law enforcement and criminal justice. The LEAA provides assistance programs for research, evaluation, technical assistance, information, training, and education and also provides assistance for juvenile justice and delinquency prevention programs. (Contact the Personnel Office, LEAA, 633 Indiana Avenue, N.W., Washington, D.C. 20531.)

Department of Labor
200 Constitution Avenue, N.W.
Washington, D.C. 20210

The department employs individuals with organizational–industrial psychology backgrounds in programs in education and training, employment standards, research, health and safety, and labor statistics. Any of the following elements of the department can be investigated by contacting the Personnel Office at the address above:

Employment and Training Administration
Labor-Management Services Administration
Employment Standards Administration
Occupational Safety and Health Administration
Labor Statistics

State Department
2201 C Street, N.W.
Washington, D.C. 20520

The department uses individuals with social science and political science backgrounds in its cultural assistance programs for other nations and in its research and analysis programs. (Contact the Personnel Office at the address above; the Permanent Mission of the United States of America to the Organization of American States at the address above; the Agency for International Development, 320 21st Street, N.W., Washington, D.C. 20523; or the United States Mission to the United Nations, 799 United Nations Plaza, New York, New York 10017.)

Department of Transportation
400 7th Street, S.W.
Washington, D.C. 20590

The department uses skills of social science majors in research and development, training, development and administration of safety standards, and systems development and technology. Administrations within the department that hire social science majors include the U.S. Coast Guard, the Federal Highway Administration, the Federal Railroad Administration, the National Highway Traffic Safety Administration, and the Urban Mass Transportation Administration (Contact all these administrations at the address above; or contact the Federal Aviation Administration, 800 Independence Avenue, S.W., Washington, D.C. 20591, which includes the National Aviation Facilities Experimental Center, Atlantic City, New Jersey 08405.)

Department of the Treasury
15th Street and Pennsylvania Avenue, N.W.
Washington, D.C. 20220

Social science majors are most frequently employed by the department in the law enforcement function; they perform the investigatory or training duties of the following agencies: U.S. Customs Service (1301 Constitution Avenue, N.W., Washington, D.C. 20229); Internal Revenue Service (1111 Constitution Avenue, N.W., Washington, D.C. 20224); U.S.

Savings Bonds Division (1111 20th Street, N.W., Washington, D.C. 20226); Bureau of Alcohol, Tobacco and Firearms (1200 Pennsylvania Avenue, N.W., Washington, D.C. 20226); and the Federal Law Enforcement Training Center (Glynco, Georgia 31520).

ACTION
806 Connecticut Avenue, N.W.
Washington, D.C. 20525

ACTION's purpose is to strengthen the impact and appeal of citizen participation in programs providing personalized services to people whose needs are compelling, both at home and abroad. It provides centralized coordination and administration of domestic and international volunteer activities sponsored by the federal government. ACTION attempts to achieve this purpose through the Peace Corps, Volunteers in Service to America (VISTA), the Retired Senior Volunteer Program (RSVP), University Year for Action (UYA), the National Student Volunteer Program (NSVP), and the Youth Challenge Program (YCP).

Commission on Civil Rights
1121 Vermont Avenue, N.W.
Washington, D.C. 20425

The commission's role is to encourage constructive steps toward equal opportunity for minority groups and women. The commission may employ individuals with social science backgrounds to investigate complaints and to collect and study information on denials of equal protection of the law because of race, color, religion, sex, or national origin.

Community Services Administration
1200 19th Street, N.W.
Washington, D.C. 20506

The overall purpose of this administration is to reduce poverty in America. It seeks to accomplish this goal by helping low-income families and individuals attain economic self-sufficiency. Social science majors may be employed in programs to develop local initiative at the community level; to provide training and technical assistance; and to advise state economic opportunity offices, senior citizen opportunities and services projects, national summer youth sports, and community economic development projects.

Energy Research and Development Administration (ERDA)
20 Massachusetts Avenue, N.W.
Washington, D.C. 20545

The purpose of ERDA is to consolidate federal activities relating to research and development on the various sources of energy and to assure public health and safety. ERDA may employ social science majors in its various environment and safety research, development, and standards programs.

Environmental Protection Agency (EPA)
401 M Street, S.W.
Washington, D.C. 20460

EPA endeavors to abate and control pollution systematically through research, monitoring, standard setting, and enforcement. Coordination of the various research programs is designed to yield a synthesis of knowledge from the biological, physical, and social sciences, which can be interpreted in terms of total human and environmental needs. Social science majors may be employed in the research and the enforcement activities of the agency.

Equal Employment Opportunity Commission (EEOC)
2401 E Street, N.W.
Washington, D.C. 20506

The EEOC investigates charges of discrimination against public and private employers exclusive of the federal government, labor organizations, joint labor-management apprenticeship programs, and public and private employment agencies. The voluntary program division provides information, educational material, consultation, and other assistance in the development of affirmative and other voluntary action programs. The commission selects its employees from various examinations and registers, including the Professional and Administrative Career Examination (PACE), midlevel, and senior-level registers, and the Equal Opportunity Specialist register. Social science majors may qualify for employment opportunities.

National Aeronautics and Space Administration (NASA)
400 Maryland Avenue, S.W.
Washington, D.C. 20546

The principal functions of NASA includes researching flight problems within and outside the earth's atmosphere; constructing, testing, and operating aeronautical and space vehicles; and conducting activities required for the exploration of space with manned and unmanned vehicles. Social science majors may be interested in opportunities with the Ames Research Center (Moffett Field, California), which has program responsibilities for flight simulation technology and life sciences, including aeronautics, exobiology, and space medicine; or the Lyndon B. Johnson Space Center (Houston, Texas), which has responsibility for the development of manned spacecraft—shuttle, manned flight operations, space medicine and biotechnology for manned flight—and earth resources applications. Advanced degrees and a strong emphasis in human-machine systems, human factors, or allied physical or biological sciences are essential requirements for job seekers with social science majors.

United States Office of Personnel Management (OPM)
1900 E Street, N.W.
Washington, D.C. 20415

The OPM administers a merit system of federal employment that includes recruiting, examining, training, and promoting people on the basis of their knowledge and skills. The OPM uses social science majors in the development, validation, and standardization of achievement and aptitude tests; recruiting and examining methods; personnel investigations; equal employment opportunity programs; employee development and training programs; incentive awards programs; personnel management; employee benefits programs; and intergovernmental personnel programs. The OPM employs numerous psychologists and social science majors in its Personnel Research and Development Center located at the OPM's headquarters in Washington, D.C.

United States Information Agency (USIA)
1750 Pennsylvania Avenue, N.W.
Washington, D.C. 20547

USIA has responsibility for the conduct of overseas information and cultural programs to promote greater understanding of the United States—its government, its people, its customs and traditions, and its policies, both foreign and domestic—through radio broadcasting, motion pictures, television, personal contact, lectures and seminars, and publications. The USIA offices abroad also carry out the overseas functions of the Department of State's educational and cultural exchange programs.

United States Postal Service (USPS)
475 L'Enfant Plaza West, S.W.
Washington, D.C. 20260

The USPS provides mail-processing and delivery services to individuals and businesses within the United States. It employs social science majors (a) in its employee relations department to develop achievement and aptitude tests and other personnel selection methods, to conduct employee training and development programs, and to perform personnel research; (b) in its research and development department to focus on human factors in the design and operation of human-operated mail-processing equipment; and (c) in its customer relations department to assist individuals and organizations in using the postal service more effectively.

Veterans Administration (VA)
810 Vermont Avenue, N.W.
Washington, D.C. 20420

The VA is responsible for the administration of a thorough system of benefits for veterans and dependents, including education and rehabilitation, and a comprehensive medical program involving a widespread system of nursing homes, clinics, and more than 170 hospitals. The VA is one of the largest federal employers of clinical and counseling psychologists and social workers. Most positions beyond such basic entry levels as psychologist aid, psychiatric aid, or social worker aid require advanced degrees and completion of an internship.

Department of Defense (DOD)
The Pentagon
Washington, D.C. 20301

The DOD is responsible for providing the military forces needed to deter war and protect the security of the United States. The major elements of these forces are the Army, Navy, Marine Corps, and Air Force, all of which employ psychologists and social science majors in a variety of clinical, social, and research activities. Accordingly, military psychologists may be thought of as psychologists who apply their skills in a military environment in the same manner as their counterparts do in the civilian environment. The requirements for personnel working in the area are generally equivalent to those of personnel working in other state and federal agencies, education, and industry. The master's level, or equivalent, is generally considered the entry level, and a sizable percentage of the work force hold the PhD. Psychologists (master's or doctorate holders) employed by the DOD may be either civil service employees or active duty officers. Many psychologists are engaged in research on fundamental issues of human behavior, while others are involved in research and development pertaining to labor planning, selection, evaluation, training, classification, motivation, leadership, career retention, human factors engineering, sensory functions, fatigue, stress, human-machine interfaces, human engineering, and safety. A number of clinical and counseling psychologists concern themselves with emotional stability, health in general, and the professional services of guidance, counseling, therapy, and special testing.

The United States Air Force employs psychologists and social science majors at the following locations:

Air Force Human Resources Laboratory, Brooks AFB, San Antonio, Texas
    Flying Training Division, Williams AFB, Arizona
    Manpower Development Division, Alexandria, Virginia
    Personnel Research Division, Lackland AFB, Texas
    Advanced Systems Division, Wright-Patterson AFB, Dayton, Ohio
    Technical Training Division, Lowry AFB, Denver, Colorado

Human Engineering Division, Aerospace Medical Research Laboratory, Wright-Patterson AFB, Dayton, Ohio

Biomedical Sciences Corps, Malcolm Grow USAF Medical Center, Andrews AFB, Washington, D.C.

Department of Life and Behavioral Sciences, U.S. Air Force Academy, Colorado 80840

The United States Army employs psychologists and social science majors at the following organizations:

U.S. Army Research Institute for the Behavioral and Social Sciences
5001 Eisenhower Avenue
Alexandria, Virginia 22333

U.S. Army Human Engineering Laboratory
Aberdeen Proving Ground, Maryland 21005

Psychology Division
U.S. Army Medical Research Laboratory
Fort Knox, Kentucky 40120

Aviation Psychological Branch
U.S. Army Medical Research Unit
U.S. Army Aeromedical Research Laboratory
Fort Rucker, Alabama 36360

Military Stress Laboratory
Army Research Institute of Environmental Medicine
Natick, Massachusetts 01760

Army Medical Department Behavioral Science
Office of the Surgeon General
Department of the Army
Directorate of Professional Service
Washington, D.C. 20314

Alcohol and Drug Abuse Prevention and Control Program
Office of the Surgeon General
Department of the Army
Washington, D.C. 20314

Office of Military Psychology and Leadership
United States Military Academy
West Point, New York 10996

The United States Navy employs psychologists and social science majors in research, clinical, and teaching capacities at the following locations:

Office of Naval Research psychological research programs:
    Office of Naval Research (Code 450)
    Department of the Navy
    Washington, D.C. 20390

Manpower and personnel research:
    Office of the Chief of Naval Operations (OP-098TL)
    Department of the Navy
    Washington, D.C. 20390

Clinical psychology programs:
    Bureau of Medicine and Surgery (Code 313)
    Department of the Navy
    Washington, D.C. 20360

Medical research programs:
    Bureau of Medicine and Surgery (Code 713)
    Department of the Navy
    Washington, D.C. 20360

Aviation psychology and human factors:
    Bureau of Medicine and Surgery (Code 513)
    Department of the Navy
    Washington, D.C. 20360

Teaching
    United States Naval Academy
    Annapolis, Maryland 21402

Chances Of Getting A Government Job

The former Civil Service Commission, in its *Bulletin on Federal Staffing Trends* (June 23, 1977) reported that hiring was down during fiscal years 1975 and 1976 and up during the first half of fiscal year 1977 until new employment ceilings and hiring limitations were imposed by President Carter in March 1977. The bulletin also reported that competition is expected to remain intense and that competitor inventories for most occupations range from adequate to surplus. The two notable exceptions are the engineering and health fields, where nationwide demand continues to exceed supply except in some specialties in certain geographic areas. In the interest of economy and public credibility, the Office of Personnel Management has a policy of accepting applications only for those occupations for which agencies anticipate a need and for which there is an inadequate supply of qualified people in their inventories.

The Office of Personnel Management's regional and area offices publish a wide variety of materials to keep the public and the agencies informed about the federal employment picture and competitor inventory conditions. Nationally, the Office of Personnel Management publishes *Federal Employment Outlook*—a summary of career fields and locales for which opportunities are either most favorable or extremely limited. This summary includes a great deal of information about specific needs in the health fields. *Trends in Federal Hiring*, a semiannual newsletter distributed to colleges and supplemented by the quarterly *Trends Bulletin*, provides detailed summaries of the employment picture at the career-entry level. The latter includes a profile of open/closed information by specialty and locale in the major nationwide examinations.

A wide variety of positions in the federal government are available to psychologists and social science majors; however, the competition is keen. Interested persons should begin to review federal job opportunities at the end of their sophomore year in college in order to select courses, work experience, and interships that will qualify them for their particular interest area. Whether one goes into federal service or not as a psychologist or social scientist, meeting the standards for a federal position will qualify the job seeker for many such positions in private industry, private practice, or state or local government. Interested persons should contact their nearest Federal Job Information Center or the personnel office of any federal agency of interest to them for vacancy announcements and particulars regarding the PACE or any other entrance examination. Above all, applicants should prepare their applications carefully to show that all required qualifications have been met.

8

Jerry L. Fryrear

Community Agency Employment Opportunities and Requirements

This chapter reports the results of a survey conducted to obtain information on employment possibilities in community health, welfare, recreational, and other social services. Of 332 agencies that responded from four cities, 55% did or would hire psychology majors with baccalaureates. An average of 5.9 openings existed per agency, and the average starting salary (1975–1976) was $7900. The skill requirements mentioned most frequently were interviewing, crisis intervention, behavior modification, and a knowledge of child development. The most frequently mentioned experience requirements were work with culturally disadvantaged and emotionally disturbed people. (See Chapter 3 of this book for advice on how to obtain such experience through volunteering.)

In 1973, J. A. Kulik reported that psychology department chairpersons estimated that approximately 40% of psychology majors sought full-time employment after graduation with a baccalaureate degree. Boneau (1968) had earlier estimated a number closer to 78%. We now know a little about the job market for those 40–78% and about the skills and experiences they need to obtain jobs; some of this information is reported in other chapters of this book. The purpose of the study described in this chapter was to add to this knowledge by (a) surveying the job market for baccalaureate psychology students in the field of community service, and (b) ascertaining the skills and experience necessary or helpful for employment in this field.

The survey described was aimed not at former students but at potential employers. The sample was restricted to community service agencies in four southern cities: New Orleans, Houston, Dallas, and Atlanta. The New Orleans and Houston surveys were carried out by telephone in 1975 and the Dallas and Atlanta surveys by mail in 1976.

Method

Sample

New Orleans. The New Orleans sample consisted of 135 agencies selected randomly from the *New Orleans Metropolitan Area Directory of*

Social Welfare and Related Services. Interviews were conducted by telephone with the personnel manager or equivalent. Of the agencies sampled, 34% were mental health agencies and 66% represented other community services.

Houston. The Houston sample consisted of 67 agencies contacted by telephone and taken randomly from the cross-directory telephone book under the headings "institutions" and "organizations." A more detailed breakdown of the Houston sample is not available.

Dallas. The Dallas sample consisted of 52 respondents to 100 mailed questionnaires. The sample of 100 was selected randomly from the *Directory of Health, Welfare, and Recreation Services for Greater Dallas*. The 52 returned questionnaires included 37% from agencies involved in mental health and 63% from other community service agencies.

Atlanta. The Atlanta sample consisted of 78 respondents of 100 mailed questionnaires. The sample of 100 was selected randomly from the *Metropolitan Atlanta Directory of Community Services*. The 78 returned questionnaries included 41% from agencies in the field of mental health and 59% from agencies involved in other community services.

The overall sample thus consisted of 332 community agencies, 33% of which are estimated to be mental health agencies. The remaining 67% represent a wide range of community services.

Questionnaires

The telephone questionnaire and mailed questionnaire were slightly different, but in both cases the respondents were asked if they hired persons with a bachelor's degree in psychology. The respondents were then asked to respond to a list of skills (see Figure 8-1) and a list of experiences (see Figure 8-2). Since telephone respondents in the first two cities mentioned crisis intervention skills as important, these skills were included in the questionnaire list mailed to the remaining two cities. All respondents were asked to estimate the number of job openings for baccalaureate psychology majors in a typical year and the average starting salary.

Results

Employment Opportunities

Responses to the question "Do you employ people with a bachelor's degree in psychology?" are presented in Table 8-1. Overall, 38% of the respondents reported that they do hire such people. An additional 17%

Jerry L. Fryrear is an assistant professor of psychology at Newcomb College, Tulane University of Louisiana.

Portions of this chapter were presented at the 1976 Annual Meeting of the American Psychological Association, Washington, D.C., September 1976. The author wishes to acknowledge the assistance of Melanie Crowder, University of Houston, and Dan Fishbein, University of Missouri.

TABLE 8-1   Percentage of Responses to the Question "Do You Employ People With a Bachelor's Degree in Psychology?

| | City | | | | |
Response	New Orleans	Houston	Dallas	Atlanta	*M*
Yes	36	28	41	46	38
No	50	43	27	29	37
Have in the past, but not now	1	6	10	5	6
Will in the future, but not now	1	3	0	3	2
Would if they had the right skills	12	20	22	17	17

Note. Percent signs are omitted.

reported that they would hire such people if they had the right skills. Thus, 55% of the agencies who were surveyed did or would have job openings for the psychology major with a baccalaureate. Of the four cities, Atlanta had the highest percentage of openings and Houston the lowest.

The average number of estimated openings per agency for one year was 5.9, with a range of 1–150. The average starting salary was $7,900 per year, with a range of $6,000–$15,000. The average numbers of yearly openings and salaries for the four cities are presented in Table 8-2.

Skills

Figure 8-1 depicts the percentages of ratings of skills as "necessary," "helpful or important," or "irrelevant," for all cities combined. The skills

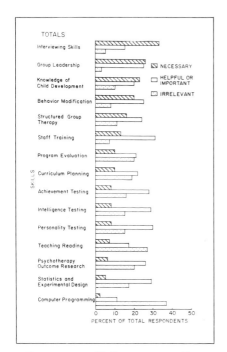

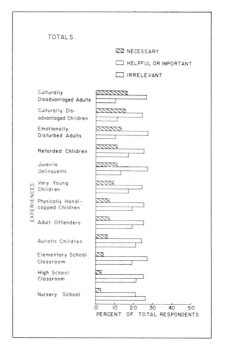

Figure 8-1.   Skill ratings for all cities combined.

Figure 8-2.   Experience ratings for all cities combined.

TABLE 8-2   Mean Number of Estimated Openings per Year and Mean Starting Annual Salary

City	Mean number of openings	Mean starting annual salary
New Orleans	6.5	$7,943
Houston	7.7	7,428
Dallas	3.4	7,822
Atlanta	6.0	8,500
All cities combined	5.9	7,900

are arranged in order of the percentages of "necessary" ratings. Interviewing skills were judged by more respondents as necessary than were group leadership skills, and so on. Computer programming had the fewest ratings of necessary and was judged irrelevant by more respondents than were the other skills. The ratings of "helpful or important" do not seem to differ a great deal among the various skills. One can speculate that most of the skills are thought to be helpful to some extent by 20% to 30% of the respondents. The pattern of ratings for each city is quite similar to that for the combined ratings. As explained above, the Dallas and Atlanta data include ratings for crisis intervention skills, which are not shown in Figure 8-1. In both cities, crisis intervention skills were judged necessary by 40% of the respondents.

Experiences

Figure 8-2 shows the percentages of ratings of experiences as "necessary," "helpful or important," or "irrelevant," for all cities combined. The experiences are arranged in order of the percentages of "necessary" ratings. Work with culturally disadvantaged adults and children was judged necessary by more respondents than the other experiences. Work in school settings was judged necessary by the fewest respondents. All the experiences were rated helpful or important by approximately equal numbers of respondents. Again, the breakdown of experience ratings by cities is similar to that for the combined ratings.

Discussion

The most obvious conclusion to be drawn from this survey is that jobs are available in community agencies for those with psychology baccalareates. Perhaps as many as half of the community agencies in cities have such openings. These jobs are in a variety of services including, but not limited to, the mental health field. The beginning salaries, while not extraordinary, seem reasonable and competitive with those of many other occupations.

A second conclusion is that no particular set of skills is universally necessary for the community-agencies job market. None of the skills surveyed were rated necessary by more than 50% of the respondents. That lack of agreement is probably due to the diversity of agencies and to the fact that the jobs themselves are not highly specialized. A rank ordering of skills in terms of percentages of ratings, however, clearly shows that interviewing, crisis intervention, and group leadership skills are desired by more agencies than computer programming, statistics and experimental design, and therapy outcome research skills. Only 8% of the respondents thought testing skills were necessary. Testing applies mainly to the mental health agencies and is probably reserved for master's- or doctoral-level psychologists.

Experiences that a student might acquire through part-time employment or volunteer work, such as work with culturally disadvantaged and emotionally disturbed people, were rated necessary more frequently than other experiences. None of the experiences, however, were thought to be necessary by a majority of the respondents. All were thought to be helpful or important by approximately equal numbers of respondents.

The information presented in this chapter should prove helpful in student advising and curriculum planning. Students who plan to work in the community service field with a bachelor's degree would be well advised to gain some expertise in interviewing, crisis intervention, group leadership, child development, and behavior modification, and to stress those areas on vitae and in job interviews. Such students would also be well advised that employment opportunities do exist in community service, contrary to frequently heard opinion.

Psychology departments that wish to train baccalaureate holders for community service may consider offering courses that include interviewing skills, group leadership, crisis intervention, and behavior modification. Furthermore, courses in statistics, experimental design, and testing do not seem to be relevant to this area. I believe a two-track or multitrack curriculum, coupled with advising students about employment opportunities and requirements, is the most appropriate undergraduate program. Students desiring to enter the community service field with a baccalaureate would take basic courses in introductory psychology, child psychology, abnormal psychology, and group dynamics and practicum courses in leadership training, interviewing, crisis intervention, and behavior modification. Ideally, field placement in a community agency during the senior year would also be provided. Such students would be advised that these courses may not be ideal preparation for graduate work and that if they are considering graduate school, a different curriculum, emphasizing research methodology and laboratory work, would be more appropriate.

More information concerning opportunities in community agencies for those with baccalaureates is desperately needed. Specifically, the survey presented in this chapter provides no information on advancement opportunities and other career considerations. Does a career ladder exist within the community service field, or does one have to eventually return to school to advance? What salary increases can one expect after six months or one year? What other skills and experiences, not included in the survey, are necessary? The timeworn statement, seen so often at the end of research discussion, is appropriate here: Additional research is needed to answer these questions.

REFERENCES

Boneau, A. The educational base: Supply for the demand. *American Psychologist*, 1968, *23*, 308–311.

Kulik, J. A. *Undergraduate education in psychology*. Washington, D.C.: American Psychological Association, 1973.

9

Carol J. Erdwins and Mark B. Mendelsohn

A Survey of Paraprofessional Positions in Human Service Settings

This chapter reports a survey of paraprofessional positions at human service agencies in the Northern Virginia portion of the Washington, D.C. metropolitan area. Similar general findings can probably be expected for any metropolitan area. In this limited sample alone, 20 agencies employing a total of 322 paraprofessionals were found. The paraprofessionals in these positions were required to perform many of the same activities, albeit with more supervision, as mental health professionals. Over 95% were engaged in some kind of therapeutic intervention and liaison work with the client's family, but psychological testing was seldom required. Salaries varied greatly, with public agencies generally offering higher starting wages, but opportunities for promotion, without further training, were limited. The authors conclude with suggestions for academic departments undertaking the development of a paraprofessional program.

In recent years, interest has increased in the use of nonprofessionally trained mental health workers within a variety of human service settings. These workers are most often designated as paraprofessionals, psychology technicians, or mental health technicians and are usually trained to the Associate of Arts (AA) or Bachelor of Arts (BA) level. A wide range of employment opportunities, from child management consultant to psychometrician, has been described for individuals with this training (Gentry, 1974; Keeley, Shemberg, & Ferber, 1973; Suinn, 1974). Interest has also been focused on the development of academic curricula and training programs to prepare graduates to fill these roles (Korn, 1974; Wasserman, McCarthy, & Ferree, 1975). In fact, several models have been specifically devised for short-term training in counseling skills at this level (Danish & Hauer, 1973; Ivey, 1972).

While many employment opportunities have been suggested for paraprofessionals, little attempt has been made to document the number of available positions and their characteristics. The limited data suggest that the picture is not entirely positive. Korn (1974) mentioned scarcity of jobs as the major problem encountered by graduates of one psychology technician program. Bouhoutsos (1970) discussed (a) the difficulty of integrating training programs, initiated within academic settings, with the demands of employment settings and (b) the marked preference on the part of many community agencies to train their own paraprofessionals rather than to hire graduates of academic programs. She concluded that these two factors account for the lack of positions open to program graduates. Bartels and Tyler (1975), in a survey of comprehensive community mental health centers and their employment of paraprofessionals, enumerated problems encountered by the agencies, such as lack of confidence by the professional staff members in the paraprofessionals' capabilities and difficult interstaff relations. Poor salaries, high turnover rates, and an inadequate career ladder for paraprofessionals were also listed as sources of concern.

As a part of developing a BA-level paraprofessional training program within the psychology department at George Mason University, we surveyed the employment opportunities available to graduates of the program within the university's metropolitan area. The information obtained sheds additional light on the job market awaiting graduates of paraprofessional training programs.

The Survey

Human service agencies within the northern Virginia portion of the Washington, D.C., metropolitan area were contacted to determine whether individuals at the paraprofessional level were on their staffs. Twenty agencies employing a total of 322 paraprofessionals were found. These facilities can be categorized as follows: (a) traditional mental health settings offering services to large numbers of persons; these settings included area community mental health centers, a training center for the mentally retarded, and an inpatient psychiatric hospital; (b) mental health facilities operating on a smaller scale and usually providing services for specific target groups; these facilities included group homes for emotionally disturbed adults, houses for runaway adolescents, and alcohol and drug treatment programs; and (c) settings that provide services for certain segments of the normal population; such settings included day care centers and nursing homes. Detailed interviews were conducted in person at each agency with an individual who was either in charge of or involved with the selection and hiring process for paraprofessionals. These interviews were based on structured questionnaires focusing on the number of positions available at the paraprofessional level, the duties involved, the type of population worked with, the salary level, and the promotion opportunities.

Results and Implications

The number of paraprofessional positions at the agencies sampled varied widely from a high of 170 to a low of 1, with a median number of 6 per

Carol J. Erdwins and Mark B. Mendelsohn are assistant professors in the Department of Psychology at George Mason University.

The authors wish to thank Haidi Sternberg for her assistance in conducting the interviews for this survey.

agency. While these numbers suggest that positions are definitely available in human service settings at this level, these positions may not be numerous enough to absorb large numbers of newly trained students.

Job Characteristics

Paraprofessional positions appear to be very demanding with regard to the type of populations worked with and the duties involved. In the majority of cases, these positions require intensive contact with populations characterized by severe, long-standing problems. Of the 322 positions in the survey, 86% involved work with severely emotionally disturbed individuals, 72% with neurologically impaired persons, 53% with the mentally retarded, and 43% with antisocial or acting-out types. The age group most frequently dealt with by this sample of paraprofessionals was adolescents (93%); 66% of the sample also worked with adult populations and 65% with children.

The survey also indicated that individuals in these positions are asked to fulfill a variety of job duties: 97% of the positions involved participation in and implementation of some kind of therapy program with individuals, 91% also involved group therapy work, and 34% involved family treatment programs. In all cases the therapy program carried out by the paraprofessional was devised and/or supervised by someone with advanced training. Thus, while paraprofessionals engage in many of the same treatment activities as professionals, they do not function with as much autonomy. The data also suggest that paraprofessionals are usually involved in long-term as well as short-term interventions and make use of a variety of treatment modalities.

The survey showed that 89% of the positions required participation in long-term treatment programs. The most frequently used therapy was behavior modification (77%), followed by client-centered techniques (36%), and reality therapy (32%).

Virtually all of these positions involved liaison work. The survey indicated that 98% of the positions included contact and work with the client's family and 91% required work with other community and social welfare agencies; to a lesser extent, communication was also required with other professionals in private practice, the school system, the courts, and health care facilities. This liaison work arises most often either in the course of gathering information about the client or in facilitating the client's therapy program. Of the positions surveyed, 87% required data collection for and about the client. In the great majority of cases this collection primarily involved obtaining information from sources other than the client, such as school and medical records; however, 23% of the positions also required diagnostic interviewing of the client.

Psychological testing was the activity least widely performed in the sample surveyed. Although 64% of the positions involved some kind of objective behavioral rating or charting, only 14% required the administration of more elaborate psychological instruments, such as vocational interest tests, academic achievement tests, and tests of intelligence. Based on this sample, paraprofessionals appear much more likely to be involved in treatment than in assessment functions.

These different job duties and their prevalence within the sample appear to correspond with the findings of a previously mentioned survey by Bartels and Tyler (1975). Both surveys suggest that, with the exception of psychological testing and evaluation, considerable overlap can be found between the activities performed by the paraprofessional and by the professional psychologist.

Salaries and Promotions

Information was also gathered on the salaries and promotion opportunities available for these positions. Annual starting salaries for full-time positions ranged widely from a high of $12,098 to a low of $5,316, with an average of $7,887. A closer analysis of the positions and agencies surveyed revealed that the greatest differences occurred between agencies funded by public monies versus private institutions. The average starting salary for the public agency positions was $8,430 per year, and the average for the private institutions was $6,212. Although paraprofessionals employed in the public sector appear to fare better than those in the private sector, statistics gathered for 1975–1976 college graduates indicate that this salary is still far below the average annual starting salary for positions in fields such as business administration ($10,416) or chemistry ($12,372); the salary is also less than the average of $9,816 for social science majors as a group (U.S. Department of Health, Education and Welfare, 1977).

With regard to opportunities for promotion, these paraprofessional positions again compare unfavorably with careers in other fields. For 10% of the positions that were surveyed, no promotions were possible, 25% of the positions held the possibility of only one promotion, and 65% of the positions held the possibility of advancing two steps up the career ladder. The average yearly salary after two years on the job, with appropriate raises and promotions, was $9,380, an increase of approximately $1,500. These percentages suggest that the career ladder for paraprofessionals is extremely limited in most cases. Within five years, most paraprofessionals will be in the highest position they will ever be able to hold without further graduate training. Reaching the pinnacle of a field by age 28 to 30, with no further promotions and perhaps only limited salary increases to anticipate, is not likely to represent a satisfying career for most college-educated individuals. This salary and promotion outlook may account, at least in part, for the average annual turnover rate of 29% computed for 90% of the positions on which these statistics were available.

Those interviewed were also asked about the kinds of training they felt would be most helpful to the paraprofessionals employed in these positions: 50% felt that relevant work experience was the single most important factor both in qualifying and being hired for the position and in functioning effectively once on the job. Other areas on which a consensus seemed to exist were knowledge of human development (mentioned by 25% of those interviewed) and knowledge of psychological tests (mentioned by 19%).

Conclusions

Durlak (1973) documented that paraprofessionals can function effectively in a variety of settings and that they represent a viable source of mental health personnel. The data from this study, as well as other sources (Bouhoutsos, 1970; Gentry, 1974), suggest also that paraprofessionals are being called upon to perform many of the same services as mental health professionals with several years of education at the graduate level. Training programs are therefore needed to enable paraprofessionals to fulfill their job responsibilities satisfactorily; however, most paraprofessional positions, as they now exist, contain serious drawbacks for the program graduate entering the field. These positions appear to combine a maximum of job responsibility with a minimum of salary and opportunity for career advancement. In addition, the number of available paraprofessional positions is not large, and subjective feedback from several respondents suggests that the generally tight job market has resulted in stiff competition for the better-paying paraprofessional positions. On the other hand, these jobs are not likely to become boring quickly. They involve direct contact with others and could potentially provide the person performing them with a great deal of personal satisfaction.

The job market as described above has meaning not only for the potential paraprofessional but also for academic departments undertaking the development of a training program. Specific suggestions that we would make are as follows:

1. Students undertaking a training program should be given as much information as possible about the employment market for paraprofessionals in their locale. This information will not only prevent dissatisfaction and unhappiness should students not find a receptive employment situation after graduation but it will also help them to make more knowledgeable choices, where possible, in their course selection and practicum training. This suggestion presumes that the employment information is available; however, the collection of these data will probably entail not only an initial survey (such as we have described here) but also continued contacts with area agencies on the part of involved faculty. This undertaking is not as onerous as it sounds, since contacts with many agencies usually exist already. Interested students may also be willing to help in carrying out the initial survey.

2. Contacts with area agencies may serve a second purpose. The agencies may use paraprofessionals more often if they are aware of the educational background and specific training of paraprofessionals in helping skills. Faculty members who have established contacts with agency

professionals will be in an ideal position to increase agency awareness in these areas.

3.   Since the salary and promotion outlook for most of the existing paraprofessional positions is probably not going to improve radically in the foreseeable future, the most feasible avenue toward career advancement for many paraprofessionals will be through further training at the graduate level. Psychology departments will have to take seriously the career ladder concept of the Vail, Colorado, Conference on Levels and Patterns of Training in Psychology: Their graduate programs will have to be designed so that employed paraprofessionals will not be penalized in their attempts to begin graduate work. Pragmatically this may mean offering courses during evening and weekend hours, accepting students on a part-time as well as a full-time basis, and, where possible, working out practica and internship experiences at the agencies employing the paraprofessional.

In effect, if an academic psychology department proposes to undertake the training of paraprofessionals, it needs to look beyond the development of a program of courses and practica experiences. The needs both of students taking the program and agencies who will be employing them must be taken into account. A smooth transition for the student and more efficient agency use of the paraprofessional may be achieved with the academic-training faculty acting as liaison.

REFERENCES

Bartels, B. D., & Tyler, D. Paraprofessionals in the community mental health center. *Professional Psychology*, 1975, *6*, 442–452.

Bouhoutsos, J. C. The nontraditionally trained mental health worker: Fad or future? *Professional Psychology*, 1970, *1*, 455–459.

Danish, S. J., & Hauer, A. L. *Helping skills: A basic training program*. New York: Behavioral Publications, 1973.

Durlak, J. A. Myths concerning the nonprofessional therapist. *Professional Psychology*, 1973, *4*, 300–304.

Gentry, W. D. Three models of training and utilization. *Professional Psychology*, 1974, *5*, 207–214.

Ivey, A. *Microcounseling: Interviewing skills manual*. Springfield, Ill.: Charles C Thomas, 1972.

Keeley, S. M., Shemberg, K. M., & Ferber, H. The training and use of undergraduates as behavior analysts in the consultative process. *Professional Psychology*, 1973, *4*, 59–63.

Korn, J. H. Training and employment of BA psychologists: Report of a symposium. *Teaching Psychology Newsletter*, February 1974, pp. 10–12.

Suinn, R. M. Training undergraduate students as community behavior modification consultants. *Journal of Consulting Psychology*, 1974, *21*, 71–77.

U.S. Department of Health, Education, and Welfare, Office of Education, National Center for Educational Statistics. *Conditions of education*. Washington, D.C.: United States Government Printing Office, 1977.

Wasserman, C. W., McCarthy, B. W., & Ferree, E. H. Student paraprofesionals as behavior change agents. *Professional Psychology*, 1975, *6*, 217–223.

10

Edward J. Jordan, Jr.

Trends in Employment of Psychology Technicians in the Veterans Administration

This chapter presents a survey of the employment of paraprofessionals with bachelor's degrees at Veterans Administration (VA) medical facilities and discusses trends in the future employment of such individuals. Of the more than 170 VA facilities surveyed, 103 employed psychology technicians. In a sample of 73 of these 103 facilities, 56% employed technicians with bachelor's degrees. Virtually all of these positions were full-time, although some were temporary. Most bachelor's-level technicians engaged in psychodiagnostic testing; the rest divided their time about evenly between research and vocational rehabilitation activities. A few assisted in treatments such as biofeedback and behavior modification. No overall trends emerged regarding future hiring; almost equal numbers of facilities expressed positive and negative views about hiring bachelor's-level technicians, and a comparable number were indifferent to the academic level of technicians. Factors possibly associated with these attitudes are discussed.

The Veterans Administration (VA) Psychology Services employ individuals at the bachelor's-degree level primarily in the position of *psychology technician*. VA hiring criteria specify that technicians must possess "a bachelor's degree from an accredited college or university with a major in an appropriate social or biological science, which included or was supplemented by 12 semester hours in psychology." The psychology technician is also required to have "a practical understanding of some of the general principles, theories, methods, and techniques of psychology" but not the grounding in theory and the ability to apply it to the solution of practical problems expected of a psychologist. The technician should have enough knowledge of principles to carry out effectively a plan devised by a psychologist in areas such as psychodiagnostic testing, behavior modification, vocational rehabilitation, or research. It is basic to the relationship between psychologists and psychology technicians that the former supervise the latter.

Those with bachelor's degrees in psychology might also be employed by the VA Psychology Services in the position of *rehabilitation technician*. The baccalaureate is not required for this position, however, and it is typically filled by sub-baccalaureate-level personnel (such as Associates in

Arts from Mental Health Associate programs) who work in drug or alcohol counseling. Many rehabilitation technician positions are not classified by the VA under Psychology Services, and those few that are seem to be for administrative convenience as much as for substantive reasons. Thus the position of rehabilitation technician is not examined in this chapter.

Individuals with bachelor's degrees in psychology and related fields can anticipate eligibility not only for appointment as psychology technicians but also for promotions each year for the first few years. The basic level for the psychology technician series is GS-5; in 1978 the starting salary at that level was $9959 per year. After a year in that grade, the technician can be placed at the GS-6 or GS-7 level, with a yearly salary (as of 1978) of $11,101 or $12,336, respectively. After another year, the technician can be placed even higher, and positions may reach to the GS-8 or GS-9 level, with annual salaries in 1978 of $13,662 or $15,090, respectively.[1] This stage represents the top of the career ladder for psychology technicians in the VA.

VA hiring procedures make matters more complicated, however. They provide that the experience requirements for grades above GS-5 may be replaced, in part or in whole, by graduate study in psychology. One such year of study brings GS-7 eligibility, and two years, GS-9. This makes it possible for master's-degree holders as well as those with bachelor's degrees to fill psychology technician positions. VA personnel policy simply does not make distinctions between the two degrees when it comes to filling psychology technician positions at levels above GS-5. Rather, a host of factors at the level of the local facility decides the academic-degree level at which applicants will be hired.

Survey of VA Facilities

Three questions about bachelor's-level psychology technicians in the VA are of interest: (a) How many are there? (b) What kinds of work do they perform? and (c) What prospects are there for future increases or decreases in their numbers? Since no data existed on the bachelor's-level group as distinct from the entire body of VA psychology technicians, it was necessary to directly survey VA Psychology Services in field health facilities to find the answers.

Edward J. Jordan, Jr., is Assistant Chief, Psychology Service, at the Veterans Administration Hospital in Washington, D.C.

The author would like to express his deep appreciation to the 73 VA chief psychologists (and in a few cases, to their surrogates) who took the time and pains to share their data and their views. The author also thanks Jule Moravec and Charles Stenger of the VA Central Office and Carol Poor of the Personnel Division at the VA Hospital in Washington, D.C., for their support, their helpful suggestions, and the access they provided to technical documents.

1. Federal salaries in the General Schedule (GS) are set yearly by presidential initiative and congressional concurrence or modification. Raises are based on such factors as increases in the cost of living and budgetary concerns. Precise projections cannot be made about future rates, but recent years have seen increases of from approximately 3% to 8% per year.

How Many Psychology Technicians Are There?

A recent VA Central Office publication, *Psychology Staffing and Services in VA Hospitals and Clinics, 1976*, identified about 40 facilities in the field that had no psychology technicians at all. These facilities, therefore, were not surveyed, and attention was turned to the 103 facilities that did employ psychology technicians at some academic level as of June 1976.

The original intention was to survey all 103 facilities, but time limitations permitted only a sample of 75. While neither random nor systematic construction can be claimed for this sample, it is probably representative within reasonable limits. It includes over 70% of the facilities and is balanced with respect to the categories of size, location, closeness to medical schools, and type of facility.

Letters asking the three questions mentioned above were sent to the 75 chief psychologists at these facilities. To minimize response cost, the letters offered the psychologists the option of responding via a subsequent phone call, although they could respond in writing if they preferred. Twenty-four chiefs did write back, and three others telephoned. Two facilities were lost from the sample when one chief failed to return a call and when another could not be reached by telephone. The remaining 46 facilities were successfully contacted by telephone.

Of the 73 VA facilities surveyed, 41 (or 56% of the sample) employed bachelor's-level psychology technicians as of February 1977. These 41 facilities employed 84 technicians who held the bachelor's degree and no technicians with higher degrees. These 84 technicians comprise about one-third of the total 254 psychology technicians employed in the hospitals and clinics surveyed. All but a handful of these positions appear to be full-time, although a large number of research positions are temporary.

What Kind of Work Do Technicians Perform?

Bachelor's-level technicians provide a wide range of services to patients and staff. The following partial list illustrates the diversity of their work: relaxation training, geriatric remotivation in community care, evaluation research in an alcohol rehabilitation program, biofeedback, social skills training, evaluations for sheltered workshops, intake interviews for psychiatric patients, tutoring of the brain-injured, and directing socialization groups. One bachelor's-level technician also carried out TIGER training (a personal effectiveness training program developed within the VA), another serviced as an Equal Employment Opportunity counselor, and another administered programmed instruction to medical students on psychiatry rotation.

Although many of these activities overlap, and several may be done by the same technician, the duties of bachelor's-level technicians can be grouped into four classes: psychodiagnostic testing, neuropsychological testing, vocational rehabilitation, and research.

1. *Psychodiagnostic testing.* The principal activity of 36 out of the total 84 bachelor's-level technicians (almost 43%) was psychodiagnostic

testing. In a few situations, these technicians administered projective tests, but on the whole the tests were objective. The degree of test-administration skill required ranged from administration of the Minnesota Multiphasic Personality Inventory to administration of the Weschler Adult Intelligence Scale. Approximately 14 other bachelor's-level technicians specialized in administration of the Halstead-Reitan Neuropsychological Battery, and many others did neuropsychological evaluations for a lesser proportion of their time. (A strict line between these two types of testing is difficult to draw, hence the use of "approximately" in the last statement. If the estimate of 14 is in error, it is on the low side.) Pooling these two classes of activity, it appears that 60% of the bachelor's-level technicians are principally doing psychodiagnostic work.

2. *Neuropsychological testing.* The area most successfully occupied by bachelor's-level personnel was neuropsychology; 77% of neuropsychology technicians surveyed held the BA or BS degree. This percentage is particularly striking when one considers that only 21% of the psychodiagnostic technicians were at the bachelor's-degree level.[2]

3. *Vocational rehabilitation.* Seventeen bachelor's-level technicians were primarily engaged in vocational rehabilitation activities, including job replacement and follow-up visits to employers in the community. Bachelor's-level people tended to be underrepresented in vocational rehabilitation; only 24% of all technicians in this area held the BA or BS, compared to the 33% expected. This low percentage confirms the VA tradition of employing master's-level personnel in vocational rehabilitation.

4. *Research.* Another 17 bachelor's-level technicians were engaged primarily in research activities. These activities included running subjects in experiments, compiling data, and analyzing results. Many of these individuals were employed on a temporary basis because they were on time-limited research grants. Bachelor's-level technicians comprised 39% of all the psychology technicians doing research.

Trends for the Future

The third survey question, which concerned trends for the future, was purposely made very broad in order to best reflect the overall chances of more BA/BS hiring. A three-category analysis was used: A *positive* response was one indicating that the chief employed bachelor's-level technicians and was willing to hire more; a *negative* response indicated that the chief either employed no bachelor's-level technicians and had no plans to hire any or that he or she disliked the idea; and a *neutral* response referred to situations in which a chief was neither for nor against the idea, employed at least one bachelor's-level technician, and saw little likelihood of hiring

---

2. The distribution of bachelor's-level technicians across the four classes of duties departed significantly from expectation, based on the fact that neuropsychology technicians represented one-third of the psychology technician group. The continuity-corrected chi-square was 11.57 ($p < .01, df = 3$).

more in the near future. No chiefs without bachelor's-level technicians indicated plans to hire any.

The responses to the third question were 36% positive, 40% negative, and 24% neutral. Thus a little over one third of the respondents apparently accepted the idea of bachelor's-level technicians, while approximately 40% of the group appeared to take a stand against hiring such technicians.

The chiefs polled gave a variety of reasons for favoring or not favoring BA or BS technicians. The following negative comments are the most representative of the reasons given for not favoring technicians. Management was seen as preoccupied with budget and hence likely to view technicians as replacements rather than assistants for staff psychologists. Many chiefs said that staff and technician positions were equally difficult to establish and that, for the same effort, one might as well try for a staff position. In some facilities with close medical school affiliation, the chief psychologists preferred to hire those with the highest credentials possible; their technicians were likely to be master's-degree holders. In situations where psychology has to compete with other health services over patient care and management, the technician's lack of status is seen as potentially detrimental.

Some chiefs reported discontent among psychology technicians over limitations on their duties and remuneration. In terms of long-range career development, the baccalaureate psychology technician's advancement ends quite soon. Some chiefs felt that a grade ceiling higher than GS-9 would be helpful in this regard, although it would require a change in federal personnel classification policy and is most unlikely in the foreseeable future. Technicians' dissatisfaction with limitations on their duties seemed to center around psychotherapy, which technicians are not authorized to do. This was an especially sore point in facilities where psychology technicians worked with psychology trainees or with rehabilitation technicians. Trainees, doctorate bound, start below the skill level of technicians yet get to perform psychotherapy relatively soon in the typical facility. Rehabilitation technicians, often with less than a bachelor's degree, typically become involved in counseling activities that are a lot more like psychotherapy than the activities psychology technicians are permitted.

Most chiefs agreed that master's-level people generally come to the job better trained. Chiefs who use bachelor's-level technicians pointed out the need to teach them on the job. The 12 semester hours of psychology specified in VA hiring requirements were seen as inadequate. Many chiefs employing BA or BS technicians did so only because they saw unusually high potential in an individual, and these chiefs actively fostered further academic advancement for such persons. Several very pleased chiefs told me of technicians, both bachelor's- and master's-level, who had gained admission to doctoral programs.

In some cases, chiefs reported that the lower starting salary of a bachelor's-level applicant was an advantage in the eyes of station management. For a period of time, management would save money, and, because technicians' raises would be scheduled over a longer time period, chiefs would have less personnel turnover.

In a few instances where institutions near a VA facility had bachelor's- or master's-level programs, their graduates seemed well received and appeared to enjoy competitive advantages for psychology technician positions.

Discussion

Graduates of baccalaureate programs in psychology have theoretical access to over 330 psychology technician positions in the VA. An estimate based on a 70% sample of health care facilities actually employing psychology technicians suggests that about one-third of the existing positions are actually held by individuals with bachelor's degrees and that bachelor's-level positions exist in over half the facilities that use psychology technicians at all. It therefore appears that the individual with a bachelor's degree in psychology has a substantial *de facto* acceptance, although, to a large extent, this acceptance indicates the operation of mostly accidental factors such as station budget, availability of particular individuals at particular times, and the local employment market. Most VA chief psychologists do not appear to have a concept of the bachelor's-level technician as a distinct entity. Where nearby educational programs provide candidates, chief psychologists are more aware of the bachelor's-level technician, but so far the number of such programs seems small and their effect is not widespread. An increase in formal academic programs at the baccalaureate level would (a) focus attention on the BA or BS individual as a potential worker, (b) provide specific training, and (c) counteract the impression that BA or BS people are not fully prepared.

The apparently greater acceptance of bachelor's-level individuals as neuropsychology technicians may be a real phenomenon, a sampling error, or an artifact of how chiefs determine whether or not technicians are primarily involved in neuropsychology work. If this greater acceptance is real, it may be related to the relative newness of this specialization in the VA, in contrast, for example, to vocational counseling, which has been traditionally linked with a master's degree. It is a mystery to this investigator why a much lower proportion of those technicians not engaged in neuropsychological work should be at the bachelor's level. Perhaps it is due to sampling error.

Although this survey uncovered no overall trend to hire more or fewer bachelor's-level psychology technicians, slightly over one-third of the chief psychologists who had hired psychology technicians were favorably inclined toward hiring more. One limitation of this survey, however, is that VA health care facilities without psychology technicians were not asked about future trends. Any positive response from that uninvestigated group would, of course, increase the opportunities for those with bachelor's degrees. Another positive sign is the general increase, within the VA, in the number of psychology technicians from 250 in 1971[3] to over 330 as of June 1976. There is no evidence to suggest that bachelor's-level individuals are excluded from this trend, so an increase in the number of openings at this level can probably be anticipated. However, the 40% negative response of chief psychologists in this survey clearly limits the extent of expansion in the number of such positions. Bachelor's-level applicants have considerable competition from master's-degree holders and, paradoxically, from sub-bachelor's-degree individuals doing certain aspects of bachelor's-level work for less salary. Nevertheless, bachelor's-level technicians are finding acceptance in the VA, their range of activities is wide (although heavily clustered around psychodiagnosis in the traditional sense), and positive forces are at work for the gradual expansion of positions for them in the future.

---

3. The author is indebted to Ronald Wilcox, Chief Psychologist, Veterans Administration Hospital, New York, New York, for these data.

11

Patricia W. Lunneborg

Jobs in Research for Those With Bachelor's Degrees in Psychology

Research jobs in psychology at the bachelor's level were investigated through 20 in-depth interviews with people holding such positions. This chapter details the minimum qualifications, describes typical work activities, and presents the satisfactions and dissatisfactions of such jobs. Advice on which psychology courses are helpful in securing such jobs, on strategies for locating research opportunities, and on the use to which these positions can be put in career development, both vertically or horizontally, is also given.

In a mail survey on the employment of psychology graduates with bachelor's degrees from the University of Washington, some respondents listed job titles that contained the word *research*. This was intriguing since graduate study is usually assumed to be necessary for research work. Thus in order to determine whether or not those who responded to this survey were engaged in legitimate research careers at the bachelor's level, I interviewed 20 individuals in the spring of 1977. The personnel department at the University of Washington provided me a list of job titles that included the term *research* and that might apply to people who majored in psychology as well as a list of individuals currently holding jobs with those titles. I then telephoned these individuals, and the first 20 who answered that they had majored in psychology were selected for the study.

The responses of these 20 were so consistent that I am satisfied the data represent a reliable profile of this career option.[1] The group included 7 men and 13 women; 17 were working full time and 3 were working part time, by choice. They had held their jobs from 4 months to 12 years and had no degrees beyond the bachelor's.

Job Titles and Minimum Qualifications

The most common job titles of bachelor's-level individuals doing psychology research were research analyst, research technician, statistical assistant, psychometrist, and research assistant. Less common titles (the jobs being much rarer) included statistician, research literature analyst, research aide, research technician supervisor, psychological technician, biofeedback and engineering technician, research associate, and grant director. All of these except research aide and statistical assistant required a bachelor's degree that included course work in statistics and research experience.

Job Activities

The survey results indicate that there are two basic types of research assistants: those who spend about 95% of their time performing the actual research tasks and those who coordinate whole projects and whose time is distributed among an array of activities. The narrowly defined responsibilities of those in the first group included interviewing mothers of retarded children, coding data from an educational evaluation project, screening subjects for physiological research, running rats in experiments, administering test batteries to potential subjects for epileptic research, and training primates in operant tasks. Respondents described these activities as monotonous, mundane, redundant, and lonely. One person said, "Doing this sort of thing doesn't make one feel too terribly important. A lot of yawning goes on." When asked how long they had held their jobs, members of this group tended to groan, "Too long." For these researchers, the rewards of their work clearly were not found in the duties that occupied most of their time.

In contrast, research assistants of the second type described their work more favorably. These people oversaw entire projects. They handled budgets, hired people, smoothed interpersonal conflicts, trained and supervised others, and oversaw data analysis. They would perhaps be more appropriately called research administrative coordinators. Their duties were not only varied but spanned many levels of complexity in dealing with both data and people. That is, their work might be as simple as entering data in a logbook or giving directions to student helpers or as complex as delivering an original paper at an international conference or training postdoctoral fellows. They described their major responsibilities as follows: "hiring, training, and supervising the field interviews of survey researchers and overseeing data analysis"; "getting the grant on its feet—scheduling, training, organizing, analyzing data, editing papers"; "supervisory, administrative duties primarily; setting up the lab and seeing that it runs smoothly"; "administration, program planning, training, public relations, and directing a $100,000 grant project."

For both types of research assistant, however, regardless of primary activities, the most positive aspect of their jobs was *seeing results*. Most felt they were involved in very important research. And because results in such research usually take years to obtain, they are regarded as quite

---

Patricia W. Lunneborg is a professor of psychology at the University of Washington.

1. This conviction was supported when the author reported these results at the 1977 APA Convention in San Francisco. Two young people commented after the presentation that she had precisely described their careers.

exciting. As one respondent said, "Getting the results is why anybody does research. The greatest thing is the rush of finally finding such and such a result after months and months." Results compensate for all the deadly hours of programming, phoning, coding, and being accessible on evenings and weekends.

The second most frequently cited positive aspect of their jobs was *autonomy*, freedom to carry out their responsibilities without close, if any, supervision. One person who spent most of her time in routine scheduling of subjects nonetheless said that what she liked best was her independence: "I'm my own boss. Everyone expects that I'll put out the best, and I do. I feel very responsible, very professional."

Third in importance were the *opportunities* these research assistants had for high-level synthesizing, analyzing, and reflecting on ideas and concepts; that is, some had published articles, given papers, and done independent research; those who had not indicated that they *could have*. Their supervisors clearly encouraged independent thought and action in addition to, or sometimes over and above, other duties.

Both types of research assistants identified low pay as the most negative feature of their jobs. (This aspect of research jobs is discussed in detail later in this chapter.)

Finding Research Jobs

Most respondents became involved in research very early in college and had worked for very low wages cleaning rat cages, assisting on projects, or washing dishes in a laboratory. Others had worked for graduate students, sometimes for research credit but sometimes just to volunteer. From such experiences they learned that the secret of finding a research job is to already be in the system and to keep checking around to find out who is getting grants to do what and who is hiring. When respondents were asked how they got their jobs, they answered, "I lay in wait for it"; "I had an inside track"; "I just kept bugging them"; "I called everyone, I went everywhere, I sent my résumé all over, I really hustled." Each one perserved in looking for a position and managed to be in the right place at the right time. Even people with no local job contacts and no lengthy research experience found their jobs the same way—by volunteering their services where they hoped to be employed, by making the rounds, and by letting people know their skills and their desire to do research.

Three elements seem to be involved in being on the spot when a job opening occurs and in securing it: perseverance, luck, and *really wanting the job*. In contrast to many job seekers who simply look into what they are qualified for and what is available, the ones who get the jobs go after what they want. One person said, "Desperation was more behind me than competence. I didn't really believe all the things I said myself but I wanted this job *so badly*. I was not insincere about that."

Requirements and the Psychology Major

The *Dictionary of Occupational Titles* (U.S. Department of Labor, 1965) states that scientific research requires sufficient intellect and interest to absorb and interpret theories and data, a penchant for detail, mathematical prowess, an inquiring mind, and a fertile imagination. Evidence of these worker requirements can be found in a person's "active participation in extracurricular science activities" (p. 466).

How closely does this description match the opinions of the survey group? Almost all respondents agreed that the first requirement for such work is fascination with the dedication to research. One respondent put it this way: "You've got to have the kind of mind that continually says, 'Now if we did such and such, what would happen?'" A keen interest in research must be supplemented by other, far less glamorous attributes, such as attention to detail, conscientiousness, and tolerance. To be a scientific researcher, one must be willing to deal patiently with paperwork and with delicate laboratory equipment. One must even be willing to be irritated.

All of the psychology majors in the survey indicated that courses in statistics were the most important in preparing them for their research jobs. Second in importance were laboratory courses and actual research projects. Respondents also mentioned that more statistics courses and more research work would have improved their job preparation. Skills in SPSS computer programs, basic electronics, and keypunching were also mentioned as valuable preparation many respondents wished they had had. Others wished they had had more fieldwork experience in order to learn clinical skills such as interviewing and communicating.

The respondents' consensus on the type of undergraduate psychology training necessary to prepare one for a career as a psychology research assistant cannot be emphasized enough. All agreed that the very courses often postponed as long as possible by students—statistics and laboratory—and the supplementary courses that often threaten grade point averages—mathematics and science—are the keys to performing competently in research jobs. Also necessary in undergraduate training is research itself, which this group thought should ideally begin in the sophomore year.

Through their informal research apprenticeships, most of the respondents learned the experimental approach and experimental design. To quote one, "There was very little academic that was helpful about my psychology degree. What was important was that the department allowed me to go into the labs and learn research. There is a big difference between knowing what they teach in classes and actually working in science. Lots of people know the material, but they can't do a thing in the lab." Actual research experience is the only way to acquire independence in experimental thinking, creativity, and the courage to submit your ideas to those in charge.

Job Satisfaction and Personal Values

"How satisfied are you with this job?" was another question the survey respondents were asked. Most reported that their satisfaction with their positions was cyclical and characterized by ups and downs. When entering a new phase of a program, they were very satisfied with the job; if they were bogged down in the middle or were near the end of a project, however, they responded with statements such as "I'm glad I was here for the project, and I'm glad I'm leaving."

While there seemed to be more overall satisfaction among the administrative-coordinator types than among the routine-laboratory types, satisfaction stemmed for both types from a critical awareness of the many job functions required to accomplish research. Satisfied research assistants preferred their roles and responsibilities over those of others and saw their jobs as perfectly suited to them at that particular time in their careers. One said, "For where I am right now in my life, my job couldn't be better. It's the best thing I could be doing." Another, who runs experiments with aging rats, stated, "I'm very happy. I fully appreciate the specialness of my situation. It's research I believe in, but I don't have to put up with politics. I couldn't have chosen a better person to work for, but I wouldn't trade place with her for anything. I get to do all the fun stuff while she has to worry about getting grants."

What kinds of personal values are fulfilled by working at bachelor's-level research in psychology? Each respondent ranked 11 (mostly intrinsic) values, and independence was clearly found to be the highest value provided by this kind of work. Next highest was a cluster that included achievement, self-expression, interpersonal relations, and creativity. At the very bottom were the work ethic (believing in work for its intrinsic moral value), along with money and dominance. Table 11-1 presents the ordering given the 11 values by the group.

Simultaneously valuing independence and interpersonal relations may at first seem contradictory; however, some jobs have both characteristics. For example, some psychologists prefer to work alone and are themselves involved in a variety of scientific activities—teaching, research, consulting, administration—that take them away from the office or laboratory. Their style is to hire intelligent, responsible, hard-working, and therefore independent, subordinates who can be trusted to function effectively in their absence. Yet when these psychologists *are* around, interaction with them is highly prized. However, even in their absence, there are usually other research assistants in nearby offices or adjoining labs to interact with.

Few research assistants indicated that money, or meeting material needs, was a work value greatly fulfilled by their jobs. Starting salaries (as of autumn 1977) ranged from about $600 a month (for the statistical assistant) to about $1,100 (for the highest level of research technician). Those paid hourly were earning about $4.50 an hour. Jobs in the middle of this range had starting salaries of between $800 and $900 a month and had

TABLE 11-1   Ordering of Work Values by Bachelor's-Level Research
                   Assistants

Order	Work value	Description
1	Independence	Being free from supervision and restriction; "standing on one's own feet."
2	Achievement	Attaining mastery of a field, self-advancement, growth.
3	Self-expression	Working in an area particularly suited to the development of one's abilities.
4	Interpersonal relations	Being with companions, other employees, colleagues.
5	Creativity	Contributing new ideas, being original and inventive.
6	Challenge	Handling difficult or complex work.
7	Social welfare	Doing something that has meaning for others, working for society or another person's benefit.
8	Recognition	Obtaining respect, prestige, social approval.
9	Money	Gaining in socioeconomic status, meeting material need.
10	Dominance	Exercising leadership, directing, having power, influence over others.
11	Work ethic	Believing in work for its intrinsic moral values.

Note. Ordering of work values by the 20 research assistants interviewed is based on average ranks as well as frequencies of receiving top and bottom values.

ceilings of about $1200. Most of these workers were suffering financially, and all complained about the shrinking pay scale at the university even though they rated money far down in their value systems.

Another extrinsic work value not fulfilled by research assistant positions was working conditions. Most of the respondents tended to work in what looked like converted closets—windowless cubby holes that could barely accommodate two people. The typical office was filled with boxes of data and stacks of flashing electronic equipment. Co-workers were always in extremely close proximity, so it was essential to get along well with them.

Using Jobs in Career Development

Respondents were asked to describe their jobs as either "grunt" jobs or "growth" jobs. In a grunt job, one tends to perform the same tasks over and over, so it is not possible to satisfy work values such as creativity and self-expression. However, people tend to take grunt jobs for personal ends; that is, they have hidden agendas for taking such positions. While 80% of the respondents characterized their jobs as mostly growth jobs and only four admitted their jobs were of the grunt variety, a common hidden agenda for most was preparation for graduate school. Their jobs enabled them to take courses free at the university where they were employed, to obtain letters of recommendation, to learn practical knowledge not taught in the classroom, and to get published.

Eleven respondents were planning to go back to school for advanced degrees, 7 were not going to seek graduate training, and 2 were trying to decide whether or not to seek further training. Of the 11 planning to go back to school, 5 planned to study psychology in applied areas such as clinical and counseling. Of the other 6 returning to school, 3 were going to medical school, and three were going to study public affairs, social work, and biological structure. When asked whether their jobs allowed for more vertical or horizontal career development, respondents were unanimous in saying that their positions could be used either way. They described the jobs as springboards both for getting into a PhD or other professional program and for developing horizontally in the profession or elsewhere. Once a research assistant's skills become known, other employers often try to hire that person for their projects.

Those in their thirties were, of course, living examples of the horizontal use of the research assistant position. The story of a younger researcher in her third year on a family-planning grant illustrates how such horizontal development can come about. She began her job to fill an interlude between undergraduate and graduate study but in the course of her work discovered the following: "I came to be valued as a full-time employee. I wasn't just doing a job, I was contributing something. It made me feel worthwhile, gave me self-esteem. I discovered that what I did well, I don't really enjoy. I am good at experimental design, statistics, and library searching, but it was just a continuation of college; it got tiring. I also discovered I was good at other things—managing, supervising, administering the overall scheme." Consequently, she changed from using her research position vertically to using it horizontally and intends to become a business manager when the grant is up.

Advice to Job Seekers

The research assistants interviewed offered the following advice to students interested in research positions:

1. Meet the basic educational requirements—statistics, laboratory, natural science, and mathematics courses and as much actual research experience as possible. Those who graduated in psychology without taking these courses will have to go back to school to take them. Technical skills can also be picked up at community colleges in such areas as chemistry, animal technology, electronics, and engineering technology. There should be no stigma attached to getting an education "backwards"; community colleges simply have vocational opportunities that are unavailable in four-year liberal arts colleges.

2. When armed with the right credentials, begin making the rounds and knocking on doors to find out what research is being done and who has the grants. It is important to keep checking back and to stay in constant touch not only with the supervisors but with the actual staff members in the desired jobs. The goal is to be the first in the door should they decide to leave.

3. Introduce oneself or, rather, *sell* oneself. Give a résumé to anyone who will take one. Most of all, convey an interest in research.

4. Seize any piecemeal, part-time opportunity in one's area of interest no matter how low the pay. To subsist during this job-search period, financial help from friends or family may be necessary. Avoid taking an unrelated, time-consuming job in order to eat; all one's time and energy should be spent pursuing a job one really wants.

5. Develop, even for part-time research jobs, such characteristics as flexibility (willingness to work evenings and weekends), conscientiousness (finishing work on time and gaining a reputation for being responsible), perseverance (gritting one's teeth and accepting the repetitive, dirty, or tedious work), and interest (reading up on the work being done and knowing the literature better than the boss).

6. Avoid going the traditional route, that is, through the university's personnel office. Filling out applications or being put on eligibility lists will not land jobs; these are after-the-fact exercises.

Future Prospects

Working as a psychological research assistant is clearly city work. Only cities have the university settings in which most of the opportunities for research work are found. Also, cities will contain most of the other prospective employers of psychology research assistants: drug companies; psychological testing outfits; acoustical research labs such as that of the Bell Telephone Company; governmental social programs in public health, drug and alcohol treatment, criminal justice, and education; aircraft and space industries looking for human-factors research assistants; and large private corporations of any kind that hire PhD research psychologists who in turn need staff.

Psychological research assistant positions will probably continue to be relatively rare, but in absolute numbers these jobs should increase, primarily for economic reasons. Universities could not afford any of these researchers if they had graduate degrees. So unless PhDs are willing to work at a job where they are underpaid ($900 a month) and underemployed, such jobs will continue to be given to those with less training.

Universities are particularly good job-hunting locales because of the constant turnover in grants. While jobs that rely on grant money can be highly insecure, many grants start up as others peter out. One research assistant in the drug abuse field said, "We're all aware that this field is the land of opportunity. I mean, it's cooking. The government is going to be putting money into this area for a long time."

Work as a psychology research assistant can be regarded as professional. The research assistants I surveyed viewed themselves and were treated by their employers as professionals (i.e., as capable of high levels of scientific endeavor—independent research and writing). They were trusted and regarded as responsible, not just punctual and reliable.

Bachelor's-level research assistant work is recommended for people who want to progress in such jobs either horizontally or vertically, as well as for those who don't know which of these paths to follow. Those who prize being self-motivating, working independently, and dedicating their talents and energy to science will find assisting in research a legitimate and extremely satisfying career.

REFERENCE

U.S. Department of Labor. *Dictionary of occupational titles* (Vol. 2, 3rd ed.). Washington, D.C.: U.S. Government Printing Office, 1965.

Robert W. Titley

Whatever Happened to the Class of '67? Psychology Baccalaureate Holders One, Five, and Ten Years After Graduation

A longitudinal survey of baccalaureate holders in psychology suggests that they fare better in the job market than many believe and than previous studies indicate. The occupational status of a group of bachelor's-level graduates was surveyed after a period of years following their graduations. Given time, work experience, and additional education, most in the group had become upwardly mobile in a wide variety of human service and other occupations. This chapter argues that career development processes continue to operate beyond the college years and that a longitudinal survey method may provide a more valid estimate of the vocational potentials of the bachelor's degree in psychology.

Vocationalism in our educational system seems pervasive and on the increase. A bumper sticker reading "Hire Education" advertises a vocationally oriented community college. Undergraduates at Colorado State University use the term *waste majors* to describe certain bachelor's-degree programs, including psychology, that appear to lead nowhere in the world of work. The employment potential of psychology baccalaureates has been the subject of numerous surveys and discussions (Boneau, 1968; Caffrey, Berger, Cole, Marx, & Senn, 1977; Cates, 1973; Cole & Van Krevelen, 1977; Daniel, 1974; Fields, 1974; Forgus, 1974; Korman, 1974; Korn, 1974; Korn & Nodine, 1975; Kulik, 1973; Malnig & Morrow, 1975; Pinkus & Korn, 1973; Thomas, 1975; Thornton, 1974; Turner, 1974; Lunneborg, 1974, Note 1; Simmons, 1974, Note 2.

Few, if any, studies on the career status of baccalaureate holders reflect the continuing vocational development of graduates over several years beyond graduation. The purpose of the survey described in this chapter was to demonstrate how a longitudinal method can tap long-term career development and test the prevailing belief that bachelor-of-psychology graduates who do not gain entry into graduate school in the field are forever destined for unrelated, low-prestige jobs, if they can find any jobs at all.

The Sample and Questionnaire

The latest known addresses of 212 of the 218 bachelor of psychology recipients from the classes of 1967, 1972, and 1977 at Colorado State University were obtained from university records. Twenty-eight of 43 1967 graduates, 66 of 103 1972 graduates, and 44 of 66 1977 graduates returned usable questionnaires, for a return rate of 65.1%. The questionnaire requested information related to education or training beyond the bachelor's degree and occupational status. To determine occupational status at time points since leaving the university, the 1967 class members were asked what jobs they held during the 1st, 5th, and 10th years after graduating. The 1972 graduates were given the same question about the 1st and 5th years. The 1977 graduates, out of school from only 1 to 6 months, were asked to list the jobs they had been able to obtain since receiving their degrees.

Respondents were classified at each time point by defined categories of occupational status. All full-time jobs reported held were also classified by defined level and occupational fields. Excluded were "summer" jobs and part-time jobs held by those pursuing full-time education.

Definitions of Occupational Status, Field, and Level

Psychology (Psy). Master's or doctorate in psychology required and held; current work primarily psychological in content and approach.

Education and human services (EHS). Educational requirement and attainment variable; current work is primarily the provision of basic educational, health, psychosocial, vocational, or spiritual services to people, or in administration or research directly related to these needs.

Business, professional, trades (BPT). Educational requirement and attainment variable; current work is primarily business, commercial, industrial, professional, scientific, artistic, legal, governmental, instructional, or consultative in content and approach; includes transportation, technical, trades, skilled and unskilled labor; may provide services to people but does not meet criteria of preceding categories.

Postgraduate education. Bachelor's degree attained; current and primary endeavor is full-time pursuit of an associate's degree, teacher certification, a second bachelor's degree, or a master's or doctoral degree from a college or university. (Excludes other forms of business, professional, trade, or technical vocational training or certification; all who reported acquiring these forms of education were working in full-time jobs.)

Unemployed. Engaged neither in full-time employment nor in postgraduate education; status either voluntary, involuntary, holding only

Robert W. Titley is an associate professor at the Department of Psychology, Colorado State University.

This chapter is reprinted with permission from the *American Psychologist*, 1978, *33*, 1094–1098.

temporary or occasional work, or "stopping out" for extended travel or other experiences.

Job level 1. Entry possible with high school education (less in some cases); training often "on-the-job"; work experience not always required, but for some openings preference would be given to those with specific or related work experience, vocational training, or skills acquired during high school or beyond; most people holding these jobs would not be college graduates.

Job level 2. Entry possible without college degree, but in many cases preference would be given to those with some college or an academic degree, related or unrelated; in cases where college is not a desired prerequisite, moderate to extensive related work experience and/or specialized knowledge and training beyond high school would be a necessity; many of the jobs in this category would be held by college graduates.

Job level 3. Entry not possible or highly unlikely without a college degree. Preference definitely given to college graduates, and certain positions may require degree plus extensive work experience; in some cases, by legislative or professional codes, minimal degree level is specified and must be earned in accredited programs designed for education and training in the specific profession; rarely would someone without a college degree be found in most of these jobs.

Results

Table 12-1 shows a similar pattern across all three classes. From about two-thirds to three-fourths entered the job market immediately, and from one-fourth to one-third began graduate study (not necessarily in psychology) during the first year following graduation. The employment rate is over 85% after 5 years for both the 1967 and 1972 groups, with the rate still around 85% at the 10th year for the 1967 alumni. Table 12-2 lists the variety of jobs that have been held by the respondents.

Table 12-3 shows a breakdown of jobs held by field and level at time points since graduation. Only a small percentage of the 1967 and 1972 graduates have earned advanced degrees in psychology and are currently

TABLE 12-1 Bachelor-of-Psychology Graduates Employed, in Postgraduate Education, and Unemployed

Year graduated	Time point since graduation	Employed		Postgraduate education		Unemployed	
		No.	%	No.	%	No.	%
1967 (n = 28)	1st year	19	68	9	32	0	0
	5th year	24	86	2	7	2	7
	10th year	24	86	1	4	3	11
1972 (n = 66)	1st year	49	74	16	24	1	2
	5th year	58	88	5	8	3	5
1977 (n = 44)	1st year	30	68	10	23	4	9

Note. The responses did not reveal in each case of unemployment whether this status was voluntary or involuntary.

TABLE 12-2   Jobs Held by Bachelor-of-Psychology Graduates by Field and Level

Level 1	Level 2	Level 3
Psychology—none	**Psychology**—None	**Psychology** psychologist— clinical counseling developmental school unspecified
Education and human services—none	**Education and human services** ambulance technician/driver director—church youth program director—youth organization library assistant manager—youth home nurse's aide paraprofessional teacher paraprofessional assistant—counseling center physical therapy aide psychiatric technician research assistant—hospital survey interviewer—health services teacher's aide tutor—youth home	**Education and human services** counselor— child/adolescent— hospital college admissions employment financial aide—college pastoral rehabilitation secondary school youth home college administrator educational program administrator employment training coordinator executive—national sorority faculty member—college mental health worker— alcohol treatment center hospital private clinic minister physician program consultant— mental health psychiatric-technician trainer research biochemist—hospital social caseworker teacher— primary recreation secondary special education
Business, professional, trades accounting clerk apprentice electrician apprentice upholsterer bakery worker bartender bicycle mechanic bookkeeper cafeteria worker carpenter construction worker cook equipment operator factory worker farmer farm worker firefighter freight handler forest service worker housepainter laborer— unspecified military—enlisted office worker personnel clerk receptionist salesclerk seamstress secretary school bus driver shipping clerk slaughterhouse worker waiter/waitress	**Business, professional, trades** accountant appraiser—real estate building contractor buyer—retail cabinetmaker cost estimator—construction employment interviewer executive secretary farm manager fire protection manager flight attendant insurance broker land developer lobbyist—agriculture management/supervision— advertising banking construction insurance manufacturing personnel restaurant sales small business theater productions management trainee— insurance retail sales master electrician military—noncommissioned officer owner—insurance agency owner/manager— small business theater productions production scheduler— manufacturing salesperson— advertising real estate	**Business, professional, trades** account executive—advertising accountant/agent— governmental agricultural extension agent audit supervisor— corporation computer analyst executive management— corporation lawyer military officer systems analyst

TABLE 12-2 (continued)

Level 1	Level 2	Level 3
	self-employed—unspecified	
	ski instructor	
	tax preparer	
	technician—geophysics	
	technologist—unspecified	

Note. Of the 138 respondents, 123 have been employed full-time since graduating and reported holding one or more of the above jobs. More than one graduate is represented in certain occupations. See text for definitions of Level 1, 2, and 3.

working in the field of psychology. Comparing the EHS with the BPT category for the 1967 group, no significant differences exist in the percentages of jobs held at any time point, even at the 5th and 10th years when the BPT percentages have declined and even when the Psy and EHS frequencies are combined for statistical comparison with the BPT field. A definite contrast is noted in the 1972 class. Eighty percent of the jobs reported held in the first year were in the BPT category, compared to 20% in EHS. The difference is significant $\chi^2(1) = 24.24$, $p < .001$. Although a shift occurred over 5 years, the relative balance still favored the BPT field, and even when the Psy and EHS categories are again combined for comparison with BPT, the difference is still significant $\chi^2(1) = 5.58$, $p < .05$. Nearly 70% of the jobs entered by the employed 1977 class members in their first year were BPT jobs, again a significant difference in comparison with the entry rate in the EHS field, $\chi^2(1) = 6.42$, $p < .05$. Raw data showed that much shifting occurs within but not across fields; that is, those who begin careers in one of the general fields tend to stay there.

Differences in entry rates across the three classes are evident in the portion of Table 12-3 that shows a breakdown of jobs by level. Over half of the jobs obtained by the 1967 class members during the first year were Level 3 positions. The 1972 graduates did not fare nearly as well upon immediate entry. Only about 5% of the jobs obtained were at Level 3. The 1977 baccalaureate holders appear to be having somewhat greater success than the 1972 class in their initial ventures into the marketplace, with 13% breaking

TABLE 12-3 Analysis of Jobs Held by Bachelor-of-Psychology Graduates by Field and Level

Year graduated	Time point since graduation	Number employed	Number of jobs reported held	Field			Level		
				Psy (%)	EHS (%)	BPT (%)	1 (%)	2 (%)	3 (%)
1967 (*n* = 28)	1st year	19	25	0	48	52	36	12	52
	5th year	24	24	8	54	38	8	21	71
	10th year	24	24	12	50	38	0	21	79
1972 (*n* = 66)	1st year	49	66	0	20	80	62	33	5
	5th year	58	58	5	29	66	7	53	40
1977 (*n* = 44)	1st year	30	45	0	31	69	53	33	13

Note. Many respondents reported more than one job held during the first year following graduation. Percentages are based on total number of jobs held by those employed at each time point. Psy = psychology; EHS = education and human services; BPT = business, professional, trades.

TABLE 12-4   Status of Currently Employed
Bachelor-of-Psychology Graduates
by Field, Level, and Sex

Employed graduates	Field			Level		
	Psy (%)	EHS (%)	BPT (%)	1 (%)	2 (%)	3 (%)
Males (n = 69)	6	28	67	16	39	45
Females (n = 43)	5	47	49	14	47	40

Note. Based on those employed and jobs held at time of survey.
Not included are 16 graduates currently in full-time postgraduate
education and 10 unemployed graduates.

into Level 3 jobs upon graduation. The most striking trend in Table 12-3 is
the obvious upward mobility of the graduates by defined levels over time.
The percentage of jobs held at Level 1 shrinks to zero for the 1967 class by
the 10th year. Nearly 80% of the positions currently held by these alumni
are at Level 3. A similar trend is obvious in the 1972 class, with a sharp
decrease in Level 1 and a marked increase in both Level 2 and 3 jobs after 5
years. It might be predicted that upward mobility will occur among those
1977 alumni who are currently but perhaps only temporarily settling for
Level 1 jobs.

An analysis by field and sex of all graduates currently in the job market
at the time of the survey is given in Table 12-4. While there is a significant
tendency for males to lean toward BPT jobs, $\chi^2(1)$ = 7.67, $p < .01$, there is
no significant difference in employment levels by sex. Raw data revealed no
significant difference in the degree to which men and women have
progressed to upper job levels over time, nor was there any evidence that
either sex is currently underrepresented among those who are accepted into
graduate school. However, 8 of the 10 graduates unemployed at the time of
the survey were women.

Discussion and Implications

The employment experiences of psychology graduates of one institution do
not provide a basis for generalizing to other populations of psychology baccalaureate holders. Nevertheless, the findings suggest that a relatively
optimistic outlook may emerge for psychology graduates if readings are
taken on their employment status several years following graduation. The
results yielded by the longitudinal method used in this survey refute the
prevaling negative beliefs existing within Colorado State University about
the fate of bachelor-of-psychology graduates who do not become
psychologists.

Time, work experience, and additional education and training are no
doubt contributors to career development and upward mobility in the job
market. Among the 94 respondents in the 1967 and 1972 classes, 56 have
completed or are enrolled in additional full-time or part-time formal
education and have earned 49 advanced degrees representing a dozen
fields ranging from business to theology. Many others have taken vocational training in areas varying from medical emergency technology to

midwifery. The data indicate that additional formal education is related to attainment of Level 3 employment. Only 21% of the 1967 and 1972 graduates currently employed at Levels 1 and 2 are holders of additional academic degrees; nearly 80% of those at Level 3 have completed formal education beyond the bachelor's degree.

The basic and ongoing processes of career development should be considered in evaluating the job market potentials of the bachelor-of-psychology graduate. It seems reasonable to recommend that future studies on the employment status of holders of the bachelor's degree use a longitudinal method rather than merely tap job status immediately following graduation. The results might provide a basis for more meaningful answers to the question "What can you do with a bachelor's degree in psychology?"

REFERENCE NOTES

1. Lunneborg, P. APA Division 2 progress report on a pilot project to develop a national survey of graduating psychology majors. University of Washington, 1971. (Mimeo)
2. Simmons, M. *Employment opportunites for BA psychologists*. Paper presented at the meeting of the American Psychological Association, Chicago, August 1975.

REFERENCES

Boneau, A. The educational base: Supply for the demand. *American Psychologist*, 1968, *23*, 308–311.

Caffrey, B., Berger, L., Cole, S., Marx, D., & Senn, D. Integrating professional programs in a traditional undergraduate psychology program. *Teaching of Psychology*, 1977, *4*, 7–13.

Cates, J. Baccalaureates in psychology: 1969 and 1970. *American Psychologist*, 1973, *28*, 262–264.

Cole, D., & Van Krevelen, A. Psychology departments in small liberal arts colleges: Results of a survey. *Teaching of Psychology*, 1977, *4*, 163–167.

Daniel, R. Surveys of psychology baccalaureate graduates. *Teaching Psychology Newsletter*, February 1974, pp. 8–10.

Fields, C. 5-10 pct. of students major in psychology, but after graduation, what do they do? *Chronicle of Higher Education*, 1974, *8*(33), 9.

Forgus, R. Career status of BA/BS graduates: Discussion. *Teaching Psychology Newsletter*, February 1974, p. 7.

Korman, M. National conference on levels and patterns of professional training in psychologys: The major themes. *American Psychologist*, 1974, *29*, 441–449.

Korn, J. Training and employment of BA psychologist: Report of a symposium. *Teaching Psychology Newsletter*, February 1974, pp. 10–12.

Korn, J., & Nodine, B. Facts and questions concerning career training of the psychology major. *Teaching of Psychology*, 1975, *2*, 117–119.

Kulik, J. *Undergraduate education in psychology*. Washington, D.C.: American Psychological Association, 1973.

Lunneborg, P. Can college graduates in psychology find employment in their field? *Vocational Guidance Quarterly*, 1974, *23*, 159–166.

Malnig, L., & Morrow, S. *What can I do with a major in . . . ?* Jersey City N.J.: Saint Peter's College Press, 1975.

Pinkus, R., & Korn, J. The preprofessional option: An alternative to graduate work in psychology. *American Psychologist*, 1973, *28*, 710–718.

Simmons, M. Job placement problems—(or what does one do with a bachelor's degree in psychology?) *Psi Chi Newsletter*, Winter 1974, pp. 3–6.

Thomas, E. An alternative approach to undergraduate training in psychology. *Teaching of Psychology*, 1975, *2*, 80–81.

Thornton, G. The BA degree in psychology in the state colleges. Where do graduates go? What do they do? *Teaching Psychology Newsletter*, February 1974, pp. 5–6.

Turner, R. What happens to the liberal arts BA in psychology who doesn't go to graduate school? *Teaching Psychology Newsletter*, February 1974, pp. 3–4.

13

James R. Davis

Where Did They All Go? A Job Survey of BA Graduates

This chapter reports a poll of all students who graduated with bachelor's degrees in psychology from the University of New Hampshire between 1968 and 1972. Almost half went on to get advanced degrees; nearly all did advanced work in departments other than psychology. The students consistently reported satisfaction with their preparation, mentioning statistics and experimental psychology courses as exceptionally useful. Most of the jobs obtained by those who did not go on to graduate school were in business, and only about one-third of these were in areas where psychology was directly relevant. Greater dissatisfaction with their college major was expressed by those not going on to graduate school, but approximately half of this group would major in psychology again if they had to do it over. The implications of these findings for current psychology majors are discussed. Curriculum changes, none requiring a major revision of the psychology department's undergraduate curriculum, are also suggested.

When I was assistant chairperson of the University of New Hampshire's psychology department, students often asked me, "What can I do with a major in psychology?" Although I administered the undergraduate program, I had no answer other than the traditional "Go to graduate school." To give students a more complete answer, I decided to find out what previous graduates of the program had done to find jobs. With the help of several undergraduates, I polled every student from the University of New Hampshire who graduated with a BA in Psychology from 1968 through 1972. (That 5-year period was chosen because both the faculty and the curriculum had been relatively stable during it.)

The University of New Hampshire has a total enrollment of 10,000; approximately 40 graduate and 350 undergraduate students are enrolled in the psychology department, which has 18 full-time faculty members. The PhD is offered in six subareas of experimental psychology, but no clinical psychology program exists. The curriculum is traditional in that it emphasizes the scientific aspects of psychology and is designed to prepare students for graduate work in psychology.

Of the 255 students who graduated with psychology majors, 160 (62%) replied. Each year of graduation was equally represented, as were both

TABLE 13-1   Degrees and Areas of Study of Respondents with
Graduate Degrees

| | No. of respondents | |
Degree and area of study	Male	Female
Master of Arts		
Clinical psychology		1
Counseling psychology		1
Criminal justice	1	
Library science		1
Public administration	1	
Social psychology		1
Speech pathology		1
Teaching (psychology)	1	1
Master of Science		
Education		
Counseling	3	5
Counselor education		4
Guidance	2	1
Educational counseling	5	
Education research methods		1
Elementary education	1	
Personnel		1
School administration	1	
School psychology	1	
Special education	1	3
Vocational rehabilitation counseling	1	
Psychology		
Clinical		1
Counselor education		1
Environmental engineering	1	
School psychology	1	1
Master of Social Work	1	2
Master of Fine Arts	1	1
Master of Business Administration	1	1
Master of Divinity	4	
JD (Law)	5	
MD (Medicine)	2	
DDS (Dentistry)	1	
PhD		
Clinical psychology	2	3
Educational psychology	1	
Unspecified	1	2

sexes. Several internal checks on the patterning of the responses convinced me that the sample was representative. The registrar supplied the cumulative grade point average (GPA) for each student who replied.

Not surprisingly, almost half (47%) of the respondents had obtained at least one advanced degree; this group included slightly more males (53%) than females (41%). The average GPA for those who obtained graduate degrees was significantly higher ($p \leq .05$) than that for those who did not (2.96 vs. 2.81). As expected, the average GPA for the females was significantly higher ($p \leq .001$) than that for the males (3.03 vs. 2.72).

I was surprised by the types of graduate degrees obtained (Table 13-1). Almost none of the former students sought advanced degrees in psychology, and of the few that did, none received degrees in experimental

James R. Davis is an associate professor of psychology at the University of New Hampshire.

psychology. Almost all of the degrees were MAs, and the majority of these were in areas leading to professions.

The types of jobs obtained by students without graduate degrees are shown in Table 13-2. For both sexes, approximately two-thirds of the jobs were in business, and the balance were in areas where a psychology major would seem to be directly relevant.

Two questions were included to assess how satisfied, generally, the students were with their major in psychology. They produced identical

TABLE 13-2   Fields Entered or Positions Obtained by Respondents Without Graduate Degrees

Field and/or position	No. of respondents	
	Male	Female
Business		
Advertising	1	2
Accounting		5
Bank teller		1
Buyer		1
Claims adjustor	1	
Clerical		11
General contractor	1	
General laborer	11	3
IRS clerk		1
IRS examiner	1	
Management/administration	5	5
News department	1	
Personnel	3	8
Public relations	1	2
Sales	2	2
Systems analyst	1	
Hospitals		
Chemotherapy assistant		1
Nurse's assistant		2
Psychiatric aide	1	
Psychiatric counselor		1
Psychiatric therapist	1	
Psychiatric ward manager	1	
Therapist		1
Teaching		
Day care		3
Elementary school	2	
High school	3	7
Research assistant		2
Special education	2	4
Substitute teacher	2	5
Teacher's aide for emotionally disturbed		3
Social work		
Halfway house matron		1
Houseparent in orphanage		1
Independent school		1
Peach Corps		1
Social worker	2	
State drug education program	1	
State mental health program		2
State vocational rehabilitation program	1	
VISTA	2	1
Youth counselor	1	
YWCA director		1
Military		
Drug abuse	2	
Medical corps	1	
Psychologist	1	
Unspecified	7	

answers. When asked whether they would major in psychology if they had a second chance, 73% of those who had taken an advanced degree said yes, no matter what type of graduate work they had done. However, only 52% of the graduates without advanced degrees said they would again major in psychology. No correlation was found between whether students would major in psychology again and the types of jobs they had obtained.

Respondents often suggested curriculum changes. These suggestions fell into four major categories. The most frequent comments concerned the addition of more clinical courses to the curriculum. (None of the faculty were working in clinical psychology, and therefore only three clinical courses were available.) The next most frequent type of suggestions concerned the addition of more experiential courses, especially in applied psychology. Numerous suggestions were made about adding education-related courses such as special education, testing, and teacher preparatory course. Finally, miscellaneous suggestions were made about changing the traditional curriculum, which were probably idiosyncratic to our program.

The survey revealed several points of interest for undergraduate students considering majoring in psychology. A psychology major is apparently satisfactory preparation for graduate work in several areas; the courses most frequently considered especially helpful in graduate school were statistics and experimental psychology. Since most students chose graduate work in areas other than psychology, it appears advisable for an undergraduate to have a dual major (or at least a strong minor subject.) For a student not planning to attend graduate school, a dual major or a strong minor in a business-related area would be useful. A student who lacks a high GPA should not be discouraged from thinking about graduate school; I was quite surprised that the average cumulative GPA for those surveyed who eventually did get a graduate degree was only 2.96.

A number of changes were made in the psychology department at the University of New Hampshire following the survey. I believe they have improved the usefulness of the program without radically changing the curriculum. Since the school is small, it was impossible to implement a graduate program in clinical psychology; instead, contacts were gradually made with clinical psychologists practicing in the area, and several of them now teach part-time, usually one course per semester. They typically teach upper-level courses such as counseling, testing, or abnormal psychology, since several full-time faculty members have enough clinical experience to teach the introductory courses.

The major addition to the curriculum was an internship program to partially meet the students' requests for experiential types of courses. The department hired a half-time faculty member whose job was to develop contacts with agencies in southern New Hampshire in which students might gain applied experiences. Each semester, including the summer, students (junior or senior psychology majors only) may sign up for a variable number of internship credits in proportion to their committment to the agency placement. The faculty member conducts a weekly seminar, and the student and the placement supervisor write a contract specifying what each expects of the other. The placement supervisor and the faculty member meet at the end of the semester to evaluate the student's performance and assign a grade. About 15 students per semester can be accomodated in the program, which has been well received by both the students and the state and private agencies.

Like many other academic psychologists, I was unaware of the increasing number of high schools that teach psychology. In conjunction with the New Hampshire Department of Education, I conducted a survey of all the high school teachers of psychology in the state. (Approximately half of the schools teach at least one semester of psychology, and several schools have a one-year course.) The survey supplied both useful data and contacts. As a result, the psychology department has had no problems placing students in practice teaching positions in high schools once secondary-education requirements have been fulfilled.

Finally, largely as the result of the efforts of graduate students, the psychology department has held a "career day" once a year for the past four years to make information available to the undergraduates about job opportunities and alternative professional programs outside of psychology.

None of these alterations required a radical change in the undergraduate curriculum, but a significant improvement in the usefulness of the psychology program has resulted. The survey approach was helpful, but the key to the changes made in the past four years was the faculty's concern for the welfare of their students. Such concern is the starting point for improving an undergraduate psychology program.

14

James A. Walsh

A Montana Perspective on Vocational Opportunities

This chapter describes the vocational plans, and the rates of success in fulfilling those plans, of undergraduate psychology majors at the University of Montana. Those graduating from the university with bachelor's degrees in psychology from 1973 through 1976 were interested in pursuing careers in five major areas: BA-level work in psychology (10%), secondary school teaching (25%), graduate school in psychology (25%–30%), other graduate or professional training (5%–10%), business, industry, or government (15%–20%), and the military (3%–6%). A 6-month follow-up of 1974 graduates showed that 60% of the individuals planning to do BA-level work in psychology had embarked upon such careers within that time. Sixty-six percent of the individuals planning to teach secondary school or to enter graduate programs in psychology or other areas had done so within 6 months, and about 85% of those planning to enter business, government, or industry had done so.

In 1972, I became chairperson of the psychology department at the University of Montana. My academic credentials were the usual ones, and the tools I brought to my task were also a pretty standard set. These included strong opinions about undergraduate and graduate curricula, a working knowledge of funding sources for research projects, a good acquaintance with the job market for new PhDs, and almost no information whatever about openings available for BA-level graduates from a university psychology program. My innocence in this latter area was confirmed my very first day in the office when a recent graduate with no job and no prospects insisted that I meet the department's "commitments" and find him work. A coincidental request from one of the state institutions enabled me to place him that same week. Unfortunately, however, of the one or two students each quarter over the next four years who wanted a job in psychology and had the B.A. degree as a credential, I could place only about 50%. Many of these students were placed in jobs available in a Title I program for the developmentally disabled, which was situated in a state institution and administered by a behaviorally oriented, recent PhD from the University of Montana. A few graduates went to work as psychiatric aides at a state hospital, and some accepted employment as group home parents.

University of Montana: Background

The University of Montana is typical of many state institutions in the Rocky Mountains and in the South and Southeast United States in terms of its size and the predominantly rural and smalltown backgrounds of its undergraduate students. With an enrollment of 8,500, the atmosphere is cordial if not intimate, and the students are a largely homogeneous group whose average age (almost exactly 20 years) is somewhat younger than that characteristic of urban student bodies. The backgrounds of most University of Montana students are either WASP or traditional Roman Catholic. However, there is a small but growing group (about 200) of Native American students from the state's seven major reservations, and six or eight of these students become psychology majors in an average quarter.

The psychology department is one of the largest departments on campus, with 19 full-time (and from 1 to 3 part-time) faculty and an undergraduate enrollment that varied from 240 to 290 from 1973 to 1976. Two degree options are available to undergraduate psychology majors: a traditional laboratory-oriented program that prepares students for graduate school and a liberal arts program that emphasizes the social science aspect of psychology and orients students toward nonacademic careers. In addition to the undergraduate majors, the department enrolls from 55 to 60 graduate students in an APA-approved clinical program and an experimental program with specialization available in several areas including learning, physiological, and social psychology.

The tradition of psychology at the University of Montana began when W. F. Book, an early experimental psychologist mentioned by Woodworth, established a laboratory at Missoula, Montana about 1900. (A number of beautiful and mysterious brass instruments remain to commemorate his tenure.) Psychology did not become a separate department from philosophy until the 1950s, however. Master's theses dating back to the 1930s or earlier are shelved in the library, but the graduate program seldom included more than 10 students until the establishment of a doctoral program in 1964 and the influx of federal training and research grant funds in the middle and late 1960s. Between 1965 and 1972, the graduate enrollment increased from about 15 students to more than 60, and the undergraduate enrollment soared from about 50 to nearly 300. This pattern of growth is similar to that which occurred at many other institutions during the same period.

Vocational Planning

During my first year as chairperson, especially following my initial experience with the undergraduate looking for work, I was surprised that

---

James A. Walsh is a professor of psychology at the University of Montana, Missoula.

although two or three students per week visited me to discuss vocational plans, only one or two per quarter wanted to talk about work in psychology at the BA level. Five other categories of job interests occurred frequently enough to cause me to think of them as distinct choices (see Table 14-1). The one most frequently mentioned to me was graduate study in psychology. In most years, from 25% to 30% of the graduating seniors informed me that they were applying for admission to a graduate program in psychology. Often they were unclear as to whether they planned to study beyond the master's degree to the doctoral level, and I did not make this distinction in the records that I began to keep in the autumn of 1972.

Another 10% or so of the seniors planned to do graduate or professional work in another area such as vocational rehabilitation, social work, secondary school counseling, education, law, or medicine. About 25% of the students in most graduating classes were also earning a secondary education credential and planned to teach psychology plus one or more other subjects, to high school students. (Many came to this decision relatively late in their undergraduate careers and did not graduate with a formal double major in psychology and education.)

Teaching at first appeared to be an unrealistic career choice in view of the oversupply of secondary school teachers. However, my wife and I did a survey and found that nearly half of the high schools in Montana offered at least one psychology course and that these classes were usually filled or overenrolled. As the job crunch in primary and secondary education became worse, University of Montana teaching graduates continued to compete well for jobs, in part because they often combined an area of concentration in psychology with an area in demand, such as home economics or physical education. They were especially likely to get jobs if they were prepared to teach women's physical education or men's home economics classes.

About 20% of the students in most graduating classes were headed for careers in business, industry, or government. Very often, these students were stepping into family enterprises. Although at least 20%–30% of University of Montana undergraduate psychology majors come from farming or ranching backgrounds, not one has ever expressed to me an intention to pursue such a career.

TABLE 14-1   Initial Vocational Plans of Graduating Seniors at the University of Montana

Vocational plan	Number of students per year			
	1973	1974	1975	1976
BA-level work in psychology	3	5	5	5
Secondary school teaching	7	9	10	12
Graduate school in psychology	10	12	13	17
Other graduate or professional school	3	3	4	3
Business, industry, government	6	7	9	9
Military	2	2	2	2
Unknown, undecided, other	3	4	5	4
Total	34	42	48	52

About 10% of the graduating seniors were undecided about a career choice, had made a choice unusual enough not to be readily classifiable, or could not be reached for an interview. By far the greatest proportion of students in this category simply could not be reached.

Vocational Success

By 1974, the pattern of initial career choices of graduating seniors in psychology at the University of Montana had become clear to me. But the occasional student coming in to complain or returning to visit the department also made it clear that not everyone had managed to enter careers of their choice. I therefore recorded actual career entry for seniors in 1974 for a 6-month period after their graduation. (Six months was usually the longest time that communication could be maintained.) The number of students who had indicated various vocational plans, those who had entered their chosen fields, and the number of students for which such information was unknown are given in Table 14-2.

Slightly over 50% of those students who wanted to work in psychology at the BA level as behavioral technicians, psychiatric aides, group-home parents, etc., found such positions within 6 months. Sixty-six percent of those seeking secondary school teaching positions, of those seeking admission to graduate programs in psychology, and of those with plans for graduate or professional education in other fields were successful. About 80% of the graduating seniors looking for a position in business, industry, or government were successful, and both students planning military careers activated their commissions. No information on career entry was available from 22% of the 1974 graduating class after 6 months.

The responses appear to corroborate the common belief that finding psychological work at the bachelor's level is more difficult than any other career choice. When such jobs were obtained, however, students found the rewards appreciable; those graduates hired as behavior technicians in 1974 are now earning an average of $1,300 per month.

Some of the figures in Table 14-2 may be somewhat misleading. For example, while six out of seven graduates desiring a career in business,

TABLE 14-2   Correspondence Between Vocational Plans and Vocational Entry for Graduating Seniors in 1974

Vocational plan	Number of students	% succeeding within 6 months
BA-level work in psychology	5	60
Secondary school teaching	9	66
Graduate school in psychology	12	66
Other graduate or professional school	3	66
Business, industry, government	7	85
Military	2	100
Unknown, undecided, other	4	—

Note. These are self-report data; approximately 25% of the reports were verified, and the others were not checked.

industry, or government service were successful in making an initial entry into these fields, many of these individuals were returning to family enterprises and two were in the "business" of pumping gasoline while looking for more attractive openings. Similarly, although 66% of the graduates who applied to graduate or professional programs in areas other than psychology were accepted, many would really have liked to do graduate work in psychology but were forced into other fields by low grades or GRE scores. Finally, completing an ROTC program while majoring in psychology seems, at least for the people surveyed here, to have insured career entry, but this probably says more about recruiting in the age of a volunteer army than it does about psychology as preparation for a military career.

In summary, the experience of University of Montana psychology graduates indicates that undergraduate training in psychology constitutes both a sound educational program and effective career preparation. While such training still provides, for University of Montana graduates at least, a smaller chance of immediately finding work in psychology as opposed to other fields, nevertheless, half of those desiring such work found it and substantial monetary rewards as well. Moreover, as well as being the primary route to graduate school in the discipline, undergraduate training in psychology also provides an entree to other graduate and professional training. Finally, these data also indicate that the notion of psychology as a new liberal arts program for those interested in business and government careers is not unfounded. (While individuals in this sample may often have had special advantages with respect to entering family enterprises, others without such connections also found good positions.)

15

Paul J. Woods

Employment Following Two Different Undergraduate Programs in Psychology

This chapter reports a survey of psychology majors and psychological services majors from a women's college. The survey asked for their judgments of the "job relevance" of their undergraduate courses and for descriptions of the kinds of employment they had obtained since graduation. Only those jobs obtained with no further training beyond the baccalaureate degree are reported, but these are extremely diverse, and a relatively large number of them are related to the field of psychology.

To better serve those students graduating with degrees in psychology and seeking employment without graduate training, the Department of Psychology at Hollins College developed a second major in addition to the traditional psychology major. Instituted in 1972 and entitled psychological services, this major was an attempt, within the limits of a small department, to serve those students whose goals were in the area of human service occupations primarily at the bachelor's- or master's-degree level. This major involved some new courses and a set of requirements almost totally different from those of the more traditional psychology major (see Table 15-1). After some experience with this double major, the department decided to do a follow-up survey of its graduates to find out what they had been doing and to obtain their assessments of the psychology program in light of their subsequent employment or graduate work. Accordingly, in 1977 a questionnaire was mailed to all psychology and psychological services majors from the classes of 1970 through 1976, a total of 180 women. (Hollins College is for women only.) After several follow-up contacts replies were obtained from 133 women. Seven of the questionnaires were returned marked "addressee unknown" or "nonforwardable" so the actual reply rate was 76.9%. Of the respondents, 73 reported that they were either in graduate school or had done some graduate work.

To reflect the purpose of this book, this chapter deals primarily with the replies from the 60 persons who reported no further study beyond the baccalaureate degree. Although the main focus is on the kinds of employment these students have obtained, some of their reactions to their undergraduate courses are included first.

TABLE 15-1   Required Courses for the Two Majors

Course	Traditional psychology major	Psychological services major
Introductory psychology	X	X
Contemporary issues	X	
Experimental methodology	X	
History and systems	X	
Senior seminar	X	
Statistics	X	X
Developmental psychology		X
Applied methodology		X
Educational psychology		X
Social psychology		X
Testing		X
Clinical and abnormal psychology		X

TABLE 15-2   Relevance of Courses to Respondents' Jobs

Course	% of respondents finding course relevant
Developmental psychology	56
Learning	50
Social psychology	50
Abnormal psychology	45
Statistics	41
Introductory psychology	39
Educational psychology	39
Testing	35
Speech pathology	26
Experimental psychology	21

Note. Courses listed are limited to those taken by at least 20 respondents.

TABLE 15-3   Value of Psychology Courses to General Education

Course	% of respondents finding course valuable
Introductory psychology	64
Developmental psychology	64
Learning	60
Speech pathology	59
Senior seminar	57
Abnormal psychology	52
Social psychology	46
Educational psychology	43
Testing	39
Statistics	32
History and systems	31
Applied methodology	27
Experimental psychology	26

Note. Courses listed are limited to those taken by at least 20 respondents.

Paul J. Woods is a professor of psychology at Hollins College.

The author wishes to express his appreciation to Patricia Buckley and Melissa Scott for their aid in tabulating the results of this survey.

Reactions to Courses

The questionnaire listed all courses offered by the department and asked the respondents to check those they recalled taking and then those that were "directly relevant and/or useful in any of the jobs you have held since graduation." The most frequently rated courses are shown in rank order in Table 15-2. Many of the "popular" courses appear, but so do less popular courses such as learning and statistics. Learning was rated relevant and/or useful by 50% of those who took it, and statistics was so rated by 41%.

Such judgments, of course, depend upon the jobs that were obtained, and there *are* other reasons for a college education than its relevance to employment. Hence, the questionnaire also asked respondents to check those courses that in their opinion "were valuable to your general education but not necessarily directly useful in any of the jobs you have held." The courses chosen most frequently in response to this inquiry are ranked in Table 15-3. All of the courses previously chosen as relevant to the respondents' jobs appear again, but a few of the percentages are different and some additional courses such as history and systems appear.

Finally, to tap the wisdom of hindsight, respondents were asked to "check those courses you did not take which in light of your experience you now wish you had taken." Those most frequently checked are shown in Table 15-4. One might conclude from this table that not many respondents felt that they had missed too many important courses. On the other hand, almost every course in the department was checked by at least one respondent. Also, a number of former psychology majors checked courses that were required for the psychological services major. These courses were required because the department felt they were relevant to human service careers, and perhaps now that they are employed, these graduates agree.

TABLE 15-4   Courses Respondents Wished They Had Taken

Course	% of respondents wishing they had taken course
Clinical[a]	37
Seminar in Communicative Behavior	37
Residential Peer Counseling	36
Learning	31
Educational[a]	30
Testing[a]	30

Note. Courses listed are limited to those not taken by at least 20 respondents.
[a] This course was required for psychological services majors, so those respondents wishing they had taken it were traditional psychology majors.

In any case, the findings in Tables 15-2 through 15-4 should be carefully considered by current psychology students planning to enter the job market upon graduation. The experiences of these respondents might be helpful in choosing electives.

Subsequent Employment

Any attempt to summarize or condense the survey findings on the subsequent employment of those who graduated from the two programs would fail, I feel, to communicate the wealth and diversity of positions the students have obtained. Hence, the positions are listed job by job in Tables 15-5 and 15-6. Both tables include responses from women who worked for a while following graduation from college and then went on to

TABLE 15-5   Employment of Psychology Majors

First job after graduation	Most recent job
Class of 1970	
Research assistant, VA hospital	Claims adjuster, insurance company
Lab assistant, mental health institute	— [a]
Psychometrics worker, hospitals and schools	— [a]
Administrative assistant, bank	Assistant to branch manager, investment banking firm
Secretary	— [a]
Employee in membership department, APA	Indexer, APA
Executive assistant, area office of Muscular Dystrophy Association	— [a]
Secretary and researcher, university medical center	Day school administrator
Air traffic control specialist	Customer relations employee
Mental health therapist, hospital	— [b]
Psychological examiner, state department of psychological services	— [b]
Salesperson, camera store	— [b]
Class of 1971	
Quality control technician, food company	— [a]
Management trainee, bank	— [a]
Field caseworker, welfare department	— [a]
Bank teller	— [a]
Learning disabilities teacher	— [b]
Administrative assistant, city information center	— [b]
Head teacher, demonstration day-care center	— [b]
Library technician, U.S. government	— [b]
Class of 1972	
Salesperson, department store	Relocation manager, relocation management company
Probation officer, juvenile court	Motivation researcher, advertising company
Owner-manager, clothing store	— [a]
Salesperson, department store	Registered representative, brokerage firm
Supervisor of Coding department, national polling organization	— [a]
Secretary, brokerage firm	Customer service employee, bank
Research technician, biological sciences research center	Assistant supervisor and EEG technician, university medical center
Mental health counselor, community mental health service	— [b]

(continued)

[a] Respondent had the same job, was unemployed, or was a homemaker.
[b] Graduate training intervened between the respondent's first job and the most recent job.

TABLE 15-5   (continued)

First job after graduation	Most recent job
Class of 1973	
Chief patient representative and editor of hospital newsletter, general hospital	— [a]
Receptionist, psychiatric clinic	Bookkeeper, family planning service
Technical clerk, power company	Disability determination specialist, department of vocational rehabilitation
Professional actress	— [a]
Assistant department manager, department store	Advertising salesperson, newspaper
English instructor	Manager, art gallery
Secretary, radio broadcasting corporation	News audience research administrator, radio broadcasting corporation
Research assistant, research institute	— [b]
Probation Counselor, City Juvenile and Domestic Relations Court	— [b]
After-care counselor, community mental health service	Emergency outreach counselor, community mental health service
Clinical counselor in psychiatry, university medical school	Research assistant, department of psychiatry
Elementary school teacher	— [a]
Class of 1974	
Administrative assistant, film lab	Administrative assistant, public relations department
Bookkeeper	Partner, accounting firm
Teacher, public school	— [a]
Life agent, insurance company	— [a]
Social service director, hospital	New accounts adviser, bank
Claims processor, insurance company	Secretary
Assistant to director, juvenile services	Youth Counselor, department of health and rehabilitation services
Lab technician, research institute	Lab technician, medical college
Teacher, private school	— [a]
Teacher's aide in special education, public school	Department manager, store
Clinical counselor, state hospital	— [a]
Restaurant manager	Head bartender
Assistant, research institute	Recruiter, correspondence school
Assistant teacher	— [b]
Teacher of emotionally disturbed, elementary school	Eligibility worker, department of social services
Class of 1975	
Teacher, private school	
Staff, religious crusade	
Class of 1976	
Mental health worker, psychiatric center	— [a]
Customer representative, savings and loan association	— [a]
Teacher, public school	— [a]
Secretary-receptionist, law firm	Trilingual secretarial assistant and researcher, international organization

[a] Respondent had the same job, was unemployed, or was a homemaker.
[b] Graduate training intervened between the respondent's first job and the most recent job.

graduate school. Only their first jobs are listed, however, since we are mainly concerned with jobs for those at the bachelor's level.

Although there are far more data for psychology majors than for psychological services majors, since the first people to complete the

TABLE 15-6   Employment of Psychological Services Majors

First job after graduation	Most recent job
Class of 1974	
Probation counselor, juvenile court	Social worker/counselor, public school
Childcare worker, residential treatment center	Waitress
Class of 1975	
Assistant manager, clothing store	—[a]
Secretary, bank	—[a]
Trainee, antipoverty agency	Planner/evaluator, antipoverty agency
Secretary to a physician	Secretary, research institute
Assistant buyer, department store	—[a]
Executive development candidate, bank and trust company	Assistant to the manager, bank and trust company
Class of 1976	
Teller, bank	—[a]
Teacher, private school	—[a]
Residential counselor, educational center	Secretary
Tester of children with learning disabilities for a psychologist	—[a]
City social worker	—[a]
Substitute teacher	—[b]
Assistant director for continuing education, community college	—[b]

[a] Respondent had the same job, was unemployed, or was a homemaker.
[b] Graduate training intervened between the respondent's first job and the most recent job.

psychological services major did not graduate until 1974, there don't appear to be any clear differences in employment patterns between the two majors. What is clear is that students from both programs found employment in a wide variety of jobs. And a surprisingly large number of those jobs were fully and directly related to the field of psychology. Thus, the results of this survey confirm the point made elsewhere in this book: People who major in psychology can seek and obtain employment in a great many areas, just as any other liberal arts graduates.

Part III

Training for Careers in Community Service, Mental Health, and Public Affairs

16

Sally Fullerton

The Bachelor's-Level Professional in Community Service Careers

With the emergence of the bachelor's-level professional in community service work, it has been necessary to identify the functions that persons at this level can perform and the kind of training they need. The School of Community Service and Public Affairs (CSPA) at the University of Oregon has been working on this for the past 10 years, and the training program it has developed is described in this chapter. Bachelor's-level professionals need generalist training broad enough to enable them to function in the rapidly changing field of human service delivery and deep enough to enable them to understand and deal with the varied and complex problems of people rather than merely to deliver a narrow specialized service. These professionals may perform a variety of functional roles including advocate, care giver, behavior changer, outreach worker, community planner, administrator, and others.

The bachelor's-level professional is a relatively new concept in the field of community service. Research findings in the 1960s indicated a greater need for professional workers in the human services than graduate schools could provide (U.S. Department of Labor, 1967). A number of bachelor's-level professional training programs and Associate of Arts (AA)-level paraprofessional training programs were developed across the country to try to meet this need.

In psychology, multilevel professional training was explored in 1973 at the Vail Conference on Levels and Patterns of Professional Training in Psychology, and many recommendations were made for the development and implementation of professional training programs. In a summary of that conference, however, it was noted that the bachelor's-degree level was the least well defined in terms of staffing needs, training, and evaluation (Korman, 1974).

The social work profession has also recently recognized the bachelor's-level professional. In 1974 the Council on Social Work Education formally acknowledged the bachelor's degree as the beginning level of professional practice by initiating a formal accreditation process for bachelor's-level training programs. As a result, a redefinition of social work roles and training is also occurring.

With the emergence of the bachelor's-level professional in community service, it is necessary (a) to determine what functions a person with that level of training can perform, (b) to design appropriate training programs, and (c) to differentiate training needs and role expectations of the various levels of professionals. From programs across the country engaged in training bachelor's-level professionals, a definition of this concept is emerging.

Since its establishment in 1967, the Lila Acheson Wallace School of Community Service and Public Affairs (CSPA) at the University of Oregon has provided bachelor's-level professional education for careers in community service. The school developed a generalist professional model, which is described here as one possible definition of the bachelor's-level professional in community service.

The school was created with the following objectives:

1.   To provide an opportunity for students to acquire the knowledge, skills, and attitudes to perform competently in community service and public affairs;

2.   To plan and prepare new or alternative courses for mature women wishing to return to the university;

3.   To develop the awareness among students from other departments and schools of the nature of social problems, current public issues, and alternative strategies of administration, reform, and intervention;

4.   To provide an opportunity through seminars, institutes, workshops, and conferences to exchange ideas with community leaders and practitioners;

5.   To encourage and support research among the faculty, under the assumption that much more needs to be known about the nature and sources of community problems; and

6.   To translate into practical policy basic knowledge from the behavioral and social sciences. (Lila Acheson Wallace School of Community Service and Public Affairs, Note 1)

The University of Oregon is a liberal arts institution that also has nine professional schools, of which CSPA is the most recently established. Creation of the CSPA was aided by a $1½ million grant from Mrs. Lila Acheson Wallace, for whom the school is named. The CSPA offers both a two-year undergraduate program for juniors and seniors interested in community service and public affairs and a master's program in public affairs. The community service program within CSPA is described here.

Conditions and Trends in Service Delivery Systems

In developing the generalist professional model, it was necessary to explore conditions and trends in various service delivery systems to which the professional training had to respond. This was done through conferences

---

Sally Fullerton is an associate professor at the School of Community Service and Public Affairs, University of Oregon.

with practicing professionals and consultants and through a review of relevant literature.

Rapid change in services and in style of service delivery is a notable feature of most service delivery systems. Many communities have directories of social services, for example, but these listings have to be revised frequently because the services change so often. Also, as federal grants come and go, new services appear and disappear. Even within the more traditional agencies, change is occurring, although sometimes slowly. New social legislation passed at the various levels of government also result in changes in services and in delivery systems.

Some of the current trends in service delivery are toward (a) less reliance on institutionalization and more emphasis on community-based programs, (b) more emphasis on prevention as well as treatment of problems, (c) greater involvement of the recipients of services in planning, and (d) more use of volunteers and paraprofessionals in the delivery of services. Working in community-based programs rather than in institutions often requires an ability both to work with less structure and direction and to work collaboratively with persons from other disciplines who have varying amounts of training. Since the focus must be on prevention as well as treatment, the service delivery professional must be able to explore the definition of what is "healthy" as well as possess an ability to recognize symptoms and design treatment plans.

Even though much change is occurring, much more is needed because recipients of service are still getting lost between the established territories of different service agencies, recidivism is still high in correctional institutions, and many people still suffer from malnutrition, poor housing, discrimination, alienation, and other problems. The generalist professional not only must be flexible enough to adjust to a rapidly changing field but must also be able to initiate and direct some of the change.

The roles and functions of professionals have been traditionally defined in terms of the agencies in which they work rather than in terms of the total needs of the clients they serve. Families have had to contend with a variety of different agencies and professional workers whose efforts are often uncoordinated with one another. It is an awesome task for clients to assess their own needs, to find the appropriate agencies that can give them assistance, to coordinate the agency services to meet their needs, and to determine alternatives when services are not available. There is a large service delivery now toward greater consideration of the client's perspective and toward increased coordination of services. The generalist professional, who has an interdisciplinary background, can play an important role in this new movement, but the role requires a broad understanding of human functioning, a knowledge of community resources, and an ability to assess the needs of clients and to help them find the resources they need.

Professional roles have also been described in terms of affiliation with established professions such as social work, clinical or counseling psychology, or nursing. To describe its own uniqueness, each profession has tried to carve out a jurisdictional territory in which to work and has tried to maintain that territory through licensing requirements. In actual practice, however, much overlapping of territories exists, and the attempt to be unique has resulted in some stereotypic descriptions. For example, clinical psychologists and counseling psychologists have sometimes tried to differentiate their functions in terms in the severity of the problems of their clients, while psychiatrists have differentiated their functions from those of both types of psychologists on the basis of ability to provide medication. However, all three may engage in some similar therapy practices with similar clients. Social workers also provide counseling, but they are more often characterized as working in the homes and neighborhoods of their clients, as opposed to psychologists who are characterized as providing counseling in their offices. Although these stereotypic descriptions are clearly not adequate for defining existing roles, one must be aware of claimed territories and license requirements when establishing a new bachelor's-level generalist role.

When new lower-level workers are added to a system, there is a tendency to have them become aides and assistants to the existing professional workers. For example, BA- and AA-level persons could be given positions as aides and assistants to graduate-level professionals. Although this practice has the advantage of being fairly nonthreatening to the professionals already in the system, it also has some serious disadvantages. One is that the tasks assigned to an assistant are often the menial, routine, boring jobs that the more highly trained person does not want to do, which makes the new roles rather uninteresting. Although it is difficult for an agency to examine its service delivery system and to identify the functions that can be performed at each level of training, such an analysis is likely to both enhance service delivery and make lower-level professional roles more challenging.

To respond to the various trends and conditions discussed above, bachelor's-level generalist community-service workers need to be flexible enough to function in a changing field and able to design and implement strategies of intervention to help direct the changes. They need to be able to understand client needs and view situations from client perspectives. They should be able to negotiate roles for themselves that complement existing professional roles rather than compete with or are subservient to them. In these ways, the bachelor's-level professional role can add a new dimension to service delivery. The generalist model of professional education in the community service program in CSPA attempts to prepare BA graduates to meet these conditions.

The Generalist Professional

A number of components of the generalist model for bachelor's-level professionals in community service are examined here: (a) the generalist versus specialist issue, (b) professional roles and settings, (c) competencies needed, (d) student selection, (e) instructional program, (f) theory and practice integration, and (g) professional identification.

Generalist Versus Specialist

Although this issue is usually stated in terms of a dichotomy, perhaps it is not an either–or question. Yehezkel Dror (1971), in a book on policy sciences, argued that it is nonproductive to view this issue as a dichotomy. He noted that in the controversy, stereotypic definitions are usually used: The specialist is pictured as having concentrated training in a single discipline, as considering all problems from a limited point of view but having great expertise in that narrow area, and as being unable to comprehend in a holistic way the complexities of real-life problems. The generalist, on the other hand, is stereotyped as having a fresh and holistic but uniformed view and as making idiosyncratic and amateur judgments based on common sense rather than knowledge. This is a variation of an old cliché that says "a generalist knows very little about a lot, and a specialist knows a lot about very little." With such definitions, the dichotomy between generalist and specialist will obviously persist.

Dror identified some components of these stereotyped definitions and suggested that rather than continue the controversy it would be more productive to examine professional roles in terms of the following components: academic knowledge, personal qualities, experience, and tacit capacities. Each professional role can be described in terms of the areas and depth of knowledge needed, the amount and kind of experience needed, and the qualities of the individual desirable for performance of the role. From his examination of the trend in professional roles, Dror concluded that a new type of professional is emerging who is a "specialist in a general approach and methodology." This same connotation of generalist is the basis of the CSPA model of the generalist professional.

The viability of this definition was affirmed by a group of practicing professionals who participated in a community service program review meeting. As one participant stated, "We need more skilled generalists or more flexible specialists." These agency personnel and others agreed that a generalist professional needs sound conceptual understanding and broadly transferable generic skills to be able to accommodate to the changing field of human services as well as meet current needs.

Using Dror's components of the definition, the bachelor's-level generalist professional can be described as follows:

1. *Academic knowledge.* It is expected that in four undergraduate years the student will acquire knowledge of a broad nature and certain generic skills as well as the ability to integrate both of these and apply them to a variety of work settings within a well-defined value framework. (These specific competencies are enumerated later in this chapter).

2. *Personal qualities.* The generalist should be open-minded, creative, and sincerely concerned about the welfare of others. The generalist is

expected to look at systems as well as individuals for possible solutions to problems and to try to see things from the client's perspective as much as possible.

3. *Experience*. It is expected that the generalist can enter the job market in an entry-level position requiring little experience other than supervised field experience and volunteer experience acquired prior to the training program.

4. *Tacit capacities*. It is expected that the generalist will work at an intermediate level of service delivery with a professional, rather than paraprofessional, level of competence and will make referrals to more highly trained persons when appropriate.

Professional Roles and Settings

A bachelor's-level generalist professional works in a variety of roles, such as caseworker, community developer, group worker, manager of transitional living facility, program coordinator, corrections officer, child care worker, program evaluator, community schools coordinator, volunteer coordinator, social service resource specialist, or human service planner.

Although these titles are suggestive of the functions performed, further analysis of these roles is useful in determining the specific expectations and competencies needed by the professional worker. In 1969, the National Institute of Mental Health sponsored a symposium to identify the roles and functions of mental health workers and the necessary related competencies. Participants in this symposium identified the 13 following functional roles, all of which are applicable to the roles in which bachelor's-level generalist professionals might work:

1. *Outreach worker*—detects people with problems, refers them to appropriate services, and follows up to make sure they continue to their maximum rehabilitation.

2. *Broker*—helps people get to the existing services and helps the services relate more easily to clients.

3. *Advocate*—pleads and fights for services, policies, and legislation for clients.

4. *Evaluator*—asseses client or community needs and problems, whether medical, psychiatric, social, education, etc. This role also includes formulating and explaining plans.

5. *Teacher-educator*—performs instructional activities ranging from simple coaching to teaching highly technical content to individuals or groups.

6. *Behavior changer*—carries out activities planned primarily to change behavior, ranging from coaching and counseling to casework, psychotherapy, and behavior therapy.

7. *Mobilizer*—helps to get new resources for clients or communities.

8. *Consultant*—works with other professions and agencies to handle problems, needs, and programs.

9. *Community planner*—works with community boards, committees, etc., to assure that community developments enhance positive mental health and self- and social actualization, or at least that these developments minimize emotional stress.

10. *Care giver*—provides services for persons who need ongoing support (i.e., financial assistance, day care, social support, 24-hour care).

11. *Data manager*—performs all aspects of data handling, gathering, tabulating, analyzing, synthesizing, program evaluation, and planning.

12. *Administrator*—carries out activities that are agency or institution oriented rather than client or community oriented (e.g., budgeting, purchasing, personnel activities).

13. *Assistant to specialist*—aids and assists the existing professions and specialities. (Southern Regional Education Board, Note 2)

The bachelor's-level professional generally works in positions that combine these functional roles; for example, a group worker in a juvenile detention setting might be primarily a care giver but might also take part in behavior changing, teaching, managing, and evaluating. An intake worker in a multiservice center might function primarily as a broker, evaluator, and advocate. A manager of a transitional living facility might be primarily an administrator but might also be involved in care giving and behavior changing. Thus, functional role analysis can give a clear perspective of what the professional will do and can also provide a basis for determining what competencies are needed.

These roles and functions of mental health workers may be performed by generalist professionals in a variety of settings, for example, traditional social service agencies such as children's services divisions, public welfare agencies, juvenile departments, prisons, parole and probation offices, mental health institutions, or Veterans Administration hospitals.

New settings are also developing. With revenue sharing, local governments are becoming more involved with social service delivery, through coordination of existing services and development of new ones. Schools are expanding their services through their community school programs. Head Start and day care programs are increasing. As institutionalization decreases, more emphasis is being placed on small group-living situations, outpatient care, and other forms of community-based services. Diversionary services are being developed as alternatives to incarceration. Volunteerism is increasing and expanding its definition far beyond the stereotype of envelope stuffing. Volunteer coordination positons are being developed in private industry as well as in the public sector. Prevention, as well as treatment, has become an important focus, and parent education, personal development, and other prevention programs are being developed. Service delivery is becoming more coordinated through multiservice centers and through the efforts of agencies and councils; positons are also available in these coordinating organizations. Community development and community mental health planning organizations are increasing. These are only some of the community-service settings in which generalist professionals may work.

Competencies

One of the resolutions passed at the Vail Conference on Levels and Patterns of Professional Training in Psychology (July 1973) was a strong endorsement of the development of competency criteria for all levels of psychology from the prebachelor's to the postdoctoral levels (Korman, 1974). The CSPA program has attempted to identify the essential competencies needed by the bachelor's-level professional in community service.

A variety of sources were used to identify these competencies. Committees of faculty from various disciplines at the University of Oregon reviewed their fields and developed recommendations. Several advisory groups of practicing community professionals also made recommendations. A committee of CSPA faculty and students systematically examined the needs that people have, the barriers that prevent some people from adequately fulfilling these needs, the interventions necessary to remove those barriers, and the competencies needed to implement those interventions. After determining which interventions were appropriate for generalist community service workers, this committee also recommended what competencies were needed.

In addition, several surveys were conducted of students who graduated from the CSPA program. These surveys attempted to find out what the students had learned in the program that helped them in their professional work and what additional competencies they needed. A survey was also mailed to several hundred professionals in human service agencies throughout the Pacific Northwest. These professionals were asked to indicate which competencies were essential for professional practice in community service. In addition, the literature was reviewed, and one particularly useful study was found that approached the competency question from the client perspective. The originator of that study was hired as a consultant to CSPA, as were a number of other persons from across the country who had experience in developing competency-based programs. In all, information was sought from faculty, practicing professionals, consultants, students, alumni, and clients in order to determine the competencies necessary for effective performance as a community service professional.

Eighteen core competencies were finally identified, and the current curriculum in CSPA is designed to enable students to acquire these. The essential competencies are as follows:

1. *Ability to communicate effectively in writing.* Performance indicators of this core competency include ability to write using standard English words and grammar, avoiding unnecessary jargon and clearly expressing thoughts and ideas. Specific indicators include ability to compose process recordings, case summaries, letters, memos, press and publicity releases, research reports, technical reports, and minutes from meetings. The ability to write plans, projects, and proposals is also considered an important aspect of this core competency.

2. *Ability to use oral communication effectively.* This competency includes the ability to listen, to understand, to use nonverbal communication as well as verbal, to communicate with others under stressful conditions, and to communicate with persons whose status, age, and background are different from one's own. It also includes the ability to formulate, present, and defend a position, to make a public presentation, and to speak extemporaneously in public.

3. *Ability to use problem-solving approaches effectively.* This core competency includes knowing various models of problem solving and having the ability to clearly define a problem, to obtain data relative to the problem, to assess factors related to the problem, to determine the interrelatedness of these factors, and to identify alternative solutions to the problem. It also includes designing and implementing plans of action, evaluating results, and modifying actions as needed.

4. *Ability to collect, organize, and interpret data.* Indicators of this competency include the ability to locate and use library resources, government documents, community directories, and other written materials available in the community and the ability to contact persons who may act as information and consulting resources. This core competency also includes the ability to design and administer questionnaires, to conduct personal surveys when appropriate, and to use unobtrusive data-gathering measures and skill in nonjudgmental observations. Also included is the ability to determine what information is needed and to limit information collection to those areas, to locate appropriate research reports and to critically evaluate them in terms of research design and interpretation of findings, and to distinguish among facts, theories, assumptions, hypotheses, and constructs.

5. *Ability to formulate appropriate goals and policy and to plan for their implementation.* This competency includes the ability to locate and use information sources, to organize and interpret the data collected, and to use data in formulating goals and policy. It also includes knowing various models of decision making and having the ability to involve others in the decision-making process where appropriate, to determine priorities and establish implementation plans and timelines, and to make decisions with inadequate information when necessary.

6. *Ability to evaluate the effectiveness of programs and of individual interventions and to use evaluation data to determine needed modifications.* This evaluative research competency includes the ability to identify objectives and to describe them in measurable terms, to formulate testable hypotheses, to know research designs and to be able to select an appropriate design for the particular evaluation task, and to know research concepts (e.g., correlation, causality, sampling, and probability) and be able to apply these concepts in designing research and interpreting findings. This competency also includes knowing alternatives to the programs and interventions being used and being able to propose appropriate alternatives in response to the needs identified in the evaluation process.

7. *Ability to use group process to accomplish a specific task or objec-*

tive. Since the generalist professional will work with many different types of groups, it is necessary that he or she know group dynamics theory and research and be able to analyze group processes, to intervene effectively when appropriate (as a leader or a member), to prepare agendas, to conduct meetings, and to facilitate group discussion and goal setting.

8. *Ability to conduct an informational interview*. This competency involves the effective verbal and nonverbal communication skills mentioned already as well as the ability to establish rapport with the interviewee, to set goals for the interview, to design and use an interview schedule, to formulate questions that elicit the desired information, and to listen and observe accurately. It also includes the ability to verify information obtained in an interview and to conduct the interview with respect for the dignity, privacy, and rights of the interviewee. Counseling interviewing skills are seen as highly desirable but not necessarily required of everyone, but all community service workers need to conduct informationl interviews at some time or other.

9. *Ability to assess individual and interpersonal functioning and to develop and implement strategies of intervention based on these assessments*. This competency requires knowing the dynamics of interpersonal relationships, identifying factors that contribute to interpersonal competence, knowing basic psychological and sociological concepts, and being able to use these concepts in understanding human behavior. It also requires a general knowledge of human development and how to facilitate it, a knowledge of the social, psychological, and economic causes of deviance, and an ability to identify breakdowns or dysfunctions of behavior and relationships. This competency includes being able to assess individual needs and to respect the privacy, dignity, and judgment of others and knowing models for changing behavior, including systemic and clinical views of personal and social change. The professional should be able to use the self as a tool for change and to understand his or her own motivation for wanting to bring about the desired changes in others.

10. *Ability to analyze existing groups and to design and implement appropriate interventions*. This competency includes the ability to use group process (a core competency already mentioned) and the ability to analyze the dynamics of an existing group such as a family and to see how changes in one area can affect the whole system. It also includes the ability to help group members establish goals and the ability to facilitate individual and group decision making and problem solving. It requires knowledge of methods of group intervention and knowledge of community resources as well.

11. *Ability to analyze organizational structure and function and to design and implement appropriate interventions*. The generalist professional needs to understand not only the individuals and groups with whom he or she works but also the organizational context of that work. This competency requires knowledge of organizational theory and concepts, an ability to analyze formal and informal organizational structures,

and an ability to describe functional and dysfunctional elements of an organization. It also involves knowledge of methods of intervention and of theories and strategies for change within organizations, knowledge of styles of leadership (and the ability to identify one's own style), and the ability to intervene effectively with persons at all levels of the organization.

12. *Ability to analyze a community and to design intervention strategies that will enhance the functioning of the community and the persons within it.* The generalist needs to see how the functioning of the community affects individual behavior. This core competency includes the ability to analyze the power structure, economic base, and various social structures of a community, the ability to conduct an assessment on community needs when appropriate, and the ability to identify and mobilize community resources as needed. The generalist should also have knowledge of his or her own values—and how these relate to predominant values, norms, and regulations of the community—and knowledge of social and community intervention strategies.

13. *Ability to examine the social-political-economic context of social issues and policies and to apply this knowledge to the solution of problems.* This core competency requires that the professional have general knowledge of the institutional structure of contemporary American society—of the political and legal processes, of governmental structures, power, and relationships—and be able to analyze the social, political, and economic structures and trends of a community. The professional should also know the conceptual basis for models of social reform, be able to identify environmental factors and resources, and be able to analyze the effects of social policy and legislation on individual and organizational behavior.

14. *Ability to make judgments based on a clearly defined value framework and professional ethics.* The generalist professional may or may not be affilitated with an established profession, but he or she should be aware of professional ethics as defined by such professions as counseling, social work, and psychology. This core competency includes having a commitment to an ethical framework that successfully integrates one's personal life-style, professional role, and civic responsibility in an evolving and complex society. The generalist professional should also be able to describe his or her value framework, to contrast it with the values of others, to identify value conflicts (e.g., between client and professional or between professional and agency), and to deal with these conflicts.

15. *Ability to develop one's own theoretical framework for understanding human behavior and facilitating human growth.* Although this competency is related to the ability to assess individual and interpersonal functioning (Competency 9) and to the ability to make judgments based on a value framework (Competency 14), it is different and important enough to be listed separately. This competency involves knowledge of psychological and sociological concepts and theories and the ability to

apply theory to practice. It also involves the ability to compare, integrate, and synthesize these concepts and to select and then organize them into a comprehensive theory for professional practice. Also included are the professional's ability to compare his or her own theory with established theoretical models (e.g., behaviorism or gestalt), the ability to observe behavior and its context and to interpret it in light of the professional's theoretical framework, and the ability to design helping strategies consistent with this theoretical framework.

16. *Ability to identify expectations of a professional role within a given human service setting and to examine and describe one's own qualifications in relationship to that role.* This competency is especially important, since the bachelor's-level professional is still a relatively new concept and not all human service organizations are familiar with this professional's qualifications. It is often up to the individual to sell his or her own qualifications to the prospective employer. This involves being able to analyze one's own qualifications (presenting them verbally and in a résumé) and one' expectations of a particular role in relationship to one's qualifications. To function effectively once in the job, the generalist should know the legal and ethical rights and responsibilities inherent in the performance of social and public service and should know the various models of human service delivery and trends in human services. The generalist should also be able to analyze the agency in terms of problems to be dealt with, clients served, roles and functions of his workers, and organization, in order to understand his or her role in relationship to the whole system.

17. *Ability to effectively plan and use one's own time and competencies.* Since human service work is demanding and "burnout" is common among professionals, it is important for the professional to know his or her strengths and limitations, to have realistic confidence in them, and to know the limitations imposed by self, role, and setting. The professional should also be willing to take risks, should understand the concept of risk taking, should be able to assess his or her effect on others, should be able to work under pressure, and should be able to establish priorities and organize activities. In addition, the professional should be able to read rapidly, should know management techniques, should be able to tolerate uncontrollable uncertainty and ambiguity, and should make referrals and delegate authority when appropriate. He or she should also have a commitment to the continuing self-development of skills, knowledge, and values.

18. *Ability to interact effectively with persons from diverse backgrounds.* The professional should demonstrate understanding and appreciation of individual, cultural, and ethnic differences and should understand causes and effects of racism and discrimination in the public and private sector. He or she should have a general knowledge of cultural and social values and be able to accept diverse views of other persons and groups.

Student Selection

Obviously, it would be impossible for a student to acquire all of the competencies described above during a two-year training program. It is therefore necessary to select for the CSPA program students who already have certain knowledge, skills, and experience. In addition, the program has many more applicants than can be accommodated with available resources, so a selective admissions process is necessary.

In establishing criteria for selection, the CSPA faculty considered grades an insufficient indicator of the many important qualities needed by human service workers. Admission of students to professional programs was also discussed by the Vail Conference participants, and their recommendation was to rely less on traditional selection criteria such as grades and to pay more attention to the experience, goals, interpersonal skills, and personal qualities of the applicants (Korman, 1974).

Admission selections in CSPA are based on evidence of appropriate (a) prior academic preparation, including a substantial background in the social sciences; (b) communication skills; (c) life experiences that include work, volunteer activity, or personal characteristics such as family background that give the applicant greater understanding of human needs and services; and (d) career objectives.

With several hundred applicants each year, it is impossible for the CSPA faculty to conduct individual interviews, so paper processing has to be relied upon. Applicants are asked to describe their career goals and to explain how CSPA could help them reach their goals. They are also asked to describe (a) their life experiences that contributed to career interests, (b) their understanding of human behavior, and (c) their ability to work in an area of community service. A transcript of completed coursework is also a required part of the application.

From these materials, an admissions committee determines if the applicant's goals are consistent with the objectives of CSPA, if the applicant shows evidence of having general knowledge about the field of human services, and if the applicant has carefully thought about his or her career objectives. An applicant would be rated highly, for example, if his or her career objectives were stated more clearly than at the vague "wanting-to-help-people" level and yet were not so rigid as to be described in terms of only one job. The statement of career objectives would also be strengthened if the applicants had coursework related to their objectives or if they had relevant practical experience through volunteer work, paid employment, or other life experiences. Sometimes persons who have been recipients of welfare, involved in correctional programs, or participated in other human services apply for admission to CSPA. These experiences are considered useful only if the applicants can describe how the experiences have contributed to their understanding of people and systems and how the applicants themselves use this understanding in the career area they have selected.

Communication skills are evaluated partially in terms of how well the applicants conceptualize and express their ideas on the application itself. In addition, performance in writing, speech, and other types of communication courses is considered, and knowledge of another language is considered valuable if the applicants can describe how it might be useful in their work.

As mentioned, the academic preparation of the applicants is very important, since the professional training program is for only two-years. The general university lower-division requirements should be completed so that time is not taken away from the two-year program to fulfill background requirements. At the University of Oregon, these lower-division requirements include health and physical education courses, writing courses, and a specified number of courses in arts and letters, social sciences, and science. The admissions committee also considers the adequacy of the social science background in terms of the individual's career objectives; for example, if the applicant is interested in direct service delivery, a good background in psychology and sociology is considered essential. Political science and economics courses are also considered important for better understanding of the systems in which community service work exists. Performance in coursework as indicated by grades is also noted but is not the only factor considered.

Persons interested in applying for admission to CSPA, therefore, are encouraged to obtain enough information about the field of community service so that they can select appropriate career goals for themselves. Sometimes this process involves taking advantage of career counseling and testing services available at the university in order to better understand their own interests and abilities. Applicants are strongly advised to acquire practical experience in their chosen area, both to gain more information about the field and to test themselves to make sure the career choice is an appropriate one. Some students find, for example, that they cannot stand the pressures of constantly working with people who have problems or that they do not like certain aspects of a job (e.g., the required paperwork). On the other hand, students whose career choices are affirmed not only gain a new sense of excitement about their chosen work but also can use their practical experience to enhance their understanding and enjoyment in the coursework they take in CSPA.

Using these criteria, CSPA found that the students selected for the program represented a wide age range and diverse personal qualities. For example, in 1977 the average age of new students entering the program in the junior year was 27 years, and the age range was from 19 to 50 years. These students also had widely differing backgrounds and personal characteristics; for example, some students in the program had been welfare recipients, alcoholics, and criminal offenders, while others came from privileged backgrounds. Physically limited students were also in the program, including some in wheelchairs and some with visual impairments or other handicaps. Men and women who wanted to change careers in midlife and women who wanted to develop careers outside the home after having raised families were also selected for the program. Also included were persons who had worked in human services already and who wanted to return to school to complete degrees and upgrade skills, as well as persons from various racial minorities, from foreign countries, and from urban and rural areas. They share a desire to provide a service that will make life better for others.

This mix of students in the classroom contributes to an exciting and meaningful learning process for faculty as well as for students. Two of the themes of the Vail Conference were that students must be prepared to function professionally in a pluralistic society and that training experiences in a multicultural context could facilitate that functioning (Korman, 1974). The mix of students in CSPA certainly gives students the opportunity to learn about persons quite different from themselves; for example, when a student who has received human services discusses service delivery with a student who has worked in a social service agency, insights are gained by both students and by other class members as well. Or when an ex-alcoholic describes the agonies of the addiction, students can understand the problem and the accompanying feelings in quite a different way than from reading about it in a textbook; in addition, the ex-alcoholic can gain support for the personal changes made and can use his or her understanding of the problem to help others.

Instructional Program

Upon completion of the bachelor's degree, students in the CSPA program are expected to have acquired the generic competencies described earlier. As indicated, the admissions process is designed to select those students who have good background skills and knowledge. The two-year instructional program in CSPA, therefore, is designed to help students acquire those competencies that they still need to become generalist professionals.

When CSPA was created an interdisciplinary focus was emphasized, for it was believed that the knowledge needed by this "new professional" should cut across the established disciplines and professions in order to provide a basis for understanding the major social, political, and economic issues related to community issues and services. As a result, faculty from different disciplines were brought together to design the program and to teach at CSPA. The present faculty members hold degrees in areas such as psychology, counseling, social work, sociology, political science, public administration, economics, education, anthropology, communications, and home economics.

The instructional program consists of a combination of core requirements and additional optional offerings, from which each student builds a program. The core requirements for all students preparing for careers in community services have been as follows:

1. Field observation (two hours);
2. Behavioral foundations for the helping professions (three hours);

3.   Strategies of intervention (two five-hour courses);

4.   Applied social research (three hours);

5.   Social welfare institutions, policies, and programs (three hours);

6.   Supervised field study (two full-time placements, each for 12 hours credit and each lasting for at least one term);

7.   Theory–practice integration seminar (two three-hour courses, one to be taken with each field placement);

8.   Three advanced methods courses (e.g., counseling, community development, administration, casework, group work, recreation, or communications);

9.   Two settings courses (related to a field of practice, a problem, or a client group, e.g., child welfare services, volunteerism, correctional systems, community mental health, child abuse, poverty solutions, or gerontology.

In designing core requirements, the community service faculty tried to provide as much flexibility as possible so that the student and his or her adviser could build a program that would meet the student's particular career interests. On the other hand all students of a professional school should have certain competencies for the following reasons:

1.   Although the student may know what he or she wants to do after graduation, the student should have generic skills that will transfer to various settings and that will accommodate new types of service delivery as the field of community services changes.

2.   If credibility with prospective employers of students is to be established, the CSPA degree needs to assure employers that the students have certain minimal competencies. The CSPA has worked carefully with prospective employers to determine what these minimal competencies should be.

3.   As professionals, the faculty members feel an obligation to the prospective clients of students: When the students move into professional roles, they should not only have sufficient knowledge and skills but also a clear value framework and code of ethics.

4.   When the program wishes to be accredited by an outside profession or accrediting organization, it has to demonstrate that it meets the standards established by those organizations. The CSPA believes that the competencies students acquire through the core requirements will meet these standards.

Theory–Practice Integration

It is particularly important in undergraduate professional training that students be assisted in applying theory to practice. Several methods for accomplishing this integration have been used in CSPA, including field observation opportunities, a major emphasis on supervised field instruction, required theory–practice integration seminars, and extensive use of simulations, case examples, and videotaped role playing in classroom instruction. In addition, students are helped to organize and apply their knowledge through several integrative systems. These instructional methods and integrative systems are described below.

Instructional methods. Meeting the needs of a diverse group of students has been a challenge for CSPA. It has required, for example, the development of teaching methods to facilitate the learning of students coming to a class with widely differing degrees of knowledge of the course content. The faculty has been working to develop a system for crediting prior learning gained outside the classroom setting. This system is not yet completed at CSPA, but some other schools across the country have initiated such systems. Credit for prior learning was also one of the recommendations of the psychologists at the Vail Conference (Korman, 1974).

A heterogeneous group of students requires a different model of teacher–student relationships—one in which the teacher facilitates the learning process but is not necessarily always the expert. As already mentioned, classes are much richer when student expertise is also drawn upon. The community is also relied upon heavily to assist in the training of students, both in field supervision and in the classroom.

The CSPA staff and students are strongly committed to the value of a combination of classroom and field learning and have designed the program accordingly. In the community service program a sequence of experiences has been developed in which the entering student first takes some introductory courses, then is given a junior-level field placement, then more coursework, and finally a senior-level field placement. The student may or may not return to campus for more coursework after the senior placement.

In CSPA the field placement is primarily an educational experience as opposed to the work-experience model of Antioch College and other schools. It is an opportunity for students to apply knowledge gained in the classroom and to gain new skills and understanding, with the direct assistance of a faculty field instructor and an agency field supervisor. Students are placed in professional work roles in these field experiences and are directly involved with clients. Contractual arrangements among the student, the agency, and the school spell out the student's responsibilities, limitations, and accountability. The contracts also include the specific learning objectives developed by the student and sometimes include the evaluation criteria.

A wide range of field placement settings has been developed for community service students, including community human resource centers; correctional diversionary programs; welfare, day care, and Head Start centers; senior services centers; community schools; Native-American and Chicano affairs centers; voluntary action centers; Veterans Administration Hospitals; parks and recreation programs; drug and alcohol programs; juvenile departments; primary prevention programs; and community centers. There are even a few field placements in private industry.

To further facilitate linkage between classroom and field experience, a theory–practice integration seminar is offered concurrently with each field placement. This seminar aims (a) to help students integrate experiences by discussing theoretical concepts learned in the classroom as they apply to the field settings in which the students are working; (b) to help students both to examine their own value frameworks in relation to the values held by the agencies in which they work and by the clients of these agencies and to resolve the value conflicts discovered; (c) to explore career possiblities with students by looking at the various roles in the agencies in which they are placed; and (d) to design strategies, using group problem-solving techniques, to resolve problems that the students encounter in their placements.

In addition to a heavy emphasis on field learning, the community service program uses other innovative instructional modes, including videotape equipment, team teaching, individual learning contracts, learning modules, special community project assignments, simulations and role playing, and other techniques that actively involve students in their own learning processes.

One new instructional design tried recently has been an integrated offering of core courses. Courses totaling 15 credit hours were combined into one integrated package for which students enrolled full time for one term. To integrate these courses, the competencies expected to be learned in each course were identified and learning modules were designed for helping students acquire each competency. An overall assignment was then developed in which students could integrate and apply all of these individual competencies. The courses selected for this package were field observation, strategies of intervention (two courses that deal with interpersonal relationships, group dynamics, organizational theory and development, community development, and the design of appropriate change strategies related to each area), and social welfare institutions, policies, and programs. The integrative assignment was as follows: Students worked in small groups to identify a service that was needed in the community and that was not currently being provided by existing agencies; they then developed a proposal for either establishing a new organization to provide this service or for substantially changing an existing agency to include this service. By working in small groups, the students had much opportunity to practice interpersonal and group skills and interventions. They had to become familiar with existing services in the community and to conduct surveys to identify some unmet need. They had to be familiar with organizational theory in order to develop a proposal of organizational structure or restructure. They had to be aware of social values and policies related to their proposed service. They had the opportunity to plan strategies of community intervention by anticipating the kinds of problems they would have in trying to gain community acceptance of their proposals and by designing methods for dealing with resistance.

This integrated learning experience was team taught be persons with backgrounds in sociology, counseling psychology, communications, and public administration. Student feedback on the experience was very positive. Many students commented that it was helpful to have what they were learning in the various classes integrated and that the concepts they learned became more meaningful as they were able to apply them to an area in which they had high personal interest.

Another learning opportunity offered to students is the chance to interact with professional practitioners from the community. In addition to assisting with the field program, professional practitioners are hired each year to teach courses in their areas of expertise, for example, the director of the children's services division has taught a course in child welfare services, and the director of the county juvenile department has taught a course in correctional systems. A group worker has taught group work methods, a caseworker has taught casework methods, and a juvenile court counselor has taught correctional systems methods. Again, student feedback on these courses has generally been positive. Judging from the number of agency personnel interested in teaching the courses, this program has apparently been beneficial to instructors as well.

Integrative systems. To facilitate application of knowledge gained by the student in various classes and field experiences, a number of integrative systems are used in CSPA. One system focuses on problem solving with heavy emphasis on analysis of the situation before selecting a method for intervening. Undergraduates tend to jump immediately into looking for solutions to problems, without a careful analysis of the problems themselves. This tendency could lead to the immature and idiosyncratic judgments that were earlier described as part of the stereotype of the generalist. Instead, CSPA emphasizes assessment and research skills for gathering information to analyze problems; in addition, broad knowledge of human development and behavior and of various social systems and issues is considered necessary as a framework for interpreting the data gathered.

A second integrative system, which would be used as part of the problem-solving analysis, considers the structural levels of intervention, including one-to-one, small group, organization, community, and broad societal levels. Any problem can be attacked at several levels, and in looking for possible solutions to problems, generalist professionals are encouraged to consider what interventions can be made at these various levels. In the past, psychologists have tended to focus on individuals' efforts to cope with the systems in which they live rather than considering the possibility that the systems might be much more faulty than the individual behavior. This focus is changing now, and new emphasis is being placed on community psychology and other systems approaches.

One example of analyzing a problem in terms of various structural levels is as follows: A professional working with a runaway child might find that the child's act of running away was the only way the child could find to call attention to an intolerable home situation. The professional might help the child learn how to cope with the home situation or might work with the family to try to improve the situation. At the organizational level, the worker might try to identify other alternatives that children can use to call attention to their family problems; at the community level, more family counseling services might need to be developed; and at the legislative level, the juvenile code might be changed so that children who resort to running away would not then have to suffer the stigma of being labeled a juvenile offender. The professional might choose any one or a combination of these levels of intervention in attacking the problem.

A third integrative system is also related to the problem-solving analysis. In addition to the structural dimensions of intervention, a time dimension also exists, ranging from primary prevention to rehabilitative services. In the past, human service programs have focused largely on rehabilitative services, but the current trend is toward looking at how problems can be prevented as well as treated. Some juvenile corrections systems, for example, have instituted parent education programs to try to help improve the family situations of adolescents who are already in trouble. These programs aim to help the adolescents avoid more serious trouble later and also to prevent the younger brothers and sisters in those families from getting into trouble. Preventive intervention can also be used to solve the problem of malnutrition. One bachelor's-level professional is conducting a program designed to teach better eating habits to preschool and school-aged children so that they will develop the kind of food likes and dislikes that will prevent them from later becoming malnourished. Some of these prevention programs are designed by working backward from specific problems (such as malnutrition or juvenile delinquency in the examples above) with the aim of reducing or preventing their occurrence. Another approach in developing prevention programs is to identify the characteristics of healthy functioning and then to design ways of enhancing the development of these characteristics. For example, since research studies have shown that a positive self-concept is related to positive performance in many different types of situations, programs have been designed to try to help small children develop more positive self-concepts.

Thus, in problem solving, the generalist professional analyzes the situation not only in terms of what interventions might be used to treat a problem but also in terms of what interventions might prevent the problem from initially occurring. This focus is especially appropriate for professionals with bachelor's-level training who may lack the expertise, maturity, and experience to treat seriously disturbed patients or hardened criminals but who can work effectively in prevention programs.

Understanding the functional role expectations within the work setting provides the professional with a fourth system for integrating skills and concepts. As indicated earlier, most professional roles include a combination of functional role responsibilities. Although most job descriptions do not clearly identify these functional role expectations, the generalist professional may find it useful to analyze his or her professional role. This analysis not only helps the professional understand relationships with others in the organization but also helps the professional know what is expected and what is beyond his or her limitations and would make additional training or referrals to others appropriate.

A fifth integrative system can be described in terms of the expected outcomes of the problem-solving process. This system is closely related to the value orientations of the professional, the client, and the agency. More and more accountability is being demanded of public service organizations, often through a management-by-objective model in which professionals are asked to define, in very specific terms, what they are trying to accomplish. No longer is it sufficient for a mental health clinic counselor, for example, to say that he or she is providing therapy. The specific outcome expected must be stated more clearly, whether it is to keep the client from being committed to a mental institution, to change specified objectionable behaviors, or to assist the client in specified growth goals. Counselors may then be held accountable for accomplishing these specific objectives. Thus, interventions to be used must be related not only to the analysis of the problem but also to the expected outcomes.

Obviously these integrative systems—a problem-solving approach, a consideration of both the structural level and the time dimension for dealing with the problem, an analysis of the functional roles and role relationships, and a determination of expected outcomes—are not mutually exclusive. But these considerations can provide the generalist professional with a way of focusing on the client and selecting the most appropriate interventions.

Professional Identification

Early in the development of the community service program and other bachelor's-level human service programs established in the 1960s, the focus was on a "new professionalism" that cut across existing professions rather than being affiliated with any particular one. Matthew Dumont described some of the characteristics of this "new professionalism" as follows: These new professionals were turning toward social change, lacked the fear of change often held by traditional professionals, and were impatient with the slow rate of change. They were indifferent to credentials and were interested in utilizing indigenous nonprofessionals in their work as well as forming coalitions with other professional groups and with client groups. They had an attitude of criticism and were not afraid of power. They were compassionate and tried to see things from the perspectives of their clients (Dumont, 1970). Many of these characteristics were emphasized in the development of the generalist model in CSPA.

One unexpected student response to this new professionalism, however, was that some students experienced difficulty in developing a professional identity. Part of the difficulty is that an appropriate label has not yet been developed for the bachelor's-level generalist professional in community service. While some professionals could communicate who they were and what they represented by generally well-known labels (e.g., social worker or psychologist), these new professionals did not have such a label.

In addition, these new professionals have not banded together to form any kind of professional organization, to develop any common code of ethics, or even to define common areas of expertise. Heavy responsibility has thus been placed on each individual to find support groups, to develop a personal code of ethics, and to communicate capabilities to others. Many students enjoyed the challenge of this new professionalism; some felt lost without an established affiliation.

Since discovering this problem, the community service program has developed a number of different opportunities to help students with their professional identification; for example, an accredited social work program is now available as one option for students. This program was added partly because the social work profession moved to recognize the bachelor's-level professional and partly because a number of community-service students desired this affiliation with an established profession. No large differences exist in content requirements for the social work and the community service option; in fact, students in each could take the same courses if they wished. The major difference between the two options is in the professional affiliation; students in the social work option learn how the generic competencies they are acquiring relate to the professional social worker role, and they are also able to make direct linkages to some social work graduate programs if they wish.

Recommendations from the Vail Conference indicate that psychology may be moving toward formal recognition of subdoctoral-level professional programs also, although two important differences between psychology and social work should be noted in this respect. Where social work has traditionally been a profession with the Master of Social Work (MSW) as the accepted professional degree, psychology has traditionally been a substantive discipline and is still in the process of conceptualizing a professional component, with the PhD as the accepted professional degree. Thus, social work has had to make fewer accommodations in accepting the idea of bachelor's-level professionalism.

Another means of assisting students in their professional identification has been the development of focus areas within the community service program. Since the field of practice in community service is so broad, it is clearly not possible for students to become knowledgeable about all the settings in which they might work. Some students find additional professional identification by focusing their work toward a particular practice setting and by affiliating with professional groups related to that setting (e.g., the Child Welfare League, correctional associations, mental health organizations). To help students who wish to focus in this way, the community service program has identified the following focus areas and has developed recommended courses of study for each area: (a) corrections, (b) community development/community mental health, (c) children and family services, (d) volunteerism, (e) gerontology, (f) program evaluation and development, and (g) social service administration. A student who wished to focus in one of these areas would complete all of the core requirements of the community service program and would select advanced methods, settings, electives, and senior field placement related specifically to the focus area. A focus area is clearly not the same as a specialization, for it is not possible in the limited time an undergraduate has to truly become a specialist in some area. The focus area does provide a way for students to better plan and organize selection of courses that relate directly to their career interests and also provides some basis for professional identification and affiliation.

When embarking on a new profession, the support of others engaged in the same profession is very important. As mentioned earlier, some of these new professionals can gain support by joining established professional organizations, but additional support groups are also important for these bachelor's-level professionals. While in the CSPA program, these professionals are encouraged to work in small groups through the use of many group assignments in classes. This arrangement not only gives them an opportunity to improve their group skills but also provides the basis for a support group while still in the program. The theory–practice integration seminars are kept small so that they may function as support groups for students facing new expectations and challenges in their field placements. In addition, there is a general student organization in CSPA, and students in some special interest areas, such as social work, have also formed organizations. This basis of support not only helps students while they are in school but teaches them how to develop support groups for themselves after they leave school. CSPA maintains some contact with its alumni through a newsletter and through occasional conferences, and this continued contact is important to some.

Evaluation

After 10 years of developing and evaluating the generalist model for the preparation of bachelor's-level professionals in community service, CSPA has gained some data about the effectiveness of the model. Criteria that could be used for evaluating the model are (a) satisfaction by graduates of the program, (b) acceptance by the professional world of students trained in this model, and (c) quality of work performed by students trained in this model.

Student Satisfaction

Student evaluation of course offerings is an ongoing process in CSPA. A student feedback instrument has been developed and is administered in each course each term the course is offered. Faculty members are generally responsive to suggestions made by students, and changes based on this student feedback are frequently made in course offerings. Student evaluation of CSPA courses is positive, indicating general satisfaction.

In additon, several specific surveys of student opinion regarding the program have been made. In 1973 a graduate student named Owens conducted a follow-up study of the graduates of CSPA as part of his doctoral dissertation (Owens, 1973). He found that CSPA graduates valued the field placement part of the curriculum—77% rated it more highly than any other part of the program. He also found that many students support the statement, "CSPA is an interdisciplinary school allowing high flexibility in coursework"; a few students recommended, however, that CSPA offer even more individualized instruction.

Since the charter of CSPA indicated that special attention be paid to mature students returning to college after a long absence, especially women, Owens looked for evidence of such enrollment. Among those who had graduated through 1972, the modal age on entering CSPA was 21, indicating relatively few older students. The average age of incoming majors was about 27 in 1977, indicating a clear shift in the student populations being served in the CSPA program. Several factors probably influenced this shift. One may have been the establishment of the selective admissions process in 1973 that considers life experience as one criterion for admission. The tightness of the job market, requiring people to upgrade their skills and complete degrees in order to retain their jobs, has probably also sent a number of older persons to the program.

Owens (1973) was also interested in determining whether CSPA graduates were successful in obtaining jobs in the human services. He found that some were employed in a wide range of human service positions but that a sizable number had not been able to find appropriate jobs. Of the 236 who responded to his questionnaire, 42% reported that their first job after graduation was closely related to their study at CSPA. A total of 53% of the respondents were currently working in positions related to their career interests, showing that in many cases a first job had been a stopgap measure taken until more suitable work could be located.

Some of the comments written on the questionnaire by the respondents reflected feelings about the job market and about the graduates' preparation at CSPA. When asked, "Are you involved in the kind of work and/or activity you anticipated before graduating from CSPA?" one graduate responded, "Yes, but it took me a year to get it . . . [it is] extremely difficult to get a job." Another said, "After job hunting for months I came to the conclusion that having a BS does not make much difference in getting a job. The skills I learned through field placement, strategies, research, and other activity-oriented classes are the most valuable to me—I could not have learned them as easily in other academic majors." Another said, "My job experiences weighed more heavily than a degree from CSPA, yet only through CSPA did I gain two references from field placement."

Of the 53% of the graduates in this 1973 survey who said their current jobs were highly related to their career interests and professional training at CSPA, the mean salary reported was $650 per month.

A more recent but more limited survey of graduates showed a higher percentage finally obtaining jobs related to their career interests. However, respondents in this group also emphasized that it often took them from six months to a year to find a suitable job and that when they first graduated they initially had to work at jobs unrelated to their career interests. One factor that made job seeking even more difficult for these graduates was their desire to remain in the Eugene, Oregon, area. Students who were willing to relocate found more job opportunities.

Acceptance by Professionals

To determine how well the professional world is accepting the CSPA program, its purpose, and its graduates, information was collected from an all-day program review meeting and from other advisory sources, such as evaluations by consultants, accreditation reviews, and informal feedback from ongoing contacts.

The all-day program review meeting was held to evaluate the existing program and to identify trends in the field of human services that might necessitate changes in the program. Participants in this meeting included personnel from state and local social service agencies and institutions as well as some community service students, alumni, and faculty members.

Some of the conclusions reached through this program review were as follows:

1. *Program areas and service delivery systems.* A clear trend can be seen toward increasing emphasis on prevention in community service programs. Program areas currently being emphasized include personnel planning and services, gerontology, community schools, leisure activities, and law enforcement. There is also a strong trend toward an increase in community-based services; institutional treatment programs are decreasing, and services are being decentralized. Coordination of services is increasing; for example, multiservice centers are being established, interagency cooperation is increasing, and there is more use of team approaches to service delivery. There is also increased emphasis on working with whole families and looking at the client's perspective, rather than just offering narrow specialized services. Local citizen involvement in decision making and service delivery is also being emphasized; for example, volunteerism is increasing and citizen boards are making program decisions and raising and allocating resources. Demands for accountability and program evaluation are increasing, with funding sources frequently forcing this accountability.

2. *Professional roles.* Practitioners at the all-day review meeting noted that "generalists" with broad administrative and direct service skills are needed. These generalists need sound conceptual understanding and generic skills. Outreach, advocacy, evaluation, planning, broker, teacher-facilitator (to train trainers), and coordinator roles are all increasing. Professionalism is still important but needs redefinition to get away from the elitist concept. There is an increasing focus in the field as well as in training programs on identification of competencies, regardless of certification. People are more frequently creating their own positions, and

part-time professional roles, especially among women, are increasing. The job market is not promising at the present time, and the field is crowded with people who can meet minimum qualifications for jobs, but a substantial need still exists for people who are well skilled, even at the bachelor's level. Continuing education is needed and should be stressed by CSPA even more than at present according to these professional practitioners.

3. *Competencies of community service graduates*. Participants at the meeting were generally very positive regarding the competencies of these graduates. The need for communication skills, individual and small-group skills, ability to understand and work within systems, research skills, administrative and organizational skills, and a strong theoretical base was emphasized.

4. *Linkage with the community*. While participants noted the need for better university–community relations, they cautioned that the program should not overemphasize the current job market because the curriculum must also prepare students for future job needs. Faculty–agency exchanges were encouraged, as were joint appointments between the university and agencies. The field placement program was highly rated by agency personnel as well as by students and alumni, and they recommended expansion of the program to include six-month, full-time placements.

5. *Community involvement*. Participants suggested a greater amount of community-based training, with CSPA taking initiative for demonstration projects, establishing consultation and skill development training for community groups, and providing a better information flow between program and agencies. Community-related projects jointly staffed by faculty, students, and persons from the community were also encouraged.

This program review supported CSPA's training model as appropriate for preparing undergraduates for professional careers in the community, since the professional community indicated its approval of CSPA's general purpose, program, and graduates. In addition to participating in this all-day evaluation meeting, professionals from the community have been members of numerous advisory committees for CSPA in which aspects of the program are reviewed and recommendations made. In almost all formal and informal reviews, the field program is the most highly praised part of the curriculum, but the remainder of the curriculum receives positive review also. The evaluators frequently stress the need for CSPA graduates to have good professional skills as well as theoretical understanding to enter the job market.

A variety of consultants from across the country have also been brought to CSPA to review its program and make recommendations. Although these persons were brought in to criticize and make recommendations, almost all have also expressed excitement with the innovative program and with the quality of the students.

In 1976, the social work program at CSPA was accredited by the Council on Social Work Education after a site-visit review, and in 1977 the Northwest Association of Schools and Colleges renewed its accreditation of the University of Oregon after a site-visit evaluation that also included a review of CSPA.

Another indication of acceptance of the program is that the civil service examiners of the state of Oregon changed their policies to allow the supervised field placements of CSPA students to qualify as work experience in their civil service ratings, thus giving CSPA students an advantage over students from other programs in seeking jobs.

Performance of the Students

One indication of student performance in field placements is that throughout the state of Oregon, requests by agencies for CSPA student field placements exceed the number of students and faculty available for such placements. Agency personnel have indicated they like having CSPA students not only for the quality of work they can perform but also because of the questions they raise about agency procedures and because of the new ideas they bring to the programs.

A small survey of graduates of the social work program was conducted in 1975. In this survey many CSPA graduates noted that because they had more skills than their bachelor's-level co-workers from other disciplines, they were being promoted to supervisory positions within two or three years of their employment. Such graduates therefore recommended that the community service program include more administrative and supervisory training in the core curriculum, a curricular change that will be implemented soon.

Many individual examples could be cited of the accomplishments of CSPA graduates in their professional roles, of the innovative programs they have developed, of the honors and recognition awarded their work, and their promotions within organizations. The evidence indicates that (a) the students are generally satisfied with their training in CSPA and that from 60% to 70% eventually find jobs directly related to their career interests, (b) that they have sufficient knowledge and skills to perform well in these professional roles, and (c) that the agencies that hire them are pleased with their performance.

REFERENCE NOTES

1. Lila Acheson Wallace School of Community Service and Public Affairs. *Dedication.* Eugene, Oreg.: May 3, 1969.
2. Southern Regional Education Board. *Roles and functions for mental health workers* (Report of a symposium). Atlanta, Ga.: Author, 1969.

REFERENCES

Dror, Y. *Ventures in policy sciences.* New York: Elsevier, 1971.
Dumont, M. The changing face of professionalism. *Social Policy,* 1970, May/June 26–31.

Korman, M. National conference on levels and patterns of professional training in psychology. *American Psychologist*, 1974, *29*, 441–449.

Owens, L. *A follow-up study of graduates of the school of community service and public affairs*. Unpublished doctoral dissertation, University of Oregon, 1973.

U.S. Department of Labor. *Manpower report of the President and a report on manpower requirements, resources utilization, and training* (L 1.42/2:1967). Washington, D.C.: U.S. Government Printing Office, 1967.

17

Mary Harvey and Bryan T. Downes

Undergraduate Education for Changing Professional Roles in Community Service and Public Affairs

Since 1967, the Lila Acheson Wallace School of Community Service and Public Affairs at the University of Oregon has emphasized an applied educational program for professional careers at the bachelor's-degree level. This Chapter considers several topics affecting the development and success of such programs as well as some of the issues likely to continue to confront those involved in bachelor's-level professional education for the "changing world of the human services." A recurrent theme is that the education of flexible, change-oriented problem solvers competent to perform new and changing (as well as traditional) roles in community and public service is not possible without institutional support.

The University of Oregon's Lila Acheson Wallace School of Community Service and Public Affairs (CSPA) offers an applied educational program, unique within the state of Oregon, for professional careers at the bachelor's-degree level. In a previous chapter, Fullerton (1978) outlines the curriculum and the early development of this educational program. The present chapter considers three topics in the development and success of such programs: (a) the need for professional education to serve diverse students and to develop a range of appropriate educational methods to support their learning; (b) the importance of an integrated, interdisciplinary, problem-centered curriculum for bachelor's-level entry into new and emerging public service careers; and (c) the faculty characteristics needed to support this type of educational program. In developing these three topics, we examine what the School of Community Service and Public Affairs is doing to address them and we consider some of the issues that will continue to confront those involved in bachelor's-level professional education.

Serving Diverse Students

The aims of multidisciplinary undergraduate education for public service careers must include concern for improving services, expanding public service employment opportunities, and diversifying service roles and methods to ensure greater public benefit. If these aims are to be realized, schools such as CSPA must encourage students with diverse cultural, economic, and educational backgrounds to participate in the educational process. Moreover, it is important that the value the institution places on student diversity be evident in the educational programs and instructional methods that address the varied learning needs of a diverse student population.

This issue is an important one for three reasons. First, it underscores the importance in undergraduate career education of maintaining a concern for equality of educational opportunity. Second, it recognizes that academic credentials are increasingly important aids to career entry—and that academic programs that fail to serve minorities and women will ultimately perpetuate job-market discrimination as well. Third, and most important, it recognizes that the characteristics of students at some point define the characteristics of service providers, which are related in serious ways to the nature and quality of services delivered.

Unmet Service Needs and Provider Characteristics

As recently as June 1977, Bertram Brown, then the Director of the National Institute of Mental Health (NIMH), stressed the continuing severity of such mental health problems as the geographic maldistribution of health care, the inadequacy of services available to minority and other neglected client populations, and the inappropriateness of traditional service methods for special (e.g., age group) populations (Brown, 1977). Each of these problems has, in turn, been associated with the demographic qualities, class biases, and training of traditional mental health professionals (Caplon & Nelson, 1973; Hollingshead & Redlick, 1958; Pearl & Riessman, 1965). Culture barriers between white, middle-class providers and nonwhite, lower-class clients have, for example, been related to the ineffectiveness of typical services, on the one hand, and to psychology's failure to develop new services, on the other (Heller & Monahan, 1977). While the literature documents the failure of an essentially white, middle-class service delivery system to meet these mental health needs, the help provided by noncredentialed paraprofessionals and understanding peers has been identified as both positive and effective (Brager, 1965; Durlack, 1971). Paraprofessionals indigenous to the community, familiar with the needs and circumstances of identified client groups, and sharing with these clients many ethnic, educational, and economic characteristics can be particularly effective service providers. Moreover, such persons can help shape new kinds of service systems—systems better suited to the

Mary Harvey is an assistant professor and Bryan T. Downes is a professor at the School of Community Service and Public Affairs, University of Oregon.

The authors would like to thank James G. Kelly, Dean of CSPA, for his constructive commentary. His ideas were extensively incorporated into the section on faculty characteristics.

needs of their communities and clients (Heller & Monahan, 1977; Pearl & Reissman, 1965).

These findings are important signals to human service educators. University programs traditionally serve demographically narrow populations. In the human services, however, *who* gets educated is as important an issue as the content of the education. Here, incorporating so-called nontraditional learners into the student population and developing educational methods that address their learning needs are more than interesting educational experiments. They are, in fact, integral to any effort to have constructive impact on the quality and nature of services delivered.

University Resistance to Educational Reform

Thoughtful and sometimes dramatic educational reforms are needed if diverse students are to be served respectfully and well. In higher education, university administrators and faculty often greet the prospect of serving nontraditional students with suspicion and alarm. Some educators fear that "nontraditional" means "deficient," that in the name of educational innovation students with academic limitations will be offered a watered-down, invalid education, and that the credibility of the university will be undermined. This resistance as well as the aloof traditions of higher education mean that public service educators need to walk a careful path when trying to serve diverse students and to legitimize nontraditional learning methods.

Educational Supports to Nontraditional Students

In CSPA, service to nontraditional students and experimentation with educational methodology has been facilitated by a number of grant programs (Kelly, Note 1). The New Careers in Mental Health (NCMH) program is a case in point.[1] Originally funded by NIMH in 1973, this program has sought with considerable success to develop and institutionalize educational and career supports to foster paraprofessional leadership in the emerging field of community mental health (Harvey & Passy, 1977; Harvey, Note 2). Within CSPA, the goals have been to help New Careerists (career-oriented paraprofessionals who work full time with local agencies and participate in higher education through the NCMH program) identify and acquire needed competencies, secure and master emerging community service roles, and ensure access to the credentials needed for career advancement.

The program's mission has required emphasis upon nontraditional student needs, development of new educational content and methods, and ongoing concern for local impact. Program successes include the creation of a new community college program, the institutionalization of a unique

---

1. The New Careers in Mental Health Program at the University of Oregon is partially funded by the National Institute of Mental Health through a grant entitled "New Careers in Mental Health" (NIMH Grant 5 T41 MH 13606-05).

approach to academic delivery for both the community college and the university (see Figure 17-1), the sponsorship of new service programs and new human resources policies in local agencies, the development of new service roles for paraprofessionals, and the legitimation of new faculty roles and new faculty–community relationships within the university. In developing these supports for New Careerists, the New Careers program has acted as a catalyst to reshape CSPA education as well—by identifying unmet student needs and demonstrating that higher education can feasibly address these needs with programs of quality. Three educational methodologies that meet the needs of New Careerists and enhance CSPA's educational offerings can be discussed:

Nontraditional learners need visible and accessible supports to participate in higher education. All students require and receive a variety of services to enable them to participate in higher education. These include but are not limited to university orientation, academic advising, financial assistance, and information about such options as the College Level Examination Program (CLEP) or independent study. New Careerists need these same services. Their primary need, however, is for these supports to be coordinated, visible, and accessible. Too often, the supports needed by nontraditional students are not centralized, not visible, and not delivered with any cognizance of nontraditional student needs. The support needs of the nontraditional learners have been highlighted by CSPA's experience with New Careerists. These individuals work full-time, enjoy limited educational release time from their agencies, and have priorities at work and home that supersede education per se and that demand education be incorporated into an ongoing pattern of living. The New Careers program has organized and/or reorganized a variety of services to enable paraprofessional involvement in higher education. The New Careers academic delivery system (see Figure 17-1). for example, not only identifies coursework available off campus but shows a variety of educational options that can be organized into degree programs by work-based adults.

Figure 17-1.   The New Careers in Mental Health academic delivery system.

A. Work-Based Education	B. Site-Delivered Core Seminars
e.g., supervised field study, independent study, in-service training	e.g., New Careers philosophy, introduction to community mental health, program development and evaluation
C. Site-Delivered Coursework (other than core)	D. Campus-Based Coursework
e.g., English composition, biological sciences, sociology	e.g., economics, special education, art

With respect to the design shown in Figure 17-1, the following highlights should be noted:

1. The credits and curriculum associated with Cell A stem entirely from on-the-job performance and work-based learning experiences. They involve virtually no use of release time.

2. The credits and curriculum associated with Cells B and C involve minimal use of release time and provide maximized educational accessibility.

3. The credits and curriculum associated with Cell D involve use of release time for travel to and from, as well as participation in, campus-based education.

The feasibility of using this system to put together entire degree programs is illustrated in Figure 17-2. Not only have classes been rescheduled and relocated to accommodate working adults but, more importantly, the New Careerists and their agencies have been involved in deciding where, when, and why to locate classes.

Academic advising has been revised by the New Careers program as well. First, the advising takes place in agency and community as well as campus settings. Moreover, academic advising in New Careers includes what to take, when, and from whom; how to take advantage of CLEP and other course-challenge opportunities; and what courses other students in the New Careers program are taking or have taken and from whom. New Careers faculty initiate group sessions in which educational needs are shared and priorities are assigned for program and/or group action. Course schedules, teaching methods, financial aid opportunities, child care, and tutorial supports all receive attention in the program as a result of New Careerist initiation and faculty response. This is possible because of the program's visibility and accessibility as a resource center. New Careerists have one phone number rather than several to dial and one person from whom to gain information rather than several. Without such organization, many New Careerists would remain alienated from the environment simply because the university would seem not a body of needed resources but rather a strange collection of fragmented demands and miniature bureaucracies.

Contractual study opportunities developed by the New Careers program enlarge the CSPA's ability to meet diverse student needs. The learning contract is a process whereby students and faculty collaborate in the design of unique educational plans. The process requires specificity of educational goals, accountability in the form of evaluation criteria, and a rationale that relates prior experience and career aspiration to larger school purpose. Moreover, it is a process that allows a relatively naive student to design an exploratory course of study and practice, while the older, more experienced student can focus on learning and build needed competencies. Learning contracts within the New Careers program have been used to design individual reading and conference or practicum

Aide	New Careerist	Traditional College Student
Works full time	Works full time	Works part time, if at all
Uses release time for in-service	Uses release time for education on campus	Spends most of time on campus or nearby
Enrolls in accredited education as the opportunity arises, if at all	Enrolls in new-career designed education program 4 terms per year (fall, winter, spring, and summer)	Enrolls in traditional education program on campus 3 terms per year (fall, winter, and spring)
May enroll each term in a probable maximum of 3–6 credit hours, generally of Cell C or D type	Is able to enroll each term in 10–13 credit hours: 4 from Cell A, 3 from Cell B, 3 from Cell C, and 3–6 from Cell D experiences	Enrolls in an average of 15 credit hours each term; all (or majority) of Cell D type
Is able to complete 12–15 credits of questionable degree applicability	Is able to complete 40–52 credit hours per year	Typically completes 45 credit hours per academic year at the above rate
Probably cannot get a degree or will take 10 or more years to do so	Is able to complete a 4-year degree in $3\frac{1}{2}$–4 years (186 hours typically required)	Is able to complete a 4-year degree program in 4 years at this rate
Is educated in two settings (work and campus) yet is unable to gain academic or career mobility from such experience	Is educated in two settings (work and campus) and is able to apply both sets of experience to degree advancement and career mobility	Is educated in one setting (campus) and is able to use credentials to obtain professional level employment

Figure 17-2.   The New Careers program as an alternative route to a credential (see Figure 17-1 for explanation of Cells A, B, C, and D).

courses, to design accredited field experiences, and to outline highly individualistic community-based degree programs.

The contractual study process has great potential: (a) It allows for individualizing education in the face of limited resources; (b) it affirms academic standards and regular evaluation; (c) it can greatly expand the resources, methods, and settings available for learning while clearly retaining faculty responsibility for direction, quality, and outcome of the educational process; (d) it incorporates the assessment of past experience into the planning of forthcoming educational ventures; and (e) it encourages a relationship between faculty and student that either recognizes the student's maturity or insists that such maturity emerge during the course of professional education. For New Careerists, it establishes a needed link between the academic and work environment—a link that can enhance the value of the paraprofessional in the work setting and that allows the school to make more judicious use of the New Careerist's past experience (e.g., using a New Careerist as a teaching assistant in an area where much experience exists). The contractual study process is, at least for New Careerists, an essential part of education.

When field-based learning is organized with attention to generalist service roles, theory–practice integration is enhanced for all students. The CSPA emphasizes practical experience and the need to integrate practical experience with theoretical concepts. Student diversity means, however, that students differ in the kind of theory–practice integration that best suits their past experience and current education and career needs. CSPA itself needs to offer educational content of clear value to each student and at the same time maintain a distance from the "fray." The CSPA cannot train for explicit careers nor should it define career possibilities solely in terms of agency practice or prevailing professional viewpoints. It must remain generalist. The CSPA must offer education that is relevant to many settings, but independent of each, and it must cultivate in all students a learning process that is both analytic and applied.

In the New Careers program—with 87 paraprofessionals from 33 agencies—the use of a functional community mental health roles model[2] has been a particularly valuable aid to conceptualizing field-based learning. A limited number of roles that describe behavior typical of many human service settings and of multiple staff levels are used to offer an organizational framework for understanding the human service field. The model fosters self-assessment by helping to identify specific learning needs and gaps in experience. It also underscores the variety of human service career opportunities. The roles stressed by the New Careers program include advocate, broker, educator, enabler or care giver, program developer, and program administrator. Each has the advantage of being valid in many settings, and each can be related to community needs as well as to agency expectations and career possibilities. The role model has particular value for organizing different kinds of field experiences for different kinds of students.

For the work-based New Careerist, academic credits can be negotiated not for work in general but for those aspects of assigned work that clearly involve roles valued by the educational setting. This negotiation provides the New Careerist with a platform from which to secure role expansion and greater experience with the agency and can, for example, enable a casework aide to secure experience in program development or community education. Moreover, the process affirms the integrity of academic standards being set and maintained by the university.

The role model serves students other than New Careerists. An inexperienced student can enter a field setting for the first time and use the role model to develop understanding of this new work environment.

---

2. The functional roles model used by the New Careers program is a locally useful modification of the original functional roles schema developed by the Southern Regional Education Board (McPheeters & King, 1967).

The model's validity in multiple placements affirms the common attributes of human service settings and human service activities, while the range of designated roles encourages student consideration of multiple career directions. Like the learning contract, the role model functions as a necessary innovation for New Careerists and serves the needs of a wider range of students as well.

Summary: New Career Education

The needs of nontraditional learners and some of the social issues attending the creation of undergraduate programs for human service career education are highlighted by the circumstances of paraprofessional human service workers. These individuals are already employed in human service settings. The literature suggests that they have much to offer with or without higher education. Nevertheless, their career prospects depend to one degree or another on (a) what value is given to their experience and competence by employing agencies, (b) what access to higher education (and its credentials) they are able to obtain, and (c) whether their agencies will enter the program and promote over them more educated but possibly less experienced college graduates from narrowly defined cultural and economic groups.

Unless paraprofessionals are included in the student population of schools such as CSPA, a negative effect of bachelor's-level career education could well be the displacement of these indigenous noncredentialed workers by middle-class college graduates and an unintended erosion of quality and variety in human service delivery. The New Careers program within CSPA has helped to demonstrate that the educational needs of New Careerists are shared by other students and that attention to these needs can improve education and foster positive contributions to the field.

The New CSPA Curriculum

Concern for impact is shaping not only the student population in CSPA but also the content of its educational program. The very nature of the problems addressed suggests the need for broadly trained generalists with interdisciplinary knowlege and applied problem-centered experiences. Furthermore, the design of bachelor's-level content has to emanate from an understanding of societal needs and the changing nature of service careers that will address these needs.

Goals of the Curriculum

The goals of undergraduate education at CSPA are as follows:

1. *Interdisciplinary.* Core and concentration area coursework within CSPA emphasizes the integration of theory and knowledge from multiple social science disciplines. The school stresses hiring faculty from multiple disciplines with interests and knowledge outside their "home" discipline.

2. *Applied and problem centered.* Theory is studied in settings and projects that permit practical application of theory and experiential shaping/revision of theory. Social science theory and professional experience are applied to the study and resolution of identified community problems.

3. *Career oriented.* Field projects/experiences introduce students to a range of career settings, options, and roles. Coursework prepares students for bachelor's-level entry into multiple, public service, career-role settings as well as for postbaccalaureate study. And coursework, fieldwork, and advising processes emphasize the continual examination of ethics and values characterizing public sector employment.

Courses, field designs, relationships with other university elements, hiring priorities, and so on are evaluated vis-à-vis the extent to which they simultaneously foster accomplishment of each of the above aims.

Structure of the Curriculum

During the first two years of community college or bachelor's-level education, students are expected to learn concepts and theories in political science, economics, sociology, and psychology, that will provide the context for their applied education in CSPA. Following careful selection, junior-year students are then enrolled in the CSPA curriculum. This curriculum provides the structure for acquiring basic, minimum competencies for performing new as well as more traditional professional roles in community services and public affairs.

Undergraduate education in CSPA takes place in three stages:

Entry and educational planning. Following admission into CSPA, each student constructs an educational plan to guide his or her studies in CSPA; the plan integrates both university and community resources. These learning contracts are developed in three-credit education and career decisions seminars taught by faculty advisers; they form the basis of an undergraduate educational program in CSPA. Simultaneously, students explore professional issues and ethics in a three-credit course on issues for professional practice, and, if appropriate, they receive credits for prior experience. During this program stage, students may begin working on the CSPA core curriculum, gathering basic experience in the field, and rounding out their background in the social sciences.

Core curriculum. In the past, requirements have varied for students in different program areas. In CSPA's new curriculum, all undergraduates complete an integrated common core. Each student is required to take a limited number of core courses during the junior year in CSPA. Each core course incorporates an interdisciplinary, applied, problem-centered, and career-oriented perspective. Core courses are usually taught by CSPA faculty, and a field-based learning component is an integral part of the core. Core curriculum course offerings include (a) community problem solving, (b) interpersonal problem-solving methods, (c) public service management, (d) applied research and evaluation (e) public service policy and programs, and (f) a field-based learning component.

The field-based learning component consists of at least 12 credit hours of supervised field experience or supervised applied research plus a three-credit-hour theory–practice integration seminar taken concurrently. Placements may be full- or part-time and for varying durations. Theory–practice integration seminars emphasize the integration and application of content learned in core courses in different field settings.

Concentration area studies and senior project. The concentration areas within CSPA revolve around four broadly defined, interdisciplinary, applied, problem-centered career areas: (a) public management and planning, (b) direct service delivery, (c) policy and program development-evaluation, (d) community development and organization, and social action programming.

In their education and career planning students attach greater specificity to these areas by identifying settings, populations, levels of government, and problems of specific interest. Concentration area studies are then designed from appropriate coursework within CSPA and other university departments. Students are required to develop at least one concentration area incorporating a minimum of 18 credit hours.

Many courses from which selections may be made exist in other departments and schools as well as in CSPA. Examples include *courses dealing with specific issues* such as environmental management, poverty solutions, child abuse, contemporary problems of death, issues in criminal justice, city growth and management, aid to developing countries, race relations, alcohol and drug abuse, and functional aspects of physical disability; *courses dealing with specific settings* such as correctional systems, child welfare services, state and local government, senior centers, metropolitan governments, federal public administration, and comparative bureaucracy in developing countries; and *courses dealing with specific populations* such as children, the elderly, ethnic minorities, and the mentally and physically handicapped.

Each student also completes a variable-credit senior project related to his/or her concentration area. This may be a second field placement, an applied research project, or a policy paper and is usually supervised directly by a CSPA faculty member. The senior project is designed to demonstrate a student's ability to apply multiple social science perspectives to the solution of community problems.

Supervised field study continues to be strongly emphasized in CSPA through the following: (a) a full time, field-unit faculty coordinator who works with faculty to develop placements and who teaches field observations, supervises some students, and identifies field needs for school response; (b) a junior-year field requirement; (c) a senior project that may be a second field placement; and (d) involvement of all CSPA faculty in field supervision.

Field-based learning is an integral part of each student's educational program, being directly related to career and educational goals. Such learning focuses on problems and direct service delivery and can involve students working with faculty members on applied research projects of mutual interest.

Curriculum and Faculty

Each year every CSPA faculty member is responsible for five aspects of the CSPA undergraduate curriculum: (a) teaching one education and career decisions seminar to advisees, (b) overseeing advisees' contract learning experiences; (c) supervising field-based learning, (d) teaching at least one core and one concentration area (or graduate) course, and (e) supervising senior projects.

The demands on faculty in CSPA are substantial. In addition to their teaching and advising responsibilities, faculty are expected to be active professionally and to engage in applied research and problem-solving outreach activities, preferably involving students when such experiences are likely to enhance their competencies.

Admissions

The program requires high-quality, mature students interested in close working relationships with faculty members and community resource people on topics of mutual interest. Efforts are made to recruit innovative students who have clear public career goals, who thrive on and seek out independent learning experiences, and who are comfortable working in an interdisciplinary context with an interdisciplinary faculty.

Students applying for admission are evaluated on their relevant academic background, experience, and writing ability. Students are prescreened to determine whether they will achieve junior-year standing by the time of admission, whether their career goals are congruent with those of CSPA's mission and curriculum, and whether they have the minimum required coursework and experience. Quality of students is not defined in terms of academic record alone but also in terms of past experiences, specialized knowledge, motivation, and a strong ethical interest in problem solving.

Summary: CSPA Curriculum

The new CSPA curriculum encourages and facilitates student integration of (a) classroom and field-based education; (b) direct service delivery and management perspectives on community problem solving; (c) competencies learned within the core; and (d) alternative theoretical perspectives garnered from planning and working with both CSPA and other university faculty. The faculty of CSPA provide a variety of educational experiences, and the program attracts many nontraditional and working students.

The program also helps undergraduate students to creatively use the resources of the University of Oregon as well as citizen and professional resources in the community. It integrates theoretical and applied learning and gives CSPA graduates the minimum competencies necessary to enter, survive, and lead the management and delivery of community and public services.

Supportive Faculty Characteristics

The educational programs being developed by CSPA are viable only if faculty have a high regard for nontraditional students, a preference for interdisciplinary work, and an interest in applied problem solving. In addition, 10 years of CSPA experience have revealed the importance of other faculty characteristics.

Faculty Value the Application of Knowledge

Faculty within the CSPA, whether they are on joint appointments with other university departments or are working full-time in CSPA, have a continuing investment in the application of knowledge. Courses use a variety of methods to test ideas and to create learning settings. The faculty value a dynamic interplay between what is learned in professional settings and what is learned in the classroom. They have a positive belief that useful ideas are developed and tested in multiple settings. The collective experience of the program is that knowledge garnered solely from practice settings may not be generalizable and that ideas developed solely in the classroom may lack practicality and usefulness. Work both in classrooms and in practice settings is needed for students to develop the proper combination of helping skills and analytical and conceptual abilities to perform entry-level professional roles as well as to insure a fair assessment of opportunities for a long-term professional career.

Faculty Value Professional Education at the Undergraduate Level

While there is a range of opinion among faculty about what should be learned, there is a strong shared opinion that undergraduate students can and should pursue professional careers. An optimistic spirit of adventuresome inquiry is communicated to students; they learn that they do not need to postpone development of a professional identity until graduate school. Faculty working with students of different ages have validated the fact that a variety of educational methods can set in motion a genuine professional perspective. Development of the students' competencies and a focused curriculum that integrates classwork and fieldwork have enhanced the faculty's view of professional education at the undergraduate level.

Faculty Value the Creation and Development of Educational Methods

In an educational environment that includes a commitment to integrating classwork and fieldwork and that places a value on professional education, a context is created in which interest is focused on developing a variety of learning formats. The CSPA educational program assumes that not all students learn from one method of teaching and that all educational methods must relate to professional roles required in the future work setting. Faculty therefore devote time and energy not only to developing a variety of field-placement opportunities but also to designing educational methods such as contract learning so that students may have alternative learning opportunities. The working premise is that an effective professional practitioner must create personal resources as a part of the work role; creating these resources to achieve an educational goal is viewed as a valid rehearsal.

The combination and interrelationships among coursework, fieldwork, and professional education have produced explicit expectations for students to be analytic, practical, and assertive as they learn how to apply what they have learned in both the classroom and the field.

Summary: Faculty Characteristics

Developing an undergraduate professional education program in a predominantly liberal arts university with faculty from a variety of disciplines and points of view continuously presents conflict. Managing the tensions of such conflict is not easy in higher education, where overlapping circles of advice and consent are expected. With endurance, competence, and sufficient agreement among faculty and university administrators, such an atypical educational system can survive. When it does, and successfully adapts to the ever-present crosscurrents of competing resources, teaching styles, educational philosophy, ways of viewing the world, and preferences to reduce the risks of social disorder, the student experiences an unusual opportunity to learn basic skills and test himself or herself as an independent practitioner who can create the social support systems that make it possible to launch a professional career.

Summary

CSPA has achieved a new education goal: implementation of an integrated curriculum for students in both community service and public affairs that prepares them for new and emerging roles in these areas. In attempting to meet society's ever-changing public service needs, CSPA designed a flexible educational program to prepare students for new entry-level professional roles in program development, management, and direct service delivery with emphasis on the design and evaluation of new preventive programs, as well as on the management of citizen-based, professional, and integrated public or quasi-public services. CSPA supports the following:

1. Integration of liberal arts and professional education;
2. A core curriculum for undergraduate professional education;
3. Field-based education;
4. A career-advising service;

5. Experimentation with the delivery of diverse educational methods;

6. Applied faculty research that focuses on public policy issues and the delivery of public and human services;

7. Undergraduate and graduate education for the working professional;

8. Multiple connections with university programs; and

9. Short-term appointments for in-career professionals.

In these efforts, CSPA works closely with other faculty at the University of Oregon to take advantage of their potential contributions to CSPA's educational goals.

CSPA's past 10 years indicate that a valid need exists for an interdisciplinary undergraduate academic program to prepare students for entry-level careers in community service and public affairs. CSPA's new educational program requires that its faculty orchestrate and provide leadership for this applied, professionally oriented, social science program. During the past decade, CSPA willingly accepted the risks involved in breaking new educational ground and challenging old assumptions while intentionally maintaining an innovative and self-evaluative attitude. These efforts will need to be intensified and continued. Although CSPA has not always achieved its goals, this fact should not detract from the need for such programs. Continuation of CSPA's missions in a manner that allows for improvement and innovation is imperative.

We have found a pressing need on campus for increased clarity about the nature of CSPA faculty roles and career expectations. A shrinking student population in combination with a continuing emphasis on the preservation and genesis of knowledge, research, and experimentation free of social and/or political concerns means that professional schools are vulnerable even though they are sought-after entities. The faculty of such schools must develop roles that make sense "in the streets" *and* "in the ivory tower"—or they must self-consciously create a place for new roles to bridge the gap and enhance both environments without corrupting the purposes of either. This kind of faculty role shaping in an environment that must also bring together faculty of diverse disciplines, integrate the strengths of the pure and applied social sciences and of social action and social research, and offer something of quality to varied student populations is a demanding challenge—one that has often frustrated CSPA students and faculty alike. By tackling this challenge and by making a commitment to tolerate both ambiguity and constant change, CSPA can, in fact, make room for the kind of education needed for positive impact on public services.

The education of flexible, change-oriented problem solvers competent to perform new and changing (as well as traditional) roles in community and public service is not possible without institutional support. Not only must adequate monetary support be forthcoming, but there must also be support for faculty and students engaging in nontraditional educational programming. This means visible, tangible support for nontraditional and working students, for field-based education, for applied problem-focused research, and for other outreach activities. In essence, the rewards to both faculty and students of engaging in professional, interdisciplinary, career, and applied problem-centered education must outweigh the costs.

REFERENCE NOTES

1. Kelly, J. G. (Chair). *Undergraduate education for professional careers: An Oregon story.* Symposium presented at the Eighty-Third Annual Meeting of the American Psychological Association, Chicago, Illinois, September 1975.
2. Harvey, M. *New careerists: Paraprofessionals as resources for improving services.* Paper presented at the meeting of the Western Psychological Association, Los Angeles, California, April 1976.

REFERENCES

Brager, G. The indigenous social worker: A new approach to the social work technician. *Social Work*, 1965, *10*, 27–32.

Brown, B. The director's report on psychiatric education. *NIMH Bulletin*, 1977, 1–24.

Caplon, N., & Nelson, S. D. On being useful: The nature and consequences of psychological research on social problems. *American Psychologist*, 1973, *28*, 199–211.

Durlack, J. *The use of nonprofessionals as therapeutic agents: Research, issues, and implications.* Unpublished doctoral dissertation, Vanderbilt University, 1971.

Fullerton, S. The bachelor's-level professional in community service careers. In P. J. Woods (Ed.), *The psychology major: Training and employment strategies.* Washington, D.C.: American Psychological Association, 1978.

Harvey, M., & Passy, L. A university-based new careers program. In D. Robin & M. Wagenfeld (Eds.), *Paraprofessionals in human service.* New York: Human Science Press, 1977.

Heller, K., & Monahan, J. *Psychology and community change.* Homewood, Ill.: Dorsey Press, 1977.

Hollingshead, A., & Redlick, R. *Social class and mental illness.* New York: Urley, 1958..

McPheeters, H, & King, J. *Roles and functions for mental health workers.* Atlanta, Ga.: Southern Regional Education Board, 1967.

Pearl, A., & Reissman, F. *New careers for the poor: The non-professional in public service.* New York: Free Press, 1965.

18

James P. McGee and Benjamin Pope

Baccalaureate Program for Mental Health Workers

This chapter traces the historical development of the movement toward using paraprofessionals in the mental heatlh field which began in the late 1950s. The early use of paraprofessionals occurred primarily in general medicine, but training programs for human services in mental health began developing as well, and some of these early programs are described. Also described is an innovative, yet academically oriented, baccalaureate-level mental health worker program. This program represents an attempt to achieve continuity between classroom instruction and clinical experience through a synthesis of coursework and supervised practica. The goal is to develop a specifically defined body of knowledge, skills, and attitudes in a program that does not displace basic college and departmental requirements.

History

The trend in the human services field toward the use of "paraprofessionals" began in the late fifties and early sixties. At that time federal-government-sponsored research commissions on manpower availability in human services determined that manpower shortages in these areas were rapidly approaching the crisis point. The major recommendations of these research committees were, first, that increasing effort and funding be devoted to the recruiting of personnel to train at the professional level, and, second, that new pools of manpower be developed by training personnel at a lower level to assist the professional in the delivery of services.

The first programs to emerge from these recommendations on developing new manpower resources were devoted to the training of subprofessional or paraprofessional medical assistants to aid physicians in the delivery of general medical health care. For example, in some rural states in this country where the public was particularly hard pressed for medical services, training programs were established to broaden the skills of people such as experienced registered nurses and former military corpsmen or medics so that they might function in a role similar to an MD general practitioner; these people were working under the regular supervision of fully qualified and licensed physicians. The basic rationale behind this approach was that it would enable physicians to dedicate their time and skills more fully to their professional functions of healing and educating while delegating to other persons with less than professional training the routine technical tasks. It was expected that this approach would result in better utilization of scarce professional manpower and more extensive and improved services to the community. Despite initial resistance, both from professional medical groups and from the public, the paraprofessional in medicine is becoming an integral component of the health delivery system. For example, in one study (Silver, 1968) it was found that the pediatric nurse practitioner could "give almost complete well-child care, as well as participate in the care of the sick child [p. 37]." In another project (Yankelovich, 1967), patients gave an overwhelming endorsement to the work of "home health aides."

While the early programs in the training and use of paraprofessionals occurred primarily in the field of general medicine, the human services in mental health soon began to develop training programs of their own. After reviewing the status of mental health services in the United States in the late fifties, the Joint Commission on Mental Illness and Health reported that the mental health delivery system as it was at that time established was woefully inadequate in its ability to meet the needs of the public.

The recommendations of the Joint Commission fell into three basic categories: First, they recommended that there should be a great deal of emphasis on prevention, that is, the reduction of severity and incidence of various mental health problems in a population. Second, they encouraged the development of new treatment models other than the traditional one-to-one counseling-psychotherapeutic method for effecting change. And finally, the Commission suggested that "in the absence of more specific and definitive scientific evidence of the causes of mental illness, psychiatry and the allied mental health professions should adopt and practice a broad liberal philosophy of what constitutes and who can do treatment [p. 61]."

The last point concerning who is qualified to provide treatment addresses the problem of manpower utilization and development and was based to a large extent on Albee's (1959) report to the Commission on Mental Health Manpower Trends. In his report Albee indicated that the outlook for the future regarding the meager supply of personnel in the traditional mental health professions was gloomy indeed. His paper presented a compelling argument that there was need for drastic change in both the training and utilization of personnel in the mental health delivery system.

James P. McGee is presently a staff psychologist at the Sheppard and Enoch Pratt Hospital in Baltimore, Maryland; Benjamin Pope is the Director of Psychological Services at the Sheppard and Enoch Pratt Hospital.

This chapter is a result of a training program for baccalaureate-level mental health workers, which was supported by a grant from the Bruner Foundation of New York City.

This chapter is reprinted from *Professional Psychology*, 1975, 6, 80–87.

Most of the early reports on the issue of limited manpower in the mental health area addressed the problem of manpower deficits within the traditional mental health delivery system which at that time was primarily the public psychiatric hospital. In addition to the above-noted manpower vacuum in the public psychiatric hospital, the recent community psychiatry movement has placed even greater demands on the already limited manpower resources of the mental health field. Community psychiatry has extended or attempted to extend mental health services to populations that have not been recipients of this commodity in the past. Mental health manpower problems are therefore currently noted both in the traditional psychiatric setting and in the new community mental health facilities. It is for these reasons that the mental health professions adopted the strategies taken earlier by those in the field of medical health care for developing manpower pools of paraprofessionals to assist in the delivery of services.

The pioneer program in which an attempt was made to train non-professionals to perform functions in the mental health field previously carried out by the members of the traditional disciplines of psychiatry, psychology, and social work was conducted at the National Institute of Mental Health by Margaret Rioch (Rioch, Elkes, & Flit, 1963). Essentially this program involved training a small number of middle-aged housewives intensively in counseling and psychotherapy. The Rioch program seemed to provide impetus for the development of numerous other mental health paraprofessional programs. These fall into two general categories; one includes projects for training indigenous mental health workers and the other, the more academically oriented mental health worker programs. The concern in this article is with the second category.

Academically Oriented Mental Health Worker Programs

Most of the early programs in this category were conducted by community colleges which granted graduates an associate's degree, usually as mental health technicians. These technicians would operate in a way first suggested by Rotter (1954) in the mid-fifties. He envisioned a mental health delivery system in which professionals (MDs and PhDs) devised treatment programs for patients which were implemented by technicians trained at the Associate of Arts level. Some AA-level mental health workers were trained to work with a broad spectrum of population groups; others were groomed to work with specific populations, for example, alcoholics or the mentally retarded; while still others were trained to perform particular skills such as administering psychological tests. Graduates of these two-year programs have proved their usefulness in a variety of mental health settings, and the popularity of this type of training is attested to by the fact that currently there are over 100 associate degree mental health programs conducted by various colleges throughout the United States. An additional 25 to 30 United States colleges and universities are now offering paraprofessional mental health training at the baccalaureate level.

Training Programs for Mental Health Workers

The training of both AA-and BA-level mental health workers is based on the conceptualization of a new role within the mental health enterprise, that of the *generalist*. Thus, the objective in most current undergraduate paraprofessional programs is not the training of social work assistants, psychology assistants, or other technicians within the jurisdiction of any single professional discipline. The mental health generalist is usually the end product of training even when a program may be channeled through a traditional department such as psychology. In the curriculum to be presented below, the generalist is perceived as a worker who is committed to a variety of mental health target populations. Although these roles can only be implemented if the worker has mastered certain skills, his roles vis-à-vis specified population groups are used to define his work rather than the skills he may command. Thus one does not refer to him as a therapist, a psychometrist, or a diagnostician. Instead one speaks of him as a worker who performs an outreach role, for example, that of a broker or an advocate of clients who require mental health services, an evaluator, a caregiver, a behavior changer. These roles are performed by the worker in the service of client populations, drawing upon whatever skills are relevant, and without regard for any assumptions made by different professions regarding their exclusive title to the performance of specific skills.

There are a multitude of administrative and curricular routes that could be followed in the attainment of the above objective. The administrative structure of the program to be outlined below is probably unique and deserves some comment. It has been enabled by a grant made by a private foundation to a private psychiatric hospital that is associated with a number of community psychiatric facilities. Although the mental health worker training program is administered by the hospital, it is a joint enterprise of the hospital and the psychology department of an adjacent state college. It is open only to undergraduate psychology majors and is designated a clinical concentration in psychology. Upon completion of its requirements each student obtains a BS in psychology from the college and a certificate as a baccalaureate mental health worker from the hospital. Because it has been possible to channel a mental health generalist program through a psychology department without diluting or derailing the psychology major, one may well ask whether such a development carried with it any broad implications for clinical training in psychology, both undergraduate and graduate. This possibility will be considered further after curricular principles and content have been examined.

The following are some innovative principles that are incorporated into various undergraduate training programs that have, as their objective, the preparation of students for work in the mental health field after graduation:

1.   Objectives of training are expressed in terms of competency to be attained in the performance of specified functions, roles, and skills and not

in terms of course content. In the present program, a behavioral formulation of learning objectives was attempted through the specification of the skills and the roles the student acquires in the various courses, practica, and field experiences that he undertakes.

2.   The work-study model, developed by Antioch College in Yellow Springs, Ohio, dates back to the late 1920s. Antioch itself has developed many variants of its model, maintaining through all of them the basic principle of continuity between academic and vocational experiences. Undergraduate mental health programs all seek to implement this continuity in one form or another.

3.   A flexible policy in the college's admission office regarding equivalency evaluation of past academic training and life experience is recurrently stressed in undergraduate mental health programs.

4.   The concept of the common-core curriculum within the human services that will prepare the mental health worker for his role in a broad range of clinical and community situations is increasingly emphasized in all training programs that purport to develop mental health generalists.

5.   The traditional *subject* as the basic curricular unit is replaced by the module or work-study bloc, a complex assembly of learning experiences including didactic work within the classroom and library work, together with closely correlated role-playing, practicum, and actual vocational experiences.

6.   Direct functional assessment of the skills and roles that are included in the objectives of a curricular unit is emphasized as an alternative to the traditional content-oriented "mid-term" and "final exam."

Some mental health training programs in the avant-garde of the innovative movement in undergraduate education exemplify the foregoing principles most dramatically. One such program is offered by Antioch College in Columbia, Maryland, and is associated with its Human Ecology Center (Antioch College, 1970). The program's objective is "to produce generalists in the mental health field with journeyman-level proficiencies in the full range of clinical and preventive professional activities [p. 1]." For admission to the program the student must have completed an AA degree in mental health and must be employed or employable in a mental-health-related setting. A distinguishing characteristic of the Antioch program is its insistence that the enrolled student hold a job in the mental health field. Thus in a sense, the relationship between the academic and the vocational is built into the program; in fact, it is a prerequisite for admission.

While a program that is radically new such as Antioch's dramatizes the kinds of innovations that need to be assimilated into undergraduate training with functional objectives it is so different in structure from those offered by conventional four-year colleges as to make its emulation difficult. The program to be described below represents an attempt to introduce the basic principles outlined above into a curriculum that articulates with and extends a conventional undergraduate training program in psychology.

An Innovative Training Program

In this program training goals are stated in terms of clinical skills and roles that students acquire as they proceed through the curriculum. An array of such skills and roles implicit in functions currently performed by two-year mental health associates was noted in a field survey conducted during the planning period. On these skills and roles are based the principal objectives of the present curriculum, implemented through its major structural units designated as *work-study blocs*. Two additional segments of the curriculum are the subjects that make up *basic college requirements* and a series of *field experiences*. Each work-study bloc is composed of one or more courses with closely related practicum experiences. It represents an attempt to achieve continuity between classroom instruction and clinical experience, through a synthesis of course-work and supervised practicum, resulting in the development of a specifically defined body of knowledge, skills, and attitudes. In the curriculum there are eight work-study blocs corresponding to seven clinical skills and one research skill. The blocs, along with the courses comprising them, are listed below. Typically a single course consists of both didactic and practicum components. However, in some instances the entire course is a practicum, for example, Clinical Interviewing II and Behavior Modification II.

Work-Study Bloc	Course(s)
1. Dyadic Helping Relationship	Introduction to Psychotherapy I & II
2. Group Interaction	Group Dynamics & Analysis of Interpersonal Relations
3. Interviewing	Clinical Interviewing I & II
4. Counseling and Work with Community Resources	Community Resources in Mental Health
5. Psychological Testing	Clinical Testing I & II
6. Activity Therapy	Introduction to Activity Therapy
7. Behavior Modification	Behavior Modification I & II
8. Research	Behavioral Statistics, Experimental Psychology, Psychology of Learning

The basic college requirements include Freshman Composition; Fundamentals of Public Speaking; five options from art, drama, English, music, philosophy, religion, and speech; three options from economics, geography, history, and political science; biology; physical education and one option from health and physical education; and one option from math or physical science. The foregoing are all basic liberal arts subjects. In addition, the following subjects are required of all psychology majors including those in the mental health workers program: General Psychology, Behavioral Statistics, Experimental Psychology, and the Psychology of Learning.

While the essence of the mental health subspeciality is contained within the previously described work-study blocs, these blocs do not in any way displace the basic college or psychology major requirements. Evidence for this is contained in the fact that graduates of this program, in addition to being trained "mental health workers," meet, in terms of under-graduate course requirements, all of the usual standards for admission to graduate training in psychology. In many instances the didactic portion of a work-study bloc is supplied by one or more basic requirements of the major. Thus the work-study bloc on research draws on three of the four required psychology major courses. In other instances, psychology electives already available in the curriculum are plugged into work-study blocs. Thus, Group Interaction draws on a group dynamics course and another course entitled Introduction and Analysis of Interpersonal Relations. In most cases, however, new courses, particularly directed toward the objectives of work-study blocs, have been introduced. For example, the bloc on Individual Therapy consists of two new courses, designed to serve the needs of the mental health subspeciality. However, precisely in curricular terms they are designated as psychology options.

In contrast to the work-study bloc practica, which are supervised clinical experiences closely related to specified subjects, the *field experiences* are brief exposures to on-the-job training in situations that are defined by institutional structure and target population rather than by specific skill or body of knowledge. The objective of a field experience is the application of a range of generic skills, knowledge, and attitudes in an actual work situation. Thus the field assignment is a more culminating experience than the practicum. In fact, it is within the field experience that separate skills are combined into the roles that constitute the generalist's function.

Field experiences are arranged in a broad array of different mental health facilities. Students are offered considerable options in their selection of field experiencies with an opportunity to assert their particular interests and preferences. Thus, during the course of the four-year program each student is certain to be assigned to at least three different mental health agencies for his field experiencies. The first in each instance is an inpatient ward in the private psychiatric hospital conducting the program. The other two agencies may be selected from a variety of community facilities including a crisis clinic, a community mental health clinic, drug abuse clinics, an alcoholism program including alcoholism clinics, quarter-way and half-way houses, institutions for mentally defective children, institutional and noninstitutional facilities of the Division of Juvenile Services, state psychiatric hospitals, residential treatment facilities for disturbed children, and others. For each field-work experience the student receives a stipend and two academic credits.

Conclusion

One may ask whether the mental health program outlined above is actually congruent with an undergraduate major in psychology. The preceding discussion of the articulation of the mental health programs with the psychology programs indicates that there is no technical obstacle to the integration of the two. But there are issues other than technical ones involved. One might be interested, for example, in how well the two trends, that is, the undergraduate psychology major and the mental health generalist curriculum, coexist. It would appear on the basis of the experience thus far with the present program that the latter actually enriches the former. Moreover, there is a body of experience accumulating that indicates the advantage in maintaining a continuity between the didactic and the practicum at every level of training. In this regard it should be noted that many undergraduate students appear to be sufficiently mature and ready to undertake supervised human service functions.

Graduate programs in clinical psychology have tended not to pay systematic attention to the problem of continuity between the clinical experience and the classroom even though the laboratory course in the physical sciences has long since established its curricular legitimacy. In fact, the conventional clinical psychology internship is based on the assumption of a break between the academic and job situtations. Emerging undergraduate mental health programs are posing a challenge to this traditional discontinuity.

Finally, the intrusion of clinical training into the undergraduate years has accelerated the process of erosion that has in any case been occurring beneath the structure of training objectives in clinical psychology. In the practitioner segment of the Boulder Model, the clinical psychologist has traditionally appeared as a psychodiagnostician and a psychotherapist. The extension of the mental health enterprise into the community has blurred this image and indeed supplemented the above two roles with a number of others prompted by service needs within the urban community. Now the concept of the generalist within mental health threatens to further confuse the image of the clinical psychologist as practitioner. To be sure, one can attempt to contain the generalist model within the undergraduate years and thus, by professional fiat, assert its nonrelevance to clinical psychology as a profession. Such a fiat, however, would simply signal a delaying operation if emerging service needs in mental health are indeed more congruent with the generalist rather than with the professional specialist model. Clearly, the ferment in undergraduate psychology training is being felt at the graduate level. Life may soon be different at both levels.

REFERENCES

Albee, G. W. *Mental health manpower trends.* New York: Basic Books, 1959.

Antioch College, Human Ecology Center, Community Mental Health Training Program. Training grant application prospectus. Unpublished paper, Antioch College, 1970.

Joint Commission on Mental Illness and Health. *Action for mental health.* New York: Basic Books, 1961.

Rioch, M., Elkes, C., & Flit, A. A. *Pilot project in training mental health counselors.* (USPHS Publ. 1254) Washington, D.C.: U.S. Department of Health, Education, and Welfare, 1965.

Rotter, J. B. *Social learning and clinical psychology*. New York: Prentice-Hall, 1954.

Silver, H. K. Pediatric Nurse-Practitioner Program. *Journal of the American Medical Association*, 1968, CCIV, 229.

Stormer, G. E. Implementing performance based learning objectives. Unpublished paper, College of Human Learning and Development, Governor's State University, Park Forest, Illinois, 1972.

Yankelovich, D. *Home Health Aide Demonstration Project evaluation*. New York: Author, 1967.

19

Raymond P. Lorion

Undergraduate Training in Community Psychology and Community Mental Health

This chapter summarizes two interrelated models of undergraduate training for human service careers. The first evolves from the community mental health movement and aims to introduce the student to the legislation, rationale, and services provided through the community mental health center system and its affiliated institutions. This training is based upon a tertiary or late secondary prevention rationale in which an identified disorder is responded to by a help-giving individual. The second model reflects the developing area of community psychology and focuses on social systems themselves as the care-giving agents. Students are encouraged to understand the development, organization, and programmatic goals of various social systems and to develop an appreciation of the strengths and weaknesses of the major social systems and of their potential for responding to human needs in an efficient and, in many cases, preventive manner. One of the major goals of the second training model is the recognition by the student of the wide range of alternative careers and institutions through which human services can be provided.

After nearly two decades, the community mental health movement has changed the nature and focus of the delivery of mental health services in many significant ways. Community mental health centers are now established in nearly half of the nation's 1500 mental health "catchment" areas, and treatment services are being used by more people than ever before (Simon, 1975). Increases have also occurred in the range of treatment strategies available to meet psychosocial needs. Psychotherapy has become a generic term for a variety of remedial services provided to individuals, groups, couples, and families. Nor is attention any longer focused exclusively on established disorders. The addition of the indirect services provided through consultation and education, for example, has expanded the reach of mental health into levels of dysfunction and segments of the community heretofore relatively uninvolved with mental health services.

Concern with preventing or minimizing the impact of psychosocial disorders has involved the mental health system with schools, day care centers, well-baby clinics, detention centers, facilities for the aged, and many other community settings. In fact, the delivery of supportive services for individual needs is not even restricted to the mental health system. A variety of community agencies involved with educational, medical, legal, and welfare services also contribute significantly to the total human services network, as do an untold number of "natural" self-help groups (Gartner, 1976).

These changes in the mental health delivery system and the accompanying expansion of human services have created a continuing need for more personnel. Traditionally, mental health treatment had been the exclusive function of professionals from psychiatry, psychology, and social work. Yet even prior to the community mental health movement, the serious imbalance between available professional human resources and the demand for mental health services concerned mental health planners. In their analyses of this problem, Albee (1959) and Arnhoff, Rubenstein, and Speisman (1969) concluded that the imbalance would not be resolved as long as professionals remained the sole treatment agents. The community mental health movement, with its expansion of facilities, treatment approaches, and target populations, exacerbated the imbalance and intensified efforts to identify alternative service delivery providers.

The solution to this problem appears to lie in the effective training and utilization of subprofessional treatment agents. During the past decade, the mental health literature has been replete with reports of the effectiveness of subprofessionals in providing psychological services to such diverse target populations as psychiatric inpatients and outpatients, children, parent groups, the mentally retarded, and drug abusers (Gartner & Riessman, 1974; Sobey, 1970). Although it has not been without problems, the subprofessional movement has demonstrated its value to the human service network and appears to be here to stay. Its ascendancy has brought into question many assumptions about the skills, training, and personal qualifications needed by those providing mental health services. Although the issue continues to be debated, there is increasing acceptance of the conclusion that professional training is necessary for treatment planning, differential diagnosis of disorder, and supervisory responsibilities. However, in many cases direct interaction between the target of the service and the deliverer of that service can be satisfactorily accomplished by subprofessional personnel under professional supervision. Thus, a new role has evolved in the human services system—that of the mental health worker, the mental health technician, the community aide, or the community counselor.

The need for these workers is obvious; less obvious are the criteria by which such workers should be selected and trained. Originally, subpro-

---

Raymond P. Lorion is Professor and Director of School/Community Psychology at the University of Tennessee.

This chapter is based in part on a paper delivered by the author as part of a symposium on undergraduate training in mental health presented at a meeting of the Midwestern Psychological Association, Chicago, May 1974.

fessionals were thought to be uniquely qualified as treatment agents because they lacked training and because they were indigenous to their catchment areas. Presumably, these characteristics facilitated a therapeutic relationship and provided clients with familiar patterns of communicating emotional dysfunction. Sobey (1970), however, questioned the sufficiency of these criteria for selecting subprofessional workers:

> It is by now common knowledge that we have romanticized the indigenous worker, and that little hard data is available on the effective employing and training of this type of worker. No evidence exists of the indigenous worker's special knowledge or insight into his fellow man, nor is there evidence that he is necessarily motivated to help his fellow man more than the "socially distant" professional. (p. 187)

Subprofessional human service workers are increasingly seeking training in associates- and bachelor's-level programs. This chapter describes two related approaches to providing liberal arts undergraduates with knowledge of and experience in human service technology. The first approach focuses on the community mental health system and emphasizes the needs and service delivery models of that system. The second approach focuses on the community at large and its various human service systems and emphasizes the variety of settings and roles through which such services can be made available. The community mental health approach and the community psychology approach overlap; the distinction between them is one of emphasis. They are neither the only nor the best ways of introducing undergraduates to careers in the human services, but it is hoped that their presentation, will stimulate others interested in such training to expand upon and improve them.

Community Mental Health Approach[1]

Since 1968 the Department of Psychology at the University of Rochester has included a two-semester seminar practicum in community mental health. This practicum is available to junior and senior psychology majors, and most students entering the course already have a basic understanding of psychology as a theoretical and empirical discipline. The course is designed to introduce the student to the literature on community mental health and to offer practical experience in providing human services.

Enrollment is usually limited to 40 advanced undergraduate psychology majors on a first-come, first-served basis. During the semester preceding that start of the course, interested students participate in an interview with the instructor and course assistants. During this meeting, the goals and procedures of the course are explained to the student in detail, as well as the time demands of anticipated practicium assignments (6–10 hours/week). Students are also informed that during the practicum semester they will be graded on a pass–fail basis and that the sole criterion

---

1. The community mental health approach described here refers to the curriculum used by the author while on the psychology faculty at the University of Rochester and is not intended as a current description of the program.

for failure is evidence of irresponsible or unprofessional behavior. Examples of such behavior are repeated unjustified absences from practicum assignments and refusal to follow supervisory instructions. Students who are unwilling or who seem unlikely to accept these requirements are not enrolled. Although such exclusions are rare, continued use of a preenrollment interview appears justified; to date, no student has failed or been asked to leave a practicum assignment. Since all practica depend on continued positive experience between the students and the community agencies, this cautionary step is perceived as an important component of the total course structure.

During the fall semester didactic materials are reviewed and current mental health treatment approaches are critically assessed. Students are expected to read the literature reviewing the relation between traditional service delivery models and the imbalance among available resources, current demand, and potential needs. Typically, classroom discussion focuses on the concept of prevention and the various treatment alternatives associated with primary, secondary, and tertiary preventive goals. Emerging roles in community mental health, particularly those of the subprofessional and the mental health consultant, are evaluated. Overall, the didactic portion of the course is designed to encourage students to question the accepted way of doing things in mental health and to approach mental health problems from as many perspectives as possible. It is hoped that they will develop flexibility both in their definitions of what a "mental health" problem is, who should respond to it, and in what ways it should be responded to in their conceptualizations of solutions to problems.

Many students have chosen to meet the term-paper requirement of this course by researching practical topics in the Rochester community. One group of students surveyed and catalogued mental health services available in the Rochester and Monroe County area. They assessed problem areas in which few resources were available and suggested additions to the existing community service network. A second group of students focused on the needs of patients released from local inpatient facilities. The students interviewed social workers, rehabilitation counselors, employment service workers and ex-patients to determine how the needs of the ex-patients were being met. A third, racially mixed group of students reviewed the issue of racism in the conceptualization and design of health services and also focused on recognizing their own racial biases.

The practicum experience, however, is the core of the course for most students. They want a chance to test their clinical intuitions and to learn what qualities they need to provide mental health services. Most of all, they seem to want confirmation that their undergraduate training has given them genuine skills. Fortunately, the Rochester and Monroe County area has many human service programs that welcome undergraduate trainees. Settings used in the practicum must meet the following requirements: (a) they must identify viable roles for trainees that allow them to participate in some service function of the agency; (b) they must screen, train, and supervise the trainee; and (c) they must accept the irregular schedules of the undergraduate. Demand for such trainees exceeds the supply; therefore, new sites are continually available to replace those that prove unsatisfactory or that can no longer provide training experiences.

Following are brief descriptions of four typical practicum settings:

1. The Infant Stimulation Project is a program targeted to disadvantaged, inner-city children who during their first two years demonstrate developmental lags in cognitive, linguistic, perceptual, or interpersonal functioning. Children in the program range in age from 10 to 30 months, and each child has an individual treatment program. Students visit the parents at home to discuss the child's needs and later to suggest how the ameliorative program can continue in the home. Students develop strong relationships with the children as they implement specific exercises for language modeling and motoric development and encourage presocial behavior.

2. The Monroe County Division for Youth is an agency charged with providing a liaison between community agencies and adolescents in need of help. Some clients are voluntary; many are court-committed. The agency is both a referral and a counseling service. After orientation and training, the students serve as caseworkers and provide clients with counseling and other services. Each student assumes primary responsibility for his or her caseload.

3. Various hospital-affiliated community mental health settings serve as practicum sites. The range of clients served by the undergraduates assigned to these settings varies from chronic institutionalized psychotics whom the trainees lead in activity groups to children whose emotional problems have necessitated their termination from a regular school program. In the latter case, the trainees have both recreational and educational duties as well as the therapeutic task of relating to children who have serious difficulties with most behavioral limits. A third type of hospital-based program uses trainees as group co-leaders in hospital day programs.

4. The Monroe Developmental Services is a federation of programs that responds to the needs of the mentally retarded and physically handicapped at various stages of development. Trainees initially select an age group (e.g., adolescents) that interests them and are then assigned a supervisor to help them develop an appropriate treatment program for this group. Typical duties range from helping children perform simple motor tasks to teaching a very retarded adult how to take a public bus without getting lost. Improvement for these clients is slow, and undergraduates working with them need constant encouragement.

Once the list of practicum assignments for a given year is definite, students rank the alternatives in order of preference for a particular population (i.e., child vs. adult) and setting (i.e., psychiatric vs. nonpsychiatric). If possible students are assigned their first or second choice. During the first semester students contact their practicum settings and work out a mutually acceptable schedule. Each student's schedule should specify a time for weekly supervisory meetings with a predetermined staff member. Students should receive constant supervisory feedback and have regular opportunities to integrate conceptually their duties into the total service delivery system of the setting. In addition, groups of 8–10 students meet biweekly with the course instructor and teaching assistants to exchange experiences and to discuss the relationship of their settings and duties to principles discussed during the first semester.

General student reaction to the practicum has been positive. Occasionally students voice dissatisfaction with a particular assignment and strongly recommend that the setting be excluded. Even in such rare cases, however, students express positive feelings about their total course experience and indicate that their dissatisfying experience was in some ways instructive. More typical, however, are the students who not only learn something but also enjoy their assignments. One student stated,

Working at ——————— has really increased my interest in mental health. Most of all, it has shown me my strong points, weak points, and even some areas where I know almost nothing. Some of what was in the books makes sense now; some of it seems too distant to be useful. I've learned some important things about what I can do and how I feel about working with people who are very different and more in need of help than anyone I have ever known.

Few benefits of the practicum assignments are tangible. Some students acquire helping skills that may later assist them in securing jobs, and occasionally, practicum assignments have led directly into full or part-time jobs in the same setting after graduation. Yet, far fewer students actually obtain positions in mental health than enroll in the course. Thus, for the majority of students the primary course benefits are intangible changes in their attitudes toward and understanding of mental health needs and services. From observing the slow pace of change in the profoundly retarded and the chronic schizophrenic students learn to value the unique contribution of those able to effect such change. Similarly, the impact of services upon those in acute need, in crisis or, in conflict is also recognized, as are the limits and potentials of the mental health system.

More important, students learn much about themselves. They gain an opportunity to explore their myths and preconceptions about those in need of mental health and mental retardation services. In many cases their ideals must be tempered by the realities of needs, resources, and client acceptance. The students also gain a chance to demonstrate to themselves that they can provide a useful, meaningful service, that their book learning can be translated into action. Often they recognize these gains during the practicum year. Some students, however, do not recognize the full impact of their helping experience until months or even years later.

Community Psychology Approach

The second approach to undergraduate training is still in a developmental stage and reflects, in many ways, changes in the community mental health movement and my own biases toward this movement over the last three years. The course structure for such a training approach is similar to that just described for the community mental health approach and thus its educational goals would also be met through a balance of didactic and practical experiences. As noted earlier, the distinction between these two training approaches lies in their respective focuses. The former approach presents past models of mental health service delivery as antecedents to the current community mental health model, and course prerequisites include traditional training in the theory and research of psychology.

In contrast, the community psychology approach presents the community mental health system as but *one of many* community systems involved in the delivery of mental health related services. Prerequisites for such training extend beyond psychology to include the other social sciences, particularly anthropology, political science, and economics. Assigned readings, classroom discussions, and practicum assignments focus on analysis of the nature and organization of the community and its many complexly interrelated social systems, such as education, the courts, health services, and welfare. The training's overarching goal is to develop in the students a recognition that mental health problems are, in many ways, responses to daily experiences within a variety of community settings. The students also learn that mental health problems affect and are affected by numerous social systems other than the mental health system. Thus, they learn to consider adjustment within the perspective of its ecological parameters.

Poverty, ethnicity, racism, and social policy are identified as highly relevant to understanding and, where possible, remediating psychosocial dysfunction. Each of the major social systems is considered in terms of its direct or indirect relevance to the mental health of the community. Consequently, practicum assignments developed within any of these systems are designed as much to provide students with an understanding of the particular system as to provide helping experience.

At first glance, it would appear that undergraduate training in community psychology provides the student with even fewer tangible (and marketable) skills than are acquired in the community mental health curriculum. Directly applicable training for a position in a mental health or mental retardation facility is clearly not provided. However, a basic lesson obtained from the community psychology training approach is that the delivery of mental health related helping services can be accomplished through a wide variety of roles in each of the major social systems. Thus, a sought-after result of a community psychology curriculum is for students to expand their perception of human services beyond the mental health system. In this way, their career alternatives are significantly increased, as is their potential for obtaining a position that "can make a difference" in someone's life. By understanding the organizational structure and consequent human impact of such social systems as education and welfare, rather than merely criticizing the ineffectiveness of bureaucracies, some of the students may in time become socially conscious members of those organizations.

Conclusion

There is no single approach to undergraduate training in the human services that is "best." In both of the approaches described here, students expand their understanding of what it means to be in need of and to provide human service. In both approaches they see the effect of "psychology" on the lives of real people with real problems. If community mental health is the focus of their study and work, they will likely limit their definition of helping services to those fields traditionally associated with psychology as a science and a profession. If community psychology is their focus, on the other hand, they will recognize the human service contributions to be made in the major social systems, and their definition of helping careers will be broadened. They may thus learn that one can "do psychology" without necessarily being "in psychology."

REFERENCES

Albee, G. W. *Mental health manpower trends*. New York: Basic Books, 1959.
Arnhoff, F. N., Rubenstein, E. A., & Speisman, J. C. (Eds.) *Manpower for mental health*. Chicago: Aldine, 1969.
Gartner, A. Self-help and mental health. *Social Policy*, 1976, 7(2), 28–40.
Gartner, A., & Riessman, F. The performance of paraprofessionals in the mental health field. In G. Caplan (Ed.), *The American handbook of psychiatry* (Vol. 2). New York: Basic Books, 1974.
Simon, G. C. Is there progress in community mental health? In L. Bellak & H. H. Barten (Eds.), *Progress in community mental health* (Vol. 3). New York: Brunner/Mazel, 1975.
Sobey, F. *The nonprofessional revolution in mental health*. New York: Columbia University Press, 1970.

20

Kenneth M. Shemberg and Stuart M. Keeley

Undergraduate Training for Community Mental Health Services

This chapter describes a 40-week undergraduate training program for subprofessional mental health workers. The program consists of three major phases: a 10-week introductory phase, a 10-week training phase, and a 20-week practicum placement. The first phase is a classroom experience providing a general overview of clinical psychology. The second phase includes both academic and practicum training in behaviorally oriented intervention techniques, interviewing and observational techniques, and interpersonal communication skills. Report writing, consultation, and professional and ethical problems are also covered. The third phase is a 20-week placement in a local mental health facility requiring 15 to 20 hours of work per week under the direct supervision of agency professionals.

Undergraduate psychology students often ask, "What can I do with my psychology training? Do I have to go to graduate school to be allowed to apply what I've learned? Why has my training been so devoid of the interesting, practical applications of psychology?" Perhaps in response to such questions and because of increasing personnel needs in the mental health fields, a variety of subprofessional programs have emerged. Some of these focus primarily on giving students an interesting and meaningful educational experience and provide little in the way of formal academic/clinical training. Hospital "companion" programs typify this approach (Umbarger, Dalsimer, Morrison, & Breggin, 1962). Other programs focus on providing such experiences while utilizing college students as preventive therapeutic agents for a designated clincial population (Cowen, Zax, & Laird, 1966). While these programs provide varying amounts of training, they usually do not represent a major academic investment by the student. A third type of program focuses on developing a large training program with major departmental investments in funding and staff time. The main goal of this approach, exemplified by associate-degree mental health programs (Baker, 1972), is to train a cadre of marketable subprofessional mental health workers.

From 1973 to 1977, we developed a subprofessional training program with many of these characteristics. Its aims are to involve and interest undergraduates in clinical activities, to produce well-trained mental health technicians who can provide a service as they progress through the final stages of the training, and to provide students with marketable skills in an expanding field (Korman, 1973).

The students are not trained as companions. Rather, they are trained in broad-based skills to provide three services within community agencies; (a) assessment of intervention programs with children, including interview and natural-environment observation skills; (b) direct intervention in the natural environment, such as carrying out a behavior management program in a classroom; and (c) mediator training (Tharp & Wetzel, 1969). Training in interpersonal skills (Carkhuff, 1969) is seen as an important prerequisite for providing the above services, but the emphasis of the program is on behavioral assessment and intervention; hence, the students are called behavior analysts. This chapter outlines the teaching approach we evolved to attain the above goals and provides examples of the settings in which students function and the roles they play in them.

Description of Training Program

The program described here has three major phases: (a) a 10-week introductory stage, (b) a 10-week training phase, and (c) a 20-week practicum placement. Each phase includes specific didactic and practical experiences designed to prepare the student for the succeeding phase. (The program trains a relatively small number of students per year, which permits an intensive personal experience for each trainee.) The following outline presents the essential features of each phase and the specific goals associated with each step in the sequence.

Phase 1

The first phase consists of a general introduction to clinical psychology, and approximately 40 students are enrolled. Selection criteria are sophomore or junior status, a minimal cumulative grade point average of 2.7, and enrollment as a psychology major.

The goals of this course are twofold: (a) to provide a broad background to the general field of professional clinical psychology with special emphasis on clincial intervention strategies, and (b) to provide a basis for selecting 12 of the students to continue with the program.

A general textbook in clinical psychology is assigned (Sundberg, Tyler, & Taplin, 1973), and as the quarter progresses additional readings are provided. This 10-week period includes didactic presentations on topics such as assessment and intervention at the individual, family, and community levels. The course is also heavily weighted with presentations of actual case materials (at least one per week), as well as video and audio

Kenneth M. Shemberg and Stuart M. Keeley are professors of psychology at Bowling Green State University.

tapes of the authors or graduate students engaging in assessment or treat-ment. Presentations by social workers from community agencies and by other psychologists working in settings such as halfway homes for delin-quents are also included.

The students take several field trips to local mental health facilities. They also spend one full day each week for five weeks as observers in the department's Psychological Services Center, where they see a broad range of real-life clinical activities including assessment, treatment planning, treatment, and community consultation.

The class meets twice a week for two-hour sessions. Two essay exami-nations form the basis for evaluating academic progress, and students earn four hours of academic credit. In the final weeks of the course, each student expressing an interest in continuing in the program completes a questionnaire on his or her social and academic history, interests and activities, and background in and motivation for mental health work. Information from this questionnaire forms the basis for a personal interview with one or both of the authors. Course grade, classroom partici-pation, motivation, and personal qualities as judged from the interview and classroom contact are the data upon which the selection of the final 12 trainees is based. Over the years since the program began, only one trainee has dropped out after having been selected.

Phase 2

Phase 2 is the "meat" of the training program. It entails two training modules—the academic module and the clinical team placement module. Trainees enroll for 8 hours of academic credit with the authors. Thus, the 10-week concentration represents one-half of the trainees' academic responsibility. The emphasis throughout is on acquiring specific technical skills that the trainees will later be required to apply.

The curriculum for the academic module in Phase 2 is designed to achieve nine basic goals. These goals and the methods for attaining them are as follows:

Goal 1: Mastering the basic principles of operant conditioning and social learning. This goal is implemented via a three-week, six-hour-per-week block. A programmed learning text (Miller, 1975) provides the primary teaching materials, and social learning materials are also used (Bandura, 1969). Students receive frequent written progress checks on the programmed text. Class time is primarily devoted to discussing the programmed text and progress checks.

Goal 2: Comprehending the contingency management model and the social learning model as they apply to behavioral modification in the natural environment. A two-hour session is devoted to a discussion of the general approach emphasizing behavioral intervention with parents and teachers of disturbed children. The major reading for this section is *Behavior Modification in the Natural Environment* (Tharp & Wetzel, 1969, Chap. 3).

Goal 3: Acquiring interview and observational skills for behavioral assessment. Students should be capable of assessing the following: (a) the behavioral repertoire of the target, (b) the stimulus situations under which focal behaviors occur, (c) the reinforcers maintaining focal behaviors, (d) the reinforcement hierarchies of target children, and (e) the potential for using specific mediators (parents, teachers, etc.) in the natural environment. This unit is comprised of two two-hour classroom sessions, multiple practicum observations in classrooms of normal and retarded children, and three practice interviews with volunteer subjects. Classroom activities focus on (a) practice exercises in pinpointing behaviors and in behavioral coding and recording strategies, and (b) observation and discussion of interviews with teachers and parents conducted by the instructors. Readings for this unit are *Behavior Modification in the Natural Environment* (Tharp & Wetzel, 1969), Chap. 5) *The Clinical Study of Social Behavior* (Peterson, 1968, Chap. 5), sample case studies from previous clinical cases, and handouts on various observational categories.

Goal 4: Acquiring the skills for developing intervention strategies for a wide variety of problem behaviors across diverse settings. Four two-hour class periods are devoted to (a) presentations of intervention programs previously carried out by the instructors, and (b) discussion of sample intervention programs written by the students for hypothetical problem behaviors. A minimum of three programs for home problems and three for school problems are written and discussed. During this section, students read widely from journals and books presenting various intervention programs.

Goal 5: Learning to carry out direct intervention and contingency management programs in situations where mediators cannot do so. In one two-hour class various approaches to direct intervention are presented. Readings include sample articles from behavioral journals and books.

Goal 6: Acquiring the skills to assist professionals in training mediators to carry out behavioral intervention. Three two-hour sessions are devoted to role playing the situations that arise as subprofessionals enter the homes or schools of referred children. Also, various approaches professionals use to train mediators are discussed, modeled, and role played, and students familiarize themselves with the readings used in such training (e.g., Becker, 1971; Buckley & Walker, 1970; Patterson & Gullion, 1968; e.g., Rettig, 1973).

Goal 7: Acquiring an awareness of the practical and interpersonal difficulties associated with intervention in the natural environment and strategies for dealing with such problems. One two-hour session is devoted to discussion of these issues, and one is devoted to role playing. The primary resources for this section are the authors' experiences in behavioral intervention.

Goal 8: Acquiring an awareness of professional and ethical problems associated with behavioral intervention and with the role of the subprofessional. Ethical and professional problems are continually referred to and exemplified throughout training. Students read the *Ethical Standards of Psychologists* (APA, 1968).

Goal 9: Acquiring skill in writing reports on assessment and interven-tion activities. This skill is taught throughout the 10 weeks. Students are required to write reports on all observational and intervention practicum experiences, which means at least one report per week. Each student receives one half-hour of individual supervision per week to discuss these written reports.

The most exciting element in Phase 2 is clearly the one-day-a-week, 10-week placement on a clinical team in the departmental services center. Clinical teams consist of two PhD clinical psychologists and from four to six graduate students at various levels of training. Typically, there are five such teams, and at least two undergraduates are assigned to each. In contrast to their Phase 1 experience in the center, the students now become integrated team members; that is, the supervisors often give trainees clinical assignments that provide actual experience in activities such as school and home observation or intervention. The students become highly identified with their teams and seriously accept the responsibilities attending the placement.

Despite the substantial reading required, the emphasis is on learning via direct observation, role playing, and/or practicum experience. Formal lecturing is minimized, and every effort is made to turn didactic sessions into group discussions that focus on readings as they apply to real-life clinical problems.

Students register for four hours on a pass–fail basis and for four hours on a graded basis. Evaluation is competency based. Frequent written progress checks are made to ensure the effectiveness of training.

Phase 3

This final phase is the most exciting and rewarding part of the program. After 20 weeks of intensive training and practicum experience, students are ready to go into the real world. Phase 3 is a two-quarter (20-week) placement in a mental health setting where undergraduates continue to learn while actually providing clinical services under professional supervision.

Students register for 6–8 academic hours per quarter on a pass–fail basis. They spend an average of 15–20 hours per week in their internship placement, meeting regularly with professional staff. Behavior analysts have been successfully placed in a number of community agencies, where they have had a variety of helping roles. These agencies and roles are described in the next section.

Community Agencies and Roles Played

Family Services Agency

The Family Services Agency is an urban, community mental health agency staffed by 12 social workers who provide a variety of services. The behavior analysts placed here have played many roles and have typically been supervised by social workers. For example, one behavior analyst was assigned to four cases that eventuated in her developing behavioral intervention programs for problem children and teaching the mediator (e.g., mother, teacher) to apply the program. In these instances, a social worker had contacted the clients and had decided on a behavioral intervention. The behavior analyst then took primary responsibility for intervention. In this role, the behavior analyst interviewed mediators, observed the child in problem settings, developed a behavioral program, and finally assisted the mediator in carrying out intervention.

Another behavior analyst was assigned a case requiring meetings with parents of a disturbed child for three two-hour sessions to instruct them in behavioral techniques. This behavior analyst also taught three two-hour classes in behavior modification to "homemakers," volunteer women working as surrogate mothers in homes where mothers were absent for lengthy periods.

Medical College

In this setting, behavior analysts have worked with teachers and parents in the psychology department's school for educationally and emotionally disturbed children. They have observed the classroom, interviewed parents and teachers, and developed intervention programs. In most cases, they have initiated direct-intervention token or activity–reward programs and have then phased in the teachers. Many kinds of behaviors have been targeted (e.g., assignment completion, tantrums, lying, enuresis). On several occasions, individual programs have evolved into total classroom interventions.

County School System

Behavior analysts have been placed in a school system psychology department staffed by three MA school psychologists. Typically, a school psychologist first determines that a case is appropriate for a behavior analyst's involvement and then prepares the teacher for that involvement, or a teacher specifically requests a behavior analyst's aid. After the assignment to a classroom is made, behavior analysts interview teachers, observe the classroom for assessment purposes, and then develop a behavioral program. Programs are discussed with supervisors and presented to teachers by the behavior analyst and the school psychologist.

Target behaviors have ranged from overt aggression to academic deficiencies. In most cases, behavior analysts have directly carried out the program, modeling operations for teachers, phasing in the teachers, observing teachers' performances, and providing feedback. Interventions range from simple rules-praise-ignore programs to complex token systems. This variability is primarily a function of the teacher's ability and/or willingness to carry out intervention.

School for the Retarded

In this day school for the educable and trainable retarded, behavior analysts have been supervised by graduate students in the clinical psychology program. Working closely with teachers, the behavior analysts first act as classroom observers and then determine which children need intervention and what intervention is most appropriate. In most of these cases, behavior analysts have carried out direct intervention programs with children who exhibit problems that are not covered by ongoing token programs in the classrooms; for example, several overcorrection programs have been implemented for self-stimulation behaviors. In addition to carrying out individual intervention programs and eventually incorporating the teachers into the program, behavior analysts frequently give teachers feedback concerning general classroom interaction; for example, a behavior analyst may be requested to observe the quality of reinforcement in the classroom.

Psychological Services Center

In this setting, the behavior analyst is typically assigned to a case and supervised by an advanced clinical psychology graduate student. The most frequent role in this setting has been one of observing and interviewing for assessment. The following are examples of settings within the center where behavior analysts are employed:

Head Start classroom. A five-year-old child was referred after being withdrawn from a Head Start program because of dangerous aggressive and destructive behavior. School personnel agreed to behavioral intervention as long as the child had an in-class "therapist." Thus, a direct intervention program was carried out by the behavior analyst who was in the classroom two days, and later three days, per week. The behavior analyst was supervised by an advanced graduate student who was doing intervention in the home. The behavior analyst's work began with time-outs, evolved into a high-rate, primary reinforcement program, and eventuated in an intermittent social reinforcement program.

Community day care center. A behavior analyst helped to manage a four-year-old who hit, threw things, yelled, ran away, and ignored directions. Behavior analyst involvement with this child eventuated in the development of group management plans for two teachers who were experiencing general classroom management problems. The behavior analyst thus carried out preintervention assessment, individual direct intervention, teacher training for individual intervention, and a teacher training classroom program and also interviewed the center director and teachers and observed the classroom. During the next four weeks, the behavior analyst developed, modeled, and phased teachers into a behavioral intervention program. The behavior analyst spent from two to three days a week modeling, observing, and providing feedback. Following individual intervention, a classroom program began, focusing on three children, and the behavior analyst spent three weeks working with the teachers on this latter phase of the assignment.

Elementary school. A behavior analyst developed a tutorial program for an eight-year-old learning-disabled child with motivational problems. This program included working with the teacher and the parents; goals were to improve spelling and reading. Parental counseling focused on facilitating the school program (e.g., parents reinforced appropriate school behavior). Over the summer the behavior analyst worked in the home on a self-help skills token program.

Roles Most Effectively Played by Behavior Analysts

Initial Assessment

Behavior analysts consistently provided invaluable assessment information from the natural environment. This information added significantly to the conceptualizing of clinical problems and to the planning of initial behavioral intervention programs. The behavior analysts effectively observed and interviewed parents, teachers, and target children to pinpoint target behaviors and to determine the relevance of important environmental antecedents and reinforcers. They also communicated valuable impressions of the attitudes and capabilities of parents and teachers as expressed in the natural environment rather than in the clinic. Thus, behavior analysts were instrumental in overcoming some of the problems associated with the discrepancies between clinical observations and behavior in the natural environment.

Ongoing Treatment Assessment

Once intervention programs were planned and instituted, behavior analysts were able to provide valuable information on treatment effectiveness that otherwise would have been lost. They were able to objectively gather data on how well a parent or teacher was carrying out a program, how the child was responding to treatment, or what (if anything) should be changed to increases treatment effectiveness. They also pinpointed additional problems in the functioning of teachers, parents, and target children, again providing otherwise unavailable but highly useful data from the natural environment.

These activities involved going into the classroom and carrying out specific behavioral operations, such as workbox techniques (Patterson, Cobb, & Ray, 1972), or going into the home to tutor a child or model tutoring techniques for parents. In the direct intervention role, the students functioned as effective treatment "arms," extending the activities of professionals directly into the natural setting. Many cases simply could not have been treated without the behavior analyst.

Behavioral Management Assistance

This role involved behavior analysts' meeting frequently with parents or teachers to provide *technical* aid. Their primary function was to teach skills such as graphing and counting behaviors and to deliver reinforcement. The behavior analysts were very useful in this role because they could extend into the natural setting the professional's didactic instructions to parents or teachers, thus dramatically improving the quality of behavioral programs.

While behavior analysts generally fulfilled their roles well and the supervisors were universally pleased, significant problems related to limitations in the kind of services behavior analysts can competently deliver were encountered.

Initially we believed that these well-trained undergraduates would be able to fulfill a *major* consultative function (Keeley, Shemberg, & Ferber, 1973); that is, we believed that they could work independently with parents and teachers, thus freeing the professional from a time-consuming process. We quickly observed that in most cases teachers and parents would not accept the students in this role. Also, it was obvious that being cast in the role of an independent consultant produced considerable anxiety in the student. Mediators still wanted contact with a professional, and students wanted more backup than we had initially planned to provide. Related to their problems with independent consultation, the behavior analysts often met with resistance to intervention that they were unable to overcome without the direct involvement of the supervisor.

In general, it became clear that we were demanding too much of the behavior analysts. Although their training program was relatively intensive, it could not be expected to prepare undergraduates (a) to deal with the problems of consultation and (b) to independently handle resistance. Adding the necessary additional training for this, both practical and didactic, would have amounted to developing a sequence equivalent to an MA clinical psychology program. Thus, we elected to focus primarily on technical training. We also tried to impress on supervisors the necessity of providing professional backup for the behavior analysts. In the few instances where this did not occur, the behavior analyst had a more difficult time providing the technical services that he or she was best prepared to deliver.

Benefits of the Program

We believe that this training program provides students with a university experience that is meaningful in terms of personal, educational, and intellectual growth. We are encouraged in this belief by the fact that a large number of the students have gone into graduate work in the mental health disciplines, and many others have taken jobs as mental health technicians. As the program has become more visible and as the demands for mental health technicians with such training have increased, more and more students are obtaining employment as a direct result of training in the program. In the past year, behavior analysts have been hired at a mental health clinic, a medical college, and several child treatment centers.

Increasing demands for mental health workers—demands that cannot be met by the limited number of professionals available—make it appear inevitable that the trained paraprofessional will become an integral part of the community service delivery model. Thus, we believe that programs like this one have a future and that graduates of such programs will find increasing career options.

REFERENCES

American Psychological Association. Ethical standards of psychologists. *American Psychologist*, 1968, *23*, 357–361.

Baker, E. J. The mental health associate: A new approach in mental health. *Community Mental Health Journal*, 1972, *8*, 281–291.

Bandura, A. *Principles of behavior modification*. New York: Holt, Rinehart, & Winston, 1969.

Becker, W. C. *Parents are teachers*. Champaign, Ill.: Research Press, 1971.

Buckley, N. K., & Walker, H. M. *Modifying classroom behavior*. Champaign, Ill.: Research Press, 1970.

Carkhuff, R. *Helping and human relations* (Vol. 1). New York: Holt, Rinehart, & Winston, 1969.

Cowen, E. L., Zax, M., & Laird, J. D. A college student volunteer program in the elementary school setting. *Community Mental Health Journal*, 1966, *2*, 319–328.

Keeley, S. M., Shemberg, K. M., & Feber, H. The training and use of undergraduates as behavior analysts in the consultative process. *Professional Psychology*, 1973, *1*, 59–63.

Korman, M. (Ed.). *Levels and patterns of professional training in psychology*. Washington, D.C.: American Psychological Association, 1973.

Miller, L. K. *Principles of everyday behavior analysis*. Monterey, Calif.: Brooks/Cole, 1975.

Patterson, G. R., Cobb, J. A., & Ray, R. S. Direct intervention in the classroom: A set of procedures for the aggressive child. In F. Clark, D. Evans, & L. Hamerlynck (Eds.), *Implementing behavioral programs for schools and clinics*. Champaign, Ill.: Research Press, 1972.

Patterson, G. R., & Gullion, M. E. *Living with children*. Champaign, Ill.: Research Press, 1968.

Peterson, D. R. *The clinical study of social behavior*. New York: Appleton-Century-Crofts, 1968.

Rettig, E. B. *ABCs for parents*. San Marino, Calif.: Associates for Behavior Change, 1973.

Sundberg, N. D., Tyler, L. E., & Taplin, J. R. *Clinical psychology: Expanding horizons* (2nd ed.). New York: Appleton-Century-Crofts, 1973.

Tharp, R. G., & Wetzel, R. J. *Behavior modification in the natural environment*. New York: Academic Press, 1969.

Umbarger, C. C., Dalsimer, J. S., Morrison, A. P., & Breggin, P. R. *College students in a mental hospital*. New York: Grune & Stratton, 1962.

21

Robert G. Eason

A Combined Degree-Certificate Program for Paraprofessional Training

This chapter describes a program that provides considerable applied training at the baccalaureate level without infringing on the traditional liberal arts requirements for the BA degree. Students take the usual array of foundation courses required of psychology majors by most departments including courses in developmental, personality, and abnormal psychology and a course in behavioral assessment, analysis, and therapy. After completing 120 units of work plus an additional nine-semester-hour practicum, students are awarded both a BA degree and a certificate of behavioral technology that qualifies them to work in such settings as halfway homes for children, adolescents, or adults, institutions for the retarded, mental hospitals, youth service bureaus, and court systems.

In the fall of 1974 the psychology department at the University of North Carolina at Greensboro initiated an applied training program leading to a bachelor of science in behavioral technology (BSBT) degree. Rather than serving as an option to the traditional BA degree, the BSBT is a second bachelor's degree that requires an additional year of work (30 semester hours) beyond the BA. Since the program's initiation, eight people have completed it, and four others currently are enrolled. Those graduates seeking positions have readily found employment in agencies that provide psychological services, and they are reportedly performing well in their jobs.

As originally conceived, the fifth-year program was designed to fill a gap between the traditional BA-degree program in psychology and the graduate programs that place emphasis on research and scholarship. For several reasons, the applied program has been modified so that training may be completed within a four-year period. The student no longer is awarded two bachelor's degrees, but rather, upon completion of the requirements for the BA plus nine semester hours of supervised practicum, the traditional degree is awarded along with a certificate in behavioral technology. While a full fifth year of applied training is clearly desirable, such training competes with graduate school, on the one hand, and with immediate employment, on the other. The program administrators believe the revised program, which constitutes a compromise, can provide high-quality, efficient applied training without infringing on the philosophy and goals of the liberal arts program. Since the revised program imposes little additional financial burden on the student, an increase in the number of qualified applicants is anticipated, enabling the university to be more selective in accepting students.

Purpose

The certificate program aims to provide the necessary knowledge and skills for individuals to function effectively as behavioral technicians (under appropriate supervision) in service-oriented institutions and settings such as prisons and detention homes, mental hospitals and clinics, institutions for the retarded, special remedial classrooms, home settings, and public schools. It is assumed that graduates of the program will be employed primarily by state and local governments through their divisions of social service, mental health, or juvenile justice. More specifically, the program is designed to prepare an individual to work in one of the following paraprofessional capacities: (a) as a cottage parent in group-care or halfway homes for children, adolescents, or adults with severe behavioral problems; (b) as a resocialization therapist or psychological assistant in institutions for the retarded or in mental hospitals; (c) as a juvenile counselor for youth service bureaus or court systems; or (d) as a behavior management specialist within the public school system. The job outlook in some, if not all, of these areas seems strong for the near future.

Applied Knowledge and Skills to Be Provided

A primary goal of the applied training program is to instill a scientific attitude toward observing, understanding, and changing personally debilitating and socially inadequate or inappropriate behaviors of individuals who have been institutionalized or who have sought help through a service agency. A comprehensive background in experimental psychology as well as general knowledge in the physical, biological, and social sciences is considered essential if the program's applied goals are to be realized.

Specific applied objectives include the acquisition of knowledge and skills that will enable the graduate to perform the following functions: (a) institute and administer, with appropriate supervision, behavior management programs requiring the systematic application of material and social reinforcement, contingency contracts, modeling, behavioral rehearsal, self-control, token economies, social reciprocity, etc.; (b) systematically use behavioral assessment techniques such as questionnaires, interviews, and naturalistic observation through a variety of data-recording procedures in an appropriate and effective manner; (c) apply appropriate rules and

Robert G. Eason is a professor of psychology at the University of North Carolina at Greensboro.

procedures concerning the ethical treatment of clients; (d) evaluate the effectiveness of behavioral intervention programs; (e) exhibit social skills deemed appropriate for maximizing the probability of success of behavioral management programs and for working within the structural, economic, and political framework of service agencies; and (f) detect behavioral cues signaling the possible onset or presence of serious behavior problems in a client or patient of which the professional staff may be unaware.

Admission to the Program

Students are admitted into the certificate program during their junior year. In order to be admitted a student must be a psychology major in good academic standing and must be judged to possess a high degree of social competency. Applicants meeting the academic criteria are carefully screened in terms of their motivation and their ability to relate to others in a comfortable, open, and sensitive manner. Application is made at the beginning of the junior year; the admission decision is made at the end of that year on the basis of firsthand information garnered by the applied faculty working with the students seeking admission.

Curriculum

The curriculum for the first two years of the program is no different from that of the usual psychology major pursuing the BA degree. During the junior and senior years, students register for courses that enable them to complete all requirements for the BA degree, but, in so doing, an array of psychology courses is chosen that also constitutes an integral part of the behavioral technology certificate training program.

In addition to courses in introductory psychology, statistics, and history and systems, all psychology majors are required to take at least one course from the following categories in order to ensure breadth in the discipline: (a) developmental or personality, (b) abnormal or social, (c) comparative or physiological, (d) operant behavior or human information processing, and (e) sensory or perceptual processes. In selecting courses that meet the requirements for the major, behavioral technology students have somewhat fewer options because they must take certain courses in developmental, personality, and abnormal psychology. In addition, they are required to take a course in behavioral assessment, analysis, and therapy.

The psychology major, including the behavioral technology student, may count 24–36 semester hours of psychology toward the BA degree. To complete the requirements for the behavioral technology certificate, the student must take an additional nine semester hours of practicum, none of which are creditable toward the 120 units required for the BA degree, that is, a total of 129 units must be earned in order to be awarded both the degree and the certificate. By taking courses during one summer session, however, the certificate requirements can easily be met within the 4-year period normally required for earning the BA degree.

Evaluation

In addition to providing applied knowledge and skills deemed appropriate for employment in agencies offering psychological services, a major strength of the program is its total lack of infringement on the university's liberal arts program and on the traditional requirements for the psychology major. Because the integrity of the liberal arts program is maintained, the behavioral technology student has the same opportunities for becoming liberally educated, for acquiring a comprehensive knowledge of the discipline of psychology, and, importantly, for gaining admission into graduate degree programs in psychology as do other majors receiving the traditional BA degree. Given the close faculty–student relationship that necessarily occurs in applied training situations, the technology student probably has an advantage over other students for acceptance into graduate school, all other qualifications being equal.

Because the technology program has been in existence only since 1974, a meaningful assessment of its value to the service agencies for which it is intended is premature. But informal feedback from those agencies employing the individuals who have completed the program has been positive. Administrators of the program have been and will continue to send out yearly questionnaires to all graduates of the applied program and to their employers to more reliably assess the employability of the graduates and the effectiveness of the applied training in meeting the needs of the service agencies.

22

John E. Kerrigan

Undergraduate Professional Education in Public Affairs Psychology

Knowledge of psychology is increasingly important to the undergraduate student preparing for an entry-level position in public affairs. Academic psychologists are thus working with public affairs psychologists to establish undergraduate psychology programs in public affairs. This chapter explains why such programs are necessary and recommends four principal educational processes: (a) curriculum development, (b) student consultation, (c) field instruction, and (d) professional development. Problems and policy implications concerning these processes are discussed, and the roles that psychologists have performed in public affairs are mentioned.

The term *public affairs* refers to those actions considered or taken by local, regional, state, national, or international governments on behalf of their constituents. These actions may be legislative, executive, or judicial. The term *public affairs psychology*, therefore, refers to the psychological dimensions of public affairs concerns and issues.

Only recently have public affairs concerns been viewed from a psychological perspective. However, it is difficult to think of any public issue that would not benefit from conceptualization, examination and analysis of its psychological dimensions. This is true in regard to public housing, highway construction, senior citizen programs, collective bargaining, community mental health programs, transportation, environment, unemployment, and a host of other community problems.

Psychologists and Public Affairs

Though seldom publicized, psychologists and the American Psychological Association (APA) have demonstrated an extensive commitment to and performed valuable services in public affairs. Four of every five psychologists earn their living in nonprofit settings, and one of every five psychologists in the United States is employed by government in an administrative, research, or service role. Some psychologists are directly involved in formulating public policy, while others administer public policy programs. Psychologists frequently testify before Congress on various public issues and provide insights to public interest groups seeking implementation of public policy (Brayfield & Lipsey, 1976).

The American Psychological Association recognized the profession of public affairs psychology in its formal adoption in 1968 of a policy statement providing guidance for its members working in public affairs (Tyler, 1969). In addition, the theme of the 1969 APA Annual Convention was "Psychology and the Problems of Society." In 1974, APA also helped establish the Association for the Advancement of Psychology (AAP), which focuses on the interrelationships of public policy and psychology. These measures have given public affairs psychology a sound base for future development.

New graduate programs in public affairs psychology at leading institutions (e.g., Michigan State University, Pennsylvania State University, Wright Graduate Institute, and Claremont Graduate School) have furthered this newly emerging profession. Academicians and professionals in public affairs also recognize that more skills and knowledge in psychology can help resolve contemporary public interest issues (Waldo, 1975; Watt, Parker, & Cantine, 1973). An increasing number of articles in public affairs texts and professional journals stress the importance of psychological considerations. Some observers attribute this growth to the early contributions of psychologist John B. Watson, who introduced the term *behaviorism* in 1925 and acted as a catalyst in establishing the behavioral emphasis in public administration. Today it is virtually impossible to find a major test in public affairs that fails to draw upon the concepts and practices of psychology.

Professionals in both fields are increasingly aware of the interdependency of public affairs and psychology. Therefore, undergraduate professional training in public affairs psychology is expected to become increasingly desirable. As more advanced-degree psychologists become involved in public affairs careers, the need for persons with undergraduate training in public affairs psychology will increase. New career ladders will be established for psychology aides, who will provide varied and useful paraprofessional assistance. Since the public is becoming more concerned with the human, or psychological, aspects of public policy, the demand for undergraduate training in this area will grow.

Advantages of Undergraduate
Professional Education in Public Affairs Psychology

Whether good or bad, the trend in education in the last decade has been toward increased specialization; more attention has been given to the direct application of education to a career, in contrast to the Cardinal

John E. Kerrigan is Dean of the College of Public Affairs and Community Service at the University of Nebraska at Omaha. Although not a psychologist, he is a student of public affairs who is keenly interested in the preparation of undergraduate students for careers in the public sector.

Newman approach to education (Newman, 1931). This phenomenon is reflected in the United States in a declining enrollment in liberal arts colleges and an increasing enrollment in professional schools. The much discussed unemployment rate of the 1970s has made many students want an education that enhances career opportunities. Furthermore, public policy, reflected in initiatives such as government support for career education tends to strengthen and enlarge those educational programs that equip the student for a career.

Credentials are given in today's society, and it is unlikely that the emphasis on them will lessen soon. A person with a traditional liberal arts education is not perceived as having the same credentials, that is, marketability, as a student with skills, knowledge, and values obtained in undergraduate professional programs such as accounting, journalism, or public affairs. Educational specialization—adding more credentials—is encouraged by present career patterns and the increased financial opportunities available to the specialist.

Public affairs is one of the fastest growing professional fields. The public sector component of the economy is expanding, providing increasing career opportunities for students. In 1950 the public sector represented 20% of the total gross national product; in 1977 it approached 40%. During this period the number of government employees increased from 6.5 million to 14 million.

The most optimistic predictions indicate a continued increase in public employment through the 1980s and 1990s; such predictions imply a market demand for trained graduates in public affairs. The attractiveness of working in public affairs is also enhanced by the job mobility within the government.

The essential role of government in today's society and its role in the future underscore the need to extract an early commitment from bright, young, and dedicated persons—the future architects and critical evaluators of public policy. That these builders and critics be equipped with a basic knowledge of psychology as it relates to personality structure, social functioning and group learning is crucial.

Components of an Undergraduate Program in Public Affairs Psychology

This section does not include a discussion of a program's substantive psychological content, course requirements, or credit hours. Rather, it presents the *process* framework for a viable undergraduate program in public affairs psychology. The four essential components of this framework are curriculum development, student consultation, field instruction, and professional development.

Curriculum Development

The undergraduate program in public affairs psychology must be professional in its orientation, yet it must recognize the validity of the liberal arts tradition and build on that tradition rather than supplant it. A sound curriculum is designed to prepare sensitive, responsible, and articulate people for public service. The student should be able to adapt, learn, and grow as individuals and professionals in the public environments where they may work; they should be able to improve society through responsible application of their talents and personalities. While psychological training can help such students, it must not be included at the expense of a liberal arts perspective.

The undergraduate curriculum in public affairs psychology, as an overlay on the liberal arts foundation, must make students aware of the complexities of public issues. In addition, the program's concentrated study should make students receptive to subsequent opportunities for professional skill development.

It should be clear from the outset that graduates of such a program will not have developed the mastery or proficiency of skills that customarily distinguishes professional education and training from a liberal arts education. However, the curriculum—which includes courses in public policy analysis, social psychology, collective bargaining, human services management, and public law and the legal environment,—encourages critical thinking and provides a professional orientation to students interested in public affairs psychology careers.

A recent national study focused on the roles of the public administrator in the 1970s and the knowledge and skills required to perform these roles (Watt, Parker, & Cantine, 1973). The 130 public administrators who participated in the study though surveys, essays, and workshop discussions saw an urgent need for "knowledge and skills which would let them cope more effectively with growing uncertainty." They recognized the increasing importance of knowledge of individual and group behavior, political institutions and processes, and values motivating people. The group also believed that to act effectively in the changing environment, the public affairs administrator needed skills that "would help him bargain and build concensus, cope with sensitive people relationships, size up organizational and community situations, perform analytical tasks in a complex world, assess community needs, and effectively delegate authority to members of the team." The qualifications and skills cited by those public administrators emphasize the need for programs in public affairs psychology.

A public affairs psychology program should give the student considerable flexibility, encourage interdisciplinary programming, and offer problem-oriented courses. The student should be able to focus on an area of public affairs psychology that suits his or her needs, interests, and career aspirations.

The most notable problem in such a curriculum results from the lack of respect it gives to the "golden calf" of student credit hours. An undergraduate program that encourages interdisciplinary programming, offers special courses with low student–faculty ratios, and requires few credit hours to be taken within the program is often intensely scrutinized by educational administrators concerned with "credit-hour production." A related problem is the cost of developing and maintaining a quality internship program.

Major policy implications for the university arise from this approach to curriculum development. The success of an educational program that employs this curriculum relies on a universal rather than provincial use of the university. Educational programs that experiment with innovative learning techniques, even though they may have fewer credit hours than the more traditional programs, should be rewarded rather than penalized (Vallance, 1972). Criteria other than student credit hours should be established for judging the merit of such experimental programs.

Student Consultation

Faculty assistance and field placement contacts are the two resources most needed by students seeking their first career placement. Some students want to begin professional careers as soon as they receive their bachelor's degrees and thus require much faculty attention. Because a formal placement service is seldom available in a professional program, each faculty member must be asked to accept and be responsible for placement service. This responsibility should be part of the written job description. Activities such as attendance at professional meetings, community-related research and service, and public affairs psychology consultation help quality faculty to find career placement for students.

Evaluation of a professional school, especially one for undergraduates, properly involves an audit of the employment record of its graduates. Positions filled after graduation by those with bachelor's degrees in public affairs psychology include the following: assistant personnel director, assistant administrative officer to a special district, human resource coordinator for a statewide agency, staffing coordinator, coordinator of senior citizen programs, relocation manager, human resource planner, assistant city manager, social services outreach coordinator, researcher for state agencies, transportation planner, law enforcement planner, assistant coordinator of a regional improvement program, mental health coordinator, community services counselor, and transportation analyst.

Students seeking the bachelor's degree in public affairs psychology should realize that finding a good job may be difficult. They will be competing with people who have master's degrees, perhaps people from their own program. This competition requires that faculty assist students in developing presentable vita and otherwise facilitating the employment process.

Explicit criteria should be developed for evaluating faculty members who give career counseling to students; such faculty should receive academic merit and recognition for this work.

Field Instruction

In a recent national study (Parker & Cantine, 1972), a group of public administrators was asked to rank experiencies that contributed most to their career performance. Four experiences were included in the survey: (a) undergraduate education, (b) graduate professional education, (c) continuing education, and (d) skills and knowledge gained on the job. The administrators agreed that skills and knowledge gained on the job made the most important contribution to performance. This same study indicated the necessity of providing students with a carefully constructed and closely supervised on-the-job educational situation.

Students in a public affairs psychology program should be required to complete a field placement assignment before graduation. The timing of this fieldwork in relation to classwork is critical. One or two academic terms should remain after the term of supervised field study has been completed so the student has an opportunity to sharpen or modify skills in the remaining classroom concentration in public affairs psychology.

The involvement of the faculty in establishing internships or field placements and in finding—not assigning—students to fill them is important. Maintaining frequent contact with both the student and the agency supervisor—at least two and often three personal visits, coupled with telephone calls to both during the academic term—is also instrumental to the success of the internships.

The field placement provides an opportunity to observe the student at work in a setting comparable to that of his or her career choice; the student's attitudes, values, and behaviors—in short, that individual's personality—are given an honest chance to interface with the expectations and demands of society and the chosen profession. The field experience, properly conceived and executed, helps the student as well as the academic supervisor decide whether a career in public affairs psychology is appropriate. For example, a student who displays no confidence in the intrinsic worth of other people should not work in public affairs.

A theory–practice integration seminar, to be taken concurrently with the internship, should also be established. Such a seminar serves two purposes. First, it enables the student to relate theoretical concepts learned in the traditional academic setting to the situations encountered during the internship. Second, it serves as a frame of reference for structuring the student's observation and analysis of the events occurring in the agency during the internship period.

Some of the most difficult problems for the university operating an internship program in public affairs psychology include the following:

1. Academic responsibility for field instruction must be assigned. Among other options, responsibility can be given to (a) one faculty member in the program, (b) the entire faculty (each student's academic adviser also serving as that student's field instructor), or (c) a field unit within the program consisting of faculty members from various disciplines.

2. An adequate training program for supervisors must be established in the public service agencies where students are placed.

3. Proper assistance must be provided to internship students in integrating theory and practice.

4. Academic respect must be ensured for the faculty member who does only field instruction.

The field instruction process has far-reaching implications for university policy. Most institutions of higher learning have come to recognize field instruction as a legitimate academic activity, yet somewhat paradoxically, they are reluctant to reward faculty for field-related services. It is, therefore, incumbent upon programs employing field instruction to document the criteria, methods, and evaluation procedures of this educational process.

Professional Development

The first three educational processes discussed are used primarily to provide students with knowledge and skills. Professional development also contributes to student knowledge and skills but focuses more on the values and attitudes that students will need in their careers.

Such a value orientation can be provided in a public affairs psychology program through a diversified, full-time faculty, adjunct professors from the community, guest lecturers, and strong links with professional institutes and state and local agencies and associations.

To assure a mix of faculty interests that will instill the values of continuing professional development in students, special qualities are needed among the regular faculty. In recruiting faculty for public affairs psychology programs, the following should be articulated in announcements of positions:

1. The faculty member is expected to help provide an interdisciplinary educational approach that recognizes and utilizes the resources that exist within the program, the university, and the community.
2. The faculty member should value the continual and active role of the student in the teaching–learning transaction.
3. The faculty member should be committed to the primacy of theory yet recognize the necessity of translating theory into practice.
4. The faculty member should value highly the need to participate in scholarly research and writing and thus contribute to the development and communication of knowledge.
5. The faculty member should welcome community service responsibilities and be satisfied in carrying them out.
6. The faculty member should believe in the necessity of changing and improving societal institutions and yet accept the frustration of inevitable constraints upon social change.

Instilling in students a sense of professional development, a critical component in the educational process of a public affairs psychology program, is not an easy task to accomplish. Insistence on the faculty qualities mentioned above will limit the number of interested and qualified applicants for faculty positions. Finding faculty who meet equally well the criteria for academicians and experienced professional practitioners also complicates matters. And once such professionals are located there is the further problem of finding adequate financial support for them if they are interested in teaching at the undergraduate level and are sincerely committed to the notion of intensive involvement in advising and counseling students on an individual basis.

Most professional schools, however, recognize the value of linking the practicing professional with the academic program. Guest lectures and adjunct professorships are two of the most common means of helping to provide this emphasis upon professional development. Yet, considerable improvement in this area is needed, including a solidification or institutionalization of the relationship between the academic and professional communities. Most thoughts about linking these two communities focus on bringing the practicing professional into the fold of academia. Little has been accomplished or even attempted with regard to sustaining academicians in the professional community. Long (1972) discussed the need for such an effort:

The social scientist who is worth his salt will need to become involved since in no other way can he observe, measure, and conceptualize the phenomenon of his concern and develop the explanatory theories a meaningful science requires. These explanatory theories can only be tested as they are applied to the world of practice and without this explanation the social scientist is in danger of bemusing himself with metaphysical and literary speculations, consoled by the plaudits of the mutual admiration society of academic conferees. His greatest loss will be in turning his back on the only available route to knowledge, and his greatest danger will be the day of reckoning when a restive public discovers that the academic kings wear no clothes.

The policy implications of encouraging professional development among students center on determination of the proper faculty mix; a certain irreducible number of full-time faculty is necessary, but the exact number is debatable. Also, while it is generally recognized that links to qualified professionals in the community are essential for student professional development, the form and intensity of these links need to be determined. Guest lectures, seminars, classes, and topical discussions jointly sponsored by the academic and professional communities, and advisory boards composed of both academics and professionals are some of the options.

Another set of policy implications centers on the interrelationship of the academic program with professional institutes, agencies, and associations. Regular faculty can provide some of the needed cross-fertilization, but formal, institutionalized agreements are necessary to provide the depth and breadth for successful professional undergraduate education.

In summary, an undergraduate public affairs psychology program should focus on the four principal educational processes of curriculum development, student consultation, field instruction, and professional development. The development, implementation, and refinement of each of these processes create some inherent operating difficulties that need to be overcome and raise some rather significant issues of educational policy that need to be resolved. These educational processes can and will be improved, however, as we learn more about such programs and about the needs of both society and the public service professions we are committed to serve.

REFERENCES

Brayfield, A. H., & Lipsey, M. W. Public affairs psychology. In P. J. Woods (Ed.), *Career opportunities for psychologists*. Washington, D.C.: American Psychological Association, 1976.

Long, N. E. Universities: Ivory towers or socially involved. In S. K. Gove & E. K. Steward (Eds.), *The university and the emerging federalism: A conference on improving university contributions to state governments*. Urbana-Champaign: Institute of Government and Public Affairs, University of Illinois, 1972.

Newman, J. H. *The idea of a university: Defined and illustrated*. London: Longmans, Green, 1931.

Parker, J. K., & Cantine, R. What are we educating for? *Public Management*, 1972, *54*(2), 14–19.

Tyler, L. An approach to public affairs: Report of the Ad hoc Committee on Public Affairs. *American Psychologist*, 1969, *24*, 1–4.

Vallance, T. R. Processes, problems, and prospects for innovating within the university: Lessons from 45 experiences. *Journal of Higher Education*, 1972, *43*(9), 6–7.

Waldo, D. Education for public administration in the seventies. In F. C. Mosher (Ed.), *American public administration: Past, present, future*. University, Ala.: University of Alabama Press, 1975.

Watt, G. W., Parker, J. K., & Cantine, R. R. Roles of the urban administrator in the 1970s and the knowledges and skills required to perform their roles. In F. N. Cleveland & T. J. Davy (Eds.), *Education for urban administration* (Monograph 16). Philadelphia, Pa.: American Academy of Political and Social Science, 1973.

23

Thomas J. Kramer and James H. Korn

A Model for a Career-Oriented
Undergraduate Psychology Program

Until recently, most undergraduate psychology programs were oriented toward pre-paring students for graduate school and less concerned about preparing them for other careers. This chapter describes a model for a career-oriented option within an undergraduate psychology program, the important components of the model, attempts to implement the model and necessary modifications to it, and the barriers to its full implementation. The model includes eight overlapping activities (conceptual application, resource identification for skill training, exposure to field settings, volunteer field work, practicum, cluster sharing and integration, assess-ment and reassessment, and job finding and four processes (career exploration, career planning, career decision making, and job seeking).

Liberal arts departments, including psychology departments, have tradi-tionally not been career oriented. If students were being prepared for anything specific, it was for further education at the graduate level, an option selected by only 25–33% of the undergraduates at most colleges. A national survey (Yankelovich, 1974) showed that career goals are becom-ing much more important for undergraduates, and students at St. Louis University confirm this trend (Educational Community Counselors Associates, Note 1).

This growing concern for careers comes at a time when the job market is very limited. However, jobs are available, and students must be pro-vided with the background necessary to increase not only the likelihood that they will be employed but also their effectiveness and satisfaction with their work. But students must first evaluate themselves and the career choices available.

Careful career planning, however, is not a skill that most students have developed. In their study of undergraduate education, Levine and Weingart (1973) found that "students seem to be passively floating through their formal education, either unwilling or unable to think about what they want in that education." They discussed off-campus learning and recommended a program that forces students to explore career areas that will "shake them from their lethargy."

We have developed a model program at St. Louis University based on previous programs that addressed problems similar to those discussed above. For example, Pinkus and Korn (1973) demonstrated the importance of job experience and specific course preparation, and Korn (1974) and Levine and Weingart (1973) summarized other program approaches. The most successful features of these other approaches are (a) student choice of interest area, (b) strong counseling and support systems, (c) gradual student initiation to off-campus experience, (d) student opportunity for genuine professional work, (e) analysis of student experience by counselor, with feedback, and (f) active job placement resources.

The program at St. Louis University includes off-campus experience both as an aid to career planning and as an essential form of general education. Many students are deeply affected by such experiences and readily transfer this learning to the classroom. However, meaningful experience will not be provided by a program that pushes unprepared students out of the university. Students must be helped to integrate off-campus experience with past and present learning, to build upon that experience in making career decisions, and to evaluate the experience.

In the field of psychology, programs that provide this experience are unusual. In 1973 less that 16% of four-year colleges listed field experience as part of their curriculum (Kulik, 1973). Even those experiences reported were often limited to volunteer work as part of a single course. Several programs that are in progress are well developed but limited in scope; for example, the behavior modification apprenticeship at Western Michigan University and the program for health workers at Towson State College in Maryland.

The Career-Oriented Program

Our model program attempts to prepare students for a broader range of settings than provided by the programs discussed earlier. It is based on successful features of existing career-oriented (as opposed to vocational) programs and includes a commitment to organizational learning through evaluation and research. Although descriptions of existing programs are easy to find, data concerning their success or failure are seldom available; we intend to provide this useful information on our program's process of learning.

Program Goals and Design

It is important to distinguish this career-oriented program from vocational preparation. Students in our program are not prepared for a specific job, as in paraprofessional training; instead, students learn to develop career-

Thomas J. Kramer and James H. Korn are professors of psychology at St. Louis University.

planning and decision-making strategies that will be useful to them whatever their vocation. We believe that a background in liberal arts and psychology is appropriate for students wishing to develop (a) sensitivity to human needs, (b) awareness of values, (c) skill in human relations, and (d) ability to plan for the future.

The program's design includes situations in which students must articulate their values, demonstrate their skills, engage in planning, and make decisions about their futures. The students have opportunities to apply what they learn and to see the usefulness of psychology by connecting academic learning with experience in the world. The development of these "application skills" is one of the most important goals of the program.

The program is based on some familiar educational and psychological concepts: learning from experience and from analysis of experience; knowledge of results (feedback) as an essential condition of learning; individualization of the learning experience; and development of a structure for learning—a career plan—against which new experiences can be compared. The relationship between student activities in courses (analysis and feedback), experience, and career planning is discussed in a later section of this chapter.

The city and county of St. Louis also benefit from this program. Although the greatest contribution of the program is to graduates who become uniquely prepared and motivated for human service in education, government, mental health, and business, the program also contributes to the community's resources. Students use community settings as learning experiences and also provide skilled help at low or no cost to agencies, schools, and other organizations. In some cases faculty also provide expert advice. In return, community resources assist the program by bringing their experience into classrooms upon request.

Planned Outcomes

Initial planning for this program began in the fall of 1973 as part of a major restructuring of the undergraduate curriculum at St. Louis University. Although students at the university had varied backgrounds, educational goals, and career goals, the traditional undergraduate program was geared toward serving the educational needs of only those students who planned to continue to graduate school in psychology or related areas. This subset of students represented only 10% of the psychology majors. A new undergraduate curriculum was approved in 1974 with three tracks, or options: the graduate preparatory option, the career-oriented option, and the personalistic option.

The graduate preparatory option was designed for students who plan to continue their education in graduate school. This option stresses basic research skills and a grounding in the traditional content areas of psychology. The career-oriented option was designed for those students who plan to enter the work force upon graduation and who are concerned about the applicability of their education to the working world. The personalistic option was designed for those students who are primarily interested in a broad liberal education and their own personal growth and development.

Implementation of the career-oriented model began in the fall of 1975. The model is now fully implemented but with several important changes from the original design. The following outline details the model as initially formulated.

Original Design for the Career-Oriented Option

I. *Activities for Program Coordinators (First Semester)*
  A. Organize resources for career planning.
    1. Designate career-oriented activities in general psychology, applied psychology, and advanced general psychology.
    2. Plan coordination of activities with guidance center.
    3. Develop career-planning modules for students and advisers.
  B. Produce guidelines for field placements and practica.
    1. List participating organizations.
    2. Have organizations approve guidelines.
    3. Test guidelines through student placements.
    4. Modify guidelines.
  C. Design and test a discussion format for analyzing job experiences and providing feedback to students.
II. *Activities for Students*
  A. First-year activities.
    1. Use and evaluate career-planning resources and present written evidence of career planning.
    2. Receive feedback.
    3. Become aware of human needs and personal values.
    4. Develop skill in human relations and the application of psychology.
    5. Use simulations and role playing to assess skills.
  B. Activities to be completed within two and one-half years.
    1. Continue with career planning.
      a. Regularly use university resources.
      b. Know about resources outside the university.
      c. Be able to analyze and evaluate experiences.
      d. Be able to articulate a career plan.
    2. Develop career strategies.
      a. Know about alternative careers.
      b. Use job experience to test alternatives.
      c. Analyze and evaluate alternatives.
      d. Show evidence of career decisions based on planning.
    3. Become more sensitive to human needs and more aware of personal values, and use this awareness in making career plans and decisions.

    4. Develop career application skills.
       a. Demonstrate competence in fieldwork.
       b. Receive evaluations from peers, faculty members, and field supervisors, and make self-evaluation.
    5. Develop skills in finding employment.
    6. Find a desirable job or enroll in graduate school.

III. *Program Goals*
    A. Goals for the first two years.
       1. Students in the program use career planning resources and consider them effective.
       2. Community organizations approve of and participate in the program.
       3. Job placement systems are effective for the students and the community.
       4. Evaluations are effective in improving the program.
    B. Long-term goals.
       1. The program is self-sustaining and is considered attractive and challenging by a diverse group of students.
       2. Community organizations consider the program a source of competent human service personnel.
       3. Graduates of the program are sensitive and skilled in human service, capable of self-development, and effective and satisfied in their careers.

We agree with Goodwin Watson (1974), who believed that traditional college instruction denies the three essential conditions for psychic reward: freedom to set one's own goal, freedom to choose appropriate means for moving toward that goal, and reliable feedback on actual progress. This program was intended to enhance those conditions and to capitalize on an advantage of nontraditional programs that Watson pointed out:

> Students cannot deceive themselves with the assumption that someone else—the professors, the authors of tests and textbooks—has already decided what is really the route to an enlightened, humane, useful, and satisfying life. Students in self-directed programs are more consciously faced, hour by hour and day by day, with the value decisions which shape the future of their own lives and of our precarious civilization. (p. 17)

Implementation of Design Through Activities

Based on the outcomes and goals described in the preceding outline, we also planned a set of activities that we hoped would implement these objectives and produce the desired outcome. In the model program, career-oriented students would engage in the following activities:

    1. Students would be exposed at a conceptual level to a broad cross-section of areas and activities in the working world where psychology has relevance and application;

    2. Students would identify resources for skill training and receive training in basic transferable skills;

    3.   Students would be introduced to organizations and settings where psychology is applied;

    4.   Students would perform volunteer work in at least one applied setting;

    5.   Students would experience intensive practicum in at least one setting;

    6.   Students would share experiences with undergraduate students, graduate students, and faculty to integrate conceptual learning with career-planning strategies;

    7.   Students would be trained to use career-planning and decision-making resources;

    8.   Students would be trained in job-finding skills and job placement.

All of these activities involve the three basic processes of this program: (a) learning through experience, (b) analysis and feedback, and (c) career development. Sequencing and coordination of these activities and processes as they were projected are diagrammed in Figure 23-1 (p. 218).

Implementation of Design Through Coursework and Faculty

Four courses were planned to provide the main structure for implementing the program: applied psychology, career development psychology, advanced general psychology, and practicum. In addition, about half of the courses included topics related to the activities and processes of this program; for example, social psychology, abnormal psychology, personality theory, industrial/organizational psychology, the psychology of exceptional children, effective group functioning in organizations, and a seminar in applied psychology.

It is important to note at this point that we had planned to implement this program totally within the psychology department. In addition, the model for the program was predicated on the assumption that a large number of the department faculty would take an active interest in working with and supervising students in a variety of fieldwork settings. As is evident in a later section of this chapter, these assumptions were somewhat naive. Fortunately, several other individuals within the university held similar values concerning career-oriented education. At about the same time that we were planning to implement the program, the College of Arts and Sciences applied for and received a grant from the Lilly Endowment, Inc. to implement a program entitled Career Oriented Value Education (COVE). A main thrust of this program was to develop curriculum and support structures that would aid the various individual faculty and departments in implementing career-oriented education. One of the main outgrowths of that grant was the creation, within the traditional placement office, of a career-planning function. The university placement office was changed to the Career Planning and Placement (CPP) Office.[1]

---

1. See Chapter 26 of this book for a description of this model program.

Figure 23-1. Sequence of activities and processes in the model program.

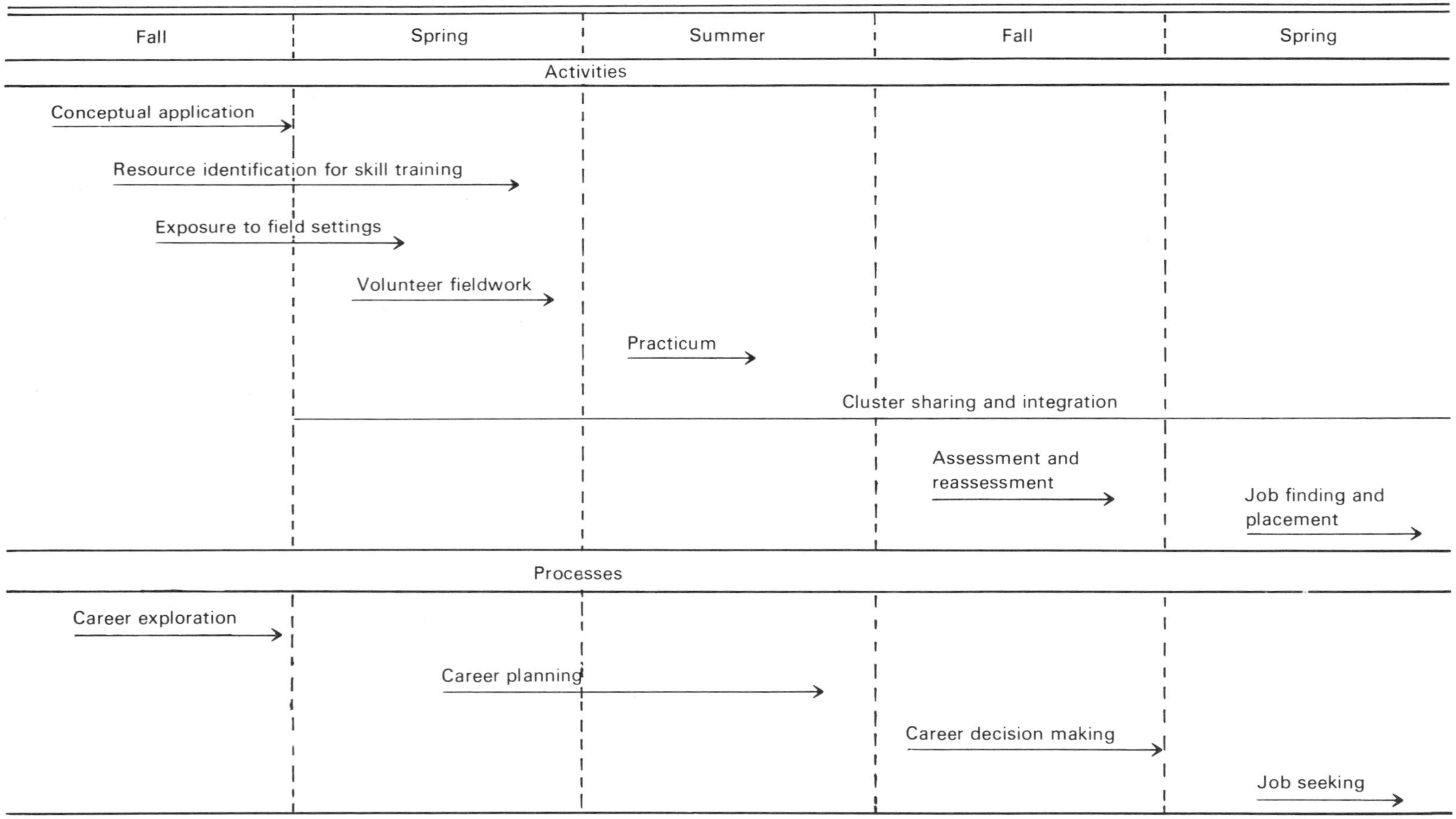

Activities

Fall	Spring	Summer	Fall	Spring
Conceptual application				
Resource identification for skill training				
Exposure to field settings				
	Volunteer fieldwork			
		Practicum		
			Cluster sharing and integration	
			Assessment and reassessment	
				Job finding and placement

Processes

Fall	Spring	Summer	Fall	Spring
Career exploration				
	Career planning			
			Career decision making	
				Job seeking

In addition to the traditional placement function, CPP developed and implemented fieldwork placements for all the students of the college. This office began to gather and collect additional resource information for career exploration, planning, and decision making. At about this same time the dean of the College of Arts and Sciences also began publicly to support the concept of fieldwork or practica for undergraduates. The developers of CPP knew of our interest in practica for students, and the timing was perfect. The CPP's development of practicum placements and the implementation of our career-oriented program overlapped considerably. We worked jointly with the CPP staff around the practicum concept and became the academic unit that provided the first students as well as the faculty supervision. In addition, we agreed to supervise a few students from other departments at the start of this program. In return, CPP developed the community contacts, negotiated a fairly broad set of practicum sites, and assisted in helping students choose an appropriate site.

Original Design Versus Actual Program

As indicated earlier in this chapter, many programs similar to the one described here do not supply data on the success or failure of the program. This section attempts to take the elements of the initial design and the projected activities of that design and compare them with the program as it is currently being implemented at St. Louis University.

Conceptual Application

In the applied psychology course of this program students are exposed to a systematic career–life planning process. For approximately one-third of the course the instructor clarifies and defines career areas and gives specific examples of how psychology applies in some of these areas. These examples are followed up by visits from those co-workers in the community who indicate to the students how psychology applies in their individual field. Finally, students are required to report on a career area of their own choosing. This career report must contain a definition of the career area, specification of a career ladder, specification of the knowledge and skills required for at least two levels of the career area, interviews of three people within the career area, a book report and outline related to the career area, and a determination of the career potential in this area.

Other courses indicate to students how psychology relates to other occupational areas. For example, as part of the introductory statistics and methods course, all students majoring in psychology are exposed to eight different data-collection strategies ranging from case studies and field research to laboratory research. This course also indicates the variety of areas in which these data-gathering strategies are used. In the learning and motivation course, theories are applied to problems of child rearing, education, and health. Students are also supplied with examples of career areas where psychology seems to have relevance: corrections, juvenile delinquency, social work, mental health, special education, mental retardation, sales, personnel, labor relations, marketing, evaluation research, and management in general.

Resource Identification for Skill Training

The model program was not designed as vocational training; therefore, the skill training provided was planned to be general and transferable rather than specific and in depth. As planned, the major focus of this training is to acquaint the student (a) with the basic skills needed in the application of psychology and (b) with resources available for acquiring these skills. The applied psychology course implements the design by identifying courses, people, books, topics, workshops, etc., and helps students to identify and anticipate their need to acquire specific skill training on their own. The importance of communications skills, group process skills, research and statistical skills, and decision-making skills is stressed where appropriate to a particular applied area.

Introduction to Fieldwork Settings

The original design of the program intended to introduce students to the range of settings in which they would be able to gain experience, to the problems they would face, and to people who would work in these settings. These plans were to be implemented through guest speakers in the applied psychology course, field trips, films, and videotapes. Other than the use of guest speakers, these aspects of the program have not been implemented. Rather, CPP serves this function; the director of CPP visits the applied psychology course, explains the purpose and function of CPP, publicizes and promotes the practicum program, and indicates to the students the importance of career planning. In addition, when students decide to explore the possibility of a practicum, they are directed to the CPP where they are given descriptions of the job responsibilities, settings, and learning opportunities available to them in field placement. After discussion with their faculty supervisor, students then interview at the practicum site. Typically, students will return to discuss the practicum with the faculty supervisor and to make a selection.

Volunteer Fieldwork

The original design called for students to choose from a pool of specific settings (agencies, organizations, etc.) in which to do volunteer work for one semester. The purpose of this work was for students to gain firsthand experience and skills that could be used in career planning and to apply psychology in a work setting.

As originally planned, this volunteer fieldwork was to be a mini-introduction to the practicum. The amount of time a student wanted to devote to volunteer work was planned to be approximately from three to five hours per week for 15 weeks. If agreeable with the various organizations, a student could choose to spend the entire 15 weeks with one organization or to spend about 5 weeks in each of three agencies. Volunteer fieldwork was meant to be a gradual introduction to field experience that would give the student an idea of the range of opportunities available in a practicum.

Volunteer work, however, has been dropped from the program sequence. Our initial experience has been that students who show an interest in fieldwork are willing to move directly into the practicum experience. The goals of the volunteer aspect of the program have now been incorporated into the practicum.

Practicum

In the original design, volunteer field experience was to be followed by a 10–12-week practicum. This practicum was planned to be equivalent to a full-time summer job in an organization where psychology had clear application. This component of the model program was based on the assumption that students had begun to identify specific settings and possible career options. The practicum was planned to intensify the student's skill learning and to allow the student to evaluate more realistically at least one career option. The additional benefit of work experience would strengthen the student's skills and job potential.

Actual implementation of the practicum has been a compromise of the original plans for the volunteer fieldwork and the practicum. Almost all students spend from 10 to 15 hours per week at a practicum site of their choosing. Most students know what is expected of them in their field placement, since it usually is negotiated as part of the interview they conduct before they accept the practicum. In addition, students negotiate with their faculty supervisor and specify their personal educational, and career goals in relationship to the practicum in terms of knowledge to be gained, attitudes or values to be investigated, and skills to be acquired. Student progress on goals and outcomes is checked by advisers throughout the semester.[2]

Cluster Sharing and Integration

The original design called for clusters of students with different levels of field experiencce to work together under the supervision of a faculty member and a graduate student.[3] The general concept, called "vertical team," states that students can learn from each other and that those with

2. The process of initial contact of the student with CPP and with the faculty supervisor, initial site negotiation, goal setting, etc., has been specified in a "Handbook for Faculty Supervision of Interns." This document has been adopted by CPP and is now sent to all faculty who supervise students on internships (see Chapter 26 of this book for a complete description of this document).

3. This concept was modeled after one that was used for several years in the authors' clinical graduate program and that is currently being used in their evaluative-applied program with excellent success.

greater experience are effective learning resources for those with lesser experience. The original plan called for clusters of from five to eight undergraduates to meet weekly for one-hour sessions with a graduate student and a faculty member. These clusters of students were to start functioning each spring semester. The cluster would include a set of undergraduate students who had been through their practicum and a set of students just starting their volunteer work. Students would function as a cluster throughout the spring, summer, and fall semesters or until they dropped out (i.e., graduated). The graduate student working with them was to be a third- or fourth-year student from one of our applied programs (clinical or evaluative-applied); the faculty supervisor would come from the same program.

This activity of the original design was never fully implemented. However, on several occasions, clusters of students working during the same semester in practicum have formed a group that meets weekly or biweekly for one or two hours. This arrangement has some benefits as well as liabilities. The cluster idea seems to work best among students who are working in similar practicum sites. These students can visit each others' institutional settings to see the similarities and differences. This exchange is profitable both for faculty and students. On the other hand, when students who are working in very different kinds of practicum sites are grouped together, the difference in experience is so great that students have difficulty seeing how one person's experience translates or is useful to a student in a different setting. The students seem to have difficulty abstracting common elements from different experiences. Currently, we are following the practical approach of clustering students with similar practica. When a student has a practicum placement that is unique and not similar to that of any other student, the faculty deals with that student on an individual basis. The primary disadvantages of this approach are that faculty supervision time is greatly increased and that such students do not learn from the experiences of other students.

Assessment and Reassessment

One of the planned purposes of the senior-year course (advanced general psychology) was to provide students with an opportunity for self-assessment with respect to their personal goals. This assessment would also give the department the opportunity to assess its own effectiveness in achieving the stated outcomes of the program. The course was to be offered during the fall semester so that the assessment information could be used before the students graduated.

As this course has developed, career planning has been integrated into a broader personal self-analysis that includes assessment of cognitive abilities, personality, values, interests, and social skills. The self-analysis serves two purposes: it integrates the knowledge of psychological theories with facts that students have learned in previous courses, and it relates career planning to student self-concepts. About one-third of the course is devoted to a continued demonstration of applied aspects of psychology. Presentations are made of some of the applied research being done in the department (e.g., sleep research, environmental psychology, depression).

Job Finding and Placement

Since some of the faculty members included in this program had extensive expertise in applied areas, the original design planned that these individuals would work closely with students in job-finding and placement activities. These individuals would provide procedures that each student could personally implement.

However, we underestimated the amount of time and the degree of commitment both of ourselves and other department members. Fortunately, CPP increased the quality and quantity of the services available to students and more than adequately performed the following job placement activities:

1. Communicated with the local business community and identified entry- and second-level positions appropriate to students in this program;

2. Educated the local community on the background, skills, and general value to them of the students;

3. Gauged the need for the outcomes of this program and collected data useful for both students and program modification;

4. Coordinated students with appropriate positions based on students' qualifications, training, performance, and desire;

5. Counseled students about job seeking and placement;

6. Established job files, sample résumés, etc.;

7. Assisted individual students in securing positions upon graduation.

Summary of Student Activities

All of the students who elected the career-oriented option were exposed to some of the essential activities described. Those students who chose to involve themselves in the field experience sequence were given increasing levels of exposure to organizations in which psychology had application. The sequence finally focused on finding jobs that were consistent with a student's individual needs, values, and talents.

Other Considerations

The program was originally planned to cover a two-year sequence. Actually, some students went through the sequence in three years while other students compressed the program into a nine-month period. The flexibility needed for the various kinds of students prevented full implementation of the cluster-sharing activity. In addition, the original design planned for most students to take their practicum during the summer months, but in fact the students worked at their practicum throughout the year. Some students desired only one in-depth fieldwork experience, while others desired two, which is acceptable under the department requirements.

Originally the program assumed that a number of faculty in the department would have some level of involvement in this sequence. However, most faculty were not prepared or were not able to make the time commitment required to provide extensive career advisement within this model.

In addition, we underestimated the amount of time needed to fully implement this program. Without the assistance of CPP the program itself would not have had the time to develop and implement practicum placements.

We were surprised by the amount of student resistance to career planning. Only a well-motivated minority of students was willing to think in terms of career alternatives and decision strategies. Even in the senior year, students were reluctant to explore career alternatives in a low-risk setting. It has been suggested (Sarason, Sarason, & Cowden, 1975) that student resistance to thinking about the future is related to the fear of aging and death. Whatever the reason, many students do not heed the advice to embark on career planning early in their educational career.

However, the program seems to have succeeded for most of the 35 students involved. Several students have acquired positions after graduation from the organization that provided the practicum. Virtually all of the students reported that they valued the career exploration and career-planning aspects of field experience. A few students discovered that they did not wish to pursue a career in an area that they once thought was of interest to them. This discovery can be regarded as a success. Many of the students have grown personally as well as intellectually as a function of this program. Currently, CPP is conducting an extensive study to compare the personal growth impact of the practicum. In conclusion, the program is in effect and working, but is conducted by a small group of committed faculty who spend less time than was originally planned with a group of students that is smaller than originally planned.

REFERENCE NOTE

1. Educational-Community Counselors Associates. *Analysis of ACT program class profile reports of enrolled and non-enrolled applicants to St. Louis University for the academic years 1970–71, 1971–72, 1972–73* (Report prepared for Project 21). St. Louis University, 1973.

REFERENCES

Korn, J. H. Training and employment of BA psychologists: Report of a symposium. *Teaching Psychology Newsletter*, February 1974, pp. 10–12.

Kulik, J. A. *Undergraduate education in psychology*. Washington, D.C.: American Psychological Association, 1973.

Levine, A., & Weingart, J. *Reform of undergraduate education*. San Francisco: Jossey-Bass, 1973.

Pinkus, R. B., & Korn, J. H. The preprofessional option: An alternative to graduate work in psychology. *American Psychologist*, 1973, *28*, 710–718.

Sarason, S. B., Sarason, E. K., & Cowden, P. Aging and the nature of work. *American Psychologist*, 1975, *30*, 584–592.

Watson, G. Origins, intent, and current developments. In S. Baskin (Ed.), *Organizing nontraditional study*. San Francisco: Jossey-Bass, 1974.

Yankelovich, D. Turbulence in the working world: Angry workers, happy grads. *Psychology Today*, December 1974, pp. 80–87.

Part IV

The Undergraduate Major:
Surveys, Models, and Problems

24

Harry J. Parker and John L. Hedl, Jr.

The Bachelor's Degree in Psychology: Its Status in the Southwest

The survey reported in this chapter, while only covering the Southwest, may be of interest and relevance to departments in other regions as well. It was designed to assess the purposes of the psychology major, the curricular emphases, the nature and selection of required fieldwork-practica, and the subsequent employment of psychology graduates for both public and private colleges and universities. Psychology department chairpersons from four-year institutions in the Southwest (Arkansas, Arizona, Kansas, Louisiana, New Mexico, Oklahoma, and Texas) were contacted by mail in 1974–1975. Eighty-one percent of the 150 schools provided usable data. In terms of general curricular purpose, the region's private schools did not differ greatly from its public schools. The major in psychology in both types of institution was used primarily as preparation for graduate school or as part of a broad-based liberal arts and sciences education. Future employment in psychologically oriented occupations, fulfillment of academic degree requirements, and preparation of high school psychology teachers were seen as less important purposes of a degree in psychology.

Since the 1960s, colleges and universities have been under societal and legislative pressure to increase the "relevance" of their academic programs as well as provide a heightened level of fiscal responsibility often labeled accountability. Undergraduate programs in psychology have been no exception to this pervasive trend. Cates (1973) noted that psychology training was perceived by 48 percent of a sample of baccalaureate degree holders to be only "somewhat related" to their immediate educational or career plans. In a survey of undergraduate students and faculty, Lipsey (1974) noted that approximately one-half of the sample identified relevance as the most important issue confronting psychology today. Relevance was interpreted in a general way to indicate perceived curricular relationships to societal problems, the "real world," etc.

To clarify the status of baccalaureate training in psychology, Parker (1973) reviewed a number of federal, state, and local job descriptions. He found that a significant number require baccalaureate-degree credentials for entry, especially in the social sciences. In another study of employment options for psychology majors, Pinkus and Korn (1973) recommended that the American Psychological Association (APA) consider a broadened view of career opportunities that could be legitimately pursued with a bachelor's degree. More specific recommendations of this study included (a) the development of a handbook for psychology advisers containing job market information at the bachelor's-degree level and (b) the expansion of manpower systems and placement to include bachelor's positions in psychology.

With this background, and as part of a task force appointed by the Texas Psychological Association (TPA) in 1974, Parker (1975) studied all Texas universities and colleges offering a major in psychology. The purposes of this study were to determine the (a) purposes of the baccalaureate degree, (b) three major occupations graduates enter via psychology preparation, (c) primary curricular emphasis(es) of the psychology major, and (d) fieldwork-practica experiences and time allotment required in the major. All 60 degree-granting private and public schools replied to the inquiry, with 27 private and 22 public schools having majors in psychology upon which to report data. The Texas study indicated that private and public schools differed significantly on two issues. First, private schools were able to identify specific occupational entries of their graduates. Second, private schools provided greater involvement with fieldwork-practica experiences than the public schools.

Since only one state was involved in this evaluation, there was a desire on the part of the TPA task force to determine if these data were characteristic of the southwestern region, and to determine if Texas was unique, similar, or different in its treatment of the undergraduate major in psychology. Accordingly, a study of the southwestern geographical region was undertaken to provide a basis for comparison with the Texas data.

Method

A total of 90 private and public baccalaureate degree-granting institutions in states identified with the southwestern region were contacted by mail in the fall of 1975. Of these schools, 77 (86%) responded to the survey. Of the respondents, 4 did not offer a psychology degree or were no longer collegiate institutions and were excluded from further consideration. The total sample included 31 private schools and 42 public schools. The response rate by states was as follows: Arkansas—13 of 16 schools; Arizona—6 of 6 schools; Kansas—19 of 24 schools; Louisiana—16 of 19 schools; New Mexico—6 of 8 schools; and Oklahoma—17 of 17 schools.

Harry J. Parker is Professor of Physical Medicine and Rehabilitation, Professor of Psychology, and Professor of Rehabilitation Science at the University of Texas Health Science Center at Dallas. John L. Hedl, Jr. is Associate Professor of Allied Health Education at the University of Texas Health Science Center at Dallas.

This study was used as a basis for Harry J. Parker's Presidential Address at the meeting of the Southwestern Psychological Association, April 30, 1976. The Texas study and the regional study grew out of the Texas Psychological Association Task Force, "Characteristics and Problems of Subdoctoral Psychology," of which Harry J. Parker was a member.

Based upon experience in the previous Texas study (Parker, 1975), the survey form was modified and expanded. Department chairpersons were asked to indicate (a) purpose(s) of the psychology major at their institution, (b) curricular emphasis(es) of their psychology major, (c) nature and selection of any required fieldwork-practica, and (d) a percentage emphasis for each curricular purpose identified. In ranking responses to questions, multiple or equivalent ranks were permitted. The survey was in letter form, signed by the authors, and directed to the chair or head of the department of psychology. It also requested the signature and title(s) of the individual completing the form.

Results and Discussion

The analyses of the present study compared the responses of the 31 private schools and 42 public schools in the southwestern region to the Texas data collected in the fall of 1974 (Parker, 1975). In certain instances, the regional data are not directly comparable to the Texas data due to minor modifications of the survey.

Reasons or Purposes for Psychology Major

Table 24-1 presents the percentage distribution of responses for Question 1 for the region and for Texas. On Question 1, private schools in the region ranked "a broad base in liberal arts and science education" (E) first, with "graduate admission" (A) a close second, followed by "employment in psychologically oriented occupations" (C), "fulfill an academic offering" (D), "prepare teachers of high school psychology" (B), and "other" (F). Texas private schools differed slightly, ranking A first and then E, C, B, D, and F. For public schools in the region, A ranked first with E, C, D, B, and F following. Texas public schools ranked A first and E a close second, followed by C, B, D, and F.

A review of these rankings suggests a rather equal emphasis between private and public schools in the region and Texas on the issue of primary purpose (i.e., graduate admission and broad base in liberal arts and sciences). It appeared that preparation of teachers of high school psychology is similarly ranked (fifth) by both private and public schools in the region, while Texas schools ranked this option one rank higher (fourth). A Spearman rho correlation coefficient of .98 was obtained for the rankings of private versus public regional institutions, reflecting the analysis above. Between the region and Texas private schools, a Spearman rho correlation coefficient of .93 was obtained, while for public schools the relationship was .98.

Employment in Psychologically Oriented Occupations

Question 2 asked, "If your major has for one of its purposes the employment of graduates in psychologically oriented occupations, please list three (3) specific occupations your graduates enter." As may be noted in

TABLE 24-1   Percentage Distribution of Ranks for Purposes of Major in Psychology

Reason or purpose for the curriculum design of the psychology major	Private school ranks							Public school ranks						
	1	2	3	4	5	6	n^a	1	2	3	4	5	6	n^b
A. Designed for graduate school admission														
Southwestern region	39	35	16	3	3	3	31	39	49	12	0	0	0	41
Texas	46	15	27	8	4	0	25	33	24	33	10	0	0	21
B. Designed to prepare teachers of high school psychology														
Southwestern region	0	0	14	38	48	0	21	4	0	14	18	64	0	28
Texas	5	9	23	9	41	14	22	6	11	22	28	33	0	18
C. Designed to prepare graduates for employment in psychologically oriented occupations in industry														
Southwestern region	14	25	32	25	4	0	28	8	17	40	26	9	0	35
Texas	22	13	17	48	0	0	23	5	36	32	21	5	0	19
D. Designed to fulfill an academic offering as established by faculties and governing officials														
Southwestern region	4	16	20	32	24	4	25	6	12	18	50	15	0	34
Texas	0	37	16	11	32	5	19	11	11	11	22	44	0	19
E. Designed to provide a broad base in behavioral science as part of a liberal arts and sciences education														
Southwestern region	53	30	10	3	3	0	30	54	20	20	5	0	2	41
Texas	52	22	13	9	0	4	23	76	10	5	0	10	0	21
F. Designed to (other, please list)														
Southwestern region	0	0	25	25	25	25	4	50	0	0	0	0	50	4
Texas	29	29	14	14	14	0	7	50	0	0	0	0	50	2

Note. All percentages have been rounded off and may not equal 100%; percentage signs are omitted.
[a] Total number of private schools = 58: 31 in the southwestern region and 27 in Texas.
[b] Total number of public schools = 64: 42 in the southwestern region and 22 in Texas.

Table 24-1, this option (C) ranked third in priority for all schools in the region and Texas, with over 83% of the schools assigning rank to this purpose among others. For the 82% of the private schools in the region who ranked the item and furnished job information, the mean rank was 2.3. Texas private schools (74%) showed a mean rank of 3.7. Ten percent of the private schools in the region and 15% in Texas did not assign a rank to this option. For the 68% of the public schools in the region who ranked the item and furnished job information, the mean rank was 3.1, whereas Texas public schools showed a mean rank of 4.3. Seventeen percent of the public schools in the region and 14% in Texas did not rank this option. These data suggest that Texas public and private schools were less oriented toward occupations than their regional counterparts.

Interestingly, within the region 18% of the private schools who ranked the item failed to provide job information, while 31% of the public schools were so identified. In Texas, 26% of the private schools and 42% of the public schools revealed this response. In addition, the public schools were less apt to include a list of three occupations (mean number listed was 2.7), whereas all private schools who ranked the item listed three entries. Collectively, these data suggest public schools to be consistently less concerned with job information and job relevance than the private schools.

Further, it was evident that the public and private school chairpersons differed in their listing of specific occupations for their graduates.

To further explicate these findings, a more detailed descriptive analysis was completed on the responses from Question 2. Specifically, a tabulation was made of the number and nature of the specific occupations cited (as asked in the survey; see Table 24-2) in comparison to the number and nature of job settings (not asked by the question; see Table 24-3) that were listed. These findings were then compared across regional and public–private school differences.

For both the private and public schools in the region and in Texas, considerable similarity was found in the occupational titles that were cited most frequently. As may be noted in Table 24-2, the occupations of

TABLE 24-2   Specific Occupations Graduates Enter Upon Completion of Major in Psychology

Specific occupation	Private schools		Public schools	
	Southwestern region (n = 23)	Texas (n = 17)	Southwestern region (n = 24)	Texas (n = 12)
Psychology aide	5	2	6	1
Personnel clerk		1	1	
Child care worker	2	2		
Caseworker	5	2	3	
Probation officer	2	1	3	1
Teacher (elementary and secondary)	1	1	2	
Counselor (vocational rehabilitation, probation, alcohol and drug)	2	2	4	1
Test construction specialist		1		
School psychologist			1	1
Counselor (unspecified)	10	4	4	
Psychological tester, rehabilitation tester, psychometrist	2		5	
Social worker	2		1	
Community planner	1		1	
House or cottage parent	2			
Clinical psychologist	1		2	
Behavior modification/ behavior management			4	
University teacher			1	
Special education worker			1	
Research assistant			1	

Note. Schools were asked to supply three specific occupations; numbers indicate frequency of their responses. Not all schools provided three occupations.

counselor and psychology aide were cited most frequently. Surprisingly, caseworker was also cited since it is generally associated with sociological or social work curricula. Further, the regional schools, both public and private, were more likely to cite specific occupations across a wider range of occupations than the Texas schools.

Curricular Emphasis of Major in Psychology

Question 3 asked the department chairpersons to rank the emphasis(es) of the major. Multiple ranks could be used (Table 24-4). In the region, private schools (N = 31) ranked "general" first, followed by "experi-

TABLE 24-3   Occupational Settings of Graduates After Completing Major in Psychology

	Private schools		Public schools	
Job setting	Southwestern region (n = 23)	Texas (n = 17)	Southwestern region (n = 24)	Texas (n = 12)
Mental health, mental retardation	6	5	5	4
Hospitals and mental hospitals		1	2	1
Social and community agencies		1		6
Welfare	3	4	2	1
Corrections		2		1
Church-related work	1	2		1
Social work	5	4	2	
Probation	1	3		
Personnel	4	2	2	3
Clinics (e.g., mental health clinics)		2		2
Industrial management business research, industry	3	1	4	5
Institutional/agency research	1	1	1	
Teaching	1		1	2
Advertising				1
Criminal justice, law enforcement	3		1	
Preschool programs	1			
Rest or nursing homes	1			
Government programs agencies	2		2	
Graduate training			1	
Medical laboratories	1		1	
Sales			2	

Note. Information in this table was derived from the responses on specific occupations shown in Table 24-2.

TABLE 24-4   Assignment of Ranks for Curricular Emphasis

	Private schools		Public schools	
Curricular emphasis	Southwestern region ($n = 31$)	Texas ($n = 27$)	Southwestern region ($n = 42$)	Texas ($n = 22$)
General	27	20	41	17
Experimental (e.g., learning, physiological, perception	25	5	38	4
Applied (e.g., mental health, community, industrial-business, personnel, behavior management	23	10	37	6
Other	6	5	9	1

Note. Numbers indicate the number of schools assigning a rank to a curricular category; schools could rank as many curricular emphases as applicable.

mental," "applied," and "other" with a mean number of 2.6 ranks. Although the Texas study did not direct the respondent to rank, but simply to indicate applicable emphases, the results are useful for comparison. Texas private schools (N = 27) most frequently cited "general," followed by "applied," "experimental," and "other" (the same order as the region) and had a mean of 1.5 checks, notably less than the region's private schools. Regional public schools (N = 42) ranked "general," "experimental," "applied," and "other" with a mean number of 3.0 ranks. Texas public schools (N = 22) ranked "general," "applied," "experimental," and "other" with a mean number of checks of 1.3.

These data indicate that the regional private and public institutions indicated more curricular or mixed emphases in the major than Texas schools. The "general" label, however, was the primary and predominant identification of the curriculum for a major in psychology in the southwest. It should be noted that some private schools that cited "other" prominently used terms like *eclectic* and *humanistic* to describe their curriculum. The frequencies of these responses were too limited to provide meaningful comparisons, however.

Percentage of Emphasis for Curriculum Ranked

Question 4 sought to determine the amount of emphasis, whether singular or multiple, in terms of percentage assigned (Table 24-5). Since these data were not secured in the Texas study, only data from the region can be analyzed. The results of this analysis indicated that private schools (N = 31) assigned the mean percentages as follows: "general" (53%), "applied" (28%), "experimental" (25%), and "other" (16%). Public schools (N = 42) assigned their mean percentages as follows: "general" (47%), "experimental" (30%), "other" (23%), and "applied" (18%). These data indicate that the public and private schools in the region allocate approximately 50% of their time and probably resources to support a general academic program in psychology.

Private schools, however, indicated a more even balance between applied and experimental aspects of their program. Public schools appeared to emphasize experimental activities to a much greater extent than applied aspects. These findings are to be expected given the purposes identified by the public schools (i.e., graduate school admission and broad-based liberal arts and science purposes).

Requirement of Fieldwork-Practica Experience

Question 5 asked, "As part of your major in psychology, do you require the student to spend time in fieldwork-practica within a mental hospital, clinic, health agency, business-industry, school, etc.?" (Table 24-6). For regional private schools (N = 31), 74% replied "no", while Texas private schools (N = 27) had 78% "no" responses. Regional public schools (N = 41) were more emphatic, with 93% saying "no", while Texas public schools (N = 22) were equally negative with 91%.

Statistically significant differences were obtained at the .02 level for frequencies from regional private and public schools, and at the .05 level for frequencies of the Texas private and public schools. No statistically significant differences existed between the frequencies cited for regional private and public schools and Texas schools.

Clearly, the private schools in the region and in Texas showed more disposition to a requirement of fieldwork-practica as part of a major in psychology. This was consistent with the private schools' identification of specific occupational citations (Table 24-2) and in greater numbers than public schools. This significant difference must be assessed for the future of psychology, and indeed the lack of exposure for the student denies an element of education. Psychology and its societal role also is seriously constrained if uses cannot be identified in our society.

Part 2 of Question 5 stated, "If yes, indicate the total hours that are required in the major" (Table 24-7). In the region, 7 private schools reported a range of 8–1,040 clock hours and a mean of 312 clock hours. Six

TABLE 24-5   Assignment of Ranks and Distribution of Percentages for Curricular Emphasis by Schools in the Southwestern Region

Curricular emphasis	Private schools (n = 31)		Public schools (n = 42)	
	No. schools assigning ranks	Average % assigned	No. schools assigning ranks	Average % assigned
General	27	53	41	47
Experimental (e.g., learning, physiological, perception)	25	25	38	30
Applied (e.g., mental health, community, industrial-business, personnel, behavior management)	23	28	37	18
Other	6	16	9	23

Note. Schools could assign more than one rank.

TABLE 24-6   Responses to a Requirement for Students to Spend Time in Fieldwork-Practica

	Private schools				Public schools			
	Southwestern region (n = 31)		Texas (n = 27)		Southwestern region (n = 42)		Texas (n = 22)	
Response	No. responses	%	No. responses	%	No. responses[a]	%	No. responses	%
Yes	8	26	6	22	3	7	2	9
No	23	74	21	78	38	93	20	91

[a] One school did not provide data.

Texas private schools reported a range of 64–240 clock hours and a mean of 102 clock hours. Regional private schools had a greater range than and over three times the mean hours of Texas schools. Three regional public schools reported a range of 6–320 clock hours and a mean of 213 hours. Only two public schools in Texas indicated a range of 6–25 clock hours, and a mean of 15.5 hours. These data clearly indicated that private schools exceeded the number of public schools in identifying the experience, and in the number of hours of experience involved. This appeared for both the regional and Texas schools.

Part 3 of Question 5 asked, "If you have a requirement for fieldwork-practica, please rank the manner in which the setting is chosen (Table 24-8). Seven regional private schools and 3 public schools provided data. While these data were too limited for broad analysis, some insights can be gained. Private schools selected "student–faculty and setting share equally in decision about a setting" first; "student individually selects the setting" and "student and faculty jointly share in a decision about a setting" were tied for next most prominent. For public schools, "student and faculty jointly share equally in a decision about a setting" and "choice of setting related to physical proximity of the school" were tied for most prominent selection.

It would appear that student and faculty share in the decision about choice of fieldwork-practica setting, which is generally regarded as ideal, if not desirable. Not surprisingly, other variations such as "student individually selects" and "faculty individually selects" were noted, suggesting that some departments of psychology are not fully committed to cooperative evaluation of the setting. No Texas comparison was available since such data were not secured.

TABLE 24-7   Clock Hours Required in Fieldwork-Practica for Psychology Major

	Private schools			Public schools		
Area	n	Range (hours)	M (hours)	n	Range (hours)	M (hours)
Southwestern region	7[a]	8–1,040	312	3	6–320	213
Texas	6	64–240	102	2	6–25	15.5

[a] One school did not provide data.

TABLE 24-8   Assignment of Ranks (1–7) for Manner of Selection of Required Fieldwork Practica Setting in the Southwestern Region

Manner of selection	Private school[o] ranks							Public school[o] ranks						
	1	2	3	4	5	6	7	1	2	3	4	5	6	7
Student individually selects setting		2	1	1							1			
Faculty individually selects setting		1	1	1						1				
Setting individually selects student					2							1		
Student and faculty jointly share decision about setting	3	1							2					
Student, faculty, and setting share equally in decision about setting	4			1										
Choice of setting related to physical proximity of school			1			1				1				1
Other							1							

Note. Schools could rank more than one of the seven categories. No Texas data are included.
[o] Eight schools reported a requirement for fieldwork-practica, but one school did not report data.
[o] Three schools reported a requirement for fieldwork-practica.

Conclusions

A review of the total region suggests that, overall, private schools do not differ too significantly from public schools. Some specific differences were noted and warrant repetition here. Private schools in the Southwest show more disposition to citing both occupational titles and settings than public schools. In view of the pressure for relevance or societal use of psychology, it raises a serious question as to why public schools are slower to recognize occupational relevance to society than private schools. The identification of job settings rather than specific occupational titles (which were requested) suggests that departments of psychology have not systematically secured employment information from graduates.

The clear identification of graduate admission as the primary purpose of the major in psychology for both private and public schools suggests further that the departments of psychology are not in stride with the job market of today and of the immediate future. "Applied" program emphases were not as prominent as "general." This finding helps explain the preservation of graduate admission as a major emphasis.

The remarkably limited emphasis upon fieldwork-practica experience as a required element in a major, particularly among public schools, was a significant finding. Certainly, lack of encounter with societal uses of psychology prevents departments of psychology from appraising job relevance. This lack of involvement makes status quo curricula understandable.

The significant inclination of private schools to involve themselves in fieldwork-practica more than public schools seems paradoxical. In many cases for private schools, financial limitation prevents the likelihood of meeting a broad range of experiences. It is also assumed that public pressure on public institutions can promote changes. Data from this study suggest that public schools are not apparently subject to any significant pressures for relevance or reality-based curricula.

As noted in the Texas study, psychology has an opportunity to determine if it wants to be a responsible profession in a contemporary society and make timely changes in its bachelor's-degree offerings. Are we up to the challenge?

REFERENCES

Cates, J. Baccalaureates in psychology: 1969 and 1970. *American Psychologist*, 1973, *28*, 262–264.

Lipsey, M. W. Research and relevance: A survey of graduate students and faculty in psychology. *American Psychologist*, 1974, *29*, 541–543.

Parker, H. J. *Employment opportunities for a baccalaureate degree in psychology.* Paper presented at the annual meeting of the Texas Psychological Association, Dallas, Texas, December 7, 1973.

Parker, H. J. The baccalaureate degree in psychology: Purpose, curricula, training and employability in Texas. *Texas Psychologist*, 1975, *27*, 25–30.

Pinkus, R. B., & Korn, J. H. The professional option: An alternative to graduate work in psychology. *American Psychologist*, 1973, *28*, 363–372.

25

Walter Mink

The Undergraduate Major: Preparation for Career or Graduate School?

This chapter reports a questionnaire survey of a sample of midwestern departments of psychology in liberal arts colleges and university graduate departments of psychology. The survey was conducted to determine these schools' perceptions of and responses to changing patterns of (a) student interest in psychology as a major and (b) career opportunities for psychology majors. Most undergraduate departments sampled offered internship, practicum, and instructional experience to their students and recognized that many of their students have career orientations. Graduate departments, however, attached no special significance to such types of undergraduate experience in their selection procedures, preferring their applicants to have undergraduate research experience. Graduate department respondents indicated traditional expectations of the role of undergraduate departments in the preparation of prospective graduate students.

Although psychology is a science of behavior that permits prediction and control, psychologists have demonstrated a surprising inability to do either with regard to the situation in higher education in the past decade. A major problem facing all undergraduate departments of psychology, especially those in liberal arts colleges, is the assessment of trends in student selection of psychology as a major and in opportunities for psychology graduates to pursue further study or to find employment related to their study.

Four developments related to psychology education from 1967 to 1977 seem to be particularly important: (a) an increase in the number of psychology majors, (b) an increase in the use of paraprofessionals in alternative and traditional human service institutions, (c) a reduction in private and public funding for graduate schools, research programs and advanced professional services, and (d) an increase in the use of undergraduates in instructional roles. This chapter considers the experiences of liberal arts colleges with these developments and the kinds of changes that some of them have made in their psychology programs in response to these developments. Specifically, it considers how undergraduate and graduate departments perceive their own and each other's missions and roles after a decade of changes in student preferences and expectations and drastic alterations in patterns of public and private funding.

A questionnaire was used to evaluate the current practices and expectations of liberal-arts-college departments of psychology and university graduate departments. Psychology department chairpersons of the member colleges of the Associated Colleges of the Midwest, the Great Lakes College Association, and the Twin-City Consortium received the questionnaire. Information was also solicited from the department chairpersons of departments with graduate programs in the Big Ten universities and four other regional universities of equivalent size.

Apparently, the questions were not viewed as trivial, since the reply rate was almost 100%; responses were received from 24 colleges and 13 universities. The more interesting trends in the responses are summarized below, while a complete tabulation of responses to both the undergraduate and graduate department questionnaires is presented at the end of this chapter.

Replies From Undergraduate Programs

1. Most of the responding institutions reported an increase in the number of psychology majors. In fact, as of 1977 the number of majors had doubled since 1965. A plateau reached in 1972 appears to have remained relatively stable in spite of some decline in overall enrollments. The majority of departments predicted that the number of psychology majors would remain stable for the next five years.

2. Even though the number of psychology majors remains high at a time when career opportunities for them seem limited, only two departments restricted the number of majors they accept.

3. Two-thirds of the departments implemented major curricular revisions in the past five years, and one-half predicted major revisions in the next five years. Revisions have generally produced an increase in the number of courses offered in both experimental-theoretical and clinical-applied areas.

4. One-half of the departments reported that they attempt to prepare students for careers at the bachelor's-degree level, and two-thirds believed that it is appropriate to prepare students for psychology-related careers at the bachelor's-degree level.

5. More than three-fourths of the departments used students in instructional roles, especially as tutors and preceptors.

6. Most departments participated in interdepartmental or interdisciplinary courses, though generally on intellectual grounds rather than career-oriented ones.

7. One-third of the departments made curricular changes designed to make students more successful in competing for entry into graduate

Walter Mink is a professor of psychology at Macalester College.

This chapter was originally a paper presented in a symposium entitled "Some Problems of Psychology Departments in Private Liberal Arts Colleges" and held at the meeting of the Midwestern Psychological Association, Chicago, Illinois, May 1976.

school, but almost all departments opposed designing the curriculum primarily for potential graduate students.

Replies From Graduate Programs

1. All but three of the responding graduate departments reduced the number of students they accepted for graduate study, but of those departments, only three anticipated further reductions.

2. In assessing the records of applicants to graduate study in psychology, graduate departments do not hold undergraduate internship experience in disfavor, but they do not view it as favorably as instructional experience, which, in turn, is not viewed as favorably as research experience.

3. Most graduate departments believed that the primary role of undergraduate departments in preparing students for graduate study should be to provide (a) a foundation in experimental-theoretical psychology, (b) exposure to many facets of psychology, and (c) independent study and research experience.

4. Undergraduate courses in experimental psychology, statistics, and other quantitative areas were considered the most important.

5. About half of the graduate departments found it appropriate to make a distinction between experimental and clinical areas in curriculum design and training.

Directions for Undergraduates

What do the data suggest about prospects for undergraduate majors? Students intending to go to graduate school should recognize that graduate departments and undergraduate liberal arts departments still share traditional ideas about the preparation of research-oriented psychologists, whether experimental or clinical. While most undergraduate departments provide for practicum or internship experience in the curriculum for their students, such experience is not given special weight by graduate programs in selecting applicants, nor is it even considered particularly important for students intending to enter clinical programs. Independent research is the undergraduate experience most likely to be viewed as distinctive by graduate departments. (There are alternative training programs for professionals in the helping professions that are not located in graduate departments. Such programs were not sent questionnaires, but it is likely that they would view undergraduate internship experience more favorably.)

What about students who do not go on to graduate study? Pinkus and Korn (1973) and Korn and Nodine (1975) have shown that there are positions in the human services for those with bachelor's degrees but that undergraduate psychology majors do not have a special advantage in competition for those positions. These authors proposed the development of career tracks to prepare undergraduate psychology majors for vocations in the human services. Departments in liberal arts colleges, however, are ambivalent about their role in career preparation. This ambivalence is not surprising, since liberal arts colleges have traditionally emphasized intellectual values and minimized "vocationalism," a function considered best left to other educational institutions. Questionnaire respondents agreed that the primary role of undergraduate departments should not be the preparation of students for graduate school. Yet only half of them made special efforts to prepare their students for careers open to those with bachelor's degrees. While most departments recognized this as an issue to which they should respond, the form of the response was not consistent across departments.

What action should an undergraduate department consider if it wants to incorporate career-oriented training into its curriculum? Rafetto (Note 1) investigated this question and discovered that the skills most sought by potential employers of bachelor's-degree holders are research and measurement skills, interpersonal skills, and communication skills. Apparently, in this age of accountability and program evaluation, the same sort of analytic and quantitative competencies valued by graduate departments are also valued by potential employers.

Rafetto indicated that a problem exists in the flow of information between undergraduate departments and the "real world": Academic psychologists are unaware of opportunities for their students, while prospective employers, in turn, are unaware of the skills and potential contributions of psychology graduates from liberal arts colleges. Perhaps psychologists need to educate themselves about the opportunities in human services for their students and to educate employers about psychology graduates' qualifications.

Given an acceptance of the belief that graduates who don't go on to graduate school should receive more attention from their psychology departments (and there are those who belive that this should not be a department's primary concern), what steps should be taken? While the questionnaire responses are not specific on this issue, a number of departments are attempting to include career training for their students. Psychology departments should find ways to share their experiences as they develop career-oriented curricular components within the liberal arts context.

REFERENCE NOTE

1. Rafetto, A. M. *Abbreviated version of RULE report.* Beloit, Wis.: Beloit College, 1976. (Mimeo)

REFERENCES

Korn, J. H., & Nodine, B. F. Facts and questions concerning career training of the psychology major. *Teaching of Psychology*, 1975, *2*, 117–119.

Pinkus, R. B., & Korn, J. H. The preprofessional option: An alternative to graduate work in psychology. *American Psychologist*, 1973, *28*, 710–718.

Results From Questionnaire Sent to Undergraduate Psychology Departments in Liberal Arts Colleges

Please indicate the number of majors graduated from your department in each of the following years [not all departments furnished complete lists of numbers of graduates]:

269	1965	658	1974
354	1968	595	1975
441	1970	656	1976
636	1972		

What do you predict the number of majors will be during the next five years?

18	About the same
2	Fewer
3	More
1	Too hard to say

Do you restrict majors in psychology or accept all who choose to major?

2	Restrict number of majors
22	No restriction on number of students

Have you made a major curricular revision in the past five years?

17	Yes
7	No

Do you comtemplate a major curricular revision in the next five years?

12	Yes
12	No

If you did revise your curriculum, did any of the following occur?

11	Increased experimental–theoretical content
8	Increased clinical–applied content
2	Decreased experimental–theoretical content
1	Decreased clinical–applied content
10	Increased experiential–practicum content
6	Other

Do you provide internship or work placement experience for psychology majors?

17	Yes
7	No

Do you think internship or work placement should be part of undergraduate majors?

__15__   Yes

__8__   No

With respect to career education expectations of undergraduate majors, what has been your experience?

__5__   No change in expectations

__7__   Increase in expectations

__9__   Decrease in expectations

Do you make any special effort to prepare majors for psychology-related careers at the BA level?

__11__   Yes

__12__   No

Do you think it appropriate for departments of psychology in liberal arts colleges to prepare students for psychology-related careers at the BA level?

__15__   Yes

__8__   No

Do you use students in instructional roles (as preceptors, tutors, seminar leaders, or originators of courses or course components)?

__19__   Yes

__5__   No

Examples: Lab assistants, proctors, all of the above

Does your department participate in interdepartmental or interdisciplinary courses?

__21__   Yes

__3__   No

If yes, please give examples of programs in which your department has participated in the past five years:

Neuroscience	Psychology and Ethics
Philosophy, Psychology and Myth	Psychology and Biology
Language and Mind	Sports in America
Humanistic Psychology and Education	Human Sexuality
Biosocial Science	Bicentennial Special
Womankind	Religion and Psychology
Social Psychology	Management of Human Resources
Social Science and the City	Psychology of Mind
Myth and Ritual	Animal Behavior
Self, Society, and Value	

(continued)

As access to graduate education has become more restricted have you made any curricular changes to make your students more competitive?

9	Yes
15	No

Do you think that undergraduate departments of psychology should structure the curriculum primarily for students who intend to enter graduate or professional study?

3	Yes
21	No

Results From Questionnaire Sent to Graduate Departments of Psychology

How do you anticipate the current reduction in acceptance of candidates for graduate study in psychology will change in the next five years?

5	No change
3	Further reductions
2	Gradual increases but not to former level
0	Increase eventually to former level
3	There has been no reduction in my department

In your selection of graduate students, what importance do you attach to internship or practicum experience?

4	Other things being equal, it would be viewed favorably
2	Other things being equal, it would be considered very important
7	Would make no difference in selection
0	Would be viewed unfavorably

In your selection of graduate students, what importance do you attach to undergraduate experience in instructional roles (preceptors, discussion leaders, student-managed courses, etc.)?

10	Other things being equal, it would be viewed favorably
0	Other things being equal, it would be considered very important
3	Would make no difference in selection
0	Would be viewed unfavorably

In comparison with undergraduate research experience, how would you view undergraduate teaching or clinical experience in graduate selection?

9	Undergraduate research experience most important
1	All considered equally valuable
0	Undergraduate research experience least important
1	None likely to be critical in selection

What do you think the role of the undergraduate department should be in preparation of students for graduate study? (Indicate more than one role if appropriate.)

12	Provide academic foundation in experimental and theoretical psychology
12	Provide broad exposure to many facets of psychology
2	Provide independent study and research experience
3	Provide opportunities to investigate career interests (through internships or practicums)
1	Provide experience in instructional roles

(continued)

What courses do you consider most important in the undergraduate curriculum for students who anticipate graduate education?

In clinical–applied areas:

Social sciences	4	Statistics	6
Humanities	1	Clinical	2
Practicum experience	3	Industrial	1
Personality	5	Measurement	2
Social	2	Behavior disorders	2
Developmental	1	Philosophy	1
Mathematics	2	Neurosis/psychosis	1

In experimental–theoretical areas:

Lab work	4	History	1
Research	3	"Hard science"	4
Mathematics	4	Cognitive	1
Learning	3	Philosophy	1
Perception	2	Biology	2
Motivation	1		
Theory	1		
Statistics	10		

How do you think undergraduate departments can best assist students in assessing their interest, motivation, and capacity for graduate study?

In Clinical–applied areas:
    Practicum or field experience

In experimental–theoretical areas:

    Statistics
    Research design
    Math
    Lab
    Research experience

Do you think making a distinction between clinical–applied areas and experimental–theoretical areas of graduate study in the previous two questions is justified?

6	Yes
7	No

Thomas J. Kramer and Ellen Harshman

A Model for Faculty Supervision
of Interns

An internship, or off-campus learning experience, can be a valuable method through which students acquire added knowledge, explore attitudes and values, or sharpen and expand skills. However, two primary barriers to an effective internship program are (a) the sizable investment of time needed to identify and negotiate an appropriate internship site for each student, and (b) the increased amount of time required of the supervising faculty member. At Saint Louis University the first barrier has been overcome by the Career Planning and Placement Center's assumption of this responsibility in cooperation with all departments. This chapter addresses the second barrier by describing a systematic, step-by-step model that faculty can follow in the supervision of interns to reduce the amount of time required. The model includes nine steps that faculty go through with each student: initial contact, negotiation of learning goals, selection of internship placement, objectives and activities, methods of evaluation, planning of ongoing contact, the learning contract, ongoing contact, final evaluation. For each step, alternatives that can be chosen by the student and faculty supervisor are described.

This chapter describes a framework from which a faculty member can construct an appropriate and sound internship supervision process. The framework is presented as it has been developed, tested, and refined through use with the Project COVE (Career-Oriented Value Education) at Saint Louis University. Although this model focuses on the faculty member's role in the internship experience, it is important to understand the organizational context in which the internship occurs and the roles of the other constituents.

Saint Louis University is an urban Catholic institution with a strong traditional liberal arts orientation. Under the auspices of the Office of the Dean, the College of Arts and Sciences in the fall of 1975 implemented several programs designed to promote career awareness and to initiate specific career development opportunities for arts and sciences undergraduates. Although such activities were new for the university, they reflected career-related innovations occurring in many similar institutions across the country (Brick & McGrath, 1969; Mayhew, 1977).

One of the most visible of the career development programs is the COVE internship option for arts and sciences undergraduates. Coordination of the COVE program—as well as other career-oriented activities, such as career days and workshops, credit courses, cooperative education and work-study, and the more traditional placement functions—takes place within the Career Planning and Placement Center (CPPC) at Saint Louis University.

The CPPC/COVE staff is responsible in most cases for developing the community contacts leading to the internship placement; for evaluating and communicating to students and faculty the details regarding the various placement possibilities; for negotiating and "matchmaking" among student, faculty member, and site; and for maintaining and monitoring systems.

When negotiations among all involved parties are final and performance criteria are agreed upon, CPPC/COVE assumes a less active role, with the internship per se focusing on the faculty supervisor, the intern, and the site supervisor. (Since one purpose of the internship is to promote greater communication between the academician and the practitioner, site and faculty supervisors are encouraged to deal with each other directly rather than through a CPPC intermediary.)

The Model

What should be learned in college? What should the teaching–learning interaction be? What are the best instructional methods? Is there a "best" learning style? These questions have been asked by educators for decades and have been the focus of those in higher education circles in the past few years as enrollments dwindle. Some answers to these questions may be applicable to large groups of students and instructors "on the average." But for the majority of individual colleges, individual instructors, and individual students, the answer to what is "best" is highly idiosyncratic. Colleges and universities stress different missions and different values under the general goal of providing a suitable learning environment. Instructors differ greatly in what they think students should learn, what they can teach best, the instructional methodology that maximizes their potential to educate, and their flexibility to adapt their teaching style to the student and/or subject matter. Similarly, students have varied interests, values, optimal learning styles, preferences for instructors, and learning needs.

Any learning interaction involves knowledge, attitudes and values, skills, or, of course, a combination of any or all of these. This variety in

Thomas J. Kramer is a professor at the Department of Psychology, Saint Louis University, and Ellen Harshman is Director of the Career Planning and Placement Center at Saint Louis University.

COVE was supported by a grant to Saint Louis University from September 1975 to June 1978 from the Lilly Endowment, Inc.

learning interactions certainly exists at the college level. An introductory history course, for example, would probably be oriented toward acquiring knowledge, whereas a research-methods course would probably stress learning how to design research and conduct statistical tests. Laboratory courses are often skill oriented. Courses in philosophy, literature, and theology usually have a strong value orientation, or the appreciation of different attitudes and values may be the essence of the course. Naturally, in each of the above examples other types of learning may occur that are secondary to the major learning purpose.

An internship, or off-campus, learning experience is a teaching–learning methodology that allows a student to acquire knowledge, attitudes and values, and skills, depending on how the internship is structured. It is an old methodology that has been used in various forms in a wide range of disciplines such as education, nursing, engineering, and marketing. In recent years this same concept has received extremely broad acceptance in liberal arts colleges across the country as an educationally sound methodology when appropriately planned and supervised. The following are the primary advantages of an intership: (a) It allows the student to see how theory can be applied to the real world, (b) it is flexible, (c) it can serve as a meaningful bridge between formal education and a career, (d) it can be individually tailored to student needs, (e) it expands the student's learning opportunities, and (f) it allows a student to acquire new skills.

The internship experience can have disadvantages, however: A sizable investment of time is needed to identify and negotiate an appropriate internship for each student, and more contact time per student is required of the supervising faculty member than for traditional lecture courses.

Saint Louis University's Project COVE has overcome one of the major barriers to the use of internships as a learning device—that of locating an appropriate internship placement. Through contacts with government agencies, community service organizations, and established businesses in the local community, a wide variety of potential internships are available to students in the university's College of Arts and Sciences. The opportunities for learning, the basic responsibilities a student will have, and the kind of on-site supervision available have been determined for most of these internships. By working through CPPC, the administrator of the internship program, the instructor, and the student can together determine internship opportunities appropriate to the student's abilities and interests and then select the internship that they think will maximally meet the student's learning needs.

As mentioned above, most student internships require the time and supervision of a faculty member if they are to be done well. The failure of most internship programs can be traced to the lack of coordination and supervision on the part of faculty. This lack of supervision is also one of the major complaints of on-site supervisors. Therefore, this chapter aims to assist faculty in (a) providing effective off-site direction and supervision to the student, (b) acting as a valuable resource to the student intern, and (c) decreasing the faculty planning time involved.

The process that is described here is recommended to all faculty who plan to supervise student interns. At each step in the process, decisions need to be made. This chapter also identifies some of the alternative decisions available to assist the faculty supervisor and the student in making and implementing the decisions most suited to their needs. The steps of the process are as follows:

1. Initial contact.
2. Negotiation of learning goals.
3. Selection of internship placement.
4. Objectives and activities.
5. Methods of evaluation.
6. Planning of ongoing contact.
7. Learning Contract.
8. Ongoing Contact.
9. Final evaluation and grade.

Before elaborating on each of these steps, it should be noted that this process is presented in idealized form. No faculty supervisor or student will move through this process in exactly the way it is described here. It is merely suggested as a model to aid faculty and students in their efforts to increase the quality and efficiency of the internship experience; they should feel free to deviate from the *sequence* of steps whenever it seems reasonable. All of these steps, however, should be included at some point in the interaction between faculty supervisor and student intern.

Initial Contact

Students may hear about and become interested in exploring the possibility of an internship through any of the following sources: (a) materials distributed by COVE or CPPC (b) a faculty member in class or an adviser, (c) another student intern, or (d) someone at an internship site.

The interested student will contact either a faculty member or CPPC for further information. Ideally, the student should go to CPPC to get a general idea of the variety of internship placements available, the amount of time required, and the kind of activities involved. Some students have unrealistic expectations of these dimensions; contact with CPPC will sketch the boundaries and terms of involvement for the student.

All students who work through the university in obtaining an internship must have a supervisor on campus, someone who assumes responsibility or at least oversees the student. Therefore, once CPPC has acquainted the student with the internship program, it will encourage the student to identify and approach a faculty member who will be able to supervise the student. A faculty member from the student's controlling department is most appropriate to function as the internship supervisor because of general familiarity with the student and knowledge of the student's interests and abilities, general educational preparation, and career goals. Some departments have two or three faculty members, each with different interests, who supervise undergraduate interns. When a student is not able to secure a faculty supervisor, a qualified individual may be designated from CPPC to supervise the student.

When approached by students who request supervision of an internship, faculty members should first direct students to CPPC to determine the scope of internships available. Once students have been to CPPC, then their understanding of the internship possibilities should be assessed. If this understanding is complete and if the reasons for wanting the internship seem appropriate, then a faculty member might tentatively agree to explore further the internship with the student.

Negotiation of Learning Goals

Selection of an internship is directly related to what the student wants to learn as an outcome of the internship placement. Some students may come to a potential faculty supervisor with a specific internship in mind, but this decision might be premature. The goals of the internship and the student qualifications for that particular placement should be clear before a final decision is made.

A wide variety of learning goals can be met through internships. At the same time, faculty tend to differ considerably about what they think are appropriate goals; the student and the faculty supervisor need to agree upon these learning goals. This particular step is probably the most important because it affects each later step.

Since in most internships several learning goals can be met, the faculty supervisor and the student possess fairly wide latitude within which to negotiate, particularly when they do not completely agree. The faculty supervisor and the student may agree on one learning goal, for example, but each may have an additional two that the other does not agree with. To compromise, three learning goals could be selected: one that both agree upon, one suggested by the faculty supervisor, and one suggested by the student.

To assist faculty and students in goal selection, a list of potential learning goals follows. Some of these learning goals may be inappropriate in some programs, but all of them can be accomplished with appropriate internship placement. Possible learning goals include (a) developing a sounder base for career decision making; (b) observing and understanding the actual operation of a particular kind of organization; (c) field testing certain skills learned in classes; (d) determining skills assets and deficiencies; (e) developing or acquiring specific skills; (f) acquiring relevant work experience; (g) acquiring knowledge, content information, or theoretical information on a topic not available at the university; (h) integrating theoretical and applied learning; (i) developing an awareness of the community as a resource for education; (j) building confidence in working in an applied setting; (k) exploring or developing attitudes or values on a particular topic or in a particular setting; and (l) learning more about oneself.

The faculty supervisor and the student should explore this list of learning goals and add to it if appropriate. Then they should select a subset from the list to be accomplished by the student on the internship.

Selection of Internship Placement

When the student and faculty supervisor have selected and agreed upon the learning goals, they should investigate with CPPC the internship placements that might be appropriate for these goals. If the student has an internship site in mind, both should explore the possibility of its satisfying the goals decided upon. If these goals can be accomplished at the preselected site, no further investigation is necessary. If not, the student will have to explore with an appropriate CPPC staff member other internship possibilities where the learning goals may be accomplished. The CPPC can clarify whether a particular learning goal can be accomplished in a particular setting.

Once the student and faculty supervisor have explored internship possibilities with CPPC in light of the learning goals, they should come to an agreement on the actual internship site. Students should fill out the form for specifying the goals to be accomplished, and the form should be signed by the faculty member and returned to CPPC.

Objectives and Activities

Once goals have been specified, how do the student and the supervisor know when these goals have been reached? If a student has specified as a goal the development of a sounder base for career decision making, then indicators of having reached that goal might be the student's ability (a) to more fully describe the desired career, (b) to perform some or all of the duties required when starting that career, and (c) to select (based on the experience of the internship) career areas for further exploration. These objectives or indicators, then, are more specific statements of a learning goal; they allow easier and more objective goal determination.

After appropriate objectives have been specified, the student should determine the activities that will be necessary to achieve each objective. For example, to develop a sounder base for making decisions about a particular career, the student and supervisor might decide that the student should read about this career, assist someone in this career area, or gain firsthand experience in performing most of the daily activities.

For each learning goal, objectives (indicators) to be achieved should be specified. For each objective a set of activities (in sequence, where appropriate) should be specified that would reasonably be expected to bring the student to the achievement of that objective. Careful and thoughtful planning of goals, objectives, and activities at the beginning of the semester will help to assure a successful internship experience for both students and faculty.

At some point during the process the on-site supervisor should be made aware of the specific learning goals, objectives, and activities of the student. Many on-site supervisors are happy to cooperate in structuring situations or making choices when appropriate to maximize learning potential for the intern. In fact, one of the more common complaints from on-site supervisors is that the student's goals are not clear enough for the supervisor to provide the maximum learning experience.

Methods of Evaluation

Two types of evaluation should occur as part of the internship: (a) progress evaluation—evaluation activities that help the student to consolidate learning as well as to indicate the degree of progress—and (b) summative evaluation—evaluation at the end of the internship that indicates how well the student was able to meet the overall learning goals.

In terms of both progress evaluation and summative evaluation, two basic dimensions need to be considered. The first dimension is the *amount of effort*—completing all assignments, working the required number of hours, showing up on time, performing all agree-upon activities. The second dimension is the *quality of effort*—the quality of a completed task, the degree of skill proficiency, or the degree of integration of the theoretical with the applied.

How will the student be able to demonstrate progress toward the objective? How does a student know the degree to which the learning goals have been achieved? Evaluation should not be considered a one-shot activity or event that occurs at the end of the semester; evaluation should be an integral part of the internship. If the planning described above has been done well, then progress evaluation becomes a useful tool to assess progress, modify upcoming activities, or replan for activities that did not seem to further progress. For each activity planned, or for a cluster of related activities, some form of evaluation should be included. Assessing progress along the way will also help the faculty supervisor to make a summative evaluation at the end of the semester.

To help the student demonstrate the degree of progress toward each objective and to determine the degree to which the student has met the final learning goals, the following methods or techniques can be used by both the student and the supervisor: (a) keeping a log or journal of activities and their outcomes; (b) reading books, journals, and other documents, and reporting on them; (c) writing a paper explaining or analyzing the internship setting by application of theoretical material; (d) verbally reporting or delivering presentations to the faculty; (e) giving demonstrations; (f) taking tests, oral or written; (g) teaching another student or a class of students; (h) teaching a faculty member; (i) writing a research paper; (j) providing documentation from work outputs at the internship site—reports, worksheets, or programs written.

Needless to say, the evaluation method should be consistent with the goal, objective, and activity. For example, it does not seem appropriate for a student to take a test for activities geared toward a goal of learning more about the self. However, for activities geared toward the goal of skill development, a demonstration involving the acquired skill might be quite appropriate. In any case, it should be clear between student and faculty supervisor what the evaluation criteria are before the student gets too involved in the internship.

Planning of Ongoing Contact

At this final stage of preinternship planning between the student and faculty member, certain questions need to be answered clearly and understood by both participants: (a) How often will the faculty supervisor and the student get together? (b) Will the faculty supervisor meet individually with the student or with a group of interns? (c) What will be the purpose of these interactions (e. g., review of internship activity, review of progress toward goals, checking of progress toward projected outcomes, faculty "educating" student, faculty serving as a resource to student)?

As is apparent, much planning needs to be done between faculty, supervisor, and student for maximum benefit on the internship. At the same time, this planning is difficult to accomplish before the student has started the internship. Often, the learning goals and placement site are selected at an initial meeting; after the student has spent a week on internship, the specific activities and objectives as well as the method of evaluation can be determined.

Learning Contract

Once all the above steps have been completed, the student and faculty supervisor should put in writing the statement of learning goals, the statement of projected outcomes, the statement of activities to be performed, and the statement of methods of evaluation. This contract should be signed by both faculty supervisor and student and communicated to CPPC.

Ongoing Contact

Throughout the semester the faculty supervisor might consider several kinds of contact with the intern. First, the faculty supervisor may find it appropriate and helpful to contact the student's on-site supervisor. Sometimes this contact can be made before the planning between the faculty supervisor and the student has been completed so that the on-site supervisor can assist in the procedure. Once the planning has been completed and the learning contract written, it is also helpful for the faculty supervisor to communicate the student's goals, objectives, activities, and methods of evaluation to the on-site supervisor. Contact with the on-site supervisor can also be made to determine whether the student is honoring the contract, what additional learning the student may need, and whether the student is making satisfactory progress.

The faculty supervisor might visit the internship site to acquire a better understanding of what the student is doing and the context in which it is being done, to meet with the on-site supervisor, and to see possibilities for learning that may not be apparent to the student or the on-site supervisor.

Throughout the semester the most important ongoing contact for the faculty supervisor is with the student. During each of these contacts the supervisor should ask the following questions:

1. What kind of progress is being made toward the learning goals and objectives?

2. Given progress and learning opportunities, do these learning goals need to be renegotiated?

3. Are projected outcomes realistic?

4. Do outcomes need to be modified?

5. What is the status of planned activities?

6. What additional resources are needed?

7. Should any changes be requested from the on-site supervisor?

8. Is the format of the contact between faculty supervisor and student appropriate?

9. When are the faculty supervisor and the student going to meet again?

In short, the faculty member and the student should review previous planning at each meeting. Quite often it is appropriate for the faculty supervisor and the student to renegotiate one or more of the decisions regarding learning goals, activities or method of evaluation. This flexible approach allows both to take advantage of unanticipated learning opportunities as well as to adjust plans when expectations are unrealistic.

Final Evaluation and Grade

We neither know of nor recommend any "best" method of intern evaluation; whether a student is to receive a letter grade or use the pass–no pass option should be a mutual decision of the intern and the faculty supervisor during the negotiation stage of the internship. This flexibility, in addition to accommodating individual preferences, will allow the evaluation process to suit each intern's unique learning goals and activities. For example, it would be much easier to assign a letter grade to a relatively objective product (e. g., a term paper or test) than it would be to grade a subjective account of what the intern has personally gained (e.g., values clarification, decision-making skills). In the latter case, a simple pass–no pass evaluation might be more appropriate (although not necessary).

Flexibility should be an important consideration in evaluation; however, one definite requirement is that the intern must have met and fulfilled the previously negotiated goals, objectives, and activities (unless unexpected circumstances beyond the student's control have interfered) in order to receive a grade and credit. Work requirements and activities negotiated at the beginning of the experience (perhaps with modifications over time that are agreed to by all participants) form the basic material, the quality, not presence, of which is evaluated. In short, the faculty supervisor must ask how well, not whether, the student has fulfilled the learning contract.

Evaluation, as stated previously, is not a one-shot event; it is progressive as well as summative. It aims to reflect both the amount and quality of effort an intern has put forth and whether the student has approached the internship with an attitude of responsibility. These details should become evident in each student's physical productions and discussions with the faculty supervisor. Therefore, the end-of-semester grade should merely be an extension of earlier progressive evaluation. Ideally, the intern's on-site supervisor will give periodic feedback to both the intern and faculty sponsor throughout the semester, as well as the required summative evaluation. The faculty member can incorporate all of this into the final evaluation.

Other Interactors

Although the role of the faculty member is described above, it is important to mention briefly the involvement and responsibilities of the site supervisor and the student, since the interaction among the three is critical to the value of the experience.

While all participants share responsibility for initiating and maintaining communication, the site supervisor's major function is to instruct and provide regular feedback to the student and faculty member on the more work-related aspects of the placement. Included in this would be such aspects as intellectual and technical preparation, but more emphasis is placed on performance criteria (e. g., ability to deal with the organization's clients, initiative, ability to cooperate with other professional workers, or problem-solving capabilities). The student's responsibilities to the site and to the faculty member center primarily around successful completion of the negotiated learning agreement.

Evaluation of the experience is viewed from the perspectives of all participants. The faculty member is responsible for certifying the academic aspects of the experience using as sources of information (a) input from the student and the site supervisor and (b) the faculty member's own observations through such prescribed student activities as a journal, a paper, or a report. The student should be prepared to make a self-evaluation regarding initial goals and objectives and to provide a written evaluation on certain points to CPPC. The student is encouraged to provide the site with specific feedback regarding the internship experience. The site supervisor will have supplied information to the student and faculty member, who will subsequently incorporate that feedback into their own evaluations. In addition, the site supervisor is encouraged to consider the experience in terms of such things as prior expectations, organizational goals, and time and format constraints. During the internship the CPPC/COVE staff are in contact with all participants and are monitoring and evaluating the experience from the point of view of program goals.

Internship placements have occurred through four semesters and two summer terms involving 90 students, 72 site supervisors, and 40 faculty members in the College of Arts and Sciences at St. Louis University.

Summary

As stated earlier, this chapter has been written to assist faculty in their work with interns. It is not intended to be a strict set of guidelines but rather an idealized model that will assist the faculty member to be a valuable resource person and an efficient, helpful off-site supervisor. It is our hope that the chapter answers many potential questions and provides a flexible range of alternatives to many aspects of supervising the intern.

REFERENCES

Brick, M., & McGrath, E. J. *Innovation in liberal arts colleges.* New York: Teachers College Press, Columbia University, 1969.
Mayhew, L. B. *Legacy of the seventies.* San Francisco: Jossey-Bass, 1977.

27

Barbara F. Nodine

An Interdisciplinary Use of the Psychology Major

The departmental goal of thorough preparation in psychology, in combination with the goal of the graduation of students with marketable skills, has been met in the undergraduate psychology program at Beaver College described in this chapter. In this program, the certification of students as special education teachers has been coordinated within the psychology major. The program is attractive to career-oriented students and also to small psychology departments because of the efficiency of its course offerings and its lack of overlap with programs offered by other departments.

Today's psychology majors are, like previous generations, fascinated with human behavior. Unlike earlier students, however, today's students want more than intellectual enrichment: They also want broad career options. Beaver College has designed a unique undergraduate program that invites these students to integrate their majors with training in special education, one of the few areas still growing and offering expanding job opportunities. At the completion of the program the students receive the BA degree in psychology plus Pennsylvania state certification to teach mentally and/or physically handicapped children and youths.

Students interested in special education complete the first three years of the psychology major and a number of elementary education pedagogy courses. Then they may choose courses that offer intensive practicum and teaching with exceptional children. This senior-year coursework, supervised by the psychology department, provides the disciplinary material of special education. Particulars of the course sequence are described below.

The program is an interdisciplinary one based on psychology and education rather than on a separate department of special education. The program designers wanted to develop broadly trained students and teachers who could draw on learning, developmental, and social and personality theory as well as pedagogical methods to apply their knowledge in educational programming for their pupils. Students are taught, of necessity, to develop an orientation to the children that is developmental and noncategorical. Teachers trained in this interdisciplinary program should have the resources for diagnosis and remediation of any learning or behavioral problem their pupils present.

Program Constraints

This program is conducted in a small liberal arts college (800 under-graduates)—not in a university where special education would be a separate department, probably on the graduate level. Two constraints exist for such a program in a small college. First, the college cannot afford and, in fact, is theoretically opposed to any course overlap that would allow different departments to teach similar material in their own ways. Such specialization is a luxury of the large university. Second, a relatively expensive, small college must offer individual attention to attract students. The program at Beaver College has been designed to operate within these two constraints. It avoids overlap by using the core courses of the psychology major and the elementary education sequence, described below, as the basis of the special education program. Most of the material of special education is taught during the senior year to students already conversant with the theory of that field through their psychology and education courses. Thus, for three years their studies utilize college resources that are already available.

The program also works within the second constraint, individual attention. Every psychology and education course offered at Beaver College has an experiential component, such as a laboratory course, an independent research project, a student tutoring experience or an opportunity to plan and teach a mini-lesson. Usually the instructor allows enough latitude in selection of this experiential component so that the student can relate his or her experience to research or teaching in special education. The staff member in the psychology department responsible for the student's senior year in special education directs the experiential part of the lower-level courses. In this way the program serves the needs and interests of each student individually, and the student's background work in psychology and education is richer for its application to the student's vocational goal. There are fewer "empty" exercises in research or pedagogy when college resources must be used with maximal efficiency.

Coursework

The core of the psychology major is a two-semester introductory psychology course and two year-long courses, with extensive laboratory work, in the second and third years (see Table 27-1). One laboratory course, Psychology as a Natural Science, involves learning, motivation, and sensory-perceptual processes and trains students in research. This course provides the foundation for the rest of the program and is the pre-requisite for most other courses. The second laboratory course, Psychology as a Social Science, deals with basic theories and data on social interaction and the effect of culture on behavior. Major approaches to the study of personality via traits, schema, and motive are also taught in this course.

Barbara F. Nodine is an associate professor of psychology and coordinator of the special education program at Beaver College.

TABLE 27-1   Core Courses in Psychology

Year	Course description	Format
Freshman	*General Psychology:* Intensive examination of all major areas of natural science and social science psychology; fulfills educational psychology requirement for education majors; some empirical work.	2 semesters; 4 hrs. per wk.; no formal lab.
Sophomore	*Psychology as a Natural Science:* Experimental design, learning, psychophysics, perception.	2 semesters; 3 hrs. per wk.; weekly lab.; independent research project.
	Quantitative Methods: Descriptive and inferential statistics taught by Keller's PSI method.	1 semester; PSI 15 units completed in 1 yr.; final exam.; student tutors.
Junior	*Psychology as a Social Science:* Social and personality theory; research methods.	2 semesters; 3 hrs. per wk.; weekly lab.; independent research project
Senior	*Special Education:* Disciplinary material of special education; practicum on theory and use of tests in special education.	2 semesters; weekly 2-hr. seminar; major paper; intern teaching.

Note. PSI = Personalized System of Instruction.

The core is accompanied by a required program in statistics using Keller's Personalized System of Instruction. Two courses, optional for traditional psychology majors but required for students seeking certification in special education, are Introduction to Exceptional Children and Cognitive Development. These two courses are of general interest to psychology majors, education majors, or others. For students selecting the special education program, they provide a background for later senior coursework.

In the elementary education sequence, students must complete the following courses: Child Development (one semester), Facilitation of Learning (one semester), Developmental Reading (two semesters), Mathematics for Elementary Education (two semesters), and Language Arts (one semester). All of these courses involve experiential learning in addition to traditional classwork. At the lower levels, this usually means observing or tutoring. In the upper courses, it means diagnosing and remediating problems in reading or mathematics, or preparing and teaching a lesson for supervision.

The capstone of the program is the senior course in special education, a systematic investigation of diagnosis, remediation, curriculum modification, classroom management, and theories on teaching exceptional children. The course orientation is developmental, in contrast to the narrow, categorical approach of courses such as Reading for the Learning Disabled, which Beaver College has never offered. This developmental approach complements the interdisciplinary background combining psychology and education and also conforms to the recently established K–12 generalist certificate of the State of Pennsylvania.

Status of Graduates

Since this program for psychology majors was designed for a specific career focus, it is instructive to look at postgraduate employment data, although it is not possible to compare the job success of these students with that of psychology majors in general because data for the latter are unavailable (Korn & Nodine, 1975). In the past four years Beaver College has graduated approximately 30 psychology majors prepared for careers in special education. Of the 20 students who applied to graduate school, all were accepted. Most entered master's programs in special education, although one entered law school, one studied elementary counseling, and one entered a psychology of reading program. In addition to being accepted into graduate school, these students have been quite successful there, several having been invited into doctoral programs and many others reporting that their rigorous psychology major has been good preparation for graduate study in special education.

These graduates' success in obtaining teaching jobs has also been high. Most have teaching jobs specifically in special education, and the jobs range over the full diversity of special education. Because they have been trained as generalists in special education, our graduates are equipped to teach emotionally disturbed and mentally retarded adolescents and children, both severe and mild cases.

A large portion of this chapter has described the specific courses at Beaver College in psychology and special education. Although the content of these courses is similar to that in other colleges, the organization of the psychology major is somewhat unusual, and that organization has made possible the unique interdisciplinary program in special education.

For other colleges with similar course content, a special education program like that at Beaver College would be feasible. The essential ingredients for integrating the departments of psychology and education into a program in special education at Beaver College were the following: (a) courses with experiential components, (b) state certification with a noncategorical option (although a college could select one category, e.g., mental retardation, and develop a program for that certificate), (c) cooperation between psychology and education departments, and (d) an educational psychologist interested in cognitive development.

REFERENCE

Korn, J. H., & Nodine, B. F. Facts and questions concerning career training of the psychology major. *Teaching of Psychology*, 1975, 2, 117–119.

28

Rosa Lynn Pinkus

Career Training and the Definition of Liberal Arts Education: Philosophy, Politics, and Money

This chapter evaluates the key components of a professional option that existed for psychology majors at Carnegie-Mellon University from 1971 through 1974. The four-year curriculum provided students with fieldwork experience and was designed to aid them in securing employment upon graduation. In spite of support by students and cooperating agencies, the option was discontinued when it competed for scarce funds and additional faculty support. This chapter outlines procedures for developing such a professional option and offers advice to departments wishing to do so.

Many undergraduate psychology majors do not plan to attend graduate school; instead they choose to pursue careers in psychology or in psychology-related professions immediately following graduation. In past years, the problems involved in providing training, career guidance, and job placement for this group have attracted much attention. The *American Psychologist* published an article (Pinkus & Korn, 1973) concerning Carnegie-Mellon University's experiences with a preprofessional option (later renamed the professional option), a four-year curriculum designed to aid students in securing employment after graduation. This chapter evaluates key components of that program and discusses why, in spite of interest by students and cooperating agencies, it was discontinued in 1974. Special attention is devoted to the difficulties that led to the demise of the professional program at Carnegie-Mellon. Since the need for professional training of BA psychologists is still a concern, this chapter also outlines the components necessary to develop and conduct a professional option and offers suggestions to departments interested in undertaking such a venture.

Components of the Program

A successful professional training option for psychology majors should include the following components: (a) a curriculum designed to educate students in applied research methods and fieldwork experience; (b) a means for counseling students in career decision making and personal awareness; (c) a means for insuring successful and ongoing community–university relations; and (d) curriculum evaluation and development.

Three years of experience at Carnegie-Mellon (1971–1974) proved that all of the above components can be handled by one half-time faculty member. General faculty cooperation, along with support from the counseling center and placement offices, is also needed. For example, faculty members can offer special training seminars in tests and measurements or counseling techniques or can take on fieldwork students for independent study. Overall, however, only one person is needed to take major responsibility for initiating projects and coordinating the program.

Evaluation of the Program

This evaluation of the program's three aspects—fieldwork, prefieldwork preparation, and knowledge gained by students—is based on data gathered from 15 in-depth questionnaires given to students who participated in the professional option during 1972 and 1973, and from open-ended letters received from five cooperating community agencies. While this sample is small, it is indicative of the undergraduate program at Carnegie-Mellon. Of the approximately 40 majors who graduated from the department in 1973, 15 students—a significant number—took part in the professional option. In 1974, the last year it was offered, approximately half of the majors were trained in the professional option.

In spite of this small sample size and the program-specific nature of the study, recent evidence suggests that the findings reported in this chapter may apply to undergraduate professional education in general. During 1976 and 1977, I participated in the teaching and evaluation of an undergraduate urban studies program at the University of Pittsburgh. Graduating approximately 120 students a year, one of this program's components was an in-depth fieldwork experience given to students in their senior year, yet many students complained that the program lacked prefieldwork training and did not screen cooperating agencies to insure successful placement. The details of the urban studies program evaluation are not important; the point to be stressed is that the suggestions made by Pinkus and Korn (1973) concerning professional training at the undergraduate level and the model curriculum then proposed (discussed below) are still valid. An evaluation of the professional option, then, even though it proved short-lived at Carnegie-Mellon, is still topical.

Fieldwork: The Key to Success

Three aspects of the fieldwork experience deserve attention: (a) when fieldwork experience should be given, (b) what constitutes adequate pre-

Rosa Lynn Pinkus is Adjunct Professor of Neurological Surgery/History and Ethics at the School of Medicine, University of Pittsburgh.

placement training, and (c) what steps need to be taken to secure and maintain outstanding fieldwork experience.

Timing of Fieldwork Experience

Preplacement training and fieldwork experience spanned two semesters and were offered as part of a two-sequence class, Psychology and the Urban Community, given during the students' senior year. (See the course description provided at the end of this chapter.) While the program's planners recognized that exposure to a professional environment would be beneficial to students at any time, they assumed that students would profit most by it in the senior year. At this time, students would be better prepared intellectually and socially for an intensive work experience. Responding to a questionnaire item, 10 out of 15 students answered that the type of fieldwork training and experiences offered in a two-semester course designed specifically for the progam should not be given earlier than the senior year. The students cited maturity, educational preparation, and previous fieldwork training as contributing to the success of their experience. Four respondents felt the sequence should be offered earlier (i.e., in the junior year), and all students commented on the need for both more guidance during the work experience and increased preparatory training.

The request for more guidance was in response to the way the second semester of the sequence was conducted. At the end of the first-semester course, students were required to make all field placement arrangements themselves and to report their duties and hours, in writing, to the professional supervisor. If this schedule was accepted, they were required to meet with the program coordinator during the middle of the following semester for a progress report and at the end of the semester for final evaluation. The coordinator was available for consultation any time during the semester if students felt they needed additional help. Students in this second semester were left on their own and did not meet in weekly seminars to convey common experiences.

Responses to the question that probed the worth of this forced independence indicated that 13 out of 15 students personally benefited from such freedom. The following was a typical comment: "I've been so structured in the last couple years that I wasn't sure I could do anything on my own. I was forced to do my own thinking and come up with answers. It gave me a feeling of responsibility." Overall, students supported the minimal guidance requirements imposed during the second semester.

These two responses indicate that the senior year was the most practical and the most educationally beneficial time in which to institute fieldwork training and experience. Such training and experience could have been given earlier but would have involved additional preparation during the first semester of the program and more guidance during the second-semester experience. Students with the proper background benefited from independence in fieldwork. Before the senior year, however, the maturity and coursework comprising this "proper background" had not yet been acquired. Moreover, for departments that want to limit faculty involvement in a professional program, the senior year requires the least amount of faculty time for training and guidance and the forced independence allows the placement adviser to carry out other functions of the program while monitoring student projects.

Preplacement Training

A second area of concern in planning this particular course sequence was what should be included in preparatory training for fieldwork. The faculty who planned the activities for the first semester of the Psychology and the Urban Community sequence assumed that students entering the course had limited exposure to information regarding the types of placements that would be available to them and the nature of fieldwork experience. They also assumed that students were unsure of their personal abilities to function in a professional setting. The course was geared to provide this information and to place students in prototype fieldwork settings so that they could assess their own readiness to enter various work situations.

The preparatory training, therefore, consisted of class visits to five cooperating agencies. Students were given a chance to make personal contact with professionals who needed their services, were told about the type of work open to them, and were encouraged to follow their interests individually. As part of the semester's requirements, students had to locate and describe an additional community agency with work matching their vocational interests and, if they wanted to continue in the program in the second semester, they had to arrange their field placement themselves.

The course planners also assumed that if students were to work in community agencies, they would need to be provided with some framework for assessing how the work fit into a broader community setting. Agency problems and bureaucratic power struggles often become a world unto themselves. Once assigned to a specific job, a student may find it difficult to maintain a broad perspective on employment matters. Furthermore, if the student has never been shown what the range of possible careers is, discouragement about what is being accomplished on the job can set in rapidly. In choosing a career, for example, it is important to know where one wants to have an impact, whether an interpersonal, institutional, political, or academic level. Most students have never considered this aspect of career choice and once they move into a specialized setting may not be exposed to such alternatives. Thus, a major part of the fieldwork training involves the teaching of a theoretical framework within which students can evaluate their work experiences.

Through use of the theme of urbanization, students were provided with a frame of reference to enhance their appreciation of the roles of the various agencies visited. This theoretical background allowed them to speculate about their own contributions to agency work.

The value of the preparatory course varied according to the backgrounds of the individual students. Some students demonstrated that they had no need for the course. They had worked previously and could intelligently outline why they wanted to work and what they wanted to accomplish. Thus, they were able to take fieldwork during the first or second semester without previous training. For those students who elected to take the preparatory course, its benefits were confirmed. Of the 15 students doing fieldwork in the second semester, 13 had taken the course. Of these 13, 10 indicated that the first half of the course prepared them for the second half by allowing them to see the relationship of their particular agency to the community as a whole. Six students indicated that agency visits gave them insight about where they might best work. Three students indicated that course content (e.g., research techniques, observational skills, and census data analysis) directly prepared them for their jobs.

Thus, the preparatory course served its purpose and is suggested as part of any professional training experience on an undergraduate level. The content of the course is less important than the inclusion of field trips and exposure to a theoretical framework within which the specific work experience can be assimilated.

The two-course sequence, Psychology and the Urban Community, received a generally positive evaluation from students. All students responded on the questionnaire that they had gained personal confidence from the experiences of the first and second semesters. This self-assurance seemed to result from making decisions independently, interacting favorably with professionals on a professional level, and working directly with "clients." The students indicated that moving out of the student role into one that had different responsibility was extremely import to them.

The success of the training is implicit in the success of the individual fieldwork experiences. All 15 students received favorable evaluations from their professional superiors. No students were found to lack the personal awareness employers cited as essential in prospective employees (Pinkus & Korn, 1973). Nine out of 15 students contributed significantly to easing cooperating agencies' workloads, and 7 out of 15, while not directly easing the workload, added to the quality of the service rendered by the agency.

Finally, the two-semester sequence gave students information about job possibilities and future career choices. It taught personal confidence and exposed students to professional environments unlike that of the university.

Securing and Maintaining Fieldwork Placements

The third component of fieldwork, good field placement, is essential to the successful functioning of a professional program. Considerable time and effort should be given to locating, screening, and selecting cooperating agencies. This preparatory search insures that students will receive training by qualified and committed agency personnel for a variety of high-level, useful tasks.

A core of five agencies was used for fieldwork in the Carnegie-Mellon program. As a result of the community survey project carried out to develop the curriculum (Pinkus & Korn, 1973), a catalog of approximately 40 additional agencies available for student participation was kept on file for use when student demand generated a need. The five core agencies were chosen because of the wide variety of job opportunities they offered. These agencies, with summaries of the training they provided, are listed below. (Although they are local Pittsburgh agencies, each represents a type of agency found in many other localities).

Pennsylvania Parole Board. Students worked with staff members on all of the tasks related to parole work—interviewing clients, visiting institutions, writing reports, and carrying out case studies.

Grubstake, Inc. In this private rehabilitation center for male offenders aged 18–30, students gained experience in administration, scoring, and interpretation of tests, in vocational and personal counseling, and in rehabilitation research. They worked with individual clients and were included in all staff meetings.

City Planning of Pittsburgh. This component of city government is concerned with planning, zoning, traffic, recreation, and other aspects of city life. Students conducted surveys, organized community groups, and contributed to a handbook on federal aid for housing. They attended planned staff meetings and presented reports before the City Council.

American Friends Service Committee. Students worked on a bail bond reform project and were involved with lawyers and community action groups in both state and federal court systems. Proposed reform measures were based on data in part collected, analyzed, and reported by students.

Applied Science Associates. This private psychological consulting firm offered a range of experience in conducting applied research. Students contributed to the writing of grant proposals and worked on specific contracts.

The 40 other agencies that offered to cooperate in the field placement of students provided good opportunities for fieldwork experience but usually placed the students in more traditional volunteer positions. The positions exposed students to the realities of professional helping agencies but often failed to use the students' capacities for initiating projects. These agencies were acceptable for fieldwork credits, but they were used only when students consented to produce additional research projects to accompany their fieldwork. These additional projects were requested when the fieldwork consisted of clerical tasks and observation of professionals at work. If such observation was structured, the time spent at the agency was regarded by the program as more profitable.

The five core agencies indicated that they were highly satisfied with the students and very supportive of the fieldwork project. Although only one Carnegie-Mellon student actually obtained employment (significantly, at an agency that had indicated in a survey that a master's degree was needed), several were considered for jobs. Eight students entered graduate or professional school and indicated that their field experience facilitated their acceptance. Four graduates obtained employment in areas related to their field placement. Two students decided not to go into a certain career because of negative fieldwork experiences.

Fieldwork placements provided students with four advantages: (a) specific training in techniques, (b) an opportunity to apply skills acquired in the classroom to real-world problems, (c) a realistic idea of the opportunities for employment and the advanced training required for various areas of work, and (d) exposure to professionals in a variety of employment settings. None of this knowledge could be acquired as fully in a classroom. The combination of information and professional poise acquired greatly enhanced the students' ability to make informed choices about their futures.

Fate of the Professional Program[1]

The professional option at Carnegie-Mellon University was organized in 1971 and expanded during the following three years. By 1974, half of the majors in the department of psychology were in the program. In 1974 the initiator of the program was not reappointed and the key fieldwork preparatory course was turned over to a new faculty member who had been hired to teach courses in social psychology. This faculty member, traditionally and thoroughly educated in academic psychology, agreed to teach the preparatory course with the understanding that it would not be a permanent commitment. Moreover, he was encouraged to teach the course to suit his desires and qualifications—a courtesy extended by the university to all incoming assistant professors. Since the course was previously named Psychology and the Urban Community and the new faculty member had some background in environmental psychology, he converted it into a seminar on environmental psychology with an emphasis on field research. Thus, the focus of getting the student out of the classroom and into the city environment was retained, but the emphasis was on teaching students how to carry out well-controlled field research. Job-related experience was not considered. In contrast to previous work-related settings, students in the seminar conducted research in such places as laundromats, dormitory game rooms, and psychiatric hospitals. Participants judged the seminar to be challenging and interesting but unrelated to subsequent career decisions.

By September 1975 no faculty member in the psychology department was willing to teach the course, and no efforts were made to recruit faculty to carry on the professional program. Students attempted to carry out a volunteer placement effort with the community agencies during 1975 and

1. The author thanks Richard Schulz, now the Director of the Institute on Aging at Portland State University, for his description of the professional option program at Carnegie-Mellon University after the author left.

1976. Without official faculty involvement, however, student interest waned and the voluntary group effort disbanded. In August 1977, the course sequence, although it had not been taught for three years, was still listed in the college catalog.

The demise of the psychology career training program at Carnegie-Mellon University can probably best be attributed to departmental neglect. Carnegie-Mellon has a small psychology department known for its research in human information-processing psychology. In such an academic milieu, a service-oriented, applied undergraduate program is at odds with the research interests of the faculty. Thus, in the hands of a new faculty member, hired primarily because of his research abilities and interests, the program evolved into a seminar on field research methods. Expecting to maintain an expanded undergraduate professional program in such an environment is unrealistic.

Career Training Versus Liberal Arts Education

Professional training at the BA level requires the cooperation of three groups: employers, students, and faculty. If any of these three does not consider career training important, a successful program cannot be easily instituted. Employers and students benefit directly from such training; it is compatible with their needs and goals. For some academic psychologists, however, career training is in conflict with their definition of liberal arts education, and the benefits of career training are less clear.

Departments, like colleges and universities, can be scaled along a philosophical continuum with regard to BA-level career training. Schools such as Harvard University or Oberlin College, for example, have undergraduate programs devoted to educating students in academic psychology. Career training in such an environment would be considered vocationalism and would not be included in the curriculum. These schools explicitly abide by the traditional view of a liberal arts education. They strive to give each student some sense of his or her intrinsic worth, and they teach courses not so that students can profit materially but because learning is in itself rewarding. These schools believe that students who have been in an environment of inquisitiveness and self-discipline for four years should be capable of finding suitable employment when they graduate. Post graduation plans are delegated to the placement offices and to the students themselves.

At the opposite end of the continuum are departments with applied professional training programs. The University of Washington, the Lila Acheson Wallace School of Community Service and Public Affairs at the University of Oregon, and the California School of Professional Psychology are examples of schools fully committed to providing students with specific career training. Positions for employment are identified in the community, and students are trained to fill them. These departments elect to present a narrowly specialized view rather than a broad-based introduction to the world of knowledge.

Most departments, such as Carnegie-Mellon's, fall in the middle of this continuum. This middle point reflects the ambiguity of these departments with regard to their goals for a liberal arts education. Some departments accept students into programs without discussing how their four years of college will prepare them for their futures. Such discussion requires a specialized knowledge of the job market that most faculty members simply do not possess. Bombarded with other professional responsibilities, academic psychologists often overlook the issue of employment for students with bachelor's degrees. These psychologists do not actively oppose career training on philosophical grounds; rather, they are simply not qualified to provide such training nor are they interested in fostering it.

When outside circumstances (e.g., a limited job market combined with more stringent graduate school admission requirements; a decrease in college enrollment) temporarily create a visible need for professional training at the BA level, then an ethical and educational problem arises for these middle-range departments. The vague educational criteria of these departments may cause students to wonder about the value of a college education at all. Departments that recognize the obligation they have to the futures of their students will take a stand regarding career training. Departments that stress the traditional liberal arts education may deal with these issues by clearly presenting their philosophical ideals to incoming students; departments with applied training programs can expand ongoing programs. But middle-range schools are caught between the two approaches.

Resolving the Conflict

Academicians cope admirably with confusion and ambiguity. They can satisfy student demand for salable skills by a compromise measure that never clearly defines educational values. The traditional view of liberal arts education allows the inclusion of minimal vocational training (i.e., fieldwork) in subjects such as psychology. thus basic content courses are given concurrently with fieldwork. This inclusion of an applied aspect into a rigorous academic curriculum can be termed "liberalizing liberal arts," that is, bringing the competence and scope of the university into the community at large. thus, a department can incorporate career training into its curriculum without making a firm commitment to it and while maintaining a liberal arts perspective.

"Liberalizing liberal arts," however, has drawbacks. A fine line exists between bringing the university into the community and bringing the community into the university. In the latter approach, the short-term market definition of demand and salability always threatens to become incorporated into a program's goals. Traditional faculty members are wary of such a "contaminating" influence basically distrust community-oriented courses.

A second drawback concerns the adverse effects of conducting a successful fieldwork program. The more employer–student support such a program receives, the more departmental resources it may require. Clearly, a department staffed with professionals who value research above applied activities and who are wary of community programs generally will not want to spend money on a program that does not reflect these basic interests. It is when money is at stake, in other words, that philosophical debates about liberal arts education finally are settled. A successful fieldwork program will force a department to take a stand on career training. (Unfortunately for the students and faculty at Carnegie-Mellon who were committed to such training, the university took a negative stand.)

This progression of events can ultimately be beneficial to the middle-range department. If it encourages faculty members to personally reassess their values concerning undergraduate education and if it puts pressure on a department to explicitly define its educational goals, then at least students and applicants can be told what type of education they will receive. Because many competent professional programs in psychology already exist, a particular department's stand for or against career training is unimportant. What *is important* is that a department honestly state its educational goals to incoming students.

In spite of departmental difficulties accompanying career programs, a variety of programs do exist that offer career training. Students who want to pursue careers in applied psychology or in psychology-related professions should—at the high school level—be encouraged to apply to schools that offer such programs. (Departments can aid these students by describing their undergraduate programs clearly and honestly.)

Departments that place themselves in the middle range of commitment to career training may find that the professional option program, outlined by Pinkus and Korn (1973) and reviewed and evaluated here, is appropriate. This inexpensive, workable curriculum geared toward training BAs for a variety of employment positions can be conducted competently by one half-time faculty member, and it is in keeping with the philosophical goals of a traditional liberal arts education. This option is admittedly a compromise of career training, but if it is recognized as such, it need not suffer the demise described above. The program can be started with departmental consensus that it will be limited in terms of student involvement, faculty commitment, and departmental funding. For departments not unanimously committed to engaging in traditional liberal arts education, it seems that a compromise program that introduces students to alternative employment futures is preferable to no program at all.

REFERENCES

Pinkus, R., & Korn, J. The preprofessional option: An alternative to graduate school in psychology. *American Psychologist*, 1973, *28*, 710–718.

Psychology and the Urban Community: Course Description

REQUIREMENTS

1. Two semesters.
2. Senior-level students.
3. Prerequisite or by permission of instructor.

GOALS

1. To introduce students to a variety of skills that will enable them to conduct applied research projects in an urban setting.
2. To take students off campus and enable them to interact with the following:
   a. Professionals with nonacademic orientation.
   b. Agencies and institutions intricately related to urban management.
   c. Broader urban environment (the world outside of Carnegie-Mellon University).
3. To develop a working relationship with off-campus agencies so that student projects will be of practical worth to the agency.

OTHER OBJECTIVES

1. To place students in a position that demands responsible, committed, long-term involvement.
2. To prepare students to conduct and formulate an independent research project.
3. To have individual students consider and explore why they are doing what they are doing.

STRUCTURE

First Semester

1. Lectures: to introduce research skills.
2. Miniprojects: 2-week projects to introduce students to several areas of urban research and allow them to use skills taught.
3. Class field trips.
4. Speakers: representing several fields of urban-related professions.

Second Semester

Fieldwork project: student-initiated topic designed so that students can (a) work as "apprentices" with off-campus professionals, (b) conduct work that is usable to both the student and the agency, and (c) put into practice content materials from previous courses and from the first-semester course.

The course procedures assume that students will have competence in a major content area—psychology, architecture, social relations, engineering—and that they will apply this competence to a metaframework of skills.

29

Patricia Keith-Spiegel and David L. Cole

Sources of Resistance
to Changing Undergraduate Career
Training in Psychology

It seems reasonable to assume that students could be taught a salable skill related to psychology during their four years of undergraduate training. But programs geared toward this goal are few and scattered. Why? This chapter presents some possibilities for consideration and debate.

Approximately 250,000 students were undergraduate psychology majors in 1977, and 52,000 bachelor's degrees were awarded in psychology in 1974 (Nazzaro, 1976). These impressive figures suggest that undergraduate programs are meeting a substantial need.

But there are other realities. Most of those with bachelor's degrees in psychology never go on to graduate school. In 1974, 130,000 applications were received by graduate programs for fewer than 15,000 openings (Nazzaro, 1976). Psychology and its professional organizations have not done much to face up to what becomes of the majority of people educated at the subdoctoral level. What attention has been paid has often been directed at efforts to keep them from misrepresenting the profession.

In 1975 the Education and Training Board of the American Psychological Association created three subcommittees on undergraduate training in psychology. These subcommittees located in three regions of the country, were to work for one year and then report to the Board. As members of the Los Angeles area subcommittee, we found that our group came up with numerous innovations to transform undergraduate training models into vehicles for useful skills leading to potential job opportunities. Yet we became increasingly aware of the probable outcome of our puffery—more ideas, more fancy documents that would only remain on paper. We then turned our attention to identifying probable resistance to change in the undergraduate training model.

The results are reported in this chapter. While many may regard our statements as controversial, pessimistic, and cantankerous, we believe that these concerns should be seriously considered. Failure to do so may result in few actual modifications in the traditional undergraduate train-

275

ing procedures that are designed largely to accommodate the small percentage of students who continue for advanced degrees.

Resistance Point 1: Survival First!

Professors, perhaps now more than ever, are absorbed both in terms of time and energy with their own career problems. Although nontenured and/or lower-ranking faculty are usually the most enthusiastic about new training models, in the face of salary concerns, staff and resource cutbacks, and the array of issues related to retention, tenure, and promotion, they may have to concentrate more heavily on their own survival. Such concentration deploys energy they might otherwise direct toward their students. Showing concern and involvement with students and program development have not been viewed as particularly meritorious activities by personnel evaluation committees, however. What seems to count much more is research and publication output. And, for many professors, high course loads and increasing numbers of students leave precious little time for research and writing. Thus it is unfortunately not surprising that a commitment to revamping undergraduate training is not at the forefront of the contemporary academic's priorities.

Resistance Point 2: Graduate Students Are More Fun

Departments offering advanced degrees often house faculties who would prefer to put their creative efforts into the graduate programs. Graduate students are more sophisticated and can assist professors with research; in addition, graduate classes are generally smaller than undergraduate classes. Departments with graduate programs report having great difficulties in attracting anyone, short of department-head fiat, to teach lower-division courses; as a result, most introductory psychology courses end up being taught by part-time faculty members and graduate students.

Thus community colleges, which have a commitment to lower-division students, are quite likely to have innovative subdoctoral programs, while schools that award graduate degrees, and even many four-year schools, are much less likely to make innovations in undergraduate education.

Patricia Keith-Spiegel is a professor of psychology at California State University, Northridge, and David L. Cole is a professor of psychology at Occidental College.

This chapter is based on a paper presented by Patricia Keith-Spiegel at the 84th annual meeting of the American Psychological Association, Washington, D.C., September 1976, and on a paper presented by David L. Cole at the 1976 meetings of the California State Psychological Association.

The authors acknowledge the ideas contributed by the other members of the Los Angeles area subcommittee on undergraduate training (created by APA's Education and Training Board)—Lisa Gray-Shellberg, Albert Urmer, and Mae Ziskin. However, responsibility for the content of this chapter remains the authors'.

Resistance Point 3: The Elusive Search for Departmental Agreement

Even in small psychology departments, faculty members seldom agree on much of anything. With the discipline of psychology containing so many subspecialties (to the point where it is sometimes difficult for psychologists to communicate with each other), it is perhaps no wonder that the process of establishing departmental priorities often falls just short of bloodshed. Thus, it is not uncommon to hear of plans being drawn up for curriculum or program changes and then to find that the department itself is hopelessly deadlocked when it comes to a vote. As a result, the status quo usually prevails and the enthusiastic innovators begin to burn out.

Resistance Point 4: Strangled by Administrative Red Tape

Even if enthusiasm (or at least general support) for an alteration in the undergraduate program can be mustered within a department, the red tape involved in effecting the change is often oppressive and depressing. What with the competition across departments to attract full-time-equivalent students (and thus funds) and the competition resulting from decreasing enrollments, other disciplines within the university may object as the plan moves up the already cumbersome administrative approval channels—particularly if features of the program impinge on what these disciplines perceive as their territory. It sometimes takes very little for a psychology department to upset the sociology, home economics, educational psychology, and biology departments!

Resistance Point 5: The Real-World Squeeze

These intradepartment and interuniversity resistances may be only the initial barriers to establishing new programs. Another formidable resistance to new psychology programs may also come from other disciplines operating in the community (e.g., from social welfare and public health workers and from nursing professionals). Many of the kinds of salable skills psychology departments might be able to develop at the bachelor's level may impinge on the territories already tagged by other disciplines. Unless psychology is willing to get out there and establish niches for its own subdoctoral personnel, it may be too late into the human services arena.

Resistance Point 6: What Professors Don't Know

Although most professors have PhDs, few are qualified to teach salable skills that will enable undergraduates to compete in the job market with bachelor's degrees. Most faculty (ourselves included) learned to teach the way they were taught, and acquiring new skills or perspectives often means dedication to a period of retraining. And after suffering all those years to be stamped as certified psychologists, admitting that we are still deficient in being able to meet contemporary students' and society's needs does not sit well with our egos. It may be easier to renounce new models rather than attempt the arduous task of preparing to adapt to them.

Resistance Point 7: Reluctance to Change Departmental Staff Make-Ups

One way to make innovative changes at the undergraduate level would be to hire faculty who already have the needed skills and expertise. But there are practical barriers and philosophical objections to solving the problem so simply. The obvious practical disadvantage is that most departments do not have the funds to hire many new faculty, and the few openings that occur are usually in the existing traditional programs. And, using the traditional criteria for filling positions in traditional areas, hiring will be relatively simple, since it is a buyer's market for traditionally trained PhDs. Why buy trouble by being innovative when it is so easy to be traditional?

The philosophical barriers to hiring new types of teaching faculty center largely around academic elitism. Hiring the best persons to conduct an innovative undergraduate program may involve choosing among applicants other than PhD psychologists. A social worker, someone with an MA in public health, or even an experienced community worker without a college degree may be the most qualified candidate. However, psychology faculty might not accept such persons as peers, nor may such persons, even if accepted, easily adapt to the rigidities of university retention and promotion criteria.

Resistance Point 8: Inconvenience

Much of the work required to train students in innovative ways requires moving out into the community, since traditional academic institutions usually do not and cannot provide for such learning experiences on campus. This, however, also requires faculty to move out from the ivory tower, and many do not want to put up with the inconvenience. Even graduate programs in such areas as community and school psychology may have trouble finding faculty volunteers for field-supervision duty, a task often rotated by fiat and grudgingly performed. There may also be considerable resistance to having to manage larger numbers of students spread all over the map. It is so much easier just to wander down the hall to a classroom to find one's students all in one place seated in neat, little rows waiting to listen to what one has to say for an hour.

Resistance Point 9: The Accreditation Problem

Even if there is a move toward bachelor's-level training programs that stress acquisition of salable skills, the question of accreditation remains a problem. Those who oppose the increasing "unionization" of psychology would strongly resist APA or another organization accrediting bachelor's-level programs. The current notion that a psychologist must have designated competencies to do designated work is based on slippery assumptions. One must question whether the effectiveness of a psychological technician, at any level of training, is based primarily on technical skill. More important may be maturity, empathy, and perspective—attributes not always present even in those completing the PhD. Training in technique may create skilled technicians and true believers but not necessarily wise people.

Resistance Point 10: Competition From Below

A major, though perhaps unspoken, source of resistance to creating viable undergraduate programs is no doubt deep-seated fears on the part of many psychologists that people trained at the bachelor's level will be able to function, at a lower level of pay, in positions formerly held by psychologists with advanced degrees. This potential for "watering down" the status and salary of those in the profession is further exacerbated by a continuous worsening of an already poor job market for advanced-degree holders and by psychologists' struggles to be recognized nationally as legitimate health service providers.

The upshot of such resistance, however, may ultimately work against the profession by creating the very nightmare psychologists have been hoping to protect themselves from. Well-meaning persons who have sought to keep psychology scientifically and professionally pure by systematically screening out all but the most tenacious and competent are becoming aware of forces now welling up against them. Because of the demand for psychological services at affordable rates, many people without extensive training and licensing are entering the field. They receive other certification and perform services similar to those performed by a licensed psychologist with a PhD.

Further, if traditional, accredited schools will not award PhDs to huge numbers of people, then, because of the demand, other institutions will. While many psychologists are disturbed by the problems created by the proliferation of unaccredited doctoral programs, they may not fully realize that the profession's elitist attitude could be responsible.

While psychologists lament that poorly prepared people are getting into the people-services business and that the already troubled consumer may be falling into the hands of people who do not know exactly what they are doing, they seem to be myopic with regard to alternatives. By focusing only on how to keep the diploma-mill graduates and license evaders out of business, the profession is avoiding any real solution to the problem.

"Volunteerism" is also part of the dilemma. Psychology wants its undergraduates to get out into the field. And the field, it appears, is ready to sop them up like a thirsty sponge. Departments receive scores of letters each year from agencies in the community saying, "Send us your students;

we will give them real-world experiences." Thus it is not even necessary to go knocking on doors to find field placement opportunities. This all seems like a happy symbiosis, but it needs to be looked at more deeply. Most community agencies are underfunded and understaffed. Psychology students are sometimes used to perform functions that require far more training then they have actually received. They often serve as group leaders, caseworkers, and testers and even perform one-to-one therapy. When psychologists can bring themselves to face this situation, they may wonder whether they are not actually providing a steady stream of undergraduates to cope, without pay, with the mental health needs of the areas near their institutions.

Resistance Point 11: What Would BA Psychologists Be Trained to Do?

Another related resistance, or at least concern, among those who would otherwise be enthusiastic about implementing new undergraduate programs surfaces when attempting to answer the question, "What should we train bachelor's-level psychologists to do?" We should be able to train students to do something useful in four years, but what?

One innovation that has been attempted in a number of community and four-year colleges is the paraprofessional program. But often the unconscious attitude is adopted that such training is aimed at the person who would accept tasks that no fully trained psychologist wants to perform. In addition, most successful paraprofessional programs have prepared students to work in inner-city areas or other places where persons with graduate degrees would not want to work anyway. Honest and large-scale paraprofessional training programs should prepare students for work in all areas of society, including those presently the domain of the PhD psychologist.

Some PhD psychologists, however, offer no resistance to career-ladder training at the subdoctoral level because it may serve to protect them against further competition from new people flooding the field. Thus it is possible that some PhDs may support lower-level, salable-skill training primarily because it might relegate the hordes currently in the psychology training pipeline to terminal job slots that do not threaten the domain of the PhD.

Conclusion

Psychology is popular among undergraduate students, both majors and nonmajors. Psychology departments offer an array of classes and develop new ones as demand arises. From an academic vantage point psychology "has it made"—given the financial resources, psychology departments can always fill their classes with students!

But looking deeper at the field, one finds it subdivided in varied and colorful ways horizontally (social, child, abnormal, physiological, humanistic, etc.) but *not* vertically. Except for a few limited MA certifications, there is only one vertical goal—the PhD. Those who stop short of this goal are considered "unfinished" and, thus, unfit. While this protects those who funnel into the top echelons, it does so at the expense of the hundreds of thousands of undergraduates who want to learn the field of psychology and who, incidentally, provide academic psychologists with their livelihood. These students deserve more than they are getting now.

REFERENCE

Nazzaro, J. R. Identity crisis in psychology. Report on teaching. *Change Magazine*, 1976, 2(8), 44–45.

30

Lisa Gray-Shellberg, Patricia Keith-Spiegel,
and Hana Kornwasser

The Undergraduate Psychology Major's Experience: What Students Can Teach Faculty

This chapter explores the student perspective on undergraduate education by assessing the views, goals, and experiences of psychology majors who responded to a 63-item questionnaire. Information obtained included these students' views of the psychology major and their reasons for choosing it, their ultimate educational and vocational goals, and their knowledge of the job market, career planning, and job information services. Responses indicated that most psychology majors have high expectations of continuing their education through the MA and PhD levels and obtaining high-paying jobs, yet most are relatively unaware of the realities of the contemporary job market in psychology. The implications of these responses for curriculum and counseling services are discussed.

It can be argued that the best way to learn what consumers of services need and want, and what their attitudes and expectations are, is to ask them directly. This approach is rare in academia, however. Our interest in the undergraduate experience led us to conduct a survey of undergraduate psychology majors regarding their attitudes toward the education they were receiving, their opinions about psychology in general, their training and career goals, their knowledge of the contemporary job market, their concerns about the future, and the persons from whom they sought guidance. The findings taught us a great deal and also pointed to numerous concerns that should be dealt with by those who have teaching and administrative responsibilities in undergraduate psychology departments.

A sample of 202 students from three institutions responded to our 63-item questionnaire that included 157 variables. The institutions were a large state university, a relatively small state college, and a small private liberal arts college.[1]

The mean age of the subjects was 25 years (median 22); 38% were males and 61% were females. Most subjects were juniors and seniors with an overall grade point average (GPA) of 2.95 and a GPA in psychology of 3.04. Thirty percent were married, and most of the married students had children.

Reasons Students Choose Psychology as a Major

Psychology was chosen as the students' main field of study for two major reasons: a desire for a career that involves helping people (31%) and an interest in the subject matter (31%). The third most frequently cited reason for choosing psychology was that it "helps me to acquire knowledge about myself and others" (16%). Using the psychology major as a vehicle for eventual teaching or research purposes was mentioned less frequently (6%). Other reasons (e.g., being influenced by a psychology course, a book, a professor, media experience, friends, relatives, or personal experience in psychotherapy) were cited by only small percentages of students.

When students were asked to cite the main reason they were in school, half of them stated "to prepare for graduate or professional training." The other half cited reasons such as wanting a college degree, attaining a broad education in the liberal arts and sciences, developing a knowledge of themselves and others, or acquiring necessary job skills and knowledge.

To determine student interest and feelings about psychology as a discipline, respondents were given a semantic differential type of measure that included three evaluative (good–bad, valuable–worthless, wise–foolish), three potency (strong–weak, hard–soft, light–heavy), and three activity (active–passive, sharp–dull, hot–cold) bipolar adjectives. On the evaluative dimension, students were quite favorable to psychology as an area of knowledge and saw it as somewhat potent and somewhat active. Females and students who planned to go to graduate school had higher evaluative and activity scores than did males and students who did not plan to go to graduate school.

Students were also asked to rate their interest level for 20 content areas of psychology. Ares of highest interest were social/personality, abnormal, clinical/counseling, child development, social problems, humanistic psychology, sex roles, and the psychology of women. The lowest areas of interest were history and systems of psychology, industrial and organizational psychology, testing and assessment, and statistics.

Lisa Gray-Shellberg is a professor of psychology at California State University Dominquez Hills, Patricia Keith-Spiegel is a professor of psychology at California State University, Northridge, and Hana Kornwasser was a student research assistant at California State University, Northridge, when this chapter was prepared.

---

1. The sample should be considered nonrandom because not every psychology major at each institution had an equal chance of learning about and thus completing the questionnaire. Also, given the length and complexity of the questionnaire, it seems reasonable to assume that the respondents were the more highly motivated majors and had a greater than usual interest in providing input about their needs, attitudes, and goals.

Throughout this chapter we avoid excessive use of statistical presentations. Two subprograms from the *Statistical Package for the Social Sciences* (SPSS) were used for data analysis: frequencies and crosstabs (Nie, Hull, Jenkins, Steinbrenner, & Bent, 1975). Whenever the relationship between two variables is discussed, the relationship is statistically significant and based on an appropriate statistical test, usually chi-square or, for ordinal level variables, Kendall's Tau B (for square tables) or Kendall's Tau C (for rectangular tables). Responses to open-ended questions were subjected to a thorough content analysis.

The majority of the students rated the courses and faculty of their psychology program as excellent or good. Library facilities were rated as adequate, while laboratory facilities were judged as requiring some improvement.

Almost all of the students (98%) rated the courses in the major as interesting, and most found these courses to be either very or moderately useful (95%) and taught at just about the right level of difficulty (79%). In general, the students felt that the faculty members were very interested that the students receive a good education, quite interested in the students' personal welfare, quite interested in motivating students to learn, but only somewhat interested in the students' futures.

Some differences were found within these variables according to sex, age, psychology grade point average, and the stated desire to obtain an MA or PhD in psychology. Females, younger majors, and majors planning to obtain higher degrees were more likely than their counterparts to be satisfied with psychology as a major and to view psychology faculty more positively on interest in students' education and welfare. Younger as compared with older students also perceived faculty as more interested in students' futures and more interested in motivating students to learn. Older students, students with a high grade point average in psychology, and students who planned to obtain higher degrees perceived their psychology courses as "easier" than did their counterparts.

The satisfaction level among students with their choice of psychology as a major was overwhelmingly high. A large majority (90%) said that they were satisfied, while only two of the respondents said that they were very dissatisfied and might change their majors.

Through several open-ended questions, majors were asked what they perceived as the "best" and "worst" aspect of their departmental program and what improvements they would like to see made. Although some of these responses were idiosyncratic to the three departments, surveyed, the flavor of the most frequently cited categories of comments is perhaps generally revealing. Favorable comments about the professors constituted the most frequently mentioned asset. Less frequently mentioned were the quality and interest level of various courses, class size (all three departments have relatively small classes), other students, and the opportunity of doing fieldwork in the community. The main discontents were with class scheduling, enrollment, and variety. Also mentioned unfavorably were competitiveness within the department, the "required" course pattern, and "too easy" courses. Another discontent cited fairly frequently was professors whose attitude, rigidity, outdated presentations, inflexibility, or egotistical stance were deplored. Most of the changes suggested by the students dealt with course, curriculum, or program changes. Students frequently mentioned that they would like to see de-emphasis on experimental courses; more focus on areas such as clinical, counseling, and social psychology; more electives and fewer required courses; more course diversity; more "practical" courses giving career information; more courses with an applied/field/volunteer emphasis; more "exciting" courses on topics such as ESP, human sexuality, ethnic studies, etc.; more rigorous program development; de-emphasis on statistics; separate major "track" programs; and better scheduling methods.

Overall, the data indicate that undergraduate psychology majors are satisfied and are pursuing their goals with enthusiasm. It is of interest to note that most of the respondents (65%) also work on outside jobs that average 16 hours per week. Further, a large proportion (61%) indicated that work, family, financial, or other personal demands made it difficult for them to pursue their education easily.

Ultimate Degree Goals

How many students plan on going to graduate school in psychology after receiving the BA degree? If the sample is at all representative, then three out of every four graduates intend to pursue the field at an advanced level. Most respondents cited, as their reason for planning to continue in school, the requirement of an advanced degree for a desired or decent job. Only 20% named the desire to obtain more education as the basis of their decision to stay in school. Women planned to continue their education just as often as men, and for the same kinds or reasons.

When students were asked if they would consider terminating their education at the BA level if a job related to their interest area that paid a living wage was available, only 46% of the students said no. Thus, it appears that the majority of those seeking advanced degrees might prefer not to continue their education if they could find relevant work with their BA degree.

One of the prime dilemmas of the graduating psychology student is assessing his or her prospects of being accepted into a graduate program. Competition is stiff because the number of applications far exceeds the available educational program slots. The respondents to our survey were, realistically or not, quite confident (63%) that they could enter a graduate program. Students planning to seek higher degrees were more confident than those without current plans for additional formal education. About one third of the students did express some doubts, but only 7% felt that they probably could not enter an advanced program. A significant positive correlation was found between both overall and psychology grade point averages and confidence about admittance to graduate school. Women and men were equally confident.

As might be expected, those wishing to continue their education can be differentiated in a number of ways from those not planning to pursue studies beyond the BA level. The graduate school aspirants, for example, were more likely to rate psychology as more valuable and satisfying, were more interested in clinical and community psychology, and were more likely to take extra electives within the psychology department. They were also more likely to have higher grade point averages in psychology. Those not choosing to pursue graduate training were more likely to have chosen psychology as a major just because the subject matter was interesting, were in school just to get a degree, and were planning on entering a career unrelated to psychology. Interestingly, no differences were found between the two groups on the value, interest, and difficulty ratings of psychology courses nor on ratings of the faculty members of their psychology departments.

The majority (67%) of the respondents would probably require financial assistance to complete their graduate programs, yet only about 33% of these expected to actually receive support from the graduate institution itself.

In summary, 80% of the respondents intended to go on to graduate school, primarily to qualify for the type of job they want. Most planned to continue even though they were aware of financial difficulties in doing so. Some kind of academic cloning process may be developing in psychology departments, with faculty members turning out carbon copies of themselves, particularly in the area of educational aspirations. Indications of possible mitigating factors can be found, however. The data from this survey indicate that many students might prefer to start their careers much earlier than did their faculty models if only they had the training and the jobs were available. The suggestion of the Vail Conference on Levels and Patterns of Training in Psychology (Korman, 1976) concerning the development of career lattices and ladders should be more seriously considered. A career ladder is vocational progression from high school, to the two-year-college level, to the four-year-college level, to the MA, and beyond. At each step the student can opt to gain salable competencies and still retain the opportunity to get back into the system in order to progress to a higher level. Such options may well be appealing to large numbers of students and may serve their needs far better than the current model.

Vocational Goals

Respondents were asked, "What is the nature of the work you hope to do as a lifetime career?" Most (40%) were interested in careers in clinical or counseling psychology. All other response categories were relatively small and included teaching jobs (5%); business-related careers (4%); school psychologists, school counselor, or educational psychologist positions (4%); researcher or experimental psychologist positions (4%); work with handicapped or retarded children (3%); careers in writing, recording, or filmmaking (3%); careers in medicine (3%); and careers in law (2%). About 4% were undecided, and the rest were classified as "other."

The degrees of confidence expressed in reaching the desired career goals were also measured: About 20% of the students thought they would obtain their goals "without question," 55% felt "fairly confident," 15% thought they "might be able to," and only 10% expressed being "somewhat worried" about achieving their career aspirations. No respondent checked the option, "I probably won't achieve my career goals."

Yet, despite the fact that most students felt confident about their career goals, four out of five reported that their educational and career plans were not very well set. Most (55%) stated that they had a general idea as to how they would proceed, one in five reported being unsure of their plans, and one in ten said they were "very confused." Many students noted that their futures largely hinged on whether or not they were accepted into graduate school.

The survey also attempted to find out what salary the respondents hoped to be earning five years after completing their education. The average student reported a desired income of $20,000 annually. Only one-fifth apparently found less than $15,000 acceptable, and another fifth hoped for a salary in excess of $25,000 per year. (Among the few sex differences found in this study is that the women's salary aspirations were significantly lower than those of the men.)

In summary, most students want to work as professional service providers, think they will achieve that goal, and expect to be relatively well paid for it. Yet their plans are nebulous—they have little knowledge about how they are going to actually progress. The comments made in response to an open-ended question about vocational goals revealed a definite need for considerably more assistance in career planning.

Support and Information for Student Career Planning

Although the formal mission of an academic institution is to transmit knowledge, ideally an institution should also provide considerable information about relevant career opportunities and how to pursue them. The survey attempted to assess the degree to which psychology majors were knowledgeable about the contemporary job market and how they obtained this knowledge.

Students were asked, "If you had to find out what graduate training programs in your area of interest existed, would you know where to start looking?" At first, the responses were at least mildly encouraging; 57% answered yes. But upon further inquiring of those who claimed knowledge of such procedures, only a handful of students actually had constructive and appropriate combinations of search ideas. Some had a few adequate ideas, but their procedures were deemed to be incomplete or not thoroughly knowledgeable. The remainder of the students had no good specific ideas (e.g., "I would look around.").

Professors were the most frequently cited source of information (19%), followed by offices or centers of counseling, placement, graduate information and career information (14%), and catalogs and manuals (14%). Less frequently cited sources were American Psychological Association publications (7.5%); the graduate schools themselves (7%); the department office (7%); library research (this often included reading of catalogs) (5.5%); "counselors" (4.5%); other students or friends (4%); specific department resources (e.g., a specific professor, a department bulletin, brochure, or newsletter, or a specific department presentation) (4%); and off-campus people in relevant fields (3.5%).

While it is not unexpected to find professors most often cited as sources of information about graduate programs, one might wonder about the extent of knowledge that most undergraduate professors have about specific graduate training programs. Keeping abreast of programs at institutions other than one's own is a big task, and many professors may even have lost touch with the current training situation at the school where they themselves were trained.

The students were asked with whom they discussed their education or career plans. The most frequently cited category was friends (87%). Professors ranked second (81%), followed by counselors (76%). parents (65%), therapists (25%), and minister, priest, or rabbi (7%).

The survey also attempted to determine if a personal friendship with a psychologist would be useful to students. Almost half of the students (47%) claimed to have such a relationship. Those who knew a psychologist were more knowledgeable about how to get into a graduate program, were more confident about getting into graduate school, were more set in their future plans, were less likely to want to terminate their education at the BA level, and generally seemed more involved in the field than were those who reported no close friendships with a psychologist.

The survey also asked students if there was at least one professor in their department with whom they could discuss or had already discussed their academic needs, interests, future plans, and the like. Approximately 75% answered yes. It was encouraging that a majority of undergraduates were able to interact directly with a professor and to discuss nonclassroom matters of concern to them, though the survey did not assess how valuable the students considered these interactions.

When asked if they knew how to look for jobs related to their interest area in psychology, 52% of the majors answered yes—an initial response rate that was mildly encouraging. But upon further inquiry of those who felt they did know this procedure, only two respondents had constructive and useful ideas. More than 50% of the respondents had adequate, although sometimes nebulous, ideas, and 38% gave very inadequate responses.

Of the sources cited for jobs related to psychology, about 33% of those responding mentioned centers or offices on campus such as the college career office. The second most frequently cited source was the faculty (or academic advisers). Fairly frequently cited sources included community agencies, hospitals, clinics, and schools. Sources ranged from the specific ("county building, Los Angeles" to the vague "I would call research centers to find out which skills I should develop in order to perform the work required"). Less frequently cited information sources were libraries; people working in the field; publications (e.g., the APA *Monitor*, vocational guides, occupations handbooks, and various state or county pamphlets); counselors; employment/unemployment offices; and friends. Many other comments were diffuse and included "everywhere" and "the Yellow Pages."

Each of the three institutions sampled has a job placement or career service available to students. Over 75% of the respondents knew of the existence of such a service; 20% reported that they had used the service and that it was useful; and 6% reported using it but not finding it helpful. About 20% of the students did not know whether their campus operated such a service.

Student perceptions of job information resources within their departments were also assessed. A small percentage (7%) thought their department filled their needs for information about jobs and training programs related to psychology, and another 25% thought the departmental resources were adequate. However, 29% thought their department provided marginal or inadequate information services, and 38% had not looked into what resources, if any, were available at the departmental level.

Since it is possible that many students would not be aware of information needed to make informed training and career plans, the survey asked whether an elective course dealing with career alternatives, graduate programs and application procedures, job opportunities, etc., would be desirable. Almost half (45%) said they would definitely choose to take such a course if it were available, and another 33% said they probably would sign up for such a course. Those not interested tended to be students who were not planning on going to graduate school, who were already set in their career plans, who were less satisfied with their choice of psychology as a major, or who had already obtained a job related to psychology.

The results of the survey revealed that information on training and careers is not often transmitted in the context of various psychology courses offered at the institutions sampled. Students were asked to check whether or not practical aspects of psychology were discussed in the classroom. Seldom did students report any discussion of topics such as available jobs related to psychology, training requirements for different kinds of psychology jobs, licensing and certification, graduate programs, job levels for those with a BA or MA degree, and ethical standards in the profession of psychology. The need for more and better-publicized resources for students in educational and career information and planning became profoundly clear from the data.

The Returning Student

Increasing numbers of undergraduate students are returning to school after a period of time spent in other pursuits. Since 75 of the respondents (64% women and 56% men) were over the age of 25 and were returning to school after a hiatus, this population can be described and the differences and similarities noted between them and the younger students who have been in college more or less continuously since graduating from high school.

Returning students were asked, "Why did you decide to come back to college?" The largest number of respondents (29%) indicated that they wanted to further career interests; a disproportionate number of these respondents were males (64%). The second largest category (18%) of responses concerned self-fulfillment. Responses in this category were largely made by females (79%) who gave reasons such as, "I felt the need for self-identification and a need for growth"; "I wanted the exposure (for myself) and the degree for the job—which is, also, for myself." Other reasons receiving mention were to enjoy learning and the learning environment; to get a degree and/or work in the field; to experience a new beginning as a widow or divorcee; to do as one pleases and to enjoy; and to further one's education.

Returning students were also asked, "What were you doing during the years after high school that you were not in college?" The majority said they were working (25%) or working and married and/or raising a family (25%); a disproportionate number of males were in the former category, and a disproportionate number of females were in the latter category. Sixteen percent of the respondents were in the military (mostly males), 12% were married and/or raising a family (mostly females), 4% were working and traveling, and 4% (all females) were putting their spouses through school plus working, going to college, and/or raising a family. The rest of the responses were categorized as "other."

As might be expected, the older students are more likely than the younger ones to be married and have children, to work more hours per week on an outside job, and to attend school on a parttime basis. Older students also view psychology more favorably as assessed by the semantic differential measure. More older students plan on going to graduate school and are more confident of gaining entry into an advanced program. Further, they are less likely to report requiring financial assistance in order to pursue their advanced training, but they do report having more demands that make it harder for them to attend school. Older students, as compared to younger ones, rate their psychology courses as easier and rate faculty less positively on such dimensions as interest in students' welfare, students' futures, and motivating students to learn.

The returning student appears to be one who is pursuing education with purpose and vigor despite other demands and difficulties. Perhaps these students also expect a great deal from their educational experience and, as a result, judge the faculty more critically than do younger students.

Conclusions

The general picture of the current undergraduate psychology major presents some general concerns. The typical student profile appears to be that of a person who is happy with his or her choice of psychology as a major, satisfied with the departmental program, and—despite the fact that attending college requires some sacrifice and endurance of other difficulties—has high hopes of continuing his or her education through to the MA or PhD level and obtaining a well-paying job as a clinical psychologist or other type of service provider. The unfortunate trend is that many students seem to be unaware of the contemporary training and job market issues and may, therefore, be vastly overestimating their chances of being a professional psychologist at a high-entry level.

We think it would be inappropriate to cite the majority of students as ignorant and uninformed and to let it go at that. Clearly, the data show that opportunities for students to learn the necessary facts to make informed and realistic choices related to their career goals are limited or inadequately publicized.

It is evident from our findings that students believe the "truth" that American academic psychologists tend to espouse—"You can't do anything in psychology with only a BA." Psychologists may have created a self-fulfilling prophecy. Since almost everyone believes that students must obtain graduate training before being able to use their psychology knowledge vocationally, undergraduate programs are often geared to prepare the student for graduate school. The possibility of developing marketable BA-level skills is ignored or denied. Thus, baccalaureate degree holders in psychology are not prepared to make immediate use of their psychology degree and must go on to graduate school, and psychologists and students are confirmed in the belief that "you can't do anything in psychology with only a BA."

Finally, more attention should be paid to the BA-level issues by the professional organizations within psychology. More concern and action need to be directed toward issues such as the creation and discovery of new psychologically related vocations and the institution of career programs at the baccalaureate level. The newly created committee on undergraduate training of the American Psychological Association should begin the long-overdue exploration of this situation. The major underlying concern is for the tens of thousands of students who, with enthusiasm and apparent good faith, earn their BA degrees in psychology and want to go on to graduate school, not fully realizing that the room at the top is not large enough to accommodate them.

REFERENCES

Korman, M. (Ed.). *Levels and patterns of professional training in psychology*. Washington, D.C.: American Psychological Association, 1976.

Nie, N. H., Hull, C. H., Jenkins, J. G., Steinbrenner, K., & Bent, D. H. *Statistical package for the social sciences*. New York: McGraw-Hill, 1975.

Part V ————————————————————

Appendixes

Appendix A

Teresa R. McDevitt and Douglas W. Bloomquist

Curriculum and Careers in Psychology: A Bibliography

The following annotated bibliography includes references that provide some answers to several important questions concerning the predicament of the undergraduate major in psychology: (a) What are psychology graduates doing? (b) What are the employment prospects for liberal arts graduates (including psychology majors)? (c) What curriculum changes are recommended for improving the employment prospects of the undergraduate?

A preliminary version of this bibliography was prepared in 1976 by the first author as part of an undergraduate independent research project on careers for the bachelor's-degree psychology graduate. The list of entries is not intended to be exhaustive. We chose to exclude books, articles in popular magazines, and papers presented at regional and APA conventions. As a result of these and other selection criteria, the majority of the references cited occur in recent issues of *The Chronicle of Higher Education*, the *American Psychologist*, and *Teaching of Psychology* (formerly the *Teaching of Psychology Newsletter*). *The Chronicle*, published 46 times a year, frequently reports on employment trends for college graduates based on large-sample surveys. Articles in *Teaching of Psychology* and the *American Psychologist* describe surveys of psychology graduates and their prospective employers; the recommendations for curriculum changes presented by these authors surely invite discussion.

The bibliography includes several articles that describe practicum or field-experience courses. The importance of including this kind of course in the undergraduate curriculum is clearly documented (in the bibliography, see the following entries: College Placement Council, 1975; Pinkus & Korn, 1973; Smith & Spatz, 1974). Other articles that describe and evaluate practicum programs can be located through other sources. The initial 717 entries provided by Johnson and Daniel (1974) have been updated annually in *Teaching of Psychology* (see Daniel, 1977; Daniel, Lux, & Knowlan, 1976; Dresser, Jones, & Daniel, 1975; Jones, Saff, & Daniel, 1974) and presently include over 1,100 references.

Annotated Bibliography

Barnette, W. L., Jr. Feedback from bachelor of arts psychology graduates. *American Psychologist*, 1961, *16*, 184–188.

Describes survey of University of Buffalo psychology graduates who received bachelor's degrees between 1948 and 1958. Reports that 68% went to graduate school (in various areas) and that most graduates regarded their BA-level training as valuable to their present occupations.

Bell, T. H. Should colleges teach salable skills? *The Chronicle of Higher Education*, April 7, 1975, p. 32.

Controversial opinions presented by the former U.S. Commissioner of Education that appear to emphasize vocational-oriented training at the expense of traditional liberal arts programs.

Cates, J. Baccalaureates in psychology, 1969 and 1970. *American Psychologist*, 1973, *28*, 262–264.

Results of extensive survey by the American Psychological Association of 4,320 baccalaureates in psychology. Presents data on educational and employment plans.

Clark, T. S. Job prospects better or worse? You choose. *The Chronicle of Higher Education*, December 15, 1975, p. 6.

Describes differing employment predictions for 1976 graduates contained in the Endicott Report and a College Placement Council survey.

College Placement Council. Liberal arts students and the job market. *The Chronicle of Higher Education*, May 5, 1975, pp. 9; 27–31.

The text of a position statement by the College Placement Council, "Four-Year Liberal Arts Graduates: Their Utilization in Business, Industry, and Government—The Problem and Some Solutions." Describes results of a 1974 survey of 698 employers who indicated that "they would hire more liberal arts graduates if they had certain business-related courses or if they had done co-op or other experiential work."

Coughlin, E. K. Job market improves for the class of '77. *The Chronicle of Higher Education*, June 20, 1977, p. 5.

Reports that 1977 college graduates received 20% more job offers than 1976 graduates. Offers for engineering, accounting, and business graduates increased the most; there was little increase in job prospects for graduates in nontechnical fields.

Daniel, R. S. Surveys of psychology baccalaureate graduates. *Teaching of Psychology Newsletter*, February 1974, pp. 8–10.

Teresa R. McDevitt is employed as a research assistant with the Geriatric Pharmacology Group at Boston State Hospital, Boston, Massachusetts; Douglas W. Bloomquist is assistant professor of psychology at Framingham State College, Massachusetts.

The authors gratefully acknowledge the ambitious efforts of Robert S. Daniel, Margo Johnson, Candace S. Jones, and others that have resulted in a continuing series of annotated bibliographies on the teaching of psychology.

Briefly summarizes survey data of psychology graduates from four private liberal arts colleges, six state colleges, and three large state universities. A high percentage of terminal BA graduates were employed in jobs in which their psychology training was used. Private colleges had the most students who went to graduate school, while state colleges had the fewest.

Draft model labels MS's, BA's "psychological assistants." *APA Monitor*, November 1975, p. 10.

States that the APA Committee on State Legislation recommends the use of the title "psychological assistant" for all those providing psychological services with less than a doctoral degree in psychology. No distinction is made between master's and bachelor's degrees.

Fields, C. M. Education and jobs: Government clarifies rules on college claims. *The Chronicle of Higher Education*, January 12, 1976, p. 8.

States that colleges that claim that a particular course of study will lead to jobs in a particular area are required to supply students with data on the employment and salaries of previously enrolled students.

Forgus, R. H. Career status of BA/BS graduates: Discussion. *Teaching of Psychology Newsletter*, February 1974, p. 7.

Estimates that 75% of psychology graduates will not be going to graduate school. Recommendations are made for adjusting psychology programs to the job market.

Goldwin, R. A. Should colleges teach salable skills? *The Chronicle of Higher Education*, April 7, 1975, p. 32.

A rebuttal to remarks by the former Commissioner of Education (see Bell, 1975, in this bibliography). Argues that learning how to learn (through a liberal studies program) is the only stable salable skill in a fluctuating job market.

Gruver, G. G. College students as therapeutic agents. *Psychological Bulletin*, 1971, *76*, 111–127.

A review of studies concerning the effectiveness of college student volunteers as therapists. Concludes that using undergraduates as nonprofessional mental health workers may help to solve the mental health personnel problem.

Jacobson, R. L. Higher education and the job crisis: Public disillusionment provokes a debate. *The Chronicle of Higher Education*, March 28, 1977, p. 3.

Describes debate at a conference of the American Association for Higher Education concerning traditional versus vocational emphasis for colleges.

The job picture: Still gloomy. *The Chronicle of Higher Education*, August 18, 1975, p. 7.

Presents the results of a survey based on job offers made to students at 156 colleges and universities from September 1974 to June 1975.

King, M. S., & Kimble, G. A. Job opportunities for undergraduate psychology majors. *American Psychologist*, 1958, *13*, 23–27.

Report of a survey in the 1950s. The results indicated that the psychology graduate was considered for jobs with other liberal arts graduates and that specific training was left up to the prospective employer.

Korn, J. H. Training and employment of BA psychologists: Report of a symposium. *Teaching of Psychology Newsletter*, February 1974, pp. 10–12.

Reviews experimental programs at four colleges that attempted to provide psychology undergraduates with professional training. Evaluations of the success of these programs are provided.

Korn, J. H., & Nodine, B. F. Facts and questions concerning career training of the psychology major. *Teaching of Psychology*, 1975, *2*, 117–119.

Provides suggestions for improving career training programs for psychology undergraduates not planning on attending graduate school. The need for faculty support and program flexibility are emphasized.

Lunneborg, P. W. Where have all the baccalaureates gone? *American Psychologist*, 1968, *23*, 826–827.

Reports 1968 survey results of 1964–1966 psychology graduates at the University of Washington. Responses from 133 of 195 graduates showed that 70% had done graduate work either in psychology (29%) or in other areas (41%). Because approximately 66% of graduates will not become psychologists, the author urges that the undergraduate psychology curriculum be modified to consider the needs of the "BA psychologist."

Lunneborg, P. W. Undergraduate psychology field work: The unwashed take over. *American Psychologist*, 1970, *25*, 1062–1064.

Describes a successful fieldwork program at the University of Washington in which students earn credit for supervised work in a community agency.

Matarazzo, J. D. Some national developments in the utilization of nontraditional mental health manpower. *American Psychologist*, 1971, *26*, 363–372.

Emphasizes the necessity for training people in areas of mental health at the prebachelor's, bachelor's, and master's level to meet the needs of society. Indicates that in recent years the role of nonprofessionals working with the mentally ill has begun to grow.

Nazzaro, J. R. Identity crisis in psychology. *Change*, 1976, *8*(2), 44–45.

Reports that in the mid-1970s an estimated 250,000 students were majoring in psychology with more than 50,000 receiving bachelor's degrees annually. Discusses changes in the undergraduate psychology curriculum during the past decade.

Nelson, R. J. Pegging education to manpower needs. *The Chronicle of Higher Education*, April 14, 1975, p. 19.

A response to an article by Scully (1975; see entry in this bibliography). States that projections about the future job market should not discourage the pursuit of higher education.

O'Brien, G. M. Job market is better than expected. *The Chronicle of Higher Education*, June 21, 1976, p. 5.

Describes a report by the College Placement Council that indicates that 1976 college graduates found about 2% fewer jobs than 1975 graduates. This drop was less than forecasted, but 17% fewer liberal arts graduates were hired than in the previous year.

Persons, R. W., Clark, C., Persons, M., Kadish, M., & Patterson, W. Training and employing undergraduates as therapists in a college counseling service. *Professional Psychology*, 1973, *4*, 170–178.

Describes a program at Antioch College in which undergraduates are trained to function as therapists in the college counseling center. The success of the program and reactions of professionals from other colleges are discussed.

Pinkus, R. B., & Korn, J. H. The preprofessional option: An alternative to graduate work in psychology. *American Psychologist*, 1973, *28*, 710–718.

Presents results of a survey regarding employment opportunities for BA-level psychology graduates in social service agencies and businesses in the Pittsburgh area. Emphasizes the value of field experience during undergraduate training.

Robinson, G. H. Another career choice for BA psychology students. *American Psychologist*, 1974, *29*, 359–360.

Suggests that an MS degree in engineering beyond a BA degree in psychology can lead to a career in the areas of engineering psychology, human factors, and ergonomics.

Semas, P. W. Job market for graduates may be best in 5 years. *The Chronicle of Higher Education*, December 13, 1976, p. 4.

Reports the results of three surveys by the College Placement Council, Frank S. Endicott, and Michigan State University, which project a 12–17% increase in job offers for college graduates in 1977. However, the survey indicate that the impact on liberal arts graduates would be "minimal" because they comprise 40% of the graduates.

Scully, M. G. A glut of college graduates? *The Chronicle of Higher Education*, March 24, 1975, pp. 1; 8.

Relates projections from the Department of Labor's Bureau of Labor Statistics that indicate that the number of college graduates in the future will far exceed the number of jobs, forcing graduates to take jobs below the level for which they are trained.

Scully, M. G. Career-oriented studies: The debate intensifies. *The Chronicle of Higher Education*, February 9, 1976, p. 3.

Opinions of both the supporters and critics of career-oriented studies are presented.

Senior's outlook grim: Jobs are even scarcer than last year. *The Chronicle of Higher Education*, March 22, 1976, p. 11.

Reports that although job offers for bachelor's-degree candidates decreased over the previous year, there were more offers than predicted. However, graduates in the humanities and social sciences experienced the greatest decline in job offers.

Simon, G. C. Some impertinent suggestions regarding the future of undergraduate education in psychology. *Teaching of Psychology Newsletter*, April 1974, pp. 5–6.

States that students' needs for valuable experiences are not being met. Argues that more practical experiences should be provided.

Smith, R. G., & Spatz, B. A review of mental health practica for undergraduates. *Teaching of Psychology Newsletter*, April 1974, pp. 7–8.

The authors suggest that the benefits of practicum or fieldwork courses for the participating student have not been emphasized in previous descriptions of such courses. They describe positive changes in attitudes and emotions commonly experienced by students.

They're hard to place: Liberal-arts graduates are paid less, too. *The Chronicle of Higher Education*, December 15, 1975, p. 6.

A discussion of the findings included in the position statement by the College Placement Council (1975; see bibliography entry).

Thomas, E. R. An alternative approach to undergraduate training in psychology. *Teaching of Psychology*, 1975, *2*, 80–81.

Estimates that 85% of undergraduate psychology students do not enter graduate programs. Describes a track system at Virginia Commonwealth University.

Thornton, G. L. The BA degree in psychology in the state colleges: Where do graduates go? What do they do? *Teaching of Psychology Newsletter*, February 1974, pp. 5–6.

Presents results of survey of psychology graduates of Pennsylvania state colleges. Recommends that colleges improve followup of their graduates and supply more assistance in job placement.

Toombs, W. Liberal arts students: Major manpower resource. *The Chronicle of Higher Education*, June 23, 1975, p. 11.

States that changes in economic policy, rather than the short-term goal of directing curricula away from the liberal arts, is the solution to the problem of underemployment of liberal arts graduates.

Turner, R. H. What happens to the liberal arts BA in psychology who doesn't go to graduate school? *Teaching of Psychology Newsletter*, February 1974, pp. 3–4.

Reports that the number of Oberlin College graduates going to graduate school decreased in the late 1960s but increased in the early 1970s.

Vetter, B. M. Projected psychology PhD's, MA's drop since last year; BA's up. *APA Monitor*, May 1973, p. 3.

Cites data from the National Center for Educational Statistics that indicate that as a percentage of all degrees granted, psychology will increase at the bachelor's level but decrease at the master's and doctoral levels.

REFERENCES

Daniel, R. S. Annotated bibliography on the teaching of psychology 1976. *Teaching of Psychology*, 1977, *4*, 210–214.

Daniel, R. S., Lux, D., & Knowlan, L. A. Annotated bibliography on the teaching of psychology 1975. *Teaching of Psychology*, 1976, *3*, 193–196.

Dresser, R. F., Jones, C. S., & Daniel, R. S. Annotated bibliography on the teaching of psychology 1974. *Teaching of Psychology*, 1975, *2*, 188–191.

Johnson, M., & Daniel, R. S. Comprehensive annotated bibliography on the teaching of psychology at the undergraduate level through 1972. JSAS *Catalog of Selected Documents in Psychology*, 1974, *4*, 108. (Ms. No. 735)

Jones, C. S., Saff, J. L., & Daniel, R. S. Annotated bibliography on the teaching of psychology 1973. *Teaching of Psychology*, 1974, *1*, 75–79.

Appendix B

U.S. Office of Personnel Management

Qualification Standards for the Psychology Series and the Psychology Aid and Technician Series

Psychology Series[1]

For positions in the Psychology occupation GS-180, grades GS-5/15: Clinical Psychologist, Counseling Psychologist, Personnel Psychologist, Engineering Psychologist, and Psychologist.

Description of Work

Psychologists engage in professional research or direct services work relating to the behavior, capacities, traits, interests and activities of both human and animal organisms. This work may involve: (1) Developing scientific principles or laws concerning the relationship of behavior to factors of environment, experience, or physiology, or to develop practical applications of findings; (2) applying phychological principles, theories, methods, or data to practical situations or problems; and (3) providing consultative services or training in psychological principles, theories, methods, and techniques.

Information regarding specializations and typical patterns of work assignments is contained in the position-classification standard for the Psychology Series, GS-180.

Education and Experience Requirements

All professional psychologist positions require at least completion of a bachelor's degree. Clinical psychologists and counseling psychologists have additional education requirements. The basic minimum requirements for all psychologist positions are stated below.

Basic Educational Requirements

Candidates for these positions must meet the minimum education requirements appropriate to the specialization in which the position is

---

1. This standard [dated January 1969 by the U.S. Civil Service Commission] supersedes the standard for this series which was issued in July 1968 by the U.S. Civil Service Commission.

classified. These are:

A. *Clinical psychologists.* For positions in grades GS-11 and above, satisfactory completion in an accredited educational institution of all the requirements for the doctoral degree (PhD or equivalent) directly related to full professional work in clinical psychology, is required.

B. *Counseling psychologists.* For positions in grades GS-9 and above, satisfactory completion in an accredited educational institution of 2 full academic years of graduate study directly related to professional work in counseling psychology, or satisfactory completion in an accredited educational institution of all the requirements for a master's degree directly related to counseling psychology, is required.

C. *Psychologists in all other specializations.* For positions in grades GS-5 and above, completion of a full 4-year course of study in an accredited college or university leading to a bachelor's or higher degree, including or supplemented by a total of 24 semester hours in psychology, is required.

Additional Requirements

Candidates for professional psychology positions must have had either professional experience or graduate education as specified below. Such professional experience or graduate education must have been in a specialized area directly related to the requirements of the position to be filled.

This experience or education must have equipped the candidate with the knowledge and ability to perform fully the work of the position for which he is being considered. For example, candidates for research positions must possess the aptitude or ability to perform professional research work at the appropriate grade level. The requirements for each grade level are:

GS-5: Candidates must meet the basic education requirements described in (C) above. No additional education or experience is required.

GS-7: In addition to the basic minimum educational requirement specified in (C) above:

(1) One full academic year of graduate study which is acceptable toward a master's or higher degree in psychology, *or*

(2) One year of experience in psychological work which included the supervised application of basic principles and techniques of psychology, *or*

This appendix is reprinted from the *U.S. Civil Service Commission Qualifications Standards Handbook X-118,* a government publication whose sections are continually updated as individual series' qualifications standards are revised.

The U.S. Civil Service Commission is now known as the U.S. Office of Personnel Management.

(3)   Any equivalent combination of education and experience.
The requirements of the standard for Superior Academic
Achievement for GS-7 in section 3, part II of this handbook,
apply.

GS-9:   *Counseling psychologist*
Candidates must meet the basic education requirements
described in (B) above. No additional education or experience
is required.
*Psychologists in all other specializations, except clinical and
counseling*
(1)   Two full academic years of graduate study which is
      creditable toward the requirements for an advanced
      degree in psychology, *or*
(2)   Two years of experience in psychological work which
      included the application of psychological principles and
      techniques. This experience must have provided clear evi-
      dence that the candidate possesses the specialized know-
      ledges and abilities required for the successful perform-
      ance of the work of the position to be filled, *or*
(3)   Completion of all the requirements for a master's degree
      directly related to the position to be filled, *or*
(4)   Any equivalent combination of education and experience.

A combination of superior academic achievement at the baccalaureate level and 1 year of appropriate professional experience is qualifying. Typically, 30 semester hours (or equivalent) of part-time graduate
study may be credited as 1 full academic year of graduate education.

GS-11:   *Clinical psychologist*
Candidates must meet the basic education requirements
described in (A) above. No additional education or experience
is required.
Counseling psychologist
(1)   Completion of the education requirements described in
      (B) above, *and* at least 1 year of professional experience
      in which the candidate has demonstrated the knowl-
      edges, skills, and abilities needed for educational, voca-
      tional, or rehabilitation counseling, *or*
(2)   Satisfactory completion, in an accredited college or
      university, of all the requirements for a doctoral degree
      (PhD or equivalent) directly related to counseling
      psychology.
Psychologists in all other specializations
(1)   Satisfactory completion, in an accredited college or
      university, of all the requirements for a doctoral degree
      (PhD or equivalent) in psychology directly related to the
      requirements of the position to be filled, *or*

(2) Three years of professional experience in which the candidate has demonstrated the knowledges, skills, and abilities required for the successful performance of the work of the position to be filled, *or*

(3) Any appropriate combination of education and experience.

For *research* positions in all specializations *except clinical*, completion of all requirements for a master's or equivalent degree based on at least 2 full academic years of graduate study when—

a. The position involves primarily *research* or very similar research-type exploratory development of a creative or advanced scientific nature.

b. The knowledges required for the work are *typically and preferably* acquired through graduate study.

c. The work is of such character that the academic preparation will equip the candidate to perform fully the professional work at the GS-11 level after a short orientation period.

GS-12: All Specializations

In addition to the requirements for GS-11 appropriate to the specialization of the position, 1 year of appropriate professional experience is required.

For *research* positions in all specializations, completion of all the requirements for a doctoral degree (PhD or equivalent) is qualifying for appointment to positions that meet the following criteria:

a. The position involves primarily research or very similar research-type exploratory development of a creative or advanced scientific nature.

b. The knowledges required for the work are typically and preferably acquired through graduate study at the doctoral (PhD or equivalent) level.

c. The work is of such character that the academic preparation will equip the candidate to perform fully the professional work at the GS-12 level after a short orientation period.

GS-13/15: All Specializations

For each successively higher grade a correspondingly higher level and quality of experience is required. This experience must demonstrate clearly the candidate's ability to perform the work of the position being filled.

Quality of Experience

For positions at any grade, the required amount of experience will not in itself be accepted as proof of qualification for a position. The candidate's record of education and experience must clearly demonstrate that he or she has the ability to perform the duties of the position. The primary consideration is the quality and level of experience.

For eligibility at grades GS-7 through GS-11 at least 1 year of the required qualifying professional experience must have been comparable in difficulty and responsibility to the second lower grade in the Federal service. For eligibility at GS-12 and above, at least 1 year of the required qualifying professional experience must have been comparable in difficulty and responsibility to the next lower grade in the Federal service.

Supervisory Positions

For supervisory positions see the qualification standard for "Supervisory Positions in General Schedule Occupations," in part III of this handbook.

Basis of Rating

No written test is required for any position in this occupation. Candidates will be rated on the basis of their education, training, experience, and personal qualifications in relation to the requirements of the specific positions for which they are being considered. Ratings will be based on competitors' statement in their applications and on any additional evidence that may be secured through qualifications inquiries.

Interview Requirements

Mature judgment and skill in interpersonal relationships is critically important to the successful accomplishment of the work in many psychologist positions. Accordingly, candidates may be required to appear for a preemployment interview to assist in evaluating such skills.

Guide for Evaluating Qualifications

The evaluation of the psychologist's training, experience, skill, and ability is crucial to effective staffing. This evaluation is complicated by the fact that patterns of individual professional growth and development and the specific requirements of individual positions vary widely. Thus, particular care must be exercised in the appraisal of the education and experience offered by candidates for these positions.

Courses covering the same theoretical concepts or principles do not always bear the same major field or course titles. Similarly, not all course work within a broadly defined specialty field of psychology is necessarily relevant to the requirements of specific positions in that specialty field. For example, candidates with course work in social, clinical, or experimental psychology together with courses in counseling psychology may fully meet the basic educational requirements for counseling psychology positions.

Candidates offering academic preparation in higher mathematics, engineering, or the physical sciences in addition to courses in psychology, may have had excellent preparation for engineering psychology positions. Similarly, some candidates may offer additional courses in such fields as sociology, anthropology, or linguistics which may be particularly germane to the specialized demands of the individual position to be filled, or to target positions in the career ladder. Such additional preparation should be taken into account both in the appraisal of the overall breadth and quality of the candidate's education and in filling particular specialized positions.

For direct services or training positions, certification as a Diplomate by the American Board of Examiners in Professional Psychology should be given appropriate weight in assessing the overall background of postdoctoral training and experience.

Where possible, evaluation of the candidate's background should be made in consultation with psychologists of high standing in their field who have had some training in examining qualifications and appraising the significance of scientific achievement. To aid in this evaluation, applicants should furnish concise summaries of the substance of their course work as well as course titles. They should also provide clear and concise information about their professional work assignments. This information should describe the nature of the professional problems they have been called upon to solve and their contribution to the problem-solving process.

Selective Placement

In considering candidates for placement it is important to bear in mind that the boundaries between specialized areas of work in the field of psychology are not absolute. Thus, education or experience gained in one specialized area may be directly relevant to the requirements of a position classified in a different speciality field. The paramount consideration is the extent to which the psychologist's total background of education and experience meets the actual requirements of the position to be filled. It is often necessary to look beyond course titles and position titles to assess this relevance.

Physical Requirements

See part II, Physical Requirements, paragraph 1; in addition, some positions may be suitable for the deaf. Applicants must also possess emotional and mental stability.

Psychology Aid and Technician Series[2]

For Psychology Aid, GS-4, and Psychology Technician, GS-5/9.

Description of Work

Psychology Aids and Psychology Technicians perform nonprofessional technical work in connection with a program of research or direct services in psychology. They use a practical understanding of some of the principles, methods, and techniques of psychology to carry out their duties in assisting professional psychologists.

---

2. Issued in February 1962 by the U.S. Civil Service Commission.

Experience

Years of Experience Required

Grade	General (years)	Specialized (years)	Total (years)
GS-4	1½	½	2
GS-5	1½	1½	3
GS-6	1½	2	3½
GS-7	1½	2½	4
GS-8	1½	3	4½
GS-9	1½	3½	5

General Experience

For any grade, experience must have been acquired through work which has provided training and experience in the observation of, and assistance in, application of techniques characteristic of work which relates to behavior, capacities, traits, interests, and activities of either humans or, under laboratory conditions, of animals. For positions involving statistical or graphic work, experience involving simple graphics or substantial arithmetic involving following some routine statistical formulae is acceptable, as is experience collecting data to assist a psychologist or statistician.

Specialized Experience

The specialized experience required must have been in connection with a program of research or direct services in psychology which gave a practical understanding of some of the principles, methods, and techniques of psychology needed to assist professional psychologists. For technician positions at grades GS-7 and above, at least 1 year of the specialized experience must have been in the specific type of psychology program (for example, engineering psychology laboratory) in which the position to be filled is located.

Quality of Experience

For all grades, at least 6 months of the experience must have been at a level of difficulty comparable to the next lower grade or, 1 year at a level comparable to the second lower grade in the Federal service.

Substitution of Education for Experience

A.   The successful completion of a full 4-year or senior high school curriculum may be substituted for 6 months of the general experience requirement.

B.   The successful completion of a full 4-year or senior high school curriculum which has included a combination of at least six ½-year courses in psychology, biology, physics, and/or algebra, trigonometry, or other mathematics courses (excluding general science) may be substituted for 1 year of the general experience requirement. High school study may not be substituted for any part of the specialized experience required at any grade.

C. Successfully completed study in an accredited college or university which averaged at least 6 semester hours per year in psychology and statistics may be substituted for the required general and specialized experience on the basis of 1 academic year of study for 9 months of experience, except that the total substitution of education (high school and college) for experience may not exceed 3 years.

Basis of Rating

Applicants will be rated on a scale of 100 on the basis of an evaluation of their experience, education, and references.

Physical Requirements

See part II, Physical Requirements, paragraph 3; in addition, some positions may be suitable for the deaf.

P.R. Codes: A-1, 3; B-1, 2, 3, 4, 5, 6, 7, 8; C-1, 2, 3; D-1; E.

Appendix C

Bruce R. Fretz and John G. Tiedemann

Federal Job Information Centers and State Personnel Offices

———— Federal Job Information Centers ————

Alabama

Southerland Bldg., 806 Governors Dr. S.W., Huntsville 35801

Alaska

Hill Bldg., 617 G St., Anchorage 99501

Arizona

522 N. Central Ave., Phoenix 85004

Arkansas

Federal Bldg., Rm. 1319, 700 W. Capitol Ave., Little Rock 72201

California

Eastern Columbia Bldg., 851 S. Broadway, Los Angeles 90014
Federal Bldg., 650 Capitol Mall, Sacramento 95814
Suite 2100, 110 West C St., San Diego 92101
Federal Bldg., Rm. 1001, 450 Golden Gate Ave., San Francisco 94102

Colorado

Post Office Bldg., Rm. 203, 1823 Stout St., Denver 80202

Connecticut

Federal Bldg., Rm. 717, 450 Main St., Hartford 06103

Delaware

Federal Bldg., 844 King St., Wilmington 19801

District of Columbia

U.S. Office of Personnel Management, 1900 E St., N.W., Washington, D.C. 20415

Florida

1000 Brickell Ave., Suite 660, Miami 33131
3101 Maguire Blvd., Orlando 32803

Georgia

Federal Bldg., 275 Peachtree St., N.E., Atlanta 30303

Guam

GCIC Bldg., Suite 201, 190 W. Soledad Ave., Agana 96910

Hawaii

1000 Bishop St., Suite 1500, Honolulu 96813

Idaho

Federal Bldg.-U.S. Courthouse, Rm. 663, 550 W. Fort St., Boise 83724

Illinois

Dirksen Bldg., Rm. 1322, 219 S. Dearborn St., Chicago 60604

Indiana

46 East Ohio St., Indianapolis 46204

Iowa

191 Federal Bldg., 210 Walnut St., Des Moines 50309

Kansas

One-Twenty Bldg., Rm. 101, 120 S. Market St., Wichita 67202

Kentucky

Federal Bldg., Rm. 167, 600 Federal Pl., Louisville 40202

Louisiana

F. Edward Hebert Bldg., 610 South St., New Orleans 70130

Maine

Federal Bldg., Rm. 611, Sewall St. & Western Ave., Augusta 04330

Maryland

Federal Bldg., Lombard St. & Hopkins Pl., Baltimore 21201
D.C. Metro Area: U.S. Office of Personnel Management, 1900 E St., N.W., Washington, D.C. 20415

Bruce R. Fretz is a professor of psychology at the University of Maryland, and John G. Tiedemann is in private practice in Washington, D.C.

Massachusetts

3 Center Plaza, Boston 02108

Michigan

Lafayette Bldg., Lobby, 144 W. Lafayette St., Detroit 48226

Minnesota

Federal Bldg., Rm. 196, Ft. Snelling, Twin Cities 55111

Mississippi

802 N. State St., Jackson 39201

Missouri

Federal Bldg., Rm. 129, 601 E. 12th St., Kansas City 64106
Federal Bldg., Rm. 1712, 1520 Market St., St. Louis 63103

Montana

IBM Bldg., 130 Neil Ave., Helena 59601

Nebraska

U.S. Courthouse and Post Office Bldg., Rm. 1014, 215 N. 17th St., Omaha
68102

Nevada

Main Post Office, Rm. 238, 50 So. Virginia St., Reno 89505

New Hampshire

Federal Bldg., Rm. 104, Daniel & Penhallow Sts., Portsmouth 03801

New Jersey

Federal Bldg., 970 Broad St., Newark 07102

New Mexico

Federal Bldg., 421 Gold Ave. S.W., Albuquerque 87101

New York

590 Grand Concourse, Bronx 10451
111 W. Huron St., Rm. 35, Buffalo 14202
90-04 161st St., Rm. 200, Jamaica 11432
Federal Bldg., 26 Federal Plaza, New York City 10007
O'Donnell Bldg., 301 Erie Blvd. W., Syracuse 13202

North Carolina

Federal Bldg., 310 New Bern Ave., P.O. Box 25069, Raleigh 27601

North Dakota

Federal Bldg., Rm. 202, 657 Second Ave. N., Fargo 58102

Ohio

Federal Bldg., 1240 Ninth St., Cleveland 44199
Grant-Deneau Bldg., Rm. 610, 40 W. Fourth St., Dayton 45402

Oklahoma

210 NW Sixth St., Oklahoma City 73102

Oregon

Multnomah Bldg., Lobby, 319 SW Pine St., Portland 97204

Pennsylvania

Federal Bldg., Rm. 168, Harrisburg 17108
William J. Green, Jr. Federal Bldg., 600 Arch St., Philadelphia 19106
Federal Bldg., 1000 Liberty Ave., Pittsburgh 15222

Puerto Rico

Pan Am Bldg., 255 Ponce de Leon Ave., Hato Rey, (San Juan) PR 00917

Rhode Island

Federal and Post Office Bldg., Rm. 310, Kennedy Plaza, Providence 02903

South Carolina

Federal Bldg., 334 Meeting St., Charleston 29403

South Dakota

Room 201, Federal Bldg.-U.S. Court House, 515 9th St., Rapid City 57701

Tennessee

Federal Bldg., 167 N. Main St., Memphis 38103

Texas

Rm. 1042, 1100 Commerce St., Dallas 75202
El Paso National Bank Bldg., 411 N. Stanton St., El Paso 79901
702 Caroline St., Houston 77002
643 East Durango Blvd., San Antonio 78205

Utah

350 South Main St., Rm. 484, Salt Lake City 84101

Vermont

Federal Bldg., Rm. 308, Elmwood Ave. & Pearl St., Burlington 05401

Virginia

415 St. Paul's Blvd., Norfolk 23510

D.C. Metro Area: U.S. Office of Personnel Management, 1900 E St., N.W., Washington, D.C. 20415

Washington

Federal Bldg., 915 Second Ave., Seattle 98174

West Virginia

Federal Bldg., 500 Quarrier St., Charleston 25301

Wisconsin

Plankinton Bldg., Rm. 205, 161 W. Wisconsin Ave., Milwaukee 53203

Wyoming

Teton Bldg., Rm. 108, 1805 Capitol Ave., Cheyenne 82001

——————————— State Personnel Offices ———————————

Alabama

J. S. Fraser, Director, State Personnel Dept., 402 State Administration Bldg., Montgomery 36130

Alaska

Patrick L. Hunt, Director, Div. of Personnel & Labor Relations, Pouch C, Juneau 99801

Arizona

Richard Rabago, Acting Assistant Director for Personnel, State of Arizona, 1831 W. Jefferson, Phoenix 85007

Arkansas

Sherman E. Tate, Administrator, Dept. of Finance & Administration, Office of Personnel Management, P.O. Box 3278, Little Rock 72203

California

Recruitment Supervisor, State Personnel Board, 801 Capitol Mall, Sacramento 95814

Colorado

Rudolph Livingston, Executive Director, Dept. of Personnel, 118 State Centennial Bldg., Denver 80203

Connecticut

C. Perry Phillips, Personnel Commissioner, Dept. of Personnel, 404 State Office Bldg., Hartford 06115

Delaware

Fred N. VanSant, Director, State Office of Personnel, Townsend Bldg., Dover 19901

District of Columbia

Mildred J. Duckwilder, Acting Director, Office of Personnel, 499 Pennsylvania Ave., N.W., Washington, D.C. 20001

Florida

Conley M. Kennison, State Personnel Director, Div. of Personnel, 435 Carlton Bldg., Tallahassee 32304

Georgia

Ralph C. Moor, Acting Director, State Merit System, Applied Services Div., 244 Washington St., Rm. 572, Atlanta 30334

Guam

John S. Salas, Administrator, Personnel Services Div., Dept. of Administration, Government of Guam, P.O. Box 884, Agana 96910

Hawaii

Donald A. Botelho, Director, Dept. of Personnel Services, Keelikolani Bldg., Honolulu 96813

Idaho

Richard L. Barrett, State Personnel Director, Idaho Personnel Commission, 700 West State St., Boise 83720

Illinois

William Boys, Director, Dept. of Personnel, 503 William G. Stratton Bldg., Springfield 62706

Indiana

Alan J. Fromuth, Director, Personnel Div., Dept. of Administration, State Office Bldg., Indianapolis 46204

Iowa

Wallace L. Keating, Director, Iowa Merit Employment Dept., Grimes State Office Bldg., East Fourteenth and Grand Ave., Des Moines 50319

Kansas

Lowell Long, Director of Personnel, Div. of Personnel, Dept. of Administration, Room 128 S., State Office Bldg., Topeka 66612

Kentucky

Addie D. Stokley, Rm. 373, New Capitol Annex, Dept. of Personnel, Frankfort 40601

Louisiana

Harold E. Forbes, Director of Personnel, Dept. of Civil Service, State Land & Natural Resources Bldg., Baton Rouge 70801

Maine

Robert J. Stolt, Commissioner, Dept. of Personnel, State Office Bldg., Augusta 04333

Maryland

Henry B. Bosz, Secretary, Maryland State Dept. of Personnel, Recruitment Div., 301 West Preston St., Baltimore 21201

Massachusetts

Edward W. Powers, Director, Civil Service Div., Dept. of Civil Service & Regulation, 294 Washington St., Boston 02108

Michigan

Richard A. Ross, State Personnel Director, Lewis Cass Bldg., 320 S. Walnut St., Lansing 48909

Minnesota

Michael O'Donnell, Acting Commissioner, Dept. of Personnel, 215 Administration Bldg., St. Paul 55155

Mississippi

Guy Groff, Jr., Mississippi Classification Commission, 8th Floor, R. E. Lee Bldg., Jackson 39201

Missouri

Edward Godar, Director, Div. of Personnel, Office of Administration, Box 388, Jefferson City 65101

Montana

C. C. Warner, Deputy Administrator, Employment Security Div., Rm. 201, Employment Security Bldg., Lockey & Roberts, Helena 59601

Nebraska

Roy Gardner, Director, Dept. of Personnel, Box 94773, Lincoln 68509

Nevada

James F. Wittenberg, Administrator, Personnel Div., Dept. of General Services, 205 Blasdell Bldg., Carson City 89701

New Hampshire

Roy Y. Lang, Director, Dept. of Personnel, 1 State House Annex, Concord 03301

New Jersey

Ralph P. Shaw, Chief Examiner and Secretary, New Jersey Dept. of Civil Service, 215 East State St., Trenton 08625

New Mexico

Glen Gares, Director, Personnel Office, 130 S. Capitol St., Sante Fe 87501

New York

Victor S. Bahou, President, New York State Civil Service Commission, State Office Bldg. Campus, Bldg. 1, Albany 12239

North Carolina

Harold H. Webb, Director, Office of State Personnel, Dept. of Administration, 116 West Jones St., Raleigh 27603

North Dakota

Richard A. Espeland, Director, Central Personnel Div., State Capitol, Bismarck 58505

Ohio

Phillip S. Hamilton, Deputy Director, Div. of Personnel, Dept. of Administrative Services, 30 East Broad St., Rm. 2842, Columbus 43215

Oklahoma

Keith B. Frosco, Director, Oklahoma Merit System Office, Jim Thorpe Memorial Office Bldg., 2101 North Lincoln Blvd., State Capitol Complex, Oklahoma City 73105

Oregon

Laurence R. Sprecher, Acting Administrator, Executive Dept., Personnel Div., 100 Public Service Bldg., Salem 97310

Pennsylvania

Charles T. Sciotto, Director, Bureau of Personnel, Office of the Governor, 517 Finance Bldg., Harrisburg 17120

Rhode Island

Leo R. McAloon, Jr., Administrator, Rhode Island Div. of Personnel, 289

South Carolina

Jack S. Mullins, Director, State Personnel Div., 1205 Pendleton St., Columbia 29201

South Dakota

Dorothy J. Howe, Commissioner, Bureau of Personnel, State Capitol, Pierre 57501

Tennessee

J. N. Doane, Commissioner, Dept. of Personnel, 1407 Andrew Jackson Bldg., Nashville 37219

Utah

Edward T. Himstreet, Director, Personnel Office, 130 State Capitol, Salt Lake City 84114

Vermont

Jacquel-Anne Chouinard, Commissioner, Dept. of Personnel, Agency of Administration, 110 State St., Montpelier 05602

Virginia

Ralph C. Robinson, Merit System Supervisor, Dept. of Personnel & Training, 206 State Finance Bldg., Richmond 23219

Washington

Leonard Nord, Director, Dept. of Personnel, 600 South Franklin St., Olympia 98504

West Virginia

Arden Hodges, Director of Personnel, Civil Service System, State Office Bldg. #6, Charleston 25305

Wisconsin

Verne H. Knoll, Deputy Director, Bureau of Personnel, Dept. of Administration, One West Wilson St., Rm. 215, Madison 53702

Wyoming

Pete J. Kithas, Administrator, Personnel Div., Dept. of Administration & Fiscal Control, Emerson Bldg., Cheyenne 82001

American Samoa

William Roberts, Director, Dept. of Manpower Resources, Government of American Samoa, Pago Pago 96799

Appendix D

Vicki M. Wilson and Patricia W. Lunneborg

Beyond the Bachelor's Degree

This practical, how-to-get-into-graduate-school appendix is aimed at guaranteeing a student's acceptance into graduate school in psychology. Based on the author's experience advising psychology majors, it takes a very firm approach to taking enough mathematics and natural science, preparing for the Graduate Record Examination, and getting extensive undergraduate research experience. Working to get competitive credentials together, using an application strategy that emphasizes applying to several schools of varying prestige, and maintaining an attitude of realistic optimism are recommended. A guide to preparing a résumé appropriate for graduate schools is included, as is a suggested schedule of activities throughout college to prepare for graduate school.

This appendix focuses on the strategies to be applied by that minority of undergraduate psychology majors seeking acceptance into psychology graduate programs. Because the myth that one "can't do *anything* with just a bachelor's degree" is widespread, it may seem surprising that those planning to enter graduate school constitute only a small proportion of psychology graduates. Yet in Kulick's (1973) review of undergraduate education in psychology, departmental chairpersons estimated that only from one-fourth to one-third of their students were oriented toward graduate school. More recently (1975–1977) at the University of Washington, fewer than 20% of each class have been applying to graduate school.

Why, then, should there be any need for strategies to get in? Remembering the fairly uncomplicated transition from high school to college, many students think that a similar transition takes place between undergraduate and graduate study. No so! The competition for acceptance into graduate school is incredibly keen. At many prestigious institutions, 100 applications are received for every position (American Psychological Association, 1976). The competition is similar to that for medical school, with one important difference. If one truly wants to continue in psychology, is willing to take the time needed for preparation, and develops a reasonable application strategy, one will probably be accepted in a graduate program, although not necessarily at one's first- or even second-choice school.

Jobs in traditional settings for psychologists are slowly drying up. Opportunities in colleges are declining slowly but steadily, as are those in

319

hospitals and clinics. The major positive change is an increase in opportunities with state and local governments (Cuca, 1975). Wood's (1976) *Career Opportunities for Psychologists*, with its emphasis on expanding and emerging nontraditional areas, is testimony to this changing market, as is Zambrano and Entine's (1976) *Career Alternatives for Academics*. So there is a good market for psychologists, but it is a different market, and fresh PhDs will have to seek new settings and work activities in which their training and expertise can be fully utilized.

The decision to attend graduate school, then, should really be a function of the desire to become a psychologist, to study psychology because it's the area in which one wants to become educated. Students should ask themselves where in their list of priorities becoming a psychologist falls. If they have other goals or obligations that have higher priority, these *may* limit their chances for acceptance into graduate study. For example, if one decides to remain in San Francisco, such a decision reduces one's chances for advanced study, since to maximize the chances of acceptance one must apply to schools of varying *geographic* location. The fact is that not everyone who would like to go on in psychology wants it more than anything else in life; there may be other things of more importance, depending on the individual. However, the fewer restrictions one puts on becoming a psychologist (i.e., I must live *here*, I must attend school *there*), the higher the probability that one will make it.

A bright spot—after asking the above question many students might look at alternative ways of meeting their career goals and discover that psychology might not be so right for them after all. They may find that a program in social work, educational psychology, business, public affairs, guidance and counseling, law, nutrition, occupational therapy, or special education may be more appropriate to their needs and desires and less difficult to enter.

After making the decision to continue in psychology, what should one do? There are three keys to achieving acceptance into a graduate program: *persistence, preparation,* and *application know-how.*

Persistence

Webster defines persistence as "stubborn or enduring continuance, as in a chosen course or purpose." Essentially it means hanging in there until one makes it. No matter what obstacles appears and regardless of whatever pessimistic advice is received, one must maintain dedication to one's academic goals and career objectives and refuse to be deterred. Schools look favorably on those who demonstrate decisiveness. One student, against our advice, decided that there was only one school for her. After applying there for three consecutive years she was finally accepted. Each time she was rejected, however, she found out the reason for the rejection

Vicki M. Wilson is an academic advisor and Patricia W. Lunneborg is an associate professor in the Department of Psychology at the University of Washington.

and worked to correct the deficiency. Her dedication and willingness to work hard finally paid off.

Preparation

Preparation is an easy word referring to a not-so-easy task. In this context it means using one's undergraduate years (not necessarily four years but possibly five or six) to build attractive credentials. As a potential graduate student one will be judged on a number of criteria that vary in weight depending on the orientation of individual departments: cumulative grade point average, psychology grade point average, Graduate Record Examination (GRE) scores, general academic coursework, science background, research experience, letters of recommendation, and clinical experience. If a department has a strong research orientation and is heavily funded by grants, it will favor people with strong science, laboratory, statistics, and research backgrounds. Since large, traditional programs *are* research-oriented, they tend to look for candidates with similar orientations. For those interested in clinical or counseling psychology, research is still important, but field experience is also necessary. It is critical to be able to offer a graduate program proof that one has "tried" the field of clinical/counseling psychology and knows what is involved. In summary, a student willing to take the time to accumulate a solid background in the "hard" sciences (math, biology, chemistry, etc.) and include in the psychology major laboratories, statistics, research, and fieldwork (if appropriate) is well on the road to acceptance by a graduate program.

Academic Background

Once students know *what* is needed, they usually want to know *how much* is needed. There is no one, right answer. *How much* of any one element is needed to make you attractive as a candidate for a graduate program depends on the emphasis of individual graduate departments. A general rule is that a minimum of 10 quarter credits each of math, physical sciences, and biological sciences is necessary. And as part of the psychology major one should take at least two solid courses in laboratory and statistics and a minimum of one year of research. Add to this a year of clinical work if appropriate. Combining all of these courses with desired electives, one can see why the undergraduate career may stretch to five years, particularly if one's decision to go to graduate school is not made early in the college career.

We came up with these seemingly arbitrary numbers from our experience in advising thousands of students. We have routinely examined the backgrounds of our undergraduates who have applied to hundreds of different programs to see which schools accept what types of backgrounds (Wilson, Note 1). We have concluded that the best approach is a conservative one—excellent preparation in all areas. Of course, exceptions to the "rules," both by students and programs, can be found. One student accepted into graduate school did not major in psychology, another refused to get involved in research, and another had a science background consisting only of oceanography. These people are to be congratulated but not modeled. Schools can also prove to be exceptions. Although this appendix concerns preparation for the typical traditional graduate program in psychology, there *are* humanistic and clinical programs that place less emphasis on science and research as undergraduate requirements.

Research and Fieldwork

Research experience as an undergraduate can be obtained by linking up with faculty in one's department and working as a research assistant. Eventually one may progress to doing one's own research and possibly even co-author some publications; graduate schools are extremely impressed by such activities. Some institutions have undergraduate-research or independent-study courses that make obtaining research experience that much easier. However, it is not the accumulation of credits that is important. What is critical is to have done research over an extended period of time and to have developed a close professional relationship with faculty members.

Students who need clinical field experience but whose schools have no practicum programs can simply open the Yellow Pages, find local mental health agencies, hospitals, or other agencies of interest and volunteer. One should make clear to the agency the type of experience desired—counseling, interviewing, testing, research, etc.—and keep looking until one finds it. This process is much easier than it sounds, since most mental health agencies are half staffed by volunteers.

Letters of Recommendation

One cannot expect to come up with three strong letters of recommendation without having cultivated a few sources. For students attending small colleges where the normal class size is less than 30, finding faculty sources is usually not a problem. However, for those attending a university where even upper-division courses can have as many as 200 students, getting to know faculty becomes a real challenge. In such universities, faculty one has worked with on research are the best sources of letters. These professors are able to evaluate one in terms of research ability, critical scholarship, written communication, professional identification, emotional stability, effective energy, and interpersonal relations. They can also provide an overall judgment of one's probability of success (Suziedelis & Kinnane, 1961). For clinical/counseling students, fieldwork supervisors are an excellent source for letters of recommendation.

What kinds of letters should applicants have? In general, one should have at least three solid academic references—these appear the most impressive (Lunneborg & Wilson, Note 2). For clinical/counseling students, two academic references and one fieldwork reference are a good base. Some schools are now asking for four letters, so be prepared.

However, as a courtesy to those reviewing one for acceptance, don't overkill by sending more than five letters—they generally will not get read.

Graduate Record Examination

The finale in one's preparation is the Graduate Record Examination (GRE), which consists of two separate tests, the Aptitude Test and the Advanced Test. The Aptitude Test, required by essentially every graduate program in psychology, contains three sections measuring verbal, quantitative, and analytical ability and results in three scores. The Advanced Test in Psychology, not required by all programs, is designed to measure knowledge and understanding of psychological principles and facts basic to advanced study and yields an overall score as well as experimental and social subscores. The verbal and quantitative scores are commonly viewed as most important. To determine if a school requires both the Aptitude and Advanced tests, consult *Graduate Study in Psychology*, published annually by the American Psychological Association.[1]

The GRE is administered six times annually with test dates in October, December, January, February, April, and June. The Aptitude Test is given the morning of each test date and the Advanced Test in the afternoon, except in February when the Advanced Test is not given. The testing office at one's college or university should have copies of the most recent *GRE Information Bulletin* (including the test application form and sample questions) published by the Educational Testing Service.[2]

Should one study for the GRE? Yes! The consensus of our advisees over the years has been that studying is critical. There are two basic purposes for studying: to increase speed and reduce anxiety. One may not learn any new material by studying, but reviewing will bring to mind material once learned but not recently used. Becoming familiar with the nature of the material will also increase one's speed and reduce the accompanying anxiety; one will know what to expect when walking into the testing room.

To study for this important exam students should buy a GRE study guide at a local bookstore. These guides aim primarily at preparation for the verbal and quantitative sections of the Aptitude Test. For the Advanced Test in Psychology, although study guides are available, we have found that reviewing as many new-edition introductory texts as possible is the best method of studying. What about timing? The GRE should be taken in October of the year preceding the fall one would like to start graduate school. Some program application deadlines are as early as December, and most cluster around January and early February, for admission the following fall. Completing the test in October leaves ample

---

1. Students interested in this book should consult their bookstore or library; or for current price and ordering information, they should write to the Order Department, American Psychological Association, 1200 Seventeenth Street, N.W., Washington, D.C. 20036.

2. A copy of the *GRE Information Bulletin* and a test application form can be obtained by writing to the Educational Testing Service, Box 955, Princeton, New Jersey 08540.

time for distributing test scores and for solving any problems that may arise.

How important is the GRE? *Very important*, but it is one of several criteria evaluated. One's attitude toward the GRE should be one of acknowledging its importance, studying hard for it, doing as well as possible, and then following through with an application strategy consistent with one's test scores. Poorer-than-expected test scores may mean toning down one's list of prospective graduate programs. In addition, the GRE should be viewed as a one-time endeavor. Even though the test can be retaken the Educational Testing Service reports all scores, and the first scores are generally regarded as the most valid. There is also a 50–50 chance for getting a poorer second score, and most students we have known did not do significantly better on a second try.

Application Schedule

At the end of this appendix is a suggested schedule for the undergraduate years (Scott & Davis-Silka, 1974). This schedule for applying to graduate school represents, an *ideal*. Unless the decision to attend graduate school is made during the first year of college, one will not be able to follow the schedule exactly. For example, if the decision to major in psychology is not made until the junior year, it will be difficult to become an attractive applicant in one year. With imagination, however, the schedule can be adapted to meet individual decision-making plans. Students applying to graduate school for the fall (when the majority of programs accept students) following June graduation should apply almost a year ahead of the anticipated admission time. Therefore, the most impressive course work must be completed by approximately December of the senior year. This does not apply to those delaying graduate study—such students will be able to submit their entire records.

Résumé and Letter of Intent

Two important elements mentioned in the suggested schedule are the résumé and the letter of intent; copies of both should be sent to prospective schools. The résumé outlines one's educational background, work and field experience, and research. A résumé should be no longer than one page—*never* more than two. A guide to preparing such a résumé can also be found at the end of this appendix.

The letter of intent is a description of (a) the development of one's academic interests, (b) research experience, (c) clinical/counseling interests and experience (if appropriate), (d) unique abilities and skills relevant to psychology (e.g., experience as a computer programmer), (e) graduate goals, (f) reasons for wanting to attend a particular graduate school, and (g) professional goals. It is *not* an autobiography. If particular programs want other information, this will be specified in their application materials.

The letter of intent has some standard parts and some that are specific to particular programs. Applicants should be aware that even a qualified individual will probably not be accepted into a program whose specific emphasis is not clearly reflected in the individual's application materials. One must be very sure of one's direction and area of specialization and build the letters of intent around them. The goals stated must be compatible with the prospective program.

Application Know-How

The final key to acceptance by a graduate school involves knowing the mechanics of applying—where to get information on prospective programs, how many programs to select, strategy in selection, financial aid, and timing. Three excellent sources of information are available. First, and most comprehensive, is *Graduate Study in Psychology*, published annually by the American Psychological Association. Along with general advice on graduate study application, it provides specific information (including departments and addresses, programs and degrees offered, application procedures, admission requirements, student statistics, degree requirements, tuition, and financial assistance) for more than 400 graduate programs in psychology in the United States and Canada. This book is a must!

A second good source of application information is psychology department faculty. Professors aware of one's interests and abilities can use their knowledge of various programs to advise one on the most appropriate schools to apply to. A third source is the library. By going through relevant journals one can find out who is writing articles that interest one and which schools these authors are affiliated with.

The result of this research should be a list of from 20 to 30 prospective programs. If one's school has catalogs from other colleges, these can be used to eliminate some programs from the list immediately. For those programs remaining, a *typed postcard* should be sent to the chairperson of each requesting information on the program, a catalog, and application and financial aid forms. This information can then be used to trim the list down to the finalists.

How many schools and what type of school should be on that final list? The list should consist of *not less than* 10 schools that represent a range in quality, geographic location, and level of degree offered. There are two main reasons for this distribution: competition and limited control over selection procedures. The keen competition has already been discussed; one simply cannot count on getting into any one program.

Even though an applicant can exercise partial control over graduate acceptance, there are some aspects of the process that are impossible to control. For example, an applicant may be rejected by a school that at the last minute decides not to take anyone in a particular area. Thus, the rejection is not because the applicant is an unattractive candidate but because the department simply has no room. Or subjective criteria may enter in. A number of objective criteria including GRE scores, cumulative and psychology grade point averages, and science background are weighted according to a graduate department's orientation and combinded to predict the success of each applicant. However, once a final group of "top" candidates exists, it is often difficult to choose from among them in an objective fashion, and subjective opinion may play a role. For example, a selection committee might choose a candidate who impressed them by making the trip to the department and being interviewed.

Another reason for applying to a wide range of schools is simply the problem of interpreting admissions criteria. For APA's *Graduate Study in Psychology*, schools rate as high, medium or low the importance they place during selection on nonobjective criteria like letters of recommendation and work experience. While each department knows precisely what it means by these rating, how does an applicant know? How high is high? Even with objective admissions criteria there can be a huge difference between meeting stated minimum requirements and being competitive. Thus, in order to allow a margin of safety for what cannot be controlled, no matter how "top" a candidate one is, one should apply to as many programs as possible (10 at a minimum).

Doctoral programs are harder to get into than master's programs. Thus, we advise *all* students to apply to some "master's only" programs. "Master's only" refers to schools that specialize in master's programs and do not offer the PhD. (Generally, if a school reports that it grants both master's degrees and doctorates it means that it is really in the business of producing PhDs.) As a guideline for choosing the 10 schools to apply to, it might be wise to include three or four PhD programs one truly would like to attend, another four or five PhD programs one would not mind attending, and two or three "master's only" programs.

Many students are confused by this application strategy because they have been told that if one cannot attend a high-prestige institution, one might as well not go to graduate school. Others may wonder about applying to master's programs when they really want PhDs. First, it would be great to be accepted by one of the top schools in the country, but there are only so many top programs and they take only so many people. In considering schools further down one's list, remember that the decision to continue in psychology was made because it is the area one really wants an education in and therefore is willing to get that education anywhere possible.

Second, master's programs are another excellent way to work toward the PhD. They are less difficult to enter and, if one's undergraduate career has been less than glowing, may just be the ticket to that doctorate. After completing the master's degree, one can then apply to PhD programs with a much better chance of entering that "one special" program, since judgment will be based on graduate-level work rather than one's undergraduate career.

What about finances—the cost of applying and the price of acceptance? Anywhere from $100 on up, depending on the number of schools applied to, will be needed for the application process. The *average* application fee is $10; add to this the cost of official transcripts (which must come from every college attended), duplication costs (for recommendations, résumés, letters of intent, etc.), postage, and even long-distance phone calls, and start saving early.

On the other hand, if one needs financial assistance while in graduate school one should apply for it, routinely asking for financial aid forms along with applications. Graduate school is a full-time job that will not leave time to pump gas or fry hamburgers five nights a week. Programs with a tradition of supplying financial aid are still providing it, although they are not as commited in their initial letters of acceptance. In addition, stating that financial support is not needed will not necessarily help one get accepted, unless the *reason* is that one has a scholarship or funding from another prestigious source.

Finally, to avoid frustration, *get started early*. Keep in mind that it will be necessary to apply essentially a year prior to entering. Begin to meet faculty early in one's undergraduate career, complete the most impressive coursework as soon as possible, start selecting prospective programs early (not two weeks before deadlines), and when asking for letters of recommendation allow time for procrastination on the part of the writer (follow up on requests just to make sure).

For those who do not want to continue their education right away, everything mentioned above still applies. Most important, by the end of their undergraduate careers such students should have letters of recommendation and GRE scores on file. Sadly, faculty disappear for a variety of reasons, and if one returns in one or two years to ask for a letter, a particular faculty member may be gone. If remaining out of school for an extended period, one may never use these letters. A whole new set may be acquired, but *if needed*, the original letters will be there. In addition, students not planning to go to graduate school immediately should take the GRE while still undergraduates or within a few months of graduation. Students out of school for any extended period get out of the habit of taking exams, and their exam-taking ability also decreases. GRE scores remain valid for five years, so students delaying their graduate education should plan accordingly.

There is no indication that not going on to graduate school immediately is detrimental to one's chances of acceptance. Factors that correlate with maturity—employment, postbaccalaureate studies, years of research and clinical experience—seem to be gaining weight in the selection process (Lunneborg & Wilson, Note 2). What *would* be detrimental would be disconnecting oneself from psychology: Always keep a foot in the door as an indication of commitment to the field. If work in psychology cannot be found, at least do volunteer research or related fieldwork. The stronger one's continued commitment to psychology, the higher one's chance of future acceptance into graduate school; the weaker these ties, the less committed to psychology one will be judged.

Realistic optimism is the approach! The key words are persistence, preparation, and application know-how. With these in mind, graduate study in psychology can be in one's future.

REFERENCE NOTES

1. Wilson, V. M. *Realistic optimism: An approach for psychology graduate program applicants* (Tech. Rep. 76-1). Seattle: Department of Psychology, University of Washington, 1976.
2. Lunneborg, P. W., & Wilson, V. M. *Is the profile of new graduate students in psychology changing?* Unpublished manuscript, Department of Psychology, University of Washington, 1977.

REFERENCES

American Psychological Association. *Graduate study in psychology 1977–1978*. Washington, D.C.: Author, 1976.

Cuca, J. M. Placement report: 1973 and 1974. *American Psychologist*, 1975, *30*, 1176–1179.

Kulik, J. A. *Undergraduate education in psychology*. Washington, D.C.: American Psychological Association, 1973.

Scott, W. C. & Davis-Silka, L. Applying to graduate school in psychology: A perspective and guide. *JSAS Catalog of Selected Documents in Psychology*, 1974, *4*, 33. (Ms. No. 597)

Suziedelis, C., & Kinnane, J. F. Faculty judgments of graduate success: A factorial study. *American Psychologist*, 1961, *16*, 181–183.

Woods, P. J. *Career opportunities for psychologists: Expanding and emerging areas*. Washington, D.C.: American Psychological Association, 1976.

Zambrano, A. L., & Entine, A. D. *A guide to career alternatives for academics*. New Rochelle, N.Y.: Change Magazine Press, 1976.

SUGGESTED SCHEDULE FOR CAREER PLANNING AND APPLYING TO GRADUATE SCHOOL

SOPHOMORE YEAR

After completing most of the general education requirements in the first year of college, work on the basic psychology-major requirements, including statistics, laboratory, and science courses.

Become acquainted with several faculty members in the department.

Write a preliminary résumé.

Attend departmental colloquia.

JUNIOR YEAR

Continue, and try to complete, basic requirements.

Begin research with faculty and continue throughout junior year.

Think about letter of recommendation resources (e.g., research supervisors, professors of small classes).

Explore opportunities for joining professional organizations (e.g., obtain faculty sponsorship for a student membership in the American Psychological Association).

Redraft the preliminary résumé.

Attend the state's annual psychological meeting.

Keep attending departmental colloquia.

Do fieldwork if interested in clinical or counseling psychology.

Begin work on a paper on one's previous research for possible publication or presentation. (Start in spring of junior year.)

SUMMER BETWEEN JUNIOR AND SENIOR YEARS

Buy study guides for the GRE and begin studying.

Begin to investigate prospective graduate programs (consult with faculty and use library resources).

Do third draft of résumé.

From research work, write paper(s) for publication or presentation.

SENIOR YEAR

Complete, as much as possible, all impressive degree requirements, research, and fieldwork by December; continue the research and fieldwork, however, because they may be helpful later on.

September: Buy the current issue of APA's *Graduate Study in Psychology* and write to prospective schools for application materials.
Register in September to take the October GRE.
Begin requesting letters of recommendation.

(continued)

Through application materials find out about any additional requirements or tests needed by individual programs.

November: Have letter of intent written and a polished résumé completed. (Have a faculty member or advisor check them for grammar, spelling, and content.)

December on: Send completed applications to schools way ahead of deadlines.
Request transcripts to be sent from all colleges attended.

If not continuing on to graduate school immediately, continue research, fieldwork, and faculty affiliations as long as possible.